PATTERN RECOGNITION:
A STATISTICAL APPROACH

PATTERN RECOGNITION: A STATISTICAL APPROACH

PIERRE A. DEVIJVER

Philips Research Laboratory,
Brussels, Belgium

and

JOSEF KITTLER

Science and Engineering Research Council
Rutherford and Appleton Laboratories
Chilton, Didcot, England

Prentice/Hall PHI International

ENGLEWOOD CLIFFS, NEW JERSEY   LONDON   NEW DELHI
SINGAPORE   SYDNEY   TOKYO   TORONTO   WELLINGTON

Library of Congress Cataloguing in Publication Data

Devijver, P., 1938–
Pattern recognition.
Includes bibliographies and index.
1. Pattern perception—Statistical methods.
I. Kittler, J., 1946– II. Title
Q327.D49 001.53'4 81-10705
ISBN 0-13-654236-0 AACR2

British Library Cataloguing in Publication Data

Devijver, P.
Pattern recognition.
1. Pattern perception
I. Title II. Kittler, J.
001.53'4 Q327
ISBN 0-13-654236-0

ISBN 0-13-654236-0

PRENTICE-HALL INTERNATIONAL, INC., *London*
PRENTICE-HALL OF AUSTRALIA PTY., LTD., *Sydney*
PRENTICE-HALL CANADA, INC., *Toronto*
PRENTICE-HALL OF INDIA PRIVATE LIMITED, *New Delhi*
PRENTICE-HALL OF JAPAN, INC., *Tokyo*
PRENTICE-HALL OF SOUTHEAST ASIA PTE., LTD., *Singapore*
PRENTICE-HALL, INC., *Englewood Cliffs, New Jersey*
WHITEHALL BOOKS LIMITED, *Wellington, New Zealand*

Printed in the United States of America

10 9 8 7 6 5 4 3 2 1

to
Véronique, Nadine and Christine
and to
Josef and Marie-France

CONTENTS

PREFACE

This book originates from lecture notes prepared for an annual summer course on Statistical Pattern Recognition which we have taught, first at Cambridge University, and lately at Oxford University, England, over a number of years. Like the course, the book is intended to cater for the tastes of a broad spectrum of readership with varying background and motivation. At one end of the scale, the material provides comprehensive information, including algorithms and procedures, for designing effective, practical pattern recognition systems. At the other end, the material is treated in depth to satisfy the inquisitiveness of the mathematically minded student who will also find challenging problems at the end of each chapter. Last but not least, it identifies research topics for those interested in the advancement of the subject.

Although the book was conceived in the context of an intensive summer course, in its present form it is well suited as a textbook for undergraduate or postgraduate courses in pattern recognition. The only prerequisite is a prior exposure to the elements of mathematics, probability theory, and statistics. The required background is usually acquired during the first years of undergraduate courses in science and engineering.

The book addresses the problems of feature evaluation, pattern classification, performance estimation, and unsupervised learning (clustering). From the outset, we felt that there was an apparent and critical need for a systematic exposition of feature evaluation methods. This subject receives here much more attention than is usually the case. This material could be included only at the price of reduced emphasis on pattern classification methods. Within this framework, we did not attempt to provide an exhaustive covering of the field. Thus, the present volume was intended as a unified exposition of carefully selected, and representative topics.

The organization of the material and the chapter outline are described in the introductory chapter. Here we wish to comment only on the chapter structuring and cross-referencing schemes. Section, subsection, figure and table numbers are prefixed by chapter number. They are referred to in this form anywhere in the book. For simplicity, equations and paragraphs are numbered with no prefix. For example, reference to Equation 5, or simply 5, in Chapter 8 relates to equation 5 in that chapter. Cross-reference to an equation in another chapter is prefixed by the number of that chapter.

The bibliography on which the material of each chapter is based is given in the penultimate section of the chapters. The list of references is always preceded by a section on bibliographical comments. The final section of each chapter is devoted to problems and exercises enabling the reader to test his comprehension of the material.

During the development of the book, we received an unqualified support and encouragement from Philips Research Laboratory, and the Science and Engineering Research Council, Rutherford and Appleton Laboratories, our respective affiliations. Our acknowledgement of support is also due to Balliol College, Oxford, where one of us held an IBM Research Fellowship during a part of this period.

November 1981

PIERRE A. DEVIJVER
Brussels

JOSEF KITTLER
Oxford

PATTERN RECOGNITION:
A STATISTICAL APPROACH

Chapter 1

INTRODUCTION

1.1. PATTERN RECOGNITION AS A FIELD OF STUDY

Much of the information we have to deal with in real life is in the form of complex patterns : faces, handwritten text, diseases, pieces of orchestral music, wines, cars, flowers, ... In psychology, the central problem within the study of pattern recognition is the biological and mental processes by which *external signals* stimulating our *sense organs* are converted into *meaningful perceptual experiences*, or, somewhat more restrictively, how we are able to assign a name of some kind to a complex stimulus. The processes which enable us to recognize complex patterns are still largely unknown. However, they are frequently admitted to proceed according to the following scheme : Before *recognition*, a pattern must first be *perceived* by our sense organs. Next, in order to represent a meaningful perceptual experience, the same pattern or a pattern in the same class must have been previously perceived. Finally, the past perception of the pattern must be remembered, and some correspondence or equivalence must somehow be established between past and present perception.

Unfortunately, research on how these operations take place in our brain and nervous system has not yet led to any conclusive model.

The advent of the digital computer, some thirty years ago, made available a machine which opened a bewildering range of opportunities for scientific advances. In particular, equipped with sensing devices (transducers and sensors) and A/D converters, the computer can be fed "observations" about the real world. It can be used to store and retrieve information. It can also establish correspondence between past and present observations. Thus, the basic constituents of the recognition scheme became available, and the idea of designing or programming machines to recognize patterns soon became one of the most ambitious and fascinating topics in the computer and information sciences.

Research in automatic pattern recognition began with a certain flourish of romanticism, and was widely publicized as "automatic learning" or even "mechanization of thought processes". Some exaggerated expectations about the possibility of modeling the brain or simulating human perception were to be deflated sooner or later. Nevertheless, at the time of this writing, machines do exist that read typed or handprinted text, sort the mail, count blood cells, analyze electocardiograms, perform visual inspection, recognize spoken words, identify speakers, etc.

By its very nature, automatic pattern recognition is a very broad field of activities with very fuzzy borders. Nevertheless, it becomes more and more evident that the majority of problems that could be effectively solved in the past share a common characteristic : Either the original problem itself can be reformulated as a problem of pattern *classification*, or it may be divided into a number of classification subproblems and sub-subproblems until, eventually, the original problem is reduced to a set of pattern classification problems. Optical character recognition is a problem in the first category where, in principle, we have one distinct *pattern class* for each of the thirty-six alphanumeric symbols.

Producing a description of a circuit diagram is a problem in the second category: Circuit diagrams consist of symbols for electronic components, connecting lines, and strings of characters for identifying symbols, lines, and terminals. Therefore, we have three pattern classification subproblems, corresponding to symbols, lines, and characters respectively. One should note, however, that in this instance, the parts cannot be added independently together to make up the whole. In addition to the "class assignment" of the basic components, *structural* information is needed to attach identifiers to symbols, lines, and terminals, and to keep track of the connections.

As evidenced by the above discussion, pattern *classification* may provide only a partial solution to the pattern *recognition* problem. However, in this book, we shall be concerned only with pattern classification.

We have not attempted thus far - and we shall not attempt - to formulate a precise description of Automatic Pattern Recognition as a field of study. The field is so diversified that it is quite impossible to capture all of its many facets in a formal definition. Instead, we hope that the various typical pattern recognition tasks alluded to in this introductory chapter will suffice to impart to the reader a good idea of the scope of the field.

It would be a mistake however to infer from our discussion that the field is restricted to deal with only those patterns that can be recognized by humans. On the one hand, the human sensory system suffers from severe biological limitations : Suffice it to say here that the ensemble of frequencies perceptible by the auditory and optical sensory apparatus constitutes a negligible part of the electromagnetic spectrum. On the other hand, despite its fantastic complexity and its bewildering efficiency at performing some recognition tasks (which have probably some survival value), the central nervous system is far less efficient at, say, performing multidigit multiplication, or visualizing structures in spaces of more than three dimensions. Conversely, there are, of course, many things that we do quite easily that computers cannot do. Nevertheless, by extending the field of automatic pattern recognition beyond that biologically available, we may be able to acquire new knowledge that would otherwise remain inaccessible.

1.2. APPROACHES TO AUTOMATIC PATTERN RECOGNITION

The diversity of pattern recognition tasks that could possibly be automated calls for an equally diversified repertoire of possible approaches.

In the simplest situations, patterns can be represented by *arrays of numbers* obtained by e.g., sampling a waveform, scanning an image at selected grid points, or performing a sequence of binary (logical) tests; and pattern classes can be represented by one or several *prototype* patterns. This prompts us to introduce a *pattern representation space* (or simply, pattern space) with as many dimensions as the number of entries in the corresponding array, and to think of a pattern as one point in that space.

Real world patterns display very high variability for reasons we shall discuss in a moment. Nevertheless, it seems plausible to assume that points representing similar patterns or patterns from the same class should tend to cluster according to some metric of the pattern space. Conversely, representations of dissimilar patterns or patterns from different classes should lie in different regions of the space.

This "wholistic" or "Gestalt" interpretation for patterns and pattern classes provided the framework for much of the early work in the field.

One of the first pattern recognition devices, the Perceptron, was based on the premise that the central nervous system acts as an intricate, random net of neurons connected through pathways selected by an adaptive mechanism of reinforcement, in which individual neurons were modeled as a threshold logic unit producing a linear dichotomization of the possible input patterns. In other words, the basic element of the Perceptron produced a two-way linear classification of the pattern space. (It may be noted that much of the anthropomorphic flavor of the terminology associated with the Perceptron has survived years of severe criticism. Although they are most of the time an abuse of the language, such expressions as "automatic learning" are still in current use.)

Already, when the field was still in its very infancy, it was also realized that statistics and probability theory had much to offer to pattern classification. Firstly, in some instances, classical, multivariate statistical distributions, defined over the pattern space, provide an adequate model for the variability of the pattern representations. By a slight, not quite legitimate extension, and by analogy with the usual statistical descriptions of information sources and channels in information theory, statistical distributions are frequently used as a model for the *pattern generating mechanism*. Secondly, the question of whether or not a given pattern "belongs" in some pattern class may naturally be treated as a test of hypothesis, or as a special case of the statistical decision theory problem. Statistical decision theory is concerned with statistical decision functions, and their figures of merit and optimality criteria. These concepts have been used largely to formulate the pattern classification problem on a mathematically rigorous, abstract basis, and to provide effective guidelines for designing pattern classifiers. For more than two decades, statistical pattern classification has been a healthy branch of pattern recognition.

Effective though as it is, the statistical approach has built-in limitations. Therefore, some other approaches have been proposed.

For instance, the theory of testing statistical hypotheses postulates that competing hypotheses are mutually exclusive. This entails that the membership of a pattern in a given class should always be decided upon by a clear-cut yes or no answer. Clearly, not all of the real life patterns admit of such coarse decisions.

Therefore it is but natural that the theory of fuzzy sets which allows for fuzzy membership functions was suggested as a way to remedy this difficulty. Fuzzy set theory has proved useful in such applications as chromosome karyotyping, and speech recognition.

Another, more important limitation of the statistical approach resides in its intrinsic weakness at handling *contextual* or *structural* information. In some instances, contextual information is embodied in the statistical dependence between successive patterns (as in c•nt•xt) in which case the theory of Markov processes can still be useful. In other instances, the structural information needed to allow the reconstruction of the whole from the knowledge of its parts (e.g., the circuit diagram) does simply not fit in any statistical framework. Recognition of this fact called for a new approach that was based on the analogy that complex patterns can be decomposed recursively in simpler subpatterns in very much the same way that a sentence can be decomposed in words which, in turn, can be decomposed in letters. The analogy directed researchers toward the theory of formal languages, much of which was found to be applicable to the pattern recognition problem. Hence the so-called *linguistic*, or *syntactic*, or *structural* approach.

In this approach, patterns are no longer represented by arrays of numbers. Instead, they are described by basic elements, the *primitive subpatterns*, together with a number of syntactic rules, the *pattern grammar*, specifying the way subpatterns can be combined together to form a legitimate pattern within the class of interest.

In principle, one grammar must be constructed for each pattern class, and patterns are represented by strings of primitives. The problem of recognition is then essentially reduced to answering the question : Does the given pattern belong to the language generated by that grammar? The process that results in an answer to that question is called *syntax analysis* or *parsing*.

Every theory necessarily involves some idealization. The syntactic method of pattern recognition is indeed quite effective when dealing with idealized (stylized) patterns. However, if pattern grammars were required to account for large amounts of distortion and noise in the input patterns, they would become extremely complicated and, possibly, ambiguous in the sense that one string (pattern) could be generated by more than one grammar. This kind of difficulty can be overcome by an approach which is in fact an outgrowth from both statistical and syntactical methodologies. This idea led to the successive development and use of stochastic grammars and attribute grammars, and paved the way towards what is presently known as the *hybrid approach* to pattern recognition.

Our necessarily brief overview of the field would be incomplete without mentioning the existence of some alternative approaches which are neither statistical nor syntactical. For example, the *geometrical method* focuses on finding data representations or organizations - together with associated data structures and algorithms - which are perceptually meaningful while the *state-space methods* are concerned with finding ways of searching effectively the hierarchical structures prevalent in many pattern recognition tasks.

Finally, clustering methods - also known as unsupervised learning methods - encompass diverse techniques for discovering regularities (or structures, or patterns) in complex data sets. They may serve to suggest either hypothetical models for the data-generating mechanism, or the existence of previously unknown pattern classes. In this sense, clustering is a tool for discovery.

1.3. THE STATISTICAL APPROACH TO PATTERN RECOGNITION

1.3.1. Pattern Similarity

As we mentioned previously, the statistical approach addresses merely the pattern classification problem, and postulates that the input to a pattern recognition machine is a set of d measurements. Thus it is usual and convenient to represent the input by a d-dimensional vector, (a point in d-space), the components of which are called the *features*. Feature measurements are acquired, and converted into a form suitable for machine processing by some data acquisition mechanism. The task of the pattern classifier is to assign the input to one out of c possible pattern classes. Two different patterns should be assigned to the same class on the basis of their being similar, and to different classes on the basis of their being dissimilar (for whatever that means for pattern similarity is sometimes very much problem-dependent).

The question of pattern similarity can be approached in a rather informal way which imposes nonetheless specific requirements on the data acquisition system. To simplify matters, let us formulate these requirements in terms of an ideal *noiseless* acquisition system.

a. Repeated observation of the same pattern should produce the same representation (point) in pattern space.

b. Any two different patterns should give rise to two different pattern representations.

c. A slight distortion of a given pattern should produce a small displacement of its representation (according to some metric of the representation space).

In fact, what these requirements are asking for is no more than biuniqueness and continuity of the acquisition process, for the purpose of transposing , in the representation space, the separating power prevailing in the universe of the patterns under consideration. (Characterization of that separating power is however quite another matter, as it may involve purely subjective judgment.)

These considerations strongly suggest that a small distance between two pattern representations is synonymous with a high degree of similarity between the corresponding patterns. However they do not allow us to make such extrapolations as "the larger the distance, the lower the degree of similarity" for this would imply the unrealistic requirement that there always exists a monotone relationship between the mathematical concept of distance in pattern space, and the (possibly subjective) concept of pattern similarity.

Note that we do not preclude the possibility of finding a justification for the extrapolation in some favorable cases. This is precisely the stage where probability and statistics come into play. Indeed, specifying the conditions such that there exists a one to one relationship between distance and similarity is quite a typical example of the use of statistics in pattern recognition.

Likewise, probability theory will enable us to assess what can be expected, in terms of performance, from the quite general premise that small distance is synonymous with high similarity. Before we turn to such considerations, a few words about the pattern variability are in order.

1.3.2. Pattern Variability

We commented previously that one of the uses of statistics in pattern recognition is to provide a mathematical model for the variability of the pattern representations. It is of interest to distinguish various sources of variability.

In the preceding subsection, our discussion was based on the assumption that pattern representations were obtained through an ideal, noiseless acquisition system. Clearly, no such system exists. Distortion and noise introduced by the acquisition system cause the *extraneous* variability of pattern representation. Examples of such artefacts are : drift in TV cameras, errors in measuring processes, additive noise in communication channels from remote inputs, quantization noise in A/D converters, etc. Additional extraneous variability may arise due to the way the data is acquired, e.g., the outlook of an electrocardiographic tracing is very much dependent upon electrode placement, reflected intensity of an image depends upon illumination conditions, etc.

To some extent, extraneous variablity is under control of the system designer. Unfortunately, this is no longer the case of the major source of variability which resides in the patterns themselves.

Very frequently, patterns in the same class differ quite a lot. It is not rare that the scope of a problem has to be reduced somehow by a number of constraints up to the point where the remaining intrinsic variability becomes manageable. A good example can be found in the history of the development of optical character recognition (OCR) machines. The first generation of OCR machines was designed to read single-font text (not to speak of fonts specifically designed for machine reading). They were followed by machines that could read multifont text. Eventually, reading of constrained handprinted text became a reality. (Automatic reading of unconstrained handwritten text remains a tremendous challenge.)

Even in the case of single-font character recognition, *intrinsic* variability of the patterns is due to such diverse causes as grain, quality, aging, and color background of the document, quality of the ribbon, type of ink, cleanliness and mechanical adjustment of the typewriter, etc. It goes without saying that the variability of multifont and handprinted characters increases by orders of magnitude.

The need to cope with the cumulative effects of intrinsic and extraneous variabilities of the pattern representations confront us with two difficult problems that will occupy us constantly in the following pages.

The first problem that comes to mind is that of extracting from the raw data the information which is most relevant for classification purposes, in the sense of minimizing the *within-class* pattern variability while enhancing the *between-class* pattern variability. This is the so-called *feature extraction* problem.

If effective features have been obtained, pattern representations should tend to assemble into well-separated groups or clusters, one cluster for each pattern class. Then, the pattern classification problem becomes one of partitioning the feature space into regions, one region for each class. Both these problems are briefly addressed hereafter. For convenience we take them in the reverse order.

1.3.3. Pattern Classification

Let us briefly outline a particularly simple example of a pattern classifier. We consider a problem of two classes, and we assume that each class can be adequately represented by one known (or given) prototype pattern or prototype point. We also assume that, due to pattern variability, each feature measurement is corrupted by independent Gaussian white noise. Under these quite restrictive conditions, pattern representations have two multivariate normal distributions centered at the prototype points, and the *likelihood* for a given point of being drawn from either distribution -or belonging to either class - is inversely proportional to the distance from the corresponding prototype point. If we have the additional information that each newly observed pattern belongs to either class with equal *a priori* probability, then it is a trivial matter to prove that a minimum distance classifier with respect to the prototype points implements a linear partitioning of the feature space, and is an optimal procedure in the decision theoretical sense of minimizing the expected probability of misclassification.

Prototype points, noise intensity, *a priori* probabilities are never "given". They have to be *estimated* from a representative sample of correctly classified patterns. In the pattern recognition terminology, estimation of the various "parameters" of a classifier is called the *learning* or *training* process. The set of samples used in this process is called the *training*, or *design* sample set.

The above discussion involved so many assumptions about the pattern generating mechanism that our "optimal" classifier is not likely to be of much practical usefulness. Thus, in subsequent chapters, we shall examine design methods that can cope with less constrained situations. A sample of pertinent questions arising in this context could be : Would it not be wise to use more than one prototype point to represent a given class? What about the idea of using each training sample as a prototype? In case the classifier structure is too complicated to be economically viable, is it possible to trade performance against ease of implementation? How should one compare competing designs?

These and other questions will occupy us for a while, and three different approaches to pattern classifier design will be examined in detail. However, the newcomer to the field should be warned that the theory of statistical pattern recognition has not yet reached the stage where it can provide guidelines as to which approach to select to solve a given real world problem.

How to "match" a pattern classifier to the environment in which it is to operate, how to characterize the range of recognitions that can be performed with a given technique, what is the price one has to pay to make implementation easy? These are very fundamental questions. As of today, the answers remain very elusive.

1.3.4. Feature Extraction

We have been assuming that patterns were represented by d-dimensional measurement vectors obtained by some, so-far unspecified data acquisition mechanism. There should be no need to insist that the selection of measurements is a very crucial step in pattern recognition system design.

Good features enhance within-class pattern similarity and between-class pattern dissimilarity. In a few cases good features are evident, e.g., to tell an O from a Q it should be sufficient to look for the presence of a tail. Unfortunately such easy cases are the exceptions rather than the rule, and the whole situation is even aggravated by the fact that there is very little theory to guide the selection of measurements.

The more complex the patterns we are dealing with, the more difficult it is to give an explicit or formal - not to say computable - answer to the question of deciding what the good measurements are. In fact, the majority of failure experienced in the field found its origin in the difficulty of discovering good features.

Despite the fact that quantity never quite compensates for quality, a very common way of getting round this difficulty is to bring to bear whatever specific knowledge about the problem, and to select *all* those measurements that could possibly provide valuable information. However, an increase in the number of measurements brings about an increasingly complex classifier structure. Concomitantly, the presence in the input data of more redundant - possibly irrelevant - information detrimentally affects the reliability of the classifier.

All these considerations justify the attention we shall devote in this book to the feature extraction problem. It is beyond the scope of this introductory chapter to discuss the problem in detail. Let us however give a preview of the kind of problems awaiting us.

In the first place, we might think of devising figures of merit reflecting the amount of classification information conveyed by individual measurements. More useful though are figures of merit for sets of measurements, because consideration of isolated measurements does not reveal redundancy in the input data. Ideally, we would like the figure of merit to be a measure of the amount of classification information that can be exploited by the classifier. Unfortunately, for most classifiers, such measures of information remain to be discovered. Examples of actual figures of merit are the ratio of between-class to within-class scatter (variability), or the probability of correct classification for an optimum classifier.

Once a figure of merit has been selected, our problem admits of two alternative formulations. Both belong to the field of optimization. First of all, we may consider selecting the best subset of d features out of the larger set of D measurements. Clearly, best is understood here in the sense of maximizing the figure of merit over all possible subsets. For moderate to large values of d and D, the number of candidate subsets is an example of the combinatorial explosion, and the problem is by no means a trivial one. Once the feature set has been selected, this approach calls for redesigning the data acquisition system.

The alternative approach - feature extraction in the true sense of the word - consists in *extracting* a number of d features, each of which is a combination of all of the initial D measurements, $d<D$. Usually, only linear combinations are considered. In other words, the approach can be viewed as projecting the original D-dimensional representation space on a d-dimensional subspace, and finding the orientation of the subspace which best preserves the information available in the complete space. As opposed to feature selection, feature extraction does not reduce the complexity of the data acquisition mechanism. Nevertheless, both techniques reduce the complexity of designing the classifier.

1.4. OVERVIEW OF THE BOOK

In this book we shall be essentially concerned with the problem of designing pattern classifiers (Chapters 2 through 4), selecting or extracting features (Chapters 5 through 9), and estimating classification performance (Chapter 10). In particular, we shall give an in-depth treatement of the Karhunen-Loeve expansion (Chapter 9), an important and useful technique at the borderline between problems in pattern representation and feature extraction. The concluding chapter is concerned with clustering techniques.

In Chapter 2 we give an outline of elementary statistical decision theory and we show how the theory provides statistical models for pattern generating mechanisms and the corresponding optimal decision (classification) processes. Optimality can be achieved only when the statistical distributions involved are known. The problem of estimating statistical distributions has been thoroughly treated in many good books. Here it is given limited attention. Its treatment is deferred to Appendix A.

Chapter 3 is entirely devoted to the so-called Nearest Neighbor decision rule. The nearest neighbor technique exchanges the need to know the statistical distributions for that of knowing a large number of correctly classified sample patterns. Roughly speaking, the analysis provides a mathematical justification for the assumption that patterns that are close together (in feature space) are likely to belong to the same pattern class.

The idea that pattern classification can be performed by a proper partitioning of the feature space suggests a straightforward analogy with the problem dealt with in the field of discriminant analysis. Accordingly, in Chapter 4, we examine several ways of designing discriminant functions. This brings to an end our discussion of pattern classification methods.

Chapter 5 is devoted to an in-depth examination of the need for feature "evaluation" methods, a general introduction to figures of merit (or feature evaluation criteria), and a description of various search algorithms for feature selection.

Next we return to the concept of within-class and between-class variabilities which was helpful in our discussion of pattern similarity, pattern classes dissimilarity and figures of merit for sets of features. The formalization of this concept in Chapter 6 leads to a number of feature extraction algorithms.

The next two chapters are concerned with feature selection and extraction algorithms which are based on a class of figures of merit that has not been alluded to thus far, namely, the so-called *distance measures* between statistical distributions, or *probabilistic distance measures*. In a word, distance measures can be construed as global characterizations for the overlap of (arbitrary large) random samples drawn from two different distributions. Several distance measures are introduced in Chapter 7 together with associated feature selection methods. Their use in feature extraction is the subject of Chapter 8. This material relies heavily on the calculus with matrix functions, some elements of which can be found in Appendix B.

The last three chapters treat distinct and rather independent problems. Chapter 9 is devoted to a thorough discussion of a very classical technique of data compression, namely, the Karhunen-Loeve expansion. In the pattern recognition context, the Karhunen-Loeve expansion enjoys a number of optimality properties which make it quite a useful tool in various domains such as optimal pattern representation in connection with data compression, and - as could be expected - feature extraction.

Chapter 10 addresses the important and difficult question of estimating the performance of a pattern recognition system. Finally, clustering methods, or unsupervised learning methods are treated in Chapter 11. As we already mentioned, clustering methods aim at discovering the existence of pattern classes in a collection of unlabeled sample patterns.

1.5. BIBLIOGRAPHICAL COMMENTS

The pattern recognition literature has grown to a point where it becomes virtually impossible to cite all pertinent references. Therefore, the list of references appearing at the end of each chapter represent no more than a small, selective and hopefully representative sample of the relevant literature.

The state of the art in the field of pattern recognition has been surveyed periodically in a number of influencial articles including Minsky (1961), Nagy (1968), and Kanal (1974), and a collection of selected reprints has been compiled by Agrawala (1977).

Readers interested in the Perceptron should consult the thought provoking text by Minsky and Papert (1969). The book by Nilsson (1965) may also serve as a very clear introduction to the subject. Statistical pattern classification is treated systematically by Fukunaga (1972), and Duda and Hart (1973). The first comprehensive treatment of syntactic pattern recognition is due to Fu (1974). Applications of syntactic methods to pictorial data can be found in the book by Pavlidis (1980). The texts by Anderberg (1973) and Hartigan (1974) concentrate on clustering methods.

Pattern recognition papers are widely scattered in a large number of journals and collection volumes. Special mention should be made of the IEEE Transactions on Pattern Analysis and Machine Intelligence, and the Pattern Recognition Journal. Finally, a wealth of information can also be found in the proceedings of the biannual International Conference on Pattern Recognition, and IEEE Conference on Pattern Recognition and Image Processing.

1.6. REFERENCES

Agrawala, A. K., (Editor), *Machine Recognition of Patterns*, IEEE Press, New York, 1977.

Anderberg, M. R., *Cluster Analysis for Applications*, Academic Press, New York, 1973.

Duda, R. O., and Hart, P. E., *Pattern Cassification and Scene Analysis*, John Wiley and Sons, New York, 1973.

Fu, K. S., *Syntactic Methods in Pattern Recognition*, Accademic Press, New York, 1974.

Fukunaga, K., *Introduction to Statistical Pattern Recognition*, Academic Press, New York, 1972.

Hartigan, J. A., *Clustering Algorithms*, John Wiley and Sons, New York, 1975.

Kanal, L., "Patterns in pattern recognition : 1968-1974", *IEEE Trans. Inform. Theory*, Vol. 20, pp. 697-722, Nov. 1974.

Minsky, M., "Steps towards artificial intelligence", *Proc. IRE*, Vol. 49, pp. 8-30, Jan. 1961.

Minsky, M., and Papert, S., *Perceptrons*, MIT Press, Cambridge (Ma), 1969.

Nagy, G., "State of the art in pattern recognition", *Proc. IEEE*, Vol. 56, pp. 836-862, May 1968.

Nilsson, N. J., *Learning Machines*, McGraw-Hill, New York, 1965.

Pavlidis, T., *Structural Pattern Recognition*, Springer Verlag, Berlin, (Second Edition), 1980.

Chapter 2

BAYES DECISION THEORY

2.1. INTRODUCTION

Over the past two decades, statistical methods have played a prominent role in the development of pattern recognition techniques. The statistical decision theory and related fields have been a forum where significant theoretical advances and innovations have taken place. These, in turn, have exerted a strong impact on pattern recognition applications. This chapter presents an elementary account of some important topics in the statistical theory of pattern recognition.

Statistical methods provide the proper framework for studying pattern recognition problems when the underlying pattern-generating mechanism can be faithfully represented by a statistical model, and the goal of the recognition consists of deciding whether or not a given pattern belongs to some prespecified class of patterns. Examples of applications which fit in this framework are plentiful : character recognition, medical diagnosis, automatic inspection of parts, speaker verification, etc. Most of our discussion in this book will take place in this framework. This, however, should not be taken as an indication that statistical methods are not useful in wider frameworks; very often, only statistical tools enable us to apprehend the extreme variability of the patterns we perceive in our everyday life. Consequently, these statistical tools are also frequently used in conjunction with sometimes radically different approaches such as the syntactic, heuristic or *ad hoc* methods of pattern recognition.

The problem we address hereafter is merely that of classifying patterns. In this chapter, the methods we use for doing this belong, to a large extent, to the *statistical decision theory*. As we just indicated, the role of the statistical decision theory consists mainly of providing the proper framework for modelling the *pattern-generating mechanism*. Besides, it also helps us formalize the *decision-making process*. So, let us begin with a formal, though quite general outline of the appropriate model of the pattern classification problem.

2.2. BASIC ELEMENTS OF THE CLASSIFICATION PROBLEM

Suppose there are c possible pattern classes $\omega_1, \omega_2, \ldots, \omega_c$ and an arbitrary pattern belongs to class ω_i with *a priori* probability P_i, $P_i \geq 0$, $\sum_{i=1}^{c} P_i = 1$. Patterns are d-component measurement vectors or *feature-vectors*. In our approach, pattern $\underline{x}$ is assumed to be a random vector taking value in d-dimensional *feature space* Ω and governed by a multivariate probability density function $p(\underline{x}|\omega_i)$ when pattern $\underline{x}$ is known to belong to class ω_i, $i=1,\ldots,c$. We already have the basic ingredients which enable us to model a very wide variety of pattern-generating mechanisms. We now consider those which make up a model for decision-making processes. To this end, we have to define the set of possible decisions and choose the classification performance criterion.

An arbitrary pattern $\underline{x}$ of unknown class ω may normally be assigned to any of the c classes. So, we have c possible decisions. Let $\hat{\omega}(\underline{x})$ be some *decision rule*, i.e., a function of $\underline{x}$ that tells us which decision to make for every possible pattern $\underline{x}$. For example, $\hat{\omega}(\underline{x})=\omega_i$ denotes the decision to assign pattern $\underline{x}$ to class ω_i. Clearly, this definition is but a thinly disguised version of the following statement : let $\hat{\omega}(\underline{x})$ be an *estimate* of the unknown, true class ω of $\underline{x}$ obtained with some decision rule. When very ambiguous situations arise as to the decision to make, it may be advantageous to allow the system to withold its decision and *reject* the pattern for exceptional handling. In such a case, we designate the reject option by writing $\hat{\omega}(\underline{x}) = \omega_0$. Our model allows now for c+1 decisions in a c class problem. Next, let $\lambda(\omega_i|\omega_j)$ be a measure of the *loss* or penalty incurred when the decision $\hat{\omega}(\underline{x})=\omega_i$ is made and the true pattern class ω is in fact ω_j, $i=0,1,\ldots,c$, $j=1,\ldots,c$.

On the ground of the above definitions, the goal of the statistical decision theory is to devise the decision rule $\hat{\omega}$ in such a way that the average loss per decision is as small as possible.

2.3. BAYES RULE FOR MINIMUM RISK

Consider the problem of classifying the arbitrary pattern $\underline{x}$ of unknown class ω. The probability of $\underline{x}$ belonging to class ω_j is the class *a posteriori* probability $P(\omega_j|\underline{x})$. This probability can be computed by the Bayes rule

1 $$P(\omega_j|\underline{x}) = \frac{p(\underline{x}|\omega_j)P_j}{p(\underline{x})},$$

where

2 $$p(\underline{x}) = \sum_{j=1}^{c} p(\underline{x}|\omega_j)P_j$$

is the unconditional probability density function governing the distribution of $\underline{x}$. Let us next consider the loss associated with one particular decision, say $\hat{\omega}(\underline{x}) = \omega_i$. Obviously this decision will entail a loss $\lambda(\omega_i|\omega_j)$ with probability $P(\omega_j|\underline{x})$. Consequently, the expected loss - usually called the *conditional risk* - of making decision $\hat{\omega}(\underline{x}) = \omega_i$ is

3 $$l^i(\underline{x}) = \sum_{j=1}^{c} \lambda(\omega_i|\omega_j)P(\omega_j|\underline{x}).$$

Now, let us recall that a decision rule is a function $\hat{\omega}(\underline{x})$ that tells us which decision to make for every possible pattern $\underline{x}$. So, one can see from 3 that one particular decision rule has conditional risk

4 $$l(\underline{x}) = \sum_{j=1}^{c} \lambda(\hat{\omega}(\underline{x})|\omega_j)P(\omega_j|\underline{x}),$$

and *average risk*

5 $$L = \int l(\underline{x})p(\underline{x})d\underline{x},$$

where $d\underline{x}$ denotes a d-space volume element and the integral extends over the entire feature space.

At this point, all that is left unspecified is the decision rule $\hat{\omega}(\underline{x})$. As already noted, the most desirable one is the rule which minimizes the average risk L. To achieve this goal, it suffices to take $\hat{\omega}(\underline{x})$ so that $l(x)$ in 4 is as small as possible for every $\underline{x}$. This is the justification for the *Bayes decision rule* $\hat{\omega}^*(\underline{x})$:

6 $$\hat{\omega}^*(\underline{x}) = \omega_i \text{ if } l^i(\underline{x}) \leq l^j(\underline{x}),\ j=1,\ldots,c.$$

This formulation of the Bayes rule is not unique since ties may possibly occur. However, as the conditional risk is not affected by the way of breaking ties, this is, after all, an unimportant matter.

From 6 we can see that the Bayes decision rule has the *minimum conditional risk*

7 $$l^*(\underline{x}) = \min_{i=0,\ldots,c} l^i(\underline{x}) = \min_{i=0,\ldots,c} \sum_{j=1}^{c} \lambda(\omega_i|\omega_j)P(\omega_j|\underline{x}),$$

and the minimum average risk - also called *the Bayes risk* -

8 $$L^* = \int l^*(\underline{x})p(\underline{x})d\underline{x}.$$

In view of these optimum properties, the Bayes decision rule is sometimes said to represent *the limit of excellence beyond which it is impossible to go.*

9 So far our model has remained very general, and the few conclusions we have reached stand inevitably on an equal level of generality. In fact we shall have to impose a number of additional restrictions in order to permit a finer analysis of the performance of the Bayes rule. Our first step will be to assume one particular loss function.

10 Suppose that we incur no loss for correct decision, $\lambda(\omega_i|\omega_i)=0$, $i=1,\ldots,c$, a unit loss for classification error, $\lambda(\omega_i|\omega_j)=1$, $i,j=1,\ldots,c$, $i\neq j$, and a constant loss λ_r for rejection, $\lambda(\omega_0|\omega_j)=\lambda_r$, $j=1,\ldots,c$. We call λ_r the *rejection threshold.* With this specification of the loss function the conditional risk $l^i(\underline{x})$ of 3 becomes

11 $$l^0(\underline{x}) = \sum_{j=1}^{c} \lambda_r P(\omega_j|\underline{x}) = \lambda_r,$$

12 $$l^i(\underline{x}) = \sum_{\substack{j=1\\ j\neq i}}^{c} P(\omega_j|\underline{x}) = 1-P(\omega_i|\underline{x}),\ i=1,\ldots,c.$$

Here we note that the conditional risk $l^i(\underline{x}) = 1-P(\omega_i|\underline{x})$ reduces to the *conditional probability of classification error*, associated with the decision $\hat{\omega}(\underline{x})=\omega_i$. In order to emphasize this fact, we shall introduce the notation $e^i(\underline{x})$ to designate this error probability. Furthermore, in order to be consistent with 7 we define the minimum conditional error probability as follows :

13 $$e^*(\underline{x}) = \min_{i=1,\ldots,c} e^i(\underline{x}) = 1- \max_{i=1,\ldots,c} P(\omega_i|\underline{x}).$$

With these definitions, the Bayes rule 6 becomes

14.a $$\hat{\omega}^*(\underline{x}) = \omega_i \text{ if } e^*(\underline{x}) = e^i(\underline{x}) \leq \lambda_r$$

14.b $$= \omega_0 \text{ if } \lambda_r < e^*(\underline{x}).$$

A somewhat more suggestive formulation of the rule is in terms of the *a posteriori* probabilities :

15.a $$\hat{\omega}^*(\underline{x}) = \omega_i \text{ if } P(\omega_i|\underline{x}) = \max_{j=1,\ldots,c} P(\omega_j|\underline{x}) \geq 1-\lambda_r$$

15.b $$= \omega_0 \text{ if } 1-\lambda_r > \max_{j=1,\ldots,c} P(\omega_j|\underline{x}).$$

16 Clearly, for c classes, $0 \leq 1-\max_j P(\omega_j|\underline{x}) \leq (c-1)/c$ with the rightmost equality corresponding to the case when all classes have equal *a posteriori* probabilities. So, for the reject option to be possibly active we must have $0 \leq \lambda_r \leq (c-1)/c$. This is the case we shall consider first.

Under the assumptions of 16 the decision rule 15 partitions the feature space into c *acceptance regions* Ω_i, i=1,...,c, and one *reject region* Ω_0. The acceptance region Ω_i consists of those samples which are classified into class ω_i :

17 $$\Omega_i = \left\{\underline{x} \,\middle|\, P(\omega_i|\underline{x}) = \max_{j=1,\ldots,c} P(\omega_j|\underline{x}) \geq 1-\lambda_r\right\}.$$

and the overall acceptance region Ω_a is the union of $\Omega_1, \Omega_2, \ldots, \Omega_c$. Likewise, the reject region Ω_0 consists of those samples which are rejected:

18 $$\Omega_0 = \left\{\underline{x} \,\middle|\, 1-\lambda_r > \max_{j=1,\ldots,c} P(\omega_j|\underline{x})\right\},$$

and

19 $$\Omega_a \cup \Omega_0 = \Omega.$$

For an arbitrary pattern $\underline{x}$, the *acceptance probability* for the decision $\hat{\omega}^*(\underline{x}) = \omega_i$ is

20
$$A^{*i} = \int_{\Omega_i} p(\underline{x})d\underline{x}, \quad i=1,\ldots,c,$$

and the overall acceptance probability, or *acceptance rate* is $A^* = \sum_{i=1}^{c} A^{*i}$ Likewise, the *reject rate* R^* is given by

21
$$R^* = \int_{\Omega_0} p(\underline{x})d\underline{x}.$$

Acceptance of the decision $\hat{\omega}^*(\underline{x})=\omega_i$ gives rise to either classification error or correct decision with probabilities

22
$$E^{*i} = \int_{\Omega_i} e^*(\underline{x})p(\underline{x})d\underline{x}$$

and

23
$$C^{*i} = \int_{\Omega_i} [1-e^*(\underline{x})]p(\underline{x})d\underline{x},$$

respectively. As for the acceptance rate, the overall probability of error, or *error rate* is $E^* = \sum_{i=1}^{c} E^{*i}$ and the overall probability of correct decision is $C^* = \sum_{i=1}^{c} C^{*i}$

24 Given the underlying distributions, the acceptance rate A^* of the Bayes rule is a function of the rejection threshold λ_r only. To see this it suffices to observe that, in 17, the boundary of the acceptance region Ω_i over which the integral of 20 is calculated depends on λ_r only. So we may write $A^*=A^*(\lambda_r)$. Clearly the same remark applies to the probabilities of rejection, classification error and correct decision. We shall henceforth write $R^*(\lambda_r)$, $E^*(\lambda_r)$ and

$C^*(\lambda_r)$. Note that these probabilities are obviously not independent of each other since they are related by the following equations:

25 $$A^*(\lambda_r) = 1 - R^*(\lambda_r)$$

26 $$A^*(\lambda_r) = E^*(\lambda_r) + C^*(\lambda_r).$$

Let us now express the Bayes risk of 8 in terms of these probabilities. As L^* will eventually appear to depend on λ_r only, we shall readily adopt the notation $L^* = L^*(\lambda_r)$ also. By using 11-14 in 8 we can write

27 $$L^*(\lambda_r) = \int l^*(\underline{x})p(\underline{x})d\underline{x}$$

$$= \int_{\Omega_a} e^*(\underline{x})p(\underline{x})d\underline{x} + \int_{\Omega_0} \lambda_r p(\underline{x})d\underline{x}$$

$$= E^*(\lambda_r) + \lambda_r R^*(\lambda_r).$$

28 This equation enables us to propose a somewhat sharper formulation of the optimality property of the Bayes decision rule : for a given pattern classification problem - in other words, for given underlying distributions - among all the rules with error rate equal to $E^*(\lambda_r)$ there exists no rule with reject rate less than $R^*(\lambda_r)$. Equivalently, among all the rules with reject rate equal to $R^*(\lambda_r)$, there exists no rule with error rate less than $E^*(\lambda_r)$. It is under this second version that the optimum property of the Bayes decision rule will prove useful in Chapter 3.

29 Equations 13-15 shed considerable light on the motivation behind the use of the reject option : the reject option is activated whenever the conditional error probability exceeds the rejection threshold λ_r. Clearly, rejection can be interpreted as a means to safeguard against excessive classification errors. However, it is important to bear in mind that the tradeoff between rejects and errors is not one to one, for some would-be correct classifications are also converted into rejections.

30 An exhaustive theoretical analysis of the *error-reject tradeoff* leading to 32 below is definitely beyond the scope of this book. So, for the time being, we shall discuss the main result of this analysis without actually proving it. However, in order to reassure the reader, we shall demonstrate 32 in the case of the illustrative example of Section 2.5 and a sketch of a general proof of the same equation will appear in the course of Chapter 3.

31 As we noted under 24, the probabilities $A^*(\lambda_r)$, $R^*(\lambda_r)$, $E^*(\lambda_r)$ and $C^*(\lambda_r)$ are functions of the rejection threshold λ_r only, and two of them suffice to characterize completely the performance of the Bayes decision rule. It is quite a remarkable fact that it is possible to go one step further and show that knowing one - just one - of these probabilities over the full range of λ_r allows us to compute the other three. This unexpected observation follows from the fact that the error and reject rates are related as follows:

32 $$E^*(\lambda_r) = -\int_0^{\lambda_r} \lambda dR^*(\lambda),$$

where the integral of the right hand side is to be considered as either an ordinary Riemann integral or a Stieltjes integral according to whether or not $R^*(\lambda)$ is differentiable with respect to λ.

33 A somewhat counterintuitive observation that follows from 32 is that the knowledge of the reject function R^* vs. λ is all that is needed to calculate the error rate $E^*(\lambda_r)$. It should therefore come as no surprise that 32 will be an important result to bear in mind when we discuss probability of error estimation in Chapter 10.

To conclude this section, we shall presently show that the rejection threshold λ_r is an upper bound of both the error rate $E^*(\lambda_r)$, and the Bayes risk $L^*(\lambda_r)$.

For any $\underline{x}$ in Ω_a, we have by 14.a

34 $$e^*(\underline{x}) \le \lambda_r.$$

By using this in 22 we obtain

$$E^{*i} \le \int_{\Omega_i} \lambda_r p(\underline{x}) d\underline{x}$$

$$= \lambda_r A^{*i}.$$

Summation over i yields

35 $$E^*(\lambda_r) \le \lambda_r A^*(\lambda_r) \le \lambda_r,$$

which is the first result we set up to prove. Next, we may substitute the leftmost inequality of 35 in 25 to obtain

36 $$L^*(\lambda_r) \le \lambda_r A^*(\lambda_r) + \lambda_r R^*(\lambda_r) = \lambda_r.$$

2.4. BAYES RULE FOR MINIMUM ERROR RATE

Let the loss function be specified by 10 and assume that the loss λ_r associated with the reject option exceeds the largest possible conditional probability of classification error, *viz.*, $(c-1)/c$. It then follows from 14 that the reject option is never activated and the Bayes decision rule constantly makes decision according to minimal conditional probability of error. We thus have

37 $$\hat{\omega}^*(\underline{x}) = \omega_i \quad \text{if} \quad P(\omega_i|\underline{x}) = \max_{j=1,\ldots,c} P(\omega_j|\underline{x}).$$

The conditional Bayes risk is

38 $$e^*(\underline{x}) = 1- \max_{j=1,\ldots,c} P(\omega_j|\underline{x}),$$

and the average Bayes risk is

39 $$E^* = \int e^*(\underline{x})p(\underline{x})d\underline{x},$$

where the integral extends again over the entire feature space.

Aside from characterizing the performance of the Bayes rule, the minimum error rate E^* can be interpreted as a measure of the *intrinsic complexity* of the classification problem. Alternatively, the probability of correct classification with the Bayes rule, *viz.*, $C^*=1-E^*$ may be viewed as a measure of the *discriminatory information* conveyed by the features making up the pattern $\underline{x}$. It is therefore natural that E^* will play a central role in many of the subsequent chapters.

2.5. THE TWO-CLASS CASE WITH MULTIVARIATE NORMAL DISTRIBUTIONS

Our next step in reducing the generality of our model will be to assume that there are only two pattern classes. Under the condition $\lambda_r \le 1/2$, the decision rule of 15 becomes

40
$$\hat{\omega}^*(\underline{x}) = \omega_1 \quad \text{if } P(\omega_1|\underline{x}) \ge 1-\lambda_r$$
$$= \omega_2 \quad \text{if } P(\omega_2|\underline{x}) \ge 1-\lambda_r$$
$$= \omega_0 \quad \text{otherwise.}$$

Alternatively, the decision rule of 40 can be expressed in terms of the *likelihood ratio* $p(\underline{x}|\omega_1)/p(\underline{x}|\omega_2)$:

41
$$\hat{\omega}^*(\underline{x}) = \omega_1 \quad \text{if } \frac{p(\underline{x}|\omega_1)}{p(\underline{x}|\omega_2)} \ge \frac{P_2}{P_1}\frac{1-\lambda_r}{\lambda_r}$$
$$= \omega_2 \qquad\qquad \le \frac{P_2}{P_1}\frac{\lambda_r}{1-\lambda_r}$$
$$= \omega_0 \quad \text{otherwise.}$$

Next, we assume that each class is normally distributed with mean vector

$$\underline{\mu}_i = \int \underline{x}p(\underline{x}|\omega_i)d\underline{x}, \; i=1,2,$$

and common covariance matrix

$$\Sigma = \int (\underline{x}-\underline{\mu}_i)(\underline{x}-\underline{\mu}_i)^t p(\underline{x}|\omega_i)d\underline{x}.$$

More specifically, we assume

42 $$p(\underline{x}|\omega_i) = (2\pi)^{-d/2}|\Sigma|^{-1/2}\exp\left[\frac{1}{2}(\underline{x}-\underline{\mu}_i)^t\Sigma^{-1}(\underline{x}-\underline{\mu}_i)\right],$$

where $(\underline{x}-\underline{\mu}_i)^t$ is the transpose of $(\underline{x}-\underline{\mu}_i)$, Σ^{-1} is the inverse of Σ, and $|\Sigma|$ is the determinant of Σ. Equation 42 will often be abbreviated as $p(\underline{x}|\omega_i)\sim\mathcal{N}(\underline{\mu}_i,\Sigma)$.

The logarithm of the likelihood ratio is

43 $$\Lambda(\underline{x}) = \log\frac{p(\underline{x}|\omega_1)}{p(\underline{x}|\omega_2)} = \left[\underline{x} - \frac{1}{2}(\underline{\mu}_1+\underline{\mu}_2)\right]^t\Sigma^{-1}(\underline{\mu}_1-\underline{\mu}_2).$$

We note that $\Lambda(\underline{x})$ is a linear function of $\underline{x}$. Let

44 $$T_1 = \log\frac{P_2}{P_1}\frac{1-\lambda_r}{\lambda_r} \quad\text{and}\quad T_2 = \log\frac{P_2}{P_1}\frac{\lambda_r}{1-\lambda_r}.$$

These definitions enable us to reformulate the Bayes decision rule 41 in the following way:

45 $$\begin{aligned}\hat{\omega}^* &= \omega_1 \quad \text{if } \Lambda(\underline{x}) \geq T_1\\ &= \omega_2 \quad \text{if } \Lambda(\underline{x}) \leq T_2\\ &= \omega_0 \quad \text{if } T_2 < \Lambda(\underline{x}) < T_1.\end{aligned}$$

Recalling 17, it is clear that the acceptance region Ω_1 is defined as $\{\underline{x}|\Lambda(\underline{x}) \geq T_1\}$. The acceptance region Ω_2 and the reject region Ω_0 are defined in a similar way. It is also clear that the equation of the *decision boundary* separating the acceptance region Ω_1 from the reject region Ω_0 is $\Lambda(\underline{x}) = T_1$. It is of interest to write this equation in full, *viz.*,

46 $$\underline{x}^t\Sigma^{-1}\left(\underline{\mu}_1-\underline{\mu}_2\right) = \frac{1}{2}\left(\underline{\mu}_1+\underline{\mu}_2\right)^t\Sigma^{-1}\left(\underline{\mu}_1-\underline{\mu}_2\right) + \log\frac{P_2}{P_1}\frac{1-\lambda_r}{\lambda_r}.$$

As could be expected, 46 is the equation of a *linear* decision boundary, i.e., a *hyperplane* in d-dimensional feature space. The same reasoning applies to the decision boundary separating the acceptance region Ω_2 from the reject region Ω_0 : this second decision boundary is also a hyperplane, the equation of which differs from 46 only in the independent term. Consequently, we obtain two parallel hyperplanes h_1 and h_2 as illustrated by Figure 2.1 for the case of two-dimensional patterns.

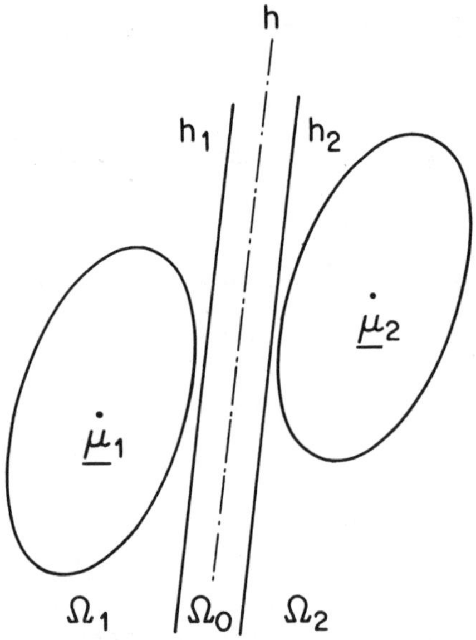

Figure 2.1. The decision boundaries and decision regions for the Bayes classifier of Equation 45.

47 A diagram for the classifier which implements the decision rule 45 is shown in Figure 2.2 and is obtained in the following manner:

Let $\underline{x}=(x_1,\ldots,x_d)^t$, $\underline{w}=\Sigma^{-1}(\underline{\mu}_1-\underline{\mu}_2)$ with $\underline{w}=(w_1,\ldots,w_d)^t$, and $w_{i,d+1}=-\left[(1/2)(\underline{\mu}_1+\underline{\mu}_2)^t\underline{w}+T_i\right]$, i=1,2. Then, the equation of hyperplane

h_i is $\underline{x}^t\underline{w}+w_{i,d+1}=0$. This formulation indicates that the classifier may be synthesized by a resistive network followed by elementary logic.

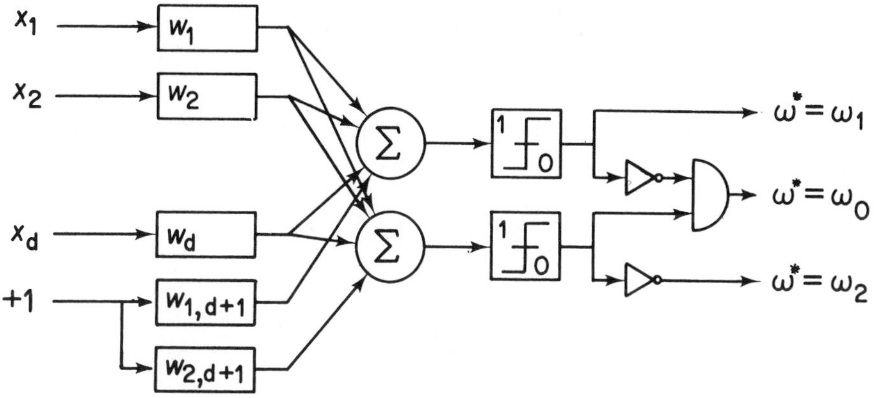

Figure 2.2. Implementation of the linear classifier in Equation 45.

We now wish to analyze the influence of the rejection threshold λ_r on the probabilities of making correct and erroneous decisions. Without loss of generality, we may calculate these probabilities in acceptance region Ω_1 only. The probability of making correct decisions is

48.a $$C^{*1} = Pr\{\omega_1, \Lambda(\underline{x}) \geq T_1\} = P_1 Pr\{\Lambda(\underline{x}) \geq T_1 | \omega_1\},$$

and the error probability is

48.b $$E^{*1} = Pr\{\omega_2, \Lambda(\underline{x}) \geq T_1\} = P_2 Pr\{\Lambda(\underline{x}) \geq T_1 | \omega_2\}.$$

Clearly, to be able to calculate these probabilities we have to determine the conditional distributions of the log-likelihood ratio $\Lambda(\underline{x})$. To this end we shall invoke a basic result in elementary multivariate statistical analysis which says that if $\underline{x}$ is distributed according to $N(\underline{\mu}_1, \Sigma)$, $\Lambda(\underline{x})$ which is a linear function of $\underline{x}$ is also normally distributed with mean

$$\int\left[\underline{x}^t \Sigma^{-1}(\underline{\mu}_1-\underline{\mu}_2) - \frac{1}{2}(\underline{\mu}_1+\underline{\mu}_2)^t \Sigma^{-1}(\underline{\mu}_1-\underline{\mu}_2)\right] p(\underline{x}|\omega_1)\,d\underline{x}$$

$$= \underline{\mu}_1^t \Sigma^{-1}(\underline{\mu}_1-\underline{\mu}_2) - \frac{1}{2}(\underline{\mu}_1+\underline{\mu}_2)^t \Sigma^{-1}(\underline{\mu}_1-\underline{\mu}_2)$$

$$= \frac{1}{2}(\underline{\mu}_1-\underline{\mu}_2)^t \Sigma^{-1}(\underline{\mu}_1-\underline{\mu}_2)$$

and variance

$$\int\left[(\underline{\mu}_1-\underline{\mu}_2)^t \Sigma^{-1}(\underline{x}-\underline{\mu}_1)(\underline{x}-\underline{\mu}_1)^t \Sigma^{-1}(\underline{\mu}_1-\underline{\mu}_2)\right] p(\underline{x}|\omega_1)\,d\underline{x}$$

$$= (\underline{\mu}_1-\underline{\mu}_2)^t \Sigma^{-1}(\underline{\mu}_1-\underline{\mu}_2).$$

The quantity $\Delta = (\underline{\mu}_1-\underline{\mu}_2)^t \Sigma^{-1}(\underline{\mu}_1-\underline{\mu}_2)$ is usually called the Mahalanobis distance measure. Then, when $\underline{x}$ belongs to class ω_1, $\Lambda(\underline{x})$ is distributed according to $N(\frac{1}{2}\Delta, \Delta)$. We could show in the same way that when $\underline{x}$ belongs to class ω_2, $\Lambda(\underline{x})$ is distributed according to $N(-\frac{1}{2}\Delta, \Delta)$. We may now write down the expressions for the probabilities in 48

49 $$C^{*1} = P_1 \int_{T_1}^{\infty} (2\pi\Delta)^{-1/2} \exp\left[\frac{-1}{2\Delta}\left(z - \frac{1}{2}\Delta\right)^2\right] dz,$$

50 $$E^{*1} = P_2 \int_{T_1}^{\infty} (2\pi\Delta)^{-1/2} \exp\left[\frac{-1}{2\Delta}\left(z + \frac{1}{2}\Delta\right)^2\right] dz.$$

These probabilities can be determined from the tables of the normal distribution.

The probabilities C^{*1} and E^{*1} are both differentiable with respect to T_1. Thus we may write

51 $$dC^{*1} = -P_1(2\pi\Delta)^{-1/2}\exp\left[-\frac{1}{2\Delta}\left(T_1 - \frac{\Delta}{2}\right)^2\right]dT_1,$$

52 $$dE^{*1} = -P_2(2\pi\Delta)^{-1/2}\exp\left[-\frac{1}{2\Delta}\left(T_1 + \frac{\Delta}{2}\right)^2\right]dT_1.$$

If we further notice that

$$-\frac{1}{2\Delta}\left(T_1 - \frac{\Delta}{2}\right)^2 = T_1 - \frac{1}{2\Delta}\left(T_1 + \frac{\Delta}{2}\right)^2,$$

we obtain from 51 and 52

$$dC^{*1} = \frac{P_1}{P_2}\exp(T_1)dE^{*1},$$

and this simplifies as follows:

53 $$dC^{*1}(\lambda_r) = \frac{1-\lambda_r}{\lambda_r}\, dE^{*1}(\lambda_r),$$

where the notation is again intended to emphasize the dependence of C^{*1} and E^{*1} on the rejection threshold. We leave it to the reader to verify that performing the same reasoning in acceptance region Ω_2 leads to the very same differential equation in terms of the probabilities E^{*2} and C^{*2}.

To see the significance of 53, consider the effect of an increase in the rejection threshold λ_r. It entails a decrease in T_1 and an increase in T_2 : the reject region shrinks as the acceptance regions expand. Both probabilities in 49 and 50 increase. However, since $\lambda_r \leq 1/2$, we have $(1-\lambda_r)/\lambda_r \geq 1$, and, by 53, the probability of correct decision increases faster than the probability of error. When λ_r reaches 1/2, the two decision boundaries, i.e., the hyperplanes h_1 and h_2, merge in a unique boundary h (see Figure 2.1). At this point $dC^{*i} = dE^{*i}$ and any further change in the decision boundary would force the error rate to increase faster than the probability of correct decision.

54 From the above discussion, it is clear that, in the important case when there are no rejects, the equation of the discriminant hyperplane h is obtained by taking $\lambda_r = 1/2$ in 46. We would evidently have come to the same formulation had we discussed the minimum error rate decision rule of 37. The hyperplane h is sometimes referred to as the Anderson discriminant plane, specifically

$$\underline{x}^t \Sigma^{-1}\left(\underline{\mu}_1-\underline{\mu}_2\right) = \frac{1}{2}\left(\underline{\mu}_1+\underline{\mu}_2\right)^t \Sigma^{-1}\left(\underline{\mu}_1-\underline{\mu}_2\right) + \log\frac{P_2}{P_1}.$$

Let us write 53 in terms of overall probabilities of error and correct decision, namely

55 $$dC^*(\lambda_r) = \frac{1-\lambda_r}{\lambda_r}\, dE^*(\lambda_r).$$

From 26 we have $C^*(\lambda_r) = A^*(\lambda_r) - E^*(\lambda_r)$. Hence

56 $$dC^*(\lambda_r) = dA^*(\lambda_r)-dE^*(\lambda_r).$$

By substituting 56 into 55 we obtain

57 $$dE^*(\lambda_r) = \lambda_r dA^*(\lambda_r) = -\lambda_r dR^*(\lambda_r).$$

Consequently

58 $$E^*(\lambda_r) = \int_0^{\lambda_r} \lambda dA^*(\lambda) = -\int_0^{\lambda_r} \lambda dR^*(\lambda).$$

Here we recognize the important result we claimed without proof in 32. It should be pointed out however that the proof outlined above applies only to the case of two normally distributed pattern classes while 32 and 58 hold irrespective of the nature of the underlying probability distributions.

2.6. BAYES DECISION THEORY IN THE DISCRETE CASE

Until now, we have been assuming that the patterns were distributed according to probability distributions which have densities. In other words, the pattern $\underline{x}$ could be any point in feature space Ω. However, in many practical situations, features may assume discrete values only. In this case, we have to replace the densities by discrete probability distributions over the possible values of pattern $\underline{x}$ and change our integrals into sums. We shall illustrate this on the basis of one classical example.

We consider a two-class problem and we assume that each component x_j of $\underline{x}$ is either 0 or 1 with conditional probabilities

59.a $$p_j = Pr\{x_j=1|\omega_1\},$$

59.b $$q_j = Pr\{x_j=1|\omega_2\}.$$

We further assume that the components of $\underline{x}$ are conditionally independent. This allows us to write the conditional probability of $\underline{x}$ in a particularly convenient way,

60.a
$$p(\underline{x}|\omega_1) = \prod_{j=1}^{d} p_j^{x_j}(1-p_j)^{1-x_j},$$

60.b
$$p(\underline{x}|\omega_2) = \prod_{j=1}^{d} q_j^{x_j}(1-q_j)^{1-x_j}.$$

Suppose we want to find the minimum error rate decision rule of Section 2.4 for these distributions. As a first step, we note that the rule of 37 can again be expressed in terms of the log-likelihood ratio $\Lambda(\underline{x})$:

61
$$\hat{\omega}^*(\underline{x}) = \omega_1 \quad \text{if } \Lambda(\underline{x}) \geq \log \frac{P_2}{P_1},$$
$$\omega_2 \quad \text{otherwise.}$$

For the distributions in 60 the likelihood ratio is given by

62
$$\frac{p(\underline{x}|\omega_1)}{p(\underline{x}|\omega_2)} = \prod_{j=1}^{d} \left(\frac{p_j}{q_j}\right)^{x_j} \left(\frac{1-p_j}{1-q_j}\right)^{1-x_j}.$$

By taking logarithms we obtain

$$\Lambda(\underline{x}) = \sum_{j=1}^{d} \left\{ x_j \log \frac{p_j}{q_j} + (1-x_j) \log \frac{1-p_j}{1-q_j} \right\}$$

63
$$= \sum_{j=1}^{d} x_j \log \frac{p_j(1-q_j)}{q_j(1-p_j)} + \sum_{j=1}^{d} \log \frac{1-p_j}{1-q_j}.$$

We observe that $\Lambda(\underline{x})$ is again linear in $\underline{x}$. Let us then use the notation introduced in 47 and let

64.a
$$w_j = \log \frac{p_j(1-q_j)}{q_j(1-p_j)}, \quad j=1,\ldots,d,$$

and

64.b $$w_{d+1} = \sum_{j=1}^{d} \log \frac{1-p_j}{1-q_j} + \log \frac{P_1}{P_2}.$$

Then the equation of the decision boundary separating the acceptance regions Ω_1 and Ω_2 is given by

65 $$\sum_{j=1}^{d} w_j x_j + w_{d+1} = 0.$$

This is, anew, the equation of a d-dimensional hyperplane.

2.7. COMMENTS

The presentation heretofore was clearly intended to demonstrate the existence of situations where a complete knowledge of the statistical model describing the pattern-generating mechanism enables the designer to determine both the optimal structure and the performance of the pattern classifier. It could be argued that, in practical applications, such a perfect knowledge of the underlying distributions is practically never available. But more on that later. One could also argue that usually the usefulness of the above results - or, for that matter, of any result derived in a comparable way - is significantly undermined by the large number of assumptions involved in their derivation. This is unfortunately an unescapable dilemma. In a sense, it is the pattern recognition version of the dilemma, well-known to communication engineers, that higher gain can only be obtained at the expense of reduced bandwith.

This point can be clearly made on the basis of the two examples we have studied in Sections 2.5 and 2.6. Suppose we wanted to enlarge the field of applicability of our study of the two normally distributed pattern classes by relaxing the assumption of equal covariance matrices. This would change the optimal decision boundaries from hyperplanes to hyperquadric surfaces. The reader would soon get a clearer appreciation of the difficulties to be expected if he wanted to try his hand at the calculation of the error probabilities in this slightly more general case. In the same line of thought, the general solution to our discrete-case problem would have been quite involved had we not assumed class-conditional independence of the components x_j of $\underline{x}$. Besides assuming the x_j's to be ternary instead of binary independent random variables would result again in the optimum decision boundary becoming a hyperquadric surface.

These comments are not intended to detract from the usefulness of working out very specific examples. This remains, in many cases, the most vivid way to outline a methodology. We would like to emphasize however that our presentation is merely intended to provide theoretical guidance on how to attack practical problems. The derivation of the optimal solution to a classification problem will, as a rule, be beyond the reach of the practitioner. He will usually have either to satisfy himself with an approximation to the optimal solution, or to resort to suboptimal classification methods such as those discussed in the following two chapters.

66 Another fundamental limitation of the approach we have discussed so far is that the simple model for the pattern-generating mechanism which we have assumed above may ignore some important aspects of the problem at hand. For example, the feature measurement process may be

sequential in nature, or the individual decisions should be influenced by the *context*. Space limitations do not allow us to discuss such points in considerable detail. Nevertheless, it is instructive to see how our model may be extended to the effect of taking such aspects into account.

2.8. SEQUENTIAL CLASSIFICATION

In this section we shall assume that the feature measurement process is sequential, as it is the case in many medical applications. We also add one further dimension to our problem by assuming that, besides the cost of classification error, there is also a *feature observation cost*. In such situations it may be desirable to allow the system to trade classification accuracy for cost. Indeed, we may wish to make a decision after n ($n<d$) measurements have been made, since the remaining $d-n$ observations may reduce the error probability only slightly while incurring additional observation cost.

There exists a number of possibilities for a desirable compromise between the cost of classification error and the observation cost. For example, such a compromise can be obtained by minimizing the number of features to be measured while achieving a sufficient classification accuracy. Another possibility is to devise the decision rule that minimizes a combination of both costs. This is the problem to which we now turn.

67 It should also be noted that sequential methods differ quite naturally according to whether or not the order of the features to be

measured has been fixed beforehand : ideally, features should be ordered in such a way as to cause the terminal decision as soon as possible. As we shall see, this requirement is again adding an extra dimension to the problem. In the first place, we shall assume that features are observed in a predetermined order.

68 Thus, suppose that the first n features have been observed and let $\xi_1,\ldots,\xi_n$ designate the values assumed by $x_1,\ldots,x_n$. Let g_j be the cost of measuring the feature x_j, and suppose our objective is to minimize the *sum* of the cost of classification error and the observation cost.

At stage n, we are confronted with the following alternative: Either we may make a *terminal*, Bayes decision based on the data $\xi_1,\ldots,\xi_n$, or we may choose to take one additional observation. In the first instance the *stopping cost* $\rho_s(\xi_1,\ldots,\xi_n)$ is

69 $$\rho_s(\xi_1,\ldots,\xi_n) = l^*(\xi_1,\ldots,\xi_n)$$

$$= \min_{i=1,\ldots,c} \sum_{j=1}^{c} \lambda(\omega_i|\omega_j)P(\omega_j|\xi_1,\ldots,\xi_n).$$

Clearly, a terminal decision will be made when $\rho_s(\xi_1,\ldots,\xi_n)$ is the *minimum cost at stage* n. Let $\rho_{min}(\xi_1,\ldots,\xi_n)$ designate this minimum cost for which we do not propose yet any formal expression.

Let us consider next the other issue of the alternative, *viz.*, continuing the process and making one additional observation. This will first result in an observation cost g_{n+1}. Next, we shall be confronted with the very same alternative expressed in terms of the data that should be available at stage n+1. This information is not completely available at stage n when we have to resolve the first alternative. Thus, the best we can hope for is to be able to calculate the conditional expected value of the minimum cost at stage n+1 under the conditions $x_1=\xi_1,\ldots,x_n=\xi_n$. This conditional expected value is given by

$$\int \rho_{min}(\xi_1,\ldots,\xi_n,x_{n+1})p(x_{n+1}|\xi_1,\ldots,\xi_n)dx_{n+1}.$$

where the integration is carried over the admissible region of x_{n+1} given $\xi_1,\ldots,\xi_n$. So the *continuing cost* $\rho_c(\xi_1,\ldots,\xi_n)$ is

70 $$\rho_c(\xi_1,\ldots,\xi_n) = \\ = g_{n+1} + \int \rho_{min}(\xi_1,\ldots,\xi_n,x_{n+1})p(x_{n+1}|\xi_1,\ldots,\xi_n)dx_{n+1}.$$

Note that, up to this point, the minimum cost function ρ_{min} remained undefined. However, by definition ρ_{min} is the minimum of the stopping and continuing costs :

71 $$\rho_{min}(\xi_1,\ldots,\xi_n) = \min\left\{\rho_s(\xi_1,\ldots,\xi_n),\rho_c(\xi_1,\ldots,\xi_n)\right\}.$$

It is this equation which gives us the clue to the expression of the minimum cost function. By substituting 69 and 70 into 71 we obtain the basic functional equation governing the sequence of minimum cost functions

72 $$\rho_{min}(\xi_1,\ldots,\xi_n) = \min \left[\begin{array}{l} \text{Continue :} \\ g_{n+1} + \int \rho'_{min}(\xi_1,\ldots,\xi_n,x_{n+1})p(x_{n+1}|\xi_1,\ldots,\xi_n)dx_{n+1} \\ \text{Stop :} \quad \min\limits_{i=1,\ldots,c} \sum\limits_{j=1}^{c} \lambda(\omega_i|\omega_j)P(\omega_j|\xi_1,\ldots,\xi_n). \end{array} \right.$$

Many of the difficulties arising with this approach are well apparent from 72. In particular, one may see that the minimum cost at stage n+1 must be determined before the computation of the minimum cost at stage n. In turn, the minimum cost at stage n+2 must be determined before the computation of the minimum cost at stage n+1. So, we have to proceed backwards, starting from

73 $$\begin{aligned}\rho_{\min}(\xi_1,\ldots,\xi_n,x_{n+1},\ldots,x_d) &= l^*(\xi_1,\ldots,\xi_n,x_{n+1},\ldots,x_d)\\ &= \min_{i=1,\ldots,c} \sum_{j=1}^{c} \lambda(\omega_i|\omega_j)P(\omega_j|\xi_1,\ldots,\xi_n,x_{n+1},\ldots,x_d).\end{aligned}$$

A number of techniques have been developed for reducing the enormous amount of computer storage required for the calculation of the cost functions - not to speak of the high-order conditional probabilities - while retaining the optimality of the proposed system. These techniques are based, for example, on the use of sufficient statistics or the assumption of Markovian dependence among feature measurements. We shall presently take an even more drastic assumption. We shall suppose that we are willing to sacrifice the optimality of the decision rule for the sake of computational simplification. One way of doing this is to assume that a terminal decision will be reached not later than the (n+ν)th stage. Clearly, this corresponds to substituting $l^*(\xi_1,\ldots,\xi_n,x_{n+1},\ldots,x_{n+\nu})$ to $\rho_{\min}(\xi_1,\ldots,\xi_n,x_{n+1},\ldots,x_{n+\nu})$ in the recursive equation 72. Thus, the suboptimal, *sequential process with two stage ahead truncation procedure* is governed by the following equations :

$\rho_{min}(\xi_1,\ldots,\xi_n)$

74
$$= \min \begin{bmatrix} \text{Continue :} \\ g_{n+1}+\int \rho_{min}(\xi_1,\ldots,\xi_n,x_{n+1})p(x_{n+1}|\xi_1,\ldots,\xi_n)dx_{n+1} \\ \text{Stop :} \quad \min\limits_{i=1,\ldots,c} \sum\limits_{j=1}^{c} \lambda(\omega_i|\omega_j)P(\omega_j|\xi_1,\ldots,\xi_n) \end{bmatrix}$$

$\rho_{min}(\xi_1,\ldots,\xi_n,x_{n+1})$

75
$$= \min \begin{bmatrix} \text{Continue :} \\ g_{n+2}+\int \min\limits_{i} \sum\limits_{j=1}^{c} \lambda(\omega_i|\omega_j)P(\omega_j|\xi_1,\ldots,\xi_n,x_{n+1},x_{n+2}) \cdot \\ \cdot p(x_{n+2}|\xi_1,\ldots\xi_n,x_{n+1})dx_{n+2} \\ \text{Stop :} \quad \min\limits_{i=1,\ldots,c} \sum\limits_{j=1}^{c} \lambda(\omega_i|\omega_j)P(\omega_j|\xi_1,\ldots,\xi_n,x_{n+1}) . \end{bmatrix}$$

Until now, we have been assuming that the order in which the features are measured has been fixed once and for all. However, the reader should easily convince himself that a given ordering cannot be uniformly good over all possible patterns. Ideally, one would like this ordering to depend on the results of the observations made so far. While this idea is very easy to state in plain words, it is rather cumbersome to formalize mathematically. To simplify matters we shall limit ourselves to the formulation of the sequential process *with on line feature ordering* in the case of the one stage ahead truncation procedure.

Suppose that $\xi_1,\ldots,\xi_n$ designate the results of the first n observations, and after each observation the remaining features - those which are yet to be measured - are renumbered to form the set

$x_{n+1},\ldots,x_d$. Next, suppose that, at stage n, the next feature to be measured is found to be x_{n+k}. In the case of the one stage ahead truncation procedure the continuation risk is

$$\rho_c(\xi_1,\ldots,\xi_n) = g_{n+k}+\int \min_i \sum_{j=1}^{c} \lambda(\omega_i|\omega_j)P(\omega_j|\xi_1,\ldots,\xi_n,x_{n+k})\cdot$$

76 $$\cdot p(x_{n+k}|\xi_1,\ldots,\xi_n)dx_{n+k}.$$

Now, since our objective is to minimize the overall cost, the optimal feature to take into consideration for measurement at the (n+1)th stage is that which results in the lowest continuation risk as expressed by the right hand side of 76. Hence the equation

$$\rho_{min}(\xi_1,\ldots,\xi_n)=$$

77 $$= \min \left[\begin{array}{l} \text{Continue :} \\ \min_k \left\{c_{n+k}+\int \min_i \sum_{j=1}^{g} \lambda(\omega_i|\omega_j)P(\omega_j|\xi_1,\ldots,\xi_n,x_{n+k})\cdot \right. \\ \left. \qquad \cdot p(x_{n+k}|\xi_1,\ldots\xi_n)dx_{n+k}\right\}, \qquad k=1,\ldots,d-n \\ \text{Stop :} \quad \min_{i=1,\ldots,c} \sum_{j=1}^{c} \lambda(\omega_i|\omega_j)P(\omega_j|\xi_1,\ldots,\xi_n). \end{array} \right.$$

Experimental evidence indicates that the additional increase in computational complexity due to on line feature ordering is generally well compensated by a further decrease in the number of features to be measured before reaching a terminal decision.

2.9. CLASSIFICATION USING CONTEXTUAL INFORMATION

In many pattern recognition problems, there exist dependencies among the successive pattern classes to be recognized. This is especially evident when the recognition of text, speech or pictures is attempted. In some cases, those dependencies may be accounted for by assuming that the underlying mechanism generating the successive pattern classes can be approximated by a kth order ergodic Markov source. For simplicity, we shall restrict ourselves to a first order Markov source, and we shall show that the sequential compound decision theory yields a recursive procedure for the determination of the class *a posteriori* probabilities required for making Bayes decisions.

78 Using the terminology associated with Markov chains, we shall say that the pattern-class generating process is in *state* ω_i at *time* τ if the τth pattern to classify is from class ω_i. Let ω^τ and $\underline{x}^\tau$ denote the class and feature vector at time τ. Before starting with the treatment of our classificaton problem, let us recall a few basic facts about Markov chains.

A *discrete parameter Markov chain* is a sequence of discrete random variables $\{\omega^\tau, \tau>0\}$ possessing the following property : for any $\tau\geq 2$ and any sequence $i_1,\ldots,i_\tau$ we have

79 $$\Pr\left\{\omega^\tau = \omega_{i_\tau} \mid \omega^1=\omega_{i_1},\ldots,\omega^{\tau-1}=\omega_{i_{\tau-1}}\right\} = \Pr\left\{\omega^\tau=\omega_{i_\tau} \mid \omega^{\tau-1}=\omega_{i_{\tau-1}}\right\}.$$

The condition 79 is usually referred to as the *Markov property*. Loosely speaking, it says that "the past should have no influence on the future except through the present". Of particular interest to us is the case when the probability in the right hand side of 79 is independent of the time index τ, thus

80 $$\Pr\left\{\omega^\tau=\omega_i \mid \omega^{\tau-1}=\omega_j\right\} = P(i\mid j),$$

for all $\tau \geq 1$ and all $i,j = 1,\ldots,c$. A discrete parameter Markov chain for which 80 holds is said to be *homogeneous* or to have *stationary transition probabilities* as stipulated by 80. We shall assume hereafter that we are dealing with a homogeneous Markov chain.

To fix ideas, let us suppose that we are concerned with the recognition of English text. Then the transition probabilities are simply the probabilities of occurrence of *bigrams* in the English language. These probabilities constitute a datum for the classification problem and represent the additional knowledge contributed by the context.

At time $\tau-1$, the state of the process is characterized by the probabilities $P\left(\omega^{\tau-1}=\omega_j|\underline{x}^1,\ldots,\underline{x}^{\tau-1}\right)$. Let us assume we know these probabilities, and proceed with the operations we have to perform at time τ.

By using the Markov property we can write:

$$P\left(\omega^{\tau}=\omega_i|\underline{x}^1,\ldots,\underline{x}^{\tau-1}\right) = \sum_{j=1}^{c} P\left(\omega^{\tau}=\omega_i,\omega^{\tau-1}=\omega_j|\underline{x}^1,\ldots,\underline{x}^{\tau-1}\right)$$

$$= \sum_{j=1}^{c} P\left(\omega^{\tau}=\omega_i|\omega^{\tau-1}=\omega_j\right)\cdot$$

$$\cdot P\left(\omega^{\tau-1}=\omega_j|\underline{x}^1,\ldots,\underline{x}^{\tau-1}\right),$$

and by using 80 we obtain

81 $$P\left(\omega^{\tau}=\omega_i|\underline{x}^1,\ldots,\underline{x}^{\tau-1}\right) = \sum_{j=1}^{c} P(i|j)P\left(\omega^{\tau-1}=\omega_j|\underline{x}^1,\ldots,\underline{x}^{\tau-1}\right).$$

Here two things must be noticed. First, the right hand side of 81 consists only of known probabilities. Second, it does not involve the observation at time τ. So the probability on the left hand side of 81 can be calculated before the observation of $\underline{x}^\tau$. It represents the *a priori* probability distribution for the state of the process at time τ. Next, this distribution has to be updated in order to account for the observation of $\underline{x}^\tau$. In order to do this we first make the assumption that $\underline{x}^1,\ldots,\underline{x}^\tau$ are conditionally independent. This implies

82 $$p\left(\underline{x}^\tau|\omega^\tau=\omega_i,\underline{x}^1,\ldots,\underline{x}^{\tau-1}\right) = p\left(\underline{x}^\tau|\omega^\tau=\omega_i\right).$$

Conditioning on $\underline{x}^1,\ldots,\underline{x}^\tau$, the *a posteriori* probability at time τ is given by

83 $$P\left(\omega^\tau=\omega_i|\underline{x}^1,\ldots,\underline{x}^\tau\right) = \frac{P\left(\omega^\tau=\omega_i,\underline{x}^\tau|\underline{x}^1,\ldots,\underline{x}^{\tau-1}\right)}{p\left(\underline{x}^\tau|\underline{x}^1,\ldots,\underline{x}^{\tau-1}\right)},$$

where for the numerator we have

$$P\left(\omega^\tau=\omega_i,\underline{x}^\tau|\underline{x}^1,\ldots,\underline{x}^{\tau-1}\right)$$

$$= P\left(\omega^\tau=\omega_i|\underline{x}^1,\ldots,\underline{x}^{\tau-1}\right)p\left(\underline{x}^\tau|\omega^\tau=\omega_i,\underline{x}^1,\ldots,\underline{x}^{\tau-1}\right)$$

84 $$= P\left(\omega^\tau=\omega_i|\underline{x}^1,\ldots,\underline{x}^{\tau-1}\right)p\left(\underline{x}^\tau|\omega^\tau=\omega_i\right),$$

and for the denominator we have

$$p\left(\underline{x}^\tau|\underline{x}^1,\ldots,\underline{x}^{\tau-1}\right) = \sum_{j=1}^{c} p\left(\underline{x}^\tau,\omega^\tau=\omega_j|\underline{x}^1,\ldots,\underline{x}^{\tau-1}\right)$$

85 $$= \sum_{j=1}^{c} P\left(\omega^\tau=\omega_j|\underline{x}^1,\ldots,\underline{x}^{\tau-1}\right)p\left(\underline{x}^\tau|\omega^\tau=\omega_j\right).$$

By substitution of 84 and 85 in 83 we obtain

86 $$P\left(\omega^\tau=\omega_i \,|\, \underline{x}^1,\ldots,\underline{x}^\tau\right) = \frac{P\left(\omega^\tau=\omega_i \,|\, \underline{x}^1,\ldots,\underline{x}^{\tau-1}\right)p\left(\underline{x}^\tau \,|\, \omega^\tau=\omega_i\right)}{\sum_{j=1}^{c} P\left(\omega^\tau=\omega_j \,|\, \underline{x}^1,\ldots,\underline{x}^{\tau-1}\right)p\left(\underline{x}^\tau \,|\, \omega^\tau=\omega_j\right)}.$$

Clearly, 86 enables us to calculate the *a posteriori* distribution at time τ. This distribution is first used to make the optimal decision at time τ. Next, it is used to initiate the calculation of the prior distribution at time $\tau+1$.

The technique we just described can be refined in a number of ways. For example, equations corresponding to 81 through 86 could be written for higher-order Markov sources. A second-order Markov source would require the use of so-called *trigram transition probabilities*, i.e., $P\left(\omega^\tau=\omega_i \,|\, \omega^{\tau-1}=\omega_j, \omega^{\tau-2}=\omega_k\right)$. The Markovian approach can also be combined with the sequential approach of the previous section. Still another possibility which we shall briefly examine is to use the *look ahead mode of decision*. In this mode, the decision about the present pattern $\underline{x}^\tau$ is postponed until we look ahead at the subsequent pattern $\underline{x}^{\tau+1}$. To implement this idea we have to calculate the probability

87 $$P\left(\omega^\tau=\omega_i \,|\, \underline{x}^1,\ldots,\underline{x}^\tau,\underline{x}^{\tau+1}\right).$$

First, we calculate $P\left(\omega^\tau=\omega_i \,|\, \underline{x}^1,\ldots,\underline{x}^\tau\right)$ as previously seen. Next, we express the probability in 87 as follows :

88 $$P\left(\omega^\tau=\omega_i \,|\, \underline{x}^1,\ldots,\underline{x}^\tau,\underline{x}^{\tau+1}\right) = \frac{p\left(\underline{x}^{\tau+1} \,|\, \omega^\tau=\omega_i\right)P\left(\omega^\tau=\omega_i \,|\, \underline{x}^1,\ldots,\underline{x}^\tau\right)}{\sum_{j=1}^{c} p\left(\underline{x}^{\tau+1} \,|\, \omega^\tau=\omega_j\right)P\left(\omega^\tau=\omega_j \,|\, \underline{x}^1,\ldots,\underline{x}^\tau\right)}.$$

The independence assumption of 82 enables us to write

89 $$p\left(\underline{x}^{\tau+1} \mid \omega^{\tau}=\omega_i\right) = \sum_{k=1}^{c} p\left(\underline{x}^{\tau+1} \mid \omega^{\tau+1}=\omega_k, \omega^{\tau}=\omega_i\right) P\left(\omega^{\tau+1}=\omega_k \mid \omega^{\tau}=\omega_i\right)$$

$$= \sum_{k=1}^{c} p\left(\underline{x}^{\tau+1} \mid \omega^{\tau+1}=\omega_k\right) P(k \mid i).$$

Eventually, by substitution of 89 in 88, it follows that

90 $$P\left(\omega^{\tau}=\omega_i \mid \underline{x}^1, \dots, \underline{x}^{\tau}, \underline{x}^{\tau+1}\right)$$

$$= \frac{\sum_{k=1}^{c} p\left(\underline{x}^{\tau+1} \mid \omega^{\tau+1}=\omega_k\right) P(k \mid i) P\left(\omega^{\tau}=\omega_i \mid \underline{x}^1, \dots, \underline{x}^{\tau}\right)}{\sum_{j=1}^{c} \sum_{k=1}^{c} p\left(\underline{x}^{\tau+1} \mid \omega^{\tau+1}=\omega_k\right) P(k \mid j) P\left(\omega^{\tau}=\omega_j \mid \underline{x}^1, \dots, \underline{x}^{\tau}\right)}$$

It should be noticed that the transition probabilities of 80 are still sufficient to compute 90, and that this equation comprises only probabilities which would have to be calculated in order to use 86 at time $\tau+1$. There follows that the improvement in the performance that results from using 90 instead of 86 is obtained without actually increasing the computational complexity of the proposed technique.

A number of alternative approaches aimed at exploiting contextual information have appeared in the pattern recognition literature. The reader should however keep in mind that contextual - or, more generally, structural - information manifests itself under a wide variety of guises, many of which cannot be modeled in a proper manner by statistical means. As an historical note, it may be of interest to remark that the need to circumvent this limitation of the statistical approach provided the motivation behind the development, in the late sixties, of the syntactic methods of pattern recognition.

2.10. ERROR PROBABILITY AND ERROR BOUNDS

We have pointed out in Section 2.4 that the error probability of the Bayes classifier was to play an important role in our investigation. However, it should be evident, from the preceding discussions, that the evaluation of the error probability is in general a very difficult task. Cases where a closed-form expression for the error probability can be found are exceptions rather than the rule, and even when it can be found, it may be too complicated to permit numerical evaluation.

An alternative approach is to seek an approximate expression for the error probability in the form of upper and/or lower bounds on error probability. The problem of error bounding can be approached from two different ways. In the following chapter we shall derive expressions of tight bounds of the error probability which are much easier to *estimate* than the error probability itself. By contrast, in this section, we discuss some error bounds which are easier to *calculate*, especially in the case of multivariate Gaussian data. These bounds are expressed in terms of *probabilistic separability or distance measures* which will be further investigated in Chapter 7.

2.10.1. The Mahalanobis Distance Measure

91 As a first example, consider a problem of two pattern classes with mean vector $\underline{u}_i$ and covariance matrix Σ_i, i=1,2. Here, we will not require the classes to be normally distributed. All that will be assumed is that the average covariance matrix

$$\Sigma = P_1\Sigma_1 + P_2\Sigma_2$$

is nonsingular. Under these conditions, we will show in Chapter 4 that the Mahalanobis distance measure

92 $$\Delta = \left(\underline{\mu}_1-\underline{\mu}_2\right)^t \Sigma^{-1}\left(\underline{\mu}_1-\underline{\mu}_2\right)$$

yields the following bound on the Bayes error E^*

93 $$\frac{2P_1P_2}{1+P_1P_2\Delta} \geq E^*.$$

Unfortunately, this bound is not very tight except when E^* is large. In counterpart, the bound is very easy to calculate. It provides a very simple way to get a rough idea of the Bayes error rate. Before closing this discussion of the Mahalanobis distance measure, let us note that it is playing, in pattern recognition, about the same role as does the signal to noise ratio in communication problems. Let us now look for more satisfying results.

2.10.2. The Bhattacharyya Coefficient

Remembering that the conditional Bayes error probability $E^*(\underline{x})$ is given by

$$e^*(\underline{x}) = 1-\max_i P(\omega_i|\underline{x}),$$

we also have for a two-class problem

94 $$e^*(\underline{x}) = \min\left[P(\omega_1|\underline{x}),P(\omega_2|\underline{x})\right].$$

By the geometric mean inequality,

95 $$e^*(\underline{x}) \leq \sqrt{P(\omega_1|\underline{x})P(\omega_2|\underline{x})},$$

and by taking expectation we get

96 $$E^* = \int e^*(\underline{x})p(\underline{x})d\underline{x} \leq \int \sqrt{P(\omega_1|\underline{x})P(\omega_2|\underline{x})}\,p(\underline{x})d\underline{x}$$

$$= \sqrt{P_1P_2} \int \sqrt{p(\underline{x}|\omega_1)p(\underline{x}|\omega_2)}\,d\underline{x}.$$

The Bhattacharyya coefficient is defined as follows:

97 $$J_B = -\log \int \sqrt{p(\underline{x}|\omega_1)p(\underline{x}|\omega_2)}\,d\underline{x}.$$

From 96, an upper-bound on E^* in terms of J_B is

98 $$E^* \le \sqrt{P_1P_2}\exp(-J_B).$$

On the other hand, we shall derive in Chapter 3 a simple proof of the lower bound of E^* appearing in 99. We thus have,

99 $$\frac{1}{2}\left[1-\sqrt{1-4P_1P_2\exp(-2J_B)}\right] \le E^* \le \sqrt{P_1P_2}\exp(-J_B).$$

100 Our reasoning, so far, may appear somewhat artificial. However, suppose now that each class is normally distributed with mean $\underline{\mu}_i$ and covariance matrix Σ_i, i=1,2. It is then a simple matter to integrate 97 in order to show that

101 $$J_B = -\log\left[|2\Sigma|^{1/2}|\Sigma_1\Sigma_2|^{-1/4}\right] + \frac{1}{4}\left(\underline{\mu}_1-\underline{\mu}_2\right)^t\left(\Sigma_1+\Sigma_2\right)^{-1}\left(\underline{\mu}_1-\underline{\mu}_2\right),$$

where

$$2\Sigma = \Sigma_1 + \Sigma_2.$$

By carrying 101 into 99 we see that the bounds of E^* in 99 can be directly evaluated from the knowledge of the parameters of the conditional distributions.

2.10.3. The Divergence Measure

Another possibility of obtaining a bound of E^* is to use the divergence measure J_D which is defined by

102 $$J_D = \int \left[p(\underline{x}|\omega_1)-p(\underline{x}|\omega_2)\right]\log \frac{p(\underline{x}|\omega_1)}{p(\underline{x}|\omega_2)}\,d\underline{x}.$$

The divergence measure yields the following crude lower bound on E^*

103 $$E^* \ge \frac{1}{8}\exp(-J_D/2).$$

A much tighter bound follows from using a slight generalization of 102, namely

104 $$J'_D = \int \left[P(\omega_1|\underline{x})-P(\omega_2|\underline{x})\right] \log \frac{P(\omega_1|\underline{x})}{P(\omega_2|\underline{x})} p(\underline{x})d\underline{x}.$$

The corresponding bound is

105 $$J'_D \geq (2E^*-1)\log\left[E^*(1-E^*)\right].$$

We shall limit ourselves to the proof of 105. By using symmetry we can write

106 $$P\left(\omega_1|\underline{x}\right)\log \frac{P(\omega_1|\underline{x})}{1-P(\omega_1|\underline{x})} + P\left(\omega_2|\underline{x}\right)\log \frac{P(\omega_2|\underline{x})}{1-P(\omega_2|\underline{x})}$$

$$= e^*(\underline{x})\log \frac{e^*(\underline{x})}{1-e^*(\underline{x})} + \left(1-e^*(\underline{x})\right)\log \frac{1-e^*(\underline{x})}{e^*(\underline{x})}.$$

It is a straightforward matter to verify that the right hand side of 106 is a convex upwards function of $e^*(\underline{x})$. Then, by virtue of the Jensen's inequality, we obtain successively

$$J'_D = \int \left[P(\omega_1|\underline{x})\log \frac{P(\omega_1|\underline{x})}{1-P(\omega_1|\underline{x})} + P(\omega_2|\underline{x})\log \frac{P(\omega_2|\underline{x})}{1-P(\omega_2|\underline{x})}\right]p(\underline{x})d\underline{x}$$

$$= \int \left[e^*(\underline{x})\log \frac{e^*(\underline{x})}{1-e^*(\underline{x})} + \left(1-e^*(\underline{x})\right)\log \frac{1-e^*(\underline{x})}{e^*(\underline{x})}\right]p(\underline{x})d\underline{x}$$

$$\geq \left(\int e^*(\underline{x})\right)\log \frac{\int e^*(\underline{x})}{1-\int e^*(\underline{x})} + \left(1-\int e^*(\underline{x})\right)\log \frac{1-\int e^*(\underline{x})}{\int e^*(\underline{x})}$$

107 $$= E^*\log \frac{E^*}{1-E^*} + (1-E^*)\log \frac{1-E^*}{E^*},$$

where, to simplify matters, we have used the notation $\int e^*(\underline{x})$ to denote

$\int e^*(\underline{x})p(\underline{x})d\underline{x}$. Finally, rearranging terms in 107 gives 105. Now, under tne assumptions of 100, J_D' is given by

108 $$J_D' = (P_1-P_2)\log \frac{P_1|\Sigma_2|^{1/2}}{P_2|\Sigma_1|^{1/2}} + \frac{1}{2}\,\mathrm{tr}\left[P_1\Sigma_1+P_2\Sigma_2\right]\left[\Sigma_2^{-1}-\Sigma_1^{-1}\right]$$
$$+ \frac{1}{2}\left(\underline{\mu}_1-\underline{\mu}_2\right)^t\left(P_1\Sigma_2^{-1}+P_2\Sigma_1^{-1}\right)\left(\underline{\mu}_1-\underline{\mu}_2\right),$$

where tr [•] denotes the trace of matrix [•]. As in the case of the Bhattacharyya coefficient, the bound can be evaluated in terms of the parameters of the conditional distributions.

2.11. ALTERNATIVES TO THE BAYESIAN APPROACH

Our discussion, thus far, has been placed constantly in a general Bayesian framework where both *a priori*, and class-conditional probability distributions are assumed to be known. However, in a number of contexts, the assumption that there exist fixed *a priori* probabilities is not a very realistic one; e.g., in some medical applications, the *a priori* distribution for a number of diseases may vary with time and place. In such circumstances, the formula of Bayes is not applicable and we must look for other approaches.

Let us consider a two-class problem, and for simplicity, the Bayes rule for minimum error-rate. We have

109 $$E^* = \sum_i E^{*i} = \sum_i \int_{\Omega_i} e^*(\underline{x})p(\underline{x})d\underline{x} = \sum_i P_j \int_{\Omega_i} p(\underline{x}|\omega_j)d\underline{x},$$

for i,j=1,2, i≠j.

The dependence of E^* on the prior distribution operates at two levels. The first one appears explicitly in the rightmost term of

109, and it is seen that with Ω_1 and Ω_2 fixed, E^* is a linear function of, say, P_1 (P_2 is uniquely determined by P_1). On the other hand, the prior distribution was also used in selecting the Bayes acceptance regions Ω_1 and Ω_2. Hence E^* also depends implicitly on P_1 through Ω_1 and Ω_2. Consequently, the functional dependence of E^* on P_1 can be very complex.

Now, for each fixed P_1, there is a best (Bayes) decision rule. However, this best decision rule will differ, in general, for different values of P_1. So, no one decision rule can be presumed to be best over all.

To further simplifiy matters, let us assume that E^* is a continuous function of P_1 on [0,1]. Then, by Weierstrass' theorem, E^* attains its maximum for some value, say P_1^* of P_1. For obvious reasons, the *a priori* distribution $\left(P_1^*, 1-P_1^*\right)$ is called the *least favorable distribution*. The Bayes decision rule with respect to the least favorable distribution minimizes the maximum of the error probability. This rule is called a *minimax* decision rule. In short, the minimax rule is the best rule to use in the worst case.

We already commented that, in general, error probability E^* is very difficult to calculate. Consequently, the problem of finding the least favorable distribution is usually a very complex one. In the simplest case considered here, we shall leave it to the reader to verify that the minimax rule follows from selecting the Bayes acceptance regions which satisfy the condition

110 $$\int_{\Omega_2} p(\underline{x}|\omega_1)d\underline{x} = \int_{\Omega_1} p(\underline{x}|\omega_2)d\underline{x},$$

and the rule can be implemented by a likelihood-ratio test. For more general cases, we shall limit ourselves to refer the reader to the specialized literature.

A second alternative to the Bayes decision rule is the Neyman-Pearson decision rule, which is thoroughly treated in many statistical texts. To put the Neyman-Pearson technique in the perspective of our present discussion, let us note that it ignores completely the *a priori* distribution and concentrates on the two error probabilities in 110. Roughly speaking, the Neyman-Pearson decision rule is the one which minimizes one of the two error probabilities subject to the condition of the other one being equal to a constant. Once again, this goal can be achieved by using an appropriate threshold in a likelihood-ratio test.

2.12. LEARNING THE UNDERLYING DISTRIBUTIONS

The theory in this chapter has been developed on the assumption that a complete description - in terms of statistical distributions - of the pattern-generating mechanism is available to the system designer. This description involves *a priori* and class-conditional distributions, transition probabilities for a Markov chain, etc.

In pattern recognition applications, however, the situation is quite different for, in fact, the knowledge of the underlying distributions is never given. Instead, it must be inferred (learned) from a given set of *design samples*. It is customary to assume that design samples are correctly classified. (Nonetheless, it is wise to bear in mind that information in the design data is frequently corrupted by some classification errors.)

In addition to the set of design samples, the designer may have some general knowledge about the pattern-generating mechanism. For instance, in some circumstances, he could reasonably assume that the class-conditional distributions belong to some parametric family of distributions. Then, the problem of estimating the densities $p(\underline{x}|\omega_i)$ becomes one of estimating the corresponding parameters. The problem of estimating the parameters of a distribution is a classical problem in statistics. It is briefly touched upon in Section 2 of Appendix A.

It is clear that, in many pattern recognition applications, the parametric assumption cannot be justified. Then the estimation problem becomes considerably more difficult. Various methods of estimating nonparametric distributions are discussed in Section 3 of Appendix A.

Clearly, the primary utility of the design samples is to enable the designer to estimate the underlying distributions. But these samples have to serve another purpose as well. For instance, they are likely to be used for *testing* the classifier in order to estimate its performance. In turn, performance estimates may be used for comparing competing designs. Our analysis of performance estimation in Chapter 10 will lead us to the conclusion that design and test samples should be statistically independent. Thus, we shall examine the question of how the samples should be partitioned between design and test sets. Therefore, it should come as no surprise that these considerations interject an extra-dimension to the design problem of estimating the underlying distributions.

2.13. BIBLIOGRAPHICAL COMMENTS

C.K. Chow (1957) is to be credited with the idea of formulating the problem of pattern recognition (specifically, the problem of character recognition) as a problem in the realm of the statistical decision theory. The analysis of the error-reject tradeoff is another important contribution of Chow (1970). Statistical decision theory, per se, is associated with the name of Wald (1950). It has been the subject matter of a number of books, e.g., Blackwell and Girshick (1954), and Ferguson (1967).

The multivariate normal case is discussed in considerable detail in the text by Anderson (1958). In the pattern recognition literature, it has been considered by too many authors to be cited here. It is also very well treated in the books by Nilsson (1965), Fukunaga (1972), and Duda and Hart (1973). Optimum decision boundaries for other parametric families of distributions were studied by Cooper (1964).

Much attention was also devoted to the case of discrete-valued features. The derivation of the optimum linear decision boundary for independent binary-valued features is usually attributed to Minsky (1961). Kazmierczak and Steinbuch (1963) used optimum quadratic decision boundaries in the case of ternary-valued independent features. Procedures for learning from binary-valued features were considered by Fukunaga and Ito (1965). For additional background material on this topic, the reader is referred to the text by Becker (1974).

Sequential decision theory was pioneerd by Wald (1947). Problems of sequential pattern classification were studied extensively by Fu and his coworkers (see Fu (1968)). Extensions of sequential methods to more complicated hierarchical structures present very challenging problems as may be seen from Kulkarni and Kanal (1978), and Tounissoux (1980).

Our exposition of classification methods using contextual information is based on the work of Raviv (1967). With the desire of exploiting context in pictorial data as a motivation, much work has been done to extend the Markov dependence approach from one-dimensional to two-dimensional problems. A substantial account of this work can be found in the text by Fu and Yu (1980).

The idea of using a probabilistic distance measure as a design criterion must be attributed to Lewis (1962), and the usefulness of these measures for bounding and estimating the Bayes error-rate was convincingly demonstrated by Kailath (1967). Various distance measures and the corresponding error-bounds were reviewed by Chen (1976).

2.14. REFERENCES

Anderson, T.W., *An Introduction to Multivariate Statistical Analysis*, John Wiley, New York, 1958.

Becker, P.W., *Recognition of Patterns*, Springer Verlag, Wien, 1974, (2d ed.).

Blackwell, D., and Girshick, M.A., *Theory of Games and Statistical Decisions*, John Wiley, New York, 1954.

Chen, C.H., "On information and distance measures, error bounds and feature selection", *Inform. Sci.*, vol. 10, pp. 159-171, 1976.

Chow, C.K., "An optimum character recognition system using decision functions", *IRE Trans. Elec. Comput.*, vol. 6, pp. 247-254, Dec. 1957.

Chow, C.K., "An optimum recognition error and reject tradeoff", *IEEE Trans. Inform. Theory*, vol. 16, pp. 41-46, Jan. 1970.

Cooper, P.W., "Hyperplanes, hyperspheres, and hyperquadrics as decision boundaries", in *Computer and Information Sciences*, J.T. Tou Ed., Spartan Book, Washington, D.C., 1964, pp. 111-138.

Duda, R.O., and Hart, P.E., *Pattern Classification and Scene Analysis*, John Wiley, New York, 1973.

Ferguson, T.S., *Mathematical Statistics : A Decision Theoretic Approach*, Academic Press, New York, 1967.

Fu, K.S., *Sequential Methods in Pattern Recognition and Machine Learning*, Academic Press, New York, 1968.

Fu, K.S., and Yu, T.S., *Statistical Pattern Classification Using Contextual Information*, Research Studies Press, Chichester, 1980.

Fukunaga, K., *Introduction to Statistical Pattern Recognition*, Academic Press, New York, 1972.

Fukunaga, K., and Ito, T., "Design theory of recognition functions in self-organizing systems", *IEEE Trans. Comput.*, vol. 14, pp. 44-52, 1965.

Kazmierczak, H., and Steinbuch, K., "Adaptive systems in pattern recognition", *IEEE Trans. Comput.*, vol. 12, pp. 822-835, Dec. 1963.

Kulkarni, A.V., and Kanal, L.N., "Admissible search strategies for parametric and nonparametric hierarchical classifiers", *Proc. Fourth. Internat. Conf. Pattern Recognition*, Kyoto, Japan, 1978, pp. 238-248.

Lewis, P.M., "The characteristic selection problem in recognition systems", *IRE Trans. Inform. Theory*, vol. 8, pp. 171-178, 1962.

Minsky, M., "Steps toward artificial intelligence", Proc. IRE, vol. 49 pp. 8-30, Jan, 1961.

Nilsson, N.J., *Learning Machines*, McGraw-Hill, New York, 1965.

Raviv, J., "Decision making in Markov chains applied to the problem of pattern recognition", *IEEE Trans. Inform. Theory*, vol. 13, pp. 536-551, Oct. 1967.

Tounissoux, D., Processus séquentiels adaptatifs de reconnaissance des formes pour l'aide au diagnostic, Doctoral Disertation, Univ. Lyon I, France, June 1980.

Wald, A., *Sequential Analysis*, John Wiley, New York, 1947.

Wald, A., *Statistical Decision Functions*, John Wiley, New York, 1950.

2.15. PROBLEMS

1. The purpose of this problem is to establish a general proof of the error-reject relationship in Equation 32. To this end, consider the effect of a decremental change in the rejection threshold from λ to $\lambda-\Delta\lambda$. The reject region expands from Ω_0 to $\Omega_0+\Delta\Omega_0$. Observe that any $\underline{x}$ in the incremental region was accepted at the threshold λ and rejected at the lower threshold $\lambda-\Delta\lambda$. Thus, $\forall \underline{x} \in \Delta\Omega_0$,

$$(1-\lambda)p(\underline{x}) \le \max_i P_i p(\underline{x}|\omega_i) < (1-\lambda+\Delta\lambda)p(\underline{x}).$$

Now, integrate this expression over the incremental region and use the result as a starting point for proving 32.

2. Determine the minimum error-rate decision rule for a problem of two classes with multivariate normal distributions with different mean vectors and different covariance matrices. Determine the functional form of the decision boundary. Next, suppose that the covariance matrices are proportional (i.e., $\Sigma_1=\alpha\Sigma_2$, α is a positive scalar, $\alpha\neq 1$), and verify that the decision boundary is a hyperellipsoid.

3. Consider a two-class problem with multivariate Pearson Type VII class-conditional distribution, i.e.,

$$p(\underline{x}|\omega_i) = \frac{\Gamma(\nu)}{\pi^{d/2}\Gamma(\nu-d/2)}|W_i|^{1/2}\left[1+(\underline{x}-\underline{\mu}_i)^t W_i(\underline{x}-\underline{\mu}_i)\right]^{-\nu},$$

where $W_i = (2\nu-d-2)^{-1}\Sigma_i^{-1}$, and the real parameter ν satisfies the condition $2\nu>d+2$. (Note that the limiting distribution as ν increases to infinity is the multivariate normal distribution.) Under which conditions is the Bayes decision boundary for minimum error-rate a) a hyperplane, b) two hyperplanes, c) a hypersphere ?

4. Let $\underline{x}$ be distributed as in Section 2.6 with $p_i=p$, $q_j=q=1-p$, $i,j=1,\ldots,d$, and $p>q$. Show that, for d odd, the minimum error probability is given by

$$E^* = \sum_{\ell=0}^{(d-1)/2} \binom{d}{\ell} p^{\ell} (1-p)^{d-\ell}.$$

5. Extend the theory of Section 2.6 to the case where each component x_j of $\underline{x}$ is a class-conditionally independent, ternary-valued, random variable.

6. Let $\pi_1,\ldots,\pi_n$ be a probability distribution, i.e., $\pi_i \geq 0$, $\sum_i \pi_i = 1$. Let $J'(\pi_1,\ldots,\pi_n)$ denote the following multihypothesis extension of the divergence measure in Section 2.10.2 :

$$J'(\pi_1,\ldots,\pi_n) = \sum_{i=1}^{n} \pi_i \log\frac{\pi_i}{1-\pi_i}.$$

By virtue of this extension, the divergence in 104 becomes

$$J_D' = \sum_{i=1}^{c} \int P(\omega_i|\underline{x}) \log\frac{P(\omega_i|\underline{x})}{1-P(\omega_i|\underline{x})} d\underline{x}.$$

(a) Demonstrate that J_D' yields the following implicit error bound

$$J_D' \geq J'(E^*,1-E^*) + E^* \log\frac{1-E^*}{c-1-E^*}.$$

(b) For the two-class case of Problem 4, show that the bound in (a) becomes

$$dJ'(p,1-p) \geq J'(E^*,1-E^*).$$

7. Verify that, in a two-class problem, the minimax decision rule follows from selecting the Bayes acceptance regions Ω_1 and Ω_2 (with respect to the least favorable *a priori* distribution) which satisfy the condition

$$\int_{\Omega_2} p(\underline{x}|\omega_1) d\underline{x} = \int_{\Omega_1} p(\underline{x}|\omega_2) d\underline{x}.$$

Chapter 3

THE NEAREST NEIGHBOR DECISION RULE

3.1. GENERAL CONSIDERATIONS

The classification techniques discussed in the preceding chapter relied heavily on the assumed knowledge of the underlying statistical distributions. By contrast, we shall now examine a family of decision rules, namely the nearest neighbor rules, which, apparently, ignore these distributions. Roughly speaking, nearest neighbor rules exchange the need to know the underlying distributions for that of knowing a large number of correctly classified patterns. In principle, this shift in viewpoint brings us a lot closer to the reality of practical problems.

The basic ideas behind the nearest neighbor rules are that samples which fall close together in feature space are likely either to belong to the same class or to have about the same *a posteriori* distributions of their respective classes. The first of these ideas gives rise to the formulation of the single nearest neighbor rule, abbreviated as 1-NNR, while the second prompts the formulation of the k-nearest neighbor rule, the k-NNR.

1 A brief description of these rules is as follows: Suppose we are given a set S_n of n pairs of independent, identically distributed random variables $(\underline{x}_1,\theta_1),\ldots,(\underline{x}_n,\theta_n)$, where the label θ may designate any of the c classes $\omega_1,\ldots,\omega_c$, θ_i is the true class of $\underline{x}_i$, and each pair is drawn from the distribution of $(\underline{x},\omega)$, as defined in Chapter 2. When we want to classify some new pattern $\underline{x}$, independent of S_n, we first determine the nearest neighbor (NN) $\underline{x}'$ to $\underline{x}$ from S_n. We then assign $\underline{x}$ to the class θ' of $\underline{x}'$. So, formally, the estimate $\hat{\omega}_1$ of the unknown class ω of $\underline{x}$ with the 1-NNR is given by

$$\hat{\omega}_1 = \theta' \quad \text{if} \quad \delta(\underline{x},\underline{x}') = \min_{i=1,\ldots,n} \delta(\underline{x},\underline{x}_i),$$

where δ is some metric of the feature space. Clearly, by relying on the first NN to $\underline{x}$ only, it may seem that we are not making a very efficient use of the information conveyed by the data in S_n. So, a natural extension of the 1-NNR, namely the k-NNR, consists in searching the k-NN to $\underline{x}$ from S_n and assigning $\underline{x}$ to the class which is most heavily represented in the labels of the k-NN.

It should be obvious that any attempt to analyze a decision rule so vaguely defined would irremediably be doomed to failure. In order to render the analysis feasible, some additional assumptions will be required. It is however quite a remarkable fact that it will be possible to analyze the performance of the NNR while keeping the number of assumptions to a strict minimum. The few theoretical restrictions that we will have to impose are merely intended to guarantee the convergence to $\underline{x}$ of the nearest neighbor $\underline{x}'$ as the cardinality of the set S_n grows arbitrarily large.

3.2. CONVERGENCE OF THE NEAREST NEIGHBORS

We shall start by discussing the conditions and the mode of convergence of the nearest neighbor $\underline{x}'_n$ to $\underline{x}$. Here, we use the notation $\underline{x}'_n$ to emphasize that $\underline{x}'$ is the 1-NN to $\underline{x}$ from a *finite* set of size n. Let us first consider a very simple case.

2 Suppose that $\underline{x}$ has a continuous unconditional probability density function $p(\underline{x})$, and $p(\underline{x})>0$. Let p_ε designate the probability that any sample falls within a hypersphere of radius ε and centered about $\underline{x}$,

$$p_\varepsilon = \int_{\delta(\underline{x},\underline{\xi})<\varepsilon} p(\underline{\xi})d\underline{\xi}.$$

Under these conditions, p_ε is some positive number. The probability that the nearest neighbor to $\underline{x}$ falls outside the hypersphere is also the probability that all n of the independent samples fall outside the hypersphere. We thus have

$$P\left\{\delta(\underline{x},\underline{x}'_n)\geq\varepsilon\right\} = \prod_{i=1}^{n} P\left\{\delta(\underline{x},\underline{x}_i)\geq\varepsilon\right\} = (1-p_\varepsilon)^n .$$

Hence

$$\lim_{n\to\infty} P\left\{\delta(\underline{x},\underline{x}'_n)\geq\varepsilon\right\} = 0$$

or

$$\underline{x}'_n \overset{n}{\to} \underline{x} \text{ in probability.}$$

If we further assume that the class-conditional probability densities are also continuous, we also have

$$P(\omega|\underline{x}'_n) \overset{n}{\to} P(\omega|\underline{x}) \text{ in probability.}$$

The *a posteriori* distribution given the 1-NN $\underline{x}'_n$ to $\underline{x}$ also converges to the *a posteriori* distribution given $\underline{x}$.

The assumption of continuity of the underlying distributions is obviously a very constraining one. Therefore, the convergence of the nearest neighbor has been studied in a number of other settings with the aim of relaxing the most restrictive assumptions and strengthening the mode of convergence. Two important results obtained along these lines are as follows.

3 When $\underline{x}$ is assumed to be distributed in a separable metric space, and, $\forall i$ $p(\underline{x}|\omega_i)$ is decomposable into a continuous component plus a series of mass points, then

4 $$\underline{x}'_n \overset{n}{\rightarrow} \underline{x} \quad \text{and} \quad P(\omega|\underline{x}'_n) \overset{n}{\rightarrow} P(\omega|\underline{x}),$$

irrespective of the metric, and where the convergence is with probability one. If, however, $\underline{x}$ is assumed to be distributed in d-dimensional Euclidean space, then 4 holds without any regularity conditions on the distribution of $\underline{x}$ or the joint distribution of $(\underline{x},\omega)$. The convergence in this case is in the kth mean, and hence in probability, under mild assumptions regarding the metric used in searching the nearest neighbor.

5 From our discussion in 2 above, it should be clear that convergence results also hold for the kth nearest neighbor for any finite value of k. The asymptotic case when $k \rightarrow \infty$ raises more subtle problems. Actually, it can be shown that asymptotic convergence is still guaranteed when we let k depend on n and impose $k_n \rightarrow \infty$, $k_n/n \rightarrow 0$ as

$n \to \infty$. It may thus be concluded that in general the convergence of the nearest neighbors is guaranteed under quite liberally unconstrained situations.

6 In the remainder of this chapter the convergence conditions will be implicitely assumed to be satisfied and most of our results will be asymptotic, $(n \to \infty)$. Aside from the independence assumption of $\underline{x}, \underline{x}_1, \ldots, \underline{x}_n$, the large sample assumption we will have to carry throughout our discussion will represent the major departure from reality. It is the price we shall have to pay to make the analysis of the NNR feasible.

3.3. THE 1-NNR

7 We shall see presently that the convergence of the NN is about all we need to determine the large-sample performance of the 1-NNR. For the purpose of simplifying the writing of many expressions we shall, from here on, use the notation $\eta_i(\underline{x})$ to designate the class *a posteriori* probability $P(\omega_i|\underline{x})$. Occasionally, we shall even use η_i instead of $\eta_i(\underline{x})$.

The *finite-sample, conditional probability of error* $e_1(\underline{x}, \underline{x}_n')$ of the 1-NNR in 1 is given by

8 $$e_1(\underline{x}, \underline{x}_n') = \Pr\left\{\omega \neq \theta' | \underline{x}, \underline{x}_n'\right\}$$

$$= \textstyle\sum_i \Pr\left\{\omega = \omega_i, \theta' \neq \omega_i | \underline{x}, \underline{x}_n'\right\}.$$

By virtue of the independence assumption we can write

9 $$e_1(\underline{x},\underline{x}'_n) = \sum_i \Pr\left\{\omega=\omega_i \mid \underline{x}\right\} \Pr\left\{\theta' \neq \omega_i \mid \underline{x}'_n\right\}$$
$$= \sum_i \eta_i(\underline{x})\left[1-\eta_i(\underline{x}'_n)\right].$$

In the large-sample case

10 $$e_1(\underline{x}) = \lim_{n\to\infty} e_1(\underline{x},\underline{x}'_n) = \sum_i \eta_i(\underline{x})\left[1-\eta_i(\underline{x})\right]$$
$$= 1 - \sum_i \eta_i(\underline{x})^2.$$

For the average asymptotic error probability, or 1-NN *error rate* E_1 we have

11 $$E_1 = \lim_{n\to\infty} \boldsymbol{E}\left\{e_1(\underline{x},\underline{x}'_n)\right\},$$

where $\boldsymbol{E}$ is the expectation operator. Since $e_1(\underline{x},\underline{x}'_n)$ is bounded, we can exchange the limit and expectation operators to obtain

12 $$E_1 = \boldsymbol{E}\left\{\lim_{n\to\infty} e_1(\underline{x},\underline{x}'_n)\right\}$$
$$= \boldsymbol{E}\left\{\sum_i \eta_i(\underline{x})\left[1-\eta_i(\underline{x})\right]\right\}$$
$$= \int \sum_{i<j}^{c} 2\eta_i(\underline{x})\eta_j(\underline{x})p(\underline{x})d\underline{x}.$$

At this point, an important question is : how does this error rate compare to the Bayes rate ? A precise answer to this question will be given in Section 3.7. Beforehand, we shall introduce more general classes of NN rules and establish some relationships which will be useful in our discussion of error bounds.

3.4. THE k-NNR, (k,ℓ)-NNR AND (k,ℓ_i)-NNR

13 The first natural extension of the 1-NNR, which was already alluded to in Section 3.1, consists in collecting the k-NN to $\underline{x}$ in S_n, and assigning $\underline{x}$ to the class which is most heavily represented in the votes of the k-NN. This rule is the k-NNR. As with the Bayes rule, we can again safeguard ourselves against excessive classification error by resorting to the *reject option*. Under this mode of operation, one classification decision is made when one class receives a number of votes which is at least equal to a *qualifying majority level* ℓ, otherwise the pattern is rejected. This rule is the (k,ℓ)-NNR. This last class of rules can still be slightly refined by letting the majority level depend on the decision to be made. That is, the decision $\hat{\omega} = \omega_i$ will be made if more than ℓ_i-NN among the k-NN to $\underline{x}$ are from class ω_i. This rule is the (k,ℓ_i)-NNR.

Before giving a unified formulation of these various rules, let us introduce a notational convention that will prove useful on many occasions throughout this chapter. For any positive integer k, let k' and k" designate respectively the least and largest integers such that

14 $$k'' \leq k/2 \leq k'.$$

Now, the NNR with and without reject may be defined in a unified manner. For simplicity, we consider a two-class problem only. Let k_i denote the number of NN belonging to class ω_i among the k-NN to $\underline{x}$ from S_n, i=1,2. Let the integers ℓ_1 and ℓ_2 be such that $k' \leq \ell_i \leq k$, where, from here on, k' satisfies the convention 14, and let $\hat{\omega}_{k,\ell_i}$ denote the estimate of ω with the (k,ℓ_i)-NNR. Likewise we will use $\hat{\omega}_{k,\ell}$ and $\hat{\omega}_k$ to denote the decision with the (k,ℓ)-NNR, and k-NNR respectively. Then $\hat{\omega}_{k,\ell_i}$ is given by

15 $$\hat{\omega}_{k,\ell_i} = \begin{cases} \omega_1 & \text{if } k_1 \geq \ell_1, \\ \omega_2 & \text{if } k_2 \geq \ell_2, \\ \omega_0 & \text{if } k_i < \ell_i,\ i=1,2, \end{cases}$$

ties in voting are broken at random.

As in Chapter 2, $\hat{\omega}_{k,\ell_i} = \omega_0$ denotes the reject option. It is easy to see that 15 embodies the different classes of rules we are interested in. Clearly, the rule 15 is the (k,ℓ_i)-NNR when $\ell_1 \neq \ell_2$ and $\ell_i > k'$ for some i. It is the (k,ℓ)-NNR when $\ell_1 = \ell_2 > k'$. It is the k-NNR when $\ell_1 = \ell_2 = k'$. We may also note that the 1-NNR of the previous section is defined by $\ell_1 = \ell_2 = k' = k = 1$. The different, possible rules are represented in Figure 3.1 for $k<10$. Note that the k-NNR's with k even have been excluded for reasons that will become clear as we proceed through the subsequent sections.

Like the Bayes decision rule of Section 2.3, the performance of the (k,ℓ_i)-NNR is characterized by *acceptance*, *reject*, and *error probabilities*, and *probability of correct decision*. We shall again concentrate mainly on acceptance and error probabilities.

16 For any $j \geq \ell_i$ let $a^i_{k,s=j}(\underline{x})$ denote the conditional, decision-dependent probability of accepting the decision $\hat{\omega}_{k,\ell_i} = \omega_i$

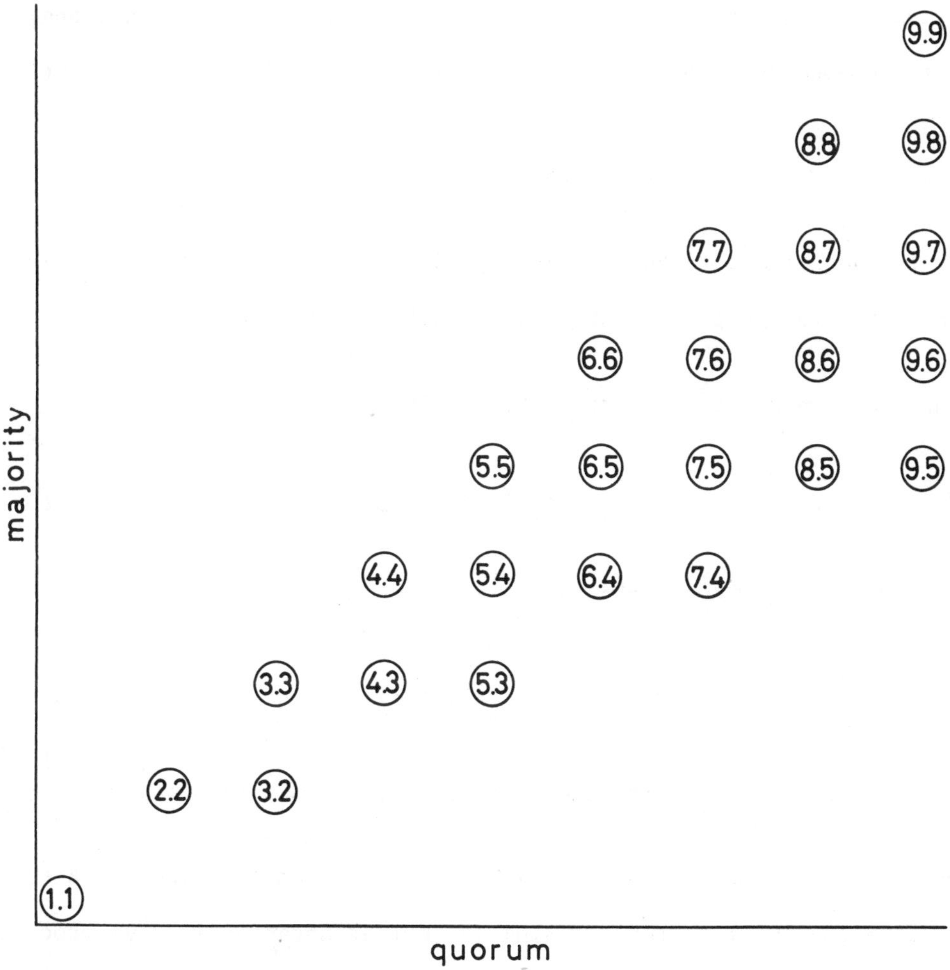

Figure 3.1. Representation of the (k, ℓ_i)—NNR

based on a score k_i=s of exactly j votes cast by the quorum of the k-NN to $\underline{x}$ from S_n. By arguing as in 8 and 9 it is easy to show that under the large-sample assumption

17
$$a^i_{k,s=j}(\underline{x}) = \binom{k}{j}\eta_i(\underline{x})^j\left[1-\eta_i(\underline{x})\right]^{k-j}, \ \forall j > k''.$$

For the k-NNR with k even, and hence k'=k/2, we also have

18
$$a^i_{k,s=k'}(\underline{x}) = \frac{1}{2}\binom{k}{k'}\eta_i(\underline{x})^{k'}\left[1-\eta_i(\underline{x})\right]^{k'}.$$

on account of the randomization of the rule in 15. The average, decision-dependent acceptance probability is clearly

19 $$A^i_{k,s=j} = \int a^i_{k,s=j}(\underline{x})p(\underline{x})d\underline{x}.$$

Now the decision-dependent acceptance probability of the (k,ℓ_i)-NNR, i.e., the average probability of accepting the decision $\hat{\omega}_{k,\ell_i} = \omega_i$ based on a score of at least ℓ_i votes, is

20 $$A^i_{k,\ell_i} = \sum_{j=\ell_i}^{k} A^i_{k,s=j}.$$

The overall acceptance rate is

21 $$A_{k,\ell_i} = \sum_{j=1}^{2} A^j_{k,\ell_j}.$$

It is clear that A_{k,ℓ_i} is the probability that an arbitrary pattern presented to the NN classifier will be accepted irrespective of the decision that will be made. Using an obvious notation we have

22 $$A_1 = A_k = A_{k,k'} = 1 \quad \forall k>1.$$

Returning to 16 and invoking again the independence assumption, the conditional, decision-dependent probability of error is given by

23.a $$e^i_{k,s=j}(\underline{x}) = P\{\omega\neq\omega_i\}a^i_{k,s=j}(\underline{x})$$

$$= \left[1-\eta_i(\underline{x})\right]\binom{k}{j}\eta_i(\underline{x})^j\left[1-\eta_i(\underline{x})\right]^{k-j}$$

23.b $$= \binom{k}{j}\eta_i(\underline{x})^j\left[1-\eta_i(\underline{x})\right]^{k-j+1}.$$

As for the acceptance, we also have

24 $$E^i_{k,s=j} = \int e^i_{k,s=j}(\underline{x})\,p(\underline{x})\,d\underline{x},$$

25 $$E^i_{k,\ell_i} = \sum_{j=\ell_i}^{k} E^i_{k,s=j},$$

26 $$E_{k,\ell_i} = \sum_{j=1}^{2} E^j_{k,\ell_j}.$$

At this point, we leave it to the reader to write down the expressions for the probabilities of correct decision C_{k,ℓ_i} and rejection R_{k,ℓ_i}.

For given underlying distributions, these probabilities are functions of k, ℓ_1 and ℓ_2 only. It is then a simple matter to verify that they satisfy the following inequalities which, for simplicity, we write down in terms of acceptance of the (k,ℓ)-NNR.

27 $$A_{k,\ell} \geq A_{k-1,\ell}$$

28 $$A_{k,\ell} \geq A_{k-1,\ell+1}$$

29 $$A_{k,\ell} \geq A_{k,\ell+1}$$

30 $$A_{k,\ell} \geq A_{k+1,\ell+1}$$

These inequalities remain true if we substitute E, C or (1-R) to A. They remain also true when they are interpreted in terms of finite-sample probabilities. They are illustrated by Figure 3.2 where the direction of the arrow indicates a decrease in A, E and C.

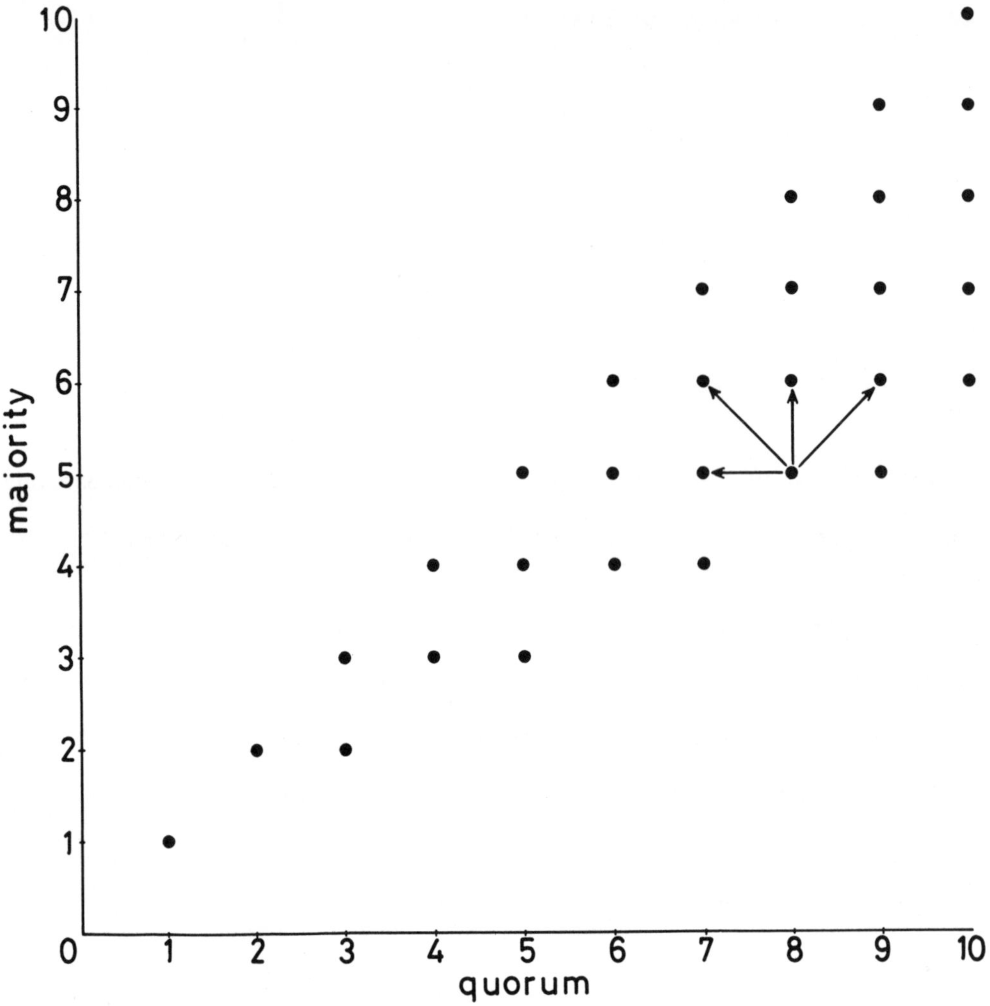

Figure 3.2. Variation of $A_{k,\ell}$ versus k and ℓ

3.5. COMMENTS

At this point, we have seen that it is, in general, a very simple matter to write down the analytic expressions for the various quantities characterizing the performance of the NNR. These expressions will prove very useful for various reasons which will appear as we proceed throughout this chapter. It should be emphasized however that any of these probabilities, say, the error rate, are by no means easier to calculate than was the Bayes error rate in the previous chapter. In most instances, the best we will be able to do is to *estimate* these probabilities from the available data.

This situation reflects on the problem of choosing the parameters k, ℓ_1 and ℓ_2 in such a way as to match the performance to prespecified requirements for a given application problem. As we usually cannot calculate the performance, we could estimate it for a number of different values of the parameters and search the optimum solution by a trial and error procedure. Until now, the theoretical guidance we could use in this process is only that which can be inferred from the inequalities 27 through 30. Needless to say, such a procedure would soon become an overwhelming computational task. Fortunately, nearest neighbor rules will prove extremely cooperative in this respect, and we shall see that the determination of the optimum parameters is greatly simplified by the existence of a bundle of simple, linear relationships connecting the performance of various rules. The derivation of these relationships is the subject matter of the next two sections.

3.6. HOMOGENEOUS RELATIONSHIPS

Our first step in this section will consist in exhibiting a number of linear relationships connecting acceptance rates. In general, the derivation of these relationships uses only classical formulae involving binomial probabilities. Therefore, the derivation of the first result only will be outlined in full.

By multiplying the right hand side of 17 by $\left[\eta_i+(1-\eta_i)\right]=1$ we obtain

$$a^i_{k,s=j}(\underline{x}) = \binom{k}{j}\eta_i(\underline{x})^j\left[1-\eta_i(\underline{x})\right]^{k-j}.$$

There follows

$$a^i_{k,s=j}(\underline{x}) = \frac{k-j+1}{k+1}\binom{k+1}{j}\eta_i(\underline{x})^j\left[1-\eta_i(\underline{x})\right]^{k-j+1}$$

$$+\frac{j+1}{k+1}\binom{k+1}{j+1}\eta_i(\underline{x})^{j+1}\left[1-\eta_i(\underline{x})\right]^{k-j}$$

31 $$= \frac{k-j+1}{k+1}\, a^i_{k+1,s=j}(\underline{x}) + \frac{j+1}{k+1}\, a^i_{k+1,s=j+1}(\underline{x}),$$

provided that $j \geq \ell_i \geq k'+1$, so the rules with no reject are presently excluded from consideration. As 31 is linear in the acceptances, we can take expectation with respect to $p(\underline{x})$ to obtain

32 $$(k+1)A^i_{k,s=j} = (k-j+1)A^i_{k+1,s=j} + (j+1)A^i_{k+1,s=j+1}.$$

We now sum 32 for $j=\ell_i,\ldots,k$. By using 20 twice we find

$$(k+1)\sum_{j=\ell_i}^{k} A^i_{k,s=j} = (k-\ell_i+1)A^i_{k+1,s=\ell_i} + (k+1)\sum_{j=\ell_i+1}^{k+1} A^i_{k+1,s=j}$$

33 $$(k+1)A^i_{k,\ell_i} = (k-\ell_i+1)A^i_{k+1,s=\ell_i} + (k+1)A^i_{k+1,\ell_i+1}.$$

Rearranging terms in 33 we finally obtain the

<u>ACCEPTANCE THEOREM</u> : for any $\ell_i \geq k'+1$,

34 $$(k+1)A^i_{k,\ell_i} = (k-\ell_i+1)A^i_{k+1,\ell_i} + \ell_i A^i_{k+1,\ell_i+1}.$$

This theorem is illustrated by Figure 3.3.

From the derivation of 34, it is clear that the acceptance theorem holds irrespective of the underlying distributions.

An equivalent formulation which will prove useful in the following section is

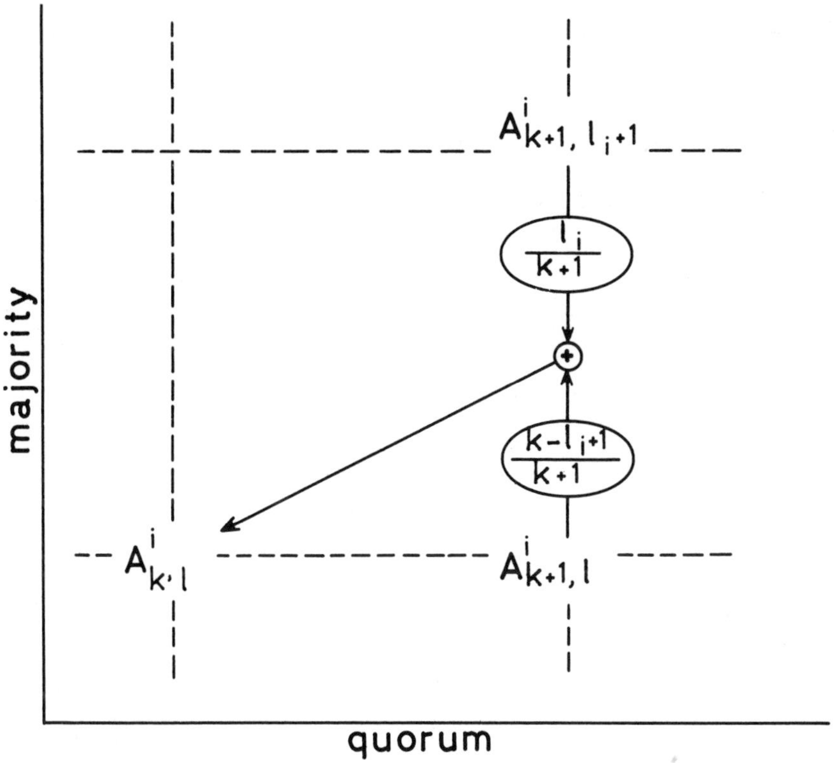

Figure 3.3. The acceptance theorem

35 $$A^i_{k,\ell_i} - A^i_{k+1,\ell_i+1} = \left(1 - \frac{\ell_i}{k+1}\right)\left[A^i_{k+1,\ell_i} - A^i_{k+1,\ell_i+1}\right].$$

36 To appreciate the usefulness of the acceptance theorem, let us note that if we knew the acceptances A^i_{k+1,ℓ_i} and A^i_{k+1,ℓ_i+1}, both along the (k+1)th column of Figure 3.1, we could use 34 to calculate A^i_{k,ℓ_i}. Besides, if we also knew A^i_{k+1,ℓ_i+2}, we could also calculate A^i_{k,ℓ_i+1} by the formula

$$(k+1)A^i_{k,\ell_i+1} = (k-\ell_i)A^i_{k+1,\ell_i+1} + (\ell_i+1)A^i_{k+1,\ell_i+2},$$

etc. So, the knowledge of the acceptances along the (k+1)th column would enable us to calculate the acceptances along the kth column. Afterwards, we could start calculating the acceptances along the (k-1)th column etc. This process, and the coefficients which have to be used, is illustrated by Figure 3.4 which has to be read in the following way

$$A^{i}_{6,5} = \frac{2}{7} A^{i}_{7,5} + \frac{5}{7} A^{i}_{7,6}.$$

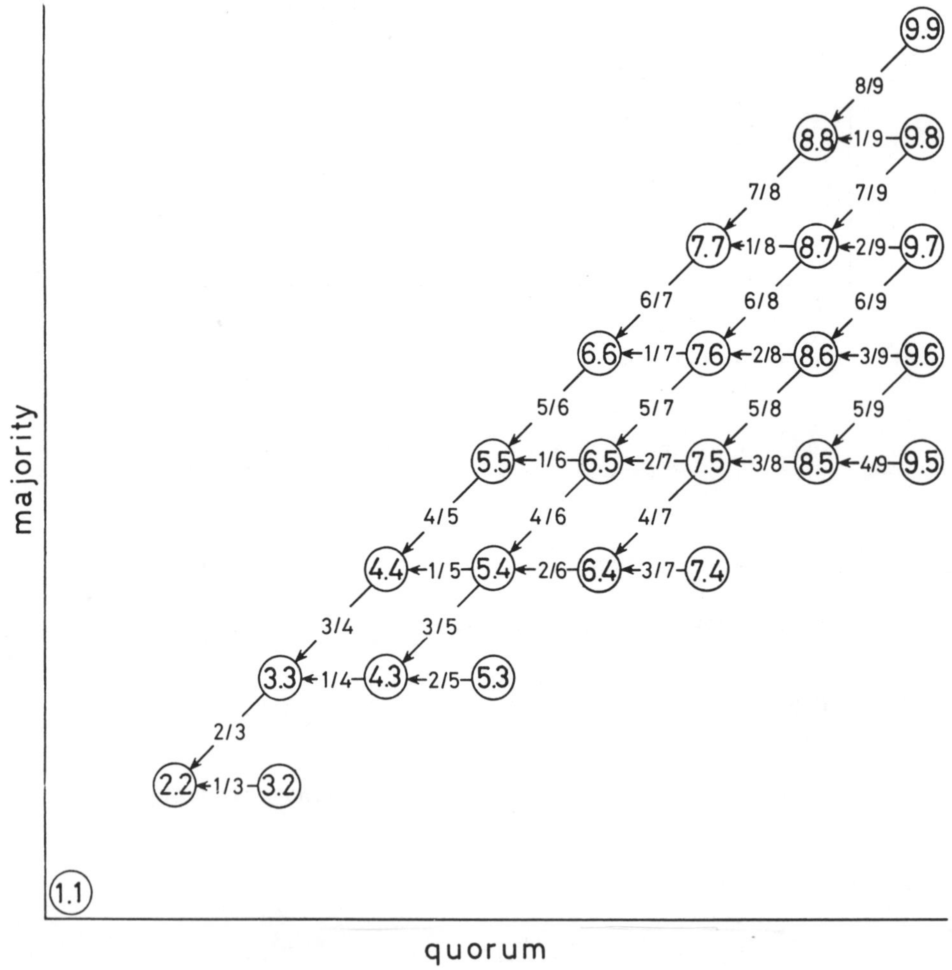

Figure 3.4. The leftwards transition theorem

We can also go one step further and establish the relationship connecting acceptance A^i_{k,ℓ_i} to those making up the (k+q)th column. This gives the following theorem:

<u>LEFTWARDS TRANSITION THEOREM FOR THE ACCEPTANCES</u> : For any k, ℓ_i and $q \geq 1$ such that

37 $$(k+q)''+1 \leq k \leq k+q-1,$$

38 $$(k+q)''+1 \leq \ell_i \leq k,$$

let us be given the $(k+q)'$ acceptance rates A^i_{k+q,ℓ_i+j}, $j=0,\dots,q$.

Then, the acceptance rate A^i_{k,ℓ_i} is given by

39 $$A^i_{k,\ell_i} = \sum_{j=0}^{q} \frac{\binom{\ell_i-1+j}{j}\binom{k-\ell_i+q-j}{q-j}}{\binom{k+q}{q}} A^i_{k+q,\ell_i+j}$$

The proof of this theorem is made very easy by considering the diagram of Figure 3.4 as a weighted directed graph. Then it may be noticed that

a. there exist $\binom{q}{j}$ paths connecting the node $(k+q,\ell_i+j)$ to the node (k,ℓ_i);

b. the product π_j of the weights associated with one of these paths is independent of the particular path chosen.

Hence, we may write

$$A^i_{k,\ell_i} = \sum_{j=0}^{q} \binom{q}{j} \pi_j \, A^i_{k+q,\ell_i+j},$$

and the problem reduces to that of determining the coefficient π_j of an arbitrary path connecting the nodes $(k+q, \ell_i+j)$ and (k, ℓ_i). Then, 39 follows from some easy combinatorial manipulations.

40 As a final remark about this theorem, it should be pointed out that the assumed knowledge of $(k+q)'$ acceptance rates enables us to calculate an additional number of

$$N = \frac{1}{2}(k+q)'[(k+q)'-1]$$

acceptance rates. This represents a first and considerable reduction in the work involved in the determination of the performance of the various NNR's.

At this point, a natural question to ask is : does the same kind of relationship exist in terms of error rates ? We shall presently see that this is indeed the case. Let us multiply 31 by $\left[1-\eta_i(\underline{x})\right]$ and use 23. We readily obtain,

41 $$e^i_{k,s=j}(\underline{x}) = \frac{k-j+1}{k+1}\, e^i_{k+1,s=j}(\underline{x}) + \frac{j+1}{k+1}\, e^i_{k+1,s=j+1}(\underline{x}).$$

This equation is perfectly identical to 31 except for the substitution of e for a. We may therefore duplicate all of the subsequent arguments to obtain first the

<u>ERROR THEOREM</u> :

42 $$(k+1)E^i_{k,\ell_i} = (k-\ell_i+1)E^i_{k+1,\ell_i} + \ell_i E^i_{k+1,\ell_i+1}.$$

Next, we also have :

LEFTWARDS TRANSITION THEOREM FOR THE ERRORS :

43 $$E^{i}_{k,\ell_i} = \sum_{j=0}^{q} \frac{\binom{\ell_i-1+j}{j}\binom{k-\ell_i+q-j}{q-j}}{\binom{k+q}{q}} E^{i}_{k+q,\ell_i+j}$$

44 Since these theorems hold in terms of acceptance and error rates, it is obvious that they also hold unchanged in terms of the probability of correct decision and, with minor modifications, in terms of reject rates of the (k,ℓ)-NNR. We may therefore generalize the conclusions reached in 40 : the knowledge of the performance of $(k+q)'$ rules enables us to calculate the performance of $(1/2)(k+q)'[(k+q)'-1]$ additional rules.

45 In our discussion of the consequences of the acceptance theorem we constantly assumed that the performance of the rules along the $(k+q)$th column of Figure 3.1 had been determined beforehand. The acceptance theorem offers us two more possibilities. First, 34 can be used along the main diagonal of Figure 3.1 in the form

46 $$A^{i}_{k+1,k} = (k+1)A^{i}_{k,k} - kA^{i}_{k+1,k+1},$$

which yields acceptances along the first subdiagonal. We may naturally think of proceeding further to the second, third subdiagonals etc. In this way we obtain the

DOWNWARDS TRANSITION THEOREM FOR THE ACCEPTANCES :

47 $$A^{i}_{k+q,\ell_i} = \sum_{j=0}^{q} (-1)^{j} \frac{\binom{\ell_i-1+j}{j}\binom{k+q}{q-j}}{\binom{k-\ell_i+q}{q}} A^{i}_{k+j,\ell_i+j}.$$

The last possibility consists in starting upwards from the ℓth line of Figure 3.1. In this case we derive the

UPWARDS TRANSITION THEOREM FOR THE ACCEPTANCES :

48 $$A^{i}_{k+q,\ell_i+q} = \sum_{j=0}^{q} (-1)^j \frac{\binom{k-\ell_i+j}{j}\binom{k+q}{q-j}}{\binom{\ell_i-1+q}{q}} A^{i}_{k+j,\ell_i} .$$

It follows from 42 that the last two theorems apply also to error rates and probabilities of correct decision.

The relationships derived in this section involve either acceptance rates only, or error rates only. Hence the section's title : homogeneous relationships. We shall now demonstrate the existence of other simple linear relationships which will enable us to relate the error rate to the acceptance rate.

3.7. ERROR-ACCEPTANCE RELATIONSHIPS

A simple and extremely important relationship connecting the conditional, decision-dependent probabilities of acceptance and error in 17 and 23 can be derived in a very straightforward manner by observing that the expression for the acceptance

$$a^{i}_{k+1,s=j}(\underline{x}) = \binom{k+1}{j} \eta_i(\underline{x})^j \left[1-\eta_i(\underline{x})\right]^{k-j+1}$$

can be transformed to

$$a^{i}_{k+1,s=j}(\underline{x}) = \frac{k+1}{k-j+1}\left[1-\eta_i(\underline{x})\right]\binom{k}{j} \eta_i(\underline{x})^j \left[1-\eta_i(\underline{x})\right]^{k-j}$$

$$= \frac{k+1}{k-j+1} e^{i}_{k,s=j}(\underline{x}),$$

or

49 $$e^i_{k,s=j}(\underline{x}) = \left(1 - \frac{j}{k+1}\right) a^i_{k+1,s=j}(\underline{x}).$$

By taking expectation we obtain

50 $$E^i_{k,s=j} = \left(1 - \frac{j}{k+1}\right) A^i_{k+1,s=j}.$$

By taking $j=\ell_i>k''$ in 50 and using 20 and 25 we find the

<u>FIRST ERROR-ACCEPTANCE THEOREM</u> :

51 $$E^i_{k,\ell_i} - E^i_{k,\ell_i+1} = \left(1 - \frac{\ell_i}{k+1}\right)\left[A^i_{k+1,\ell_i} - A^i_{k+1,\ell_i+1}\right]$$

In the case of the k-NNR which until now was excluded from consideration, it is readily shown that we have

52 $$E_{2k'-1,s=k'} = 2E_{2k',s=k'} = A_{2k',s=k'}.$$

Consequently

53.a $$E_{2k'-1} - E_{2k'-1,k'+1} = 2\left(E_{2k'} - E_{2k',k'+1}\right)$$

53.b $$= A_{2k'} - A_{2k',k'+1}.$$

We may notice that the right hand side of 51 is identical to that of 35. By equating the left hand sides of these equations we obtain the

<u>SECOND ERROR-ACCEPTANCE THEOREM</u> :

54 $$E^i_{k,\ell_i} - E^i_{k,\ell_i+1} = A^i_{k,\ell_i} - A^i_{k+1,\ell_i+1}.$$

The two error-acceptance theorems are illustrated by Figure 3.5 where, as before, the direction of the arrows indicates a decrease in error rate or acceptance rate.

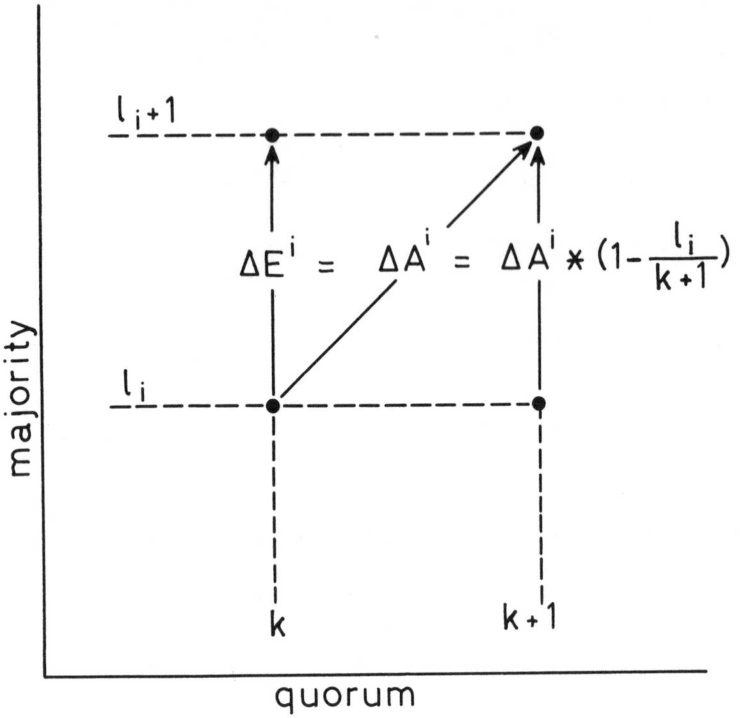

Figure 3.5. The error-acceptance theorems

55 From the results we have acquired so far, it should be evident that we will eventually be able to calculate the error rate from the knowledge of the acceptance rate only. In this respect, 49 is quite illuminating since it says that the conditional error probability when the decision is based on a majority of j out of k votes is a specified fraction of the conditional acceptance probability when the decision is based on a majority of j out of k+1 votes. Somewhat paradoxically, this acceptance probability does not depend on the true class of the pattern being classified. Anticipating Chapter 10, we may expect this equation to allow us to estimate the error rate from decisions made on unclassified patterns.

Before considering general consequences of the error- acceptance theorems, let us discuss a few special cases. First by taking ℓ_i=k in 54 and using the boundary condition $E^i_{k,k+1}=0$, we find

56 $$E^i_{k,k} = A^i_{k,k} - A^i_{k+1,k+1}.$$

which is one of the simplest relationships connecting error and acceptance rates. For the (k,ℓ)-NNR, an equivalent result is

57 $$E_{k,k} = R_{k+1,k+1} - R_{k,k}.$$

In particular, for k = 1 we have $R_{1,1}$ = 0, and 57 becomes

58 $$E_1 = R_{2,2}.$$

The error rate with the 1-NNR is equal to the reject rate with the (2,2)-NNR.

Let us consider next the more general conclusions we can draw from the error-acceptance theorems. To this end we shall regard 51 and 54 as difference equations which we shall integrate along the kth column. In each case we shall take the boundary condition $E^i_{k,k+1}$ = 0 into account. Starting with the simplest relationship, *viz.*, 54, we obtain

$$\sum_{j=\ell_i}^{k}\left[E^i_{k,j} - E^i_{k,j+1}\right] = \sum_{j=\ell_i}^{k}\left[A^i_{k,j} - A^i_{k+1,j+1}\right].$$

All terms in the left hand side cancel except E^i_{k,ℓ_i}, thus yielding the following result:

<u>FIRST ERROR-ACCEPTANCE TRADEOFF THEOREM</u> : for any $\ell_i \geq k''+1$,

59 $$E^i_{k,\ell_i} = \sum_{j=\ell_i}^{k} \left[A^i_{k,j} - A^i_{k+1,j+1}\right].$$

The derivation of this theorem is illustrated by Figure 3.6 for the case k=8.

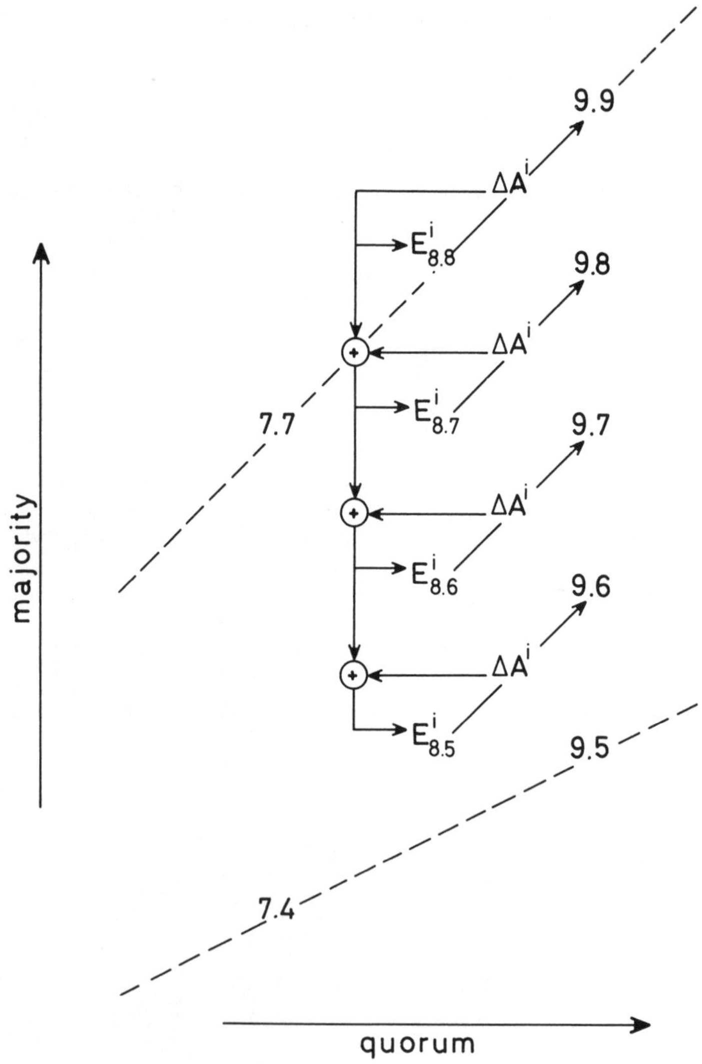

Figure 3.6. The first error-acceptance tradeoff theorem

This tradeoff theorem permits us to make two interesting observations. In the first place we see that the error rate of a NN rule based on k-NN can be calculated from the knowledge of the acceptance rates of the rules based on k and (k+1)-NN. However, as this property of the NNR will be further be improved in a moment, we shall not discuss it here. In the second place, let us interpret 59 in terms of simple events. By definition, we have

60 $$E^i_{k,\ell_i} = \Pr\left\{\hat{\omega}_{k,\ell_i}=\omega_i,\ \omega\neq\omega_i\right\}.$$

Next, a little thought reveals that the right hand side of 59 is the probability that, for an arbitrary pattern, the decision $\hat{\omega}=\omega_i$ was accepted by the (k,j)-NNR, and rejected by the (k+1,j+1)-NNR, for $j=\ell_i,\ldots,k$. In other words, the (k+1)th NN did not agree with the majority of the k-NN. Formally, let $\underline{x}^{'j'}$ denote the jth NN to $\underline{x}$ from S_n and $\theta^{'j'}$ be the class of $\underline{x}^{'j'}$. Then, we have

61 $$\sum_{j=\ell_i}^{k}\left[A^i_{k,j} - A^i_{k+1,j+1}\right] = \Pr\left\{\hat{\omega}_{k,\ell_i}=\omega_i,\ \theta^{'k+1'}\neq\omega_i\right\}.$$

By carrying 60 and 61 into 59 we obtain

62 $$\Pr\left\{\hat{\omega}_{k,\ell_i}=\omega_i,\ \omega\neq\omega_i\right\} = \Pr\left\{\hat{\omega}_{k,\ell_i}=\omega_i,\ \theta^{'k+1'}\neq\omega_i\right\}.$$

We may notice that, in calculating the error rate, the first error-acceptance tradeoff theorem simply exchanges the need to know the class ω of the pattern being classified for that of knowing the class $\theta^{'k+1'}$ of the (k+1)th neighbor. This is one simple demonstration of the fact that the error rate of the k-NNR can be calculated irrespective of the class of the patterns being classified.

Let us next consider the result of integrating the difference equation of 51. By proceeding as with the derivation of 59 we obtain the

SECOND ERROR-ACCEPTANCE TRADEOFF THEOREM :

63.a $$E^{i}_{k,\ell_i} = \sum_{j=\ell_i}^{k} \left(1 - \frac{j}{k+1}\right)\left[A^{i}_{k+1,j} - A^{i}_{k+1,j+1}\right]$$

63.b $$= \sum_{j=\ell_i}^{k} \left(1 - \frac{j}{k+1}\right)A^{i}_{k+1,s=j}.$$

The derivation of this theorem is illustrated by Figure 3.7.

The second error-acceptance tradeoff theorem deserves a number of comments.

64 First, we see that the knowledge of the acceptance rates along the (k+1)th column only enables us to calculate the error rates along the kth column. If we now combine this with the leftwards transition theorem of the previous section we are led to the surprising conclusion that the (k+1)' acceptance rates $A^{i}_{k+1,j}$, $(k+1)' \le j \le k+1$, convey all the information necessary to calculate the performance of $(1/2)(k+1)'[(k+1)'-1]$ additional (q,m)-NNR with $(k+1)' \le q,m \le k$. This observation constitutes our ultimate step in the process of reducing the computational task associated with the determination of the performance of the various NNR's.

Second, by translating 63 in terms of simple events we get

65 $$\Pr\left\{\hat{\omega}_{k,\ell_i}=\omega_i, \omega\neq\omega_i\right\} = \sum_{j=\ell_i}^{k} \left(1 - \frac{j}{k+1}\right) \Pr\left\{\hat{\omega}_{q,j}=\omega_i \mid q=k+1, k_i=j\right\}.$$

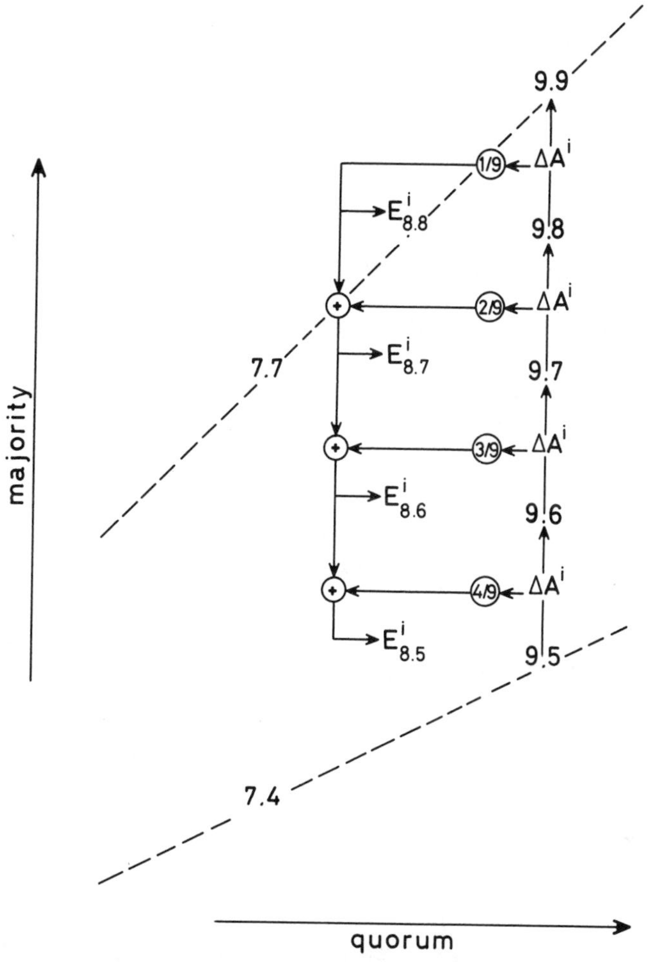

Figure 3.7. The second error-acceptance tradeoff theorem

Again we see that the true class ω of the pattern being classified has disappeared from the right hand side of 65. Moreover, if we extend the theorem to the case of the k-NNR by combining 63 and 53, we find that for k odd

66.a $$E_k = \sum_{j=k'}^{k} \left(1 - \frac{j}{k+1}\right) A_{k+1,s=j} + \frac{1}{2} A_{k+1,s=k'}$$

66.b $$= \sum_{j=(k+1)'}^{k+1} \left(1 - \frac{j}{k+1}\right) A_{k+1,s=j} + \frac{1}{2} A_{k+1,s=(k+1)'}.$$

Now, in the spirit of 65, the sum in 66.b may be interpreted as the expected value of the proportion of votes from among the (k+1)-NN which do not concur with the decision being made, and where expectation is taken with respect to the acceptance probability distribution. Equations 63 through 66 will prove very useful on a number of occasions, in particular from the viewpoint of error estimation. For the sake of completeness let us also note that for k even, 66.b becomes

67 $$E_k = \sum_{j=(k+1)'}^{k+1} \left(1 - \frac{j}{k+1}\right) A_{k+1,s=j} + \frac{(k+1)'}{2(k+1)} A_{k+1,s=(k+1)'}.$$

68 Last but not least, let us also remark that for the (k,ℓ)-NNR with $\ell > k'$, the second error-acceptance tradeoff theorem reads

69 $$E_{k,\ell} = \sum_{j=\ell}^{k} \left(1 - \frac{j}{k+1}\right) A_{k+1,s=j}.$$

This equation bears much resemblance to Equation 2.58. Actually, it can be shown that the latter is the asymptotic version of the former in the following sense. First we let $k_n \to \infty$, and $(k_n/n) \to 0$ as $n \to \infty$ as stipulated in Paragraph 5. Next, as $k \to \infty$ we further require that $\ell \to \infty$ with $(\ell/k) = 1-\lambda_r$. Under these conditions it can be proved that a) $E_{k,\ell} \to E^*(\lambda_r)$, b) $A_{k,\ell} \to A^*(\lambda_r)$, and c) Equation 2.58 is the asymptotic version of 69. In statistical terminology, the properties under a) and b) imply that the k_n-NNR is consistent in Bayes risk. Moreover, in parallel with the derivation in Chapter 2, we can also use 69 to the effect of obtaining bounds on $E_{k,\ell}$:

$$E_{k,\ell} = \sum_{j=\ell}^{k}\left(1 - \frac{j}{k+1}\right)\left[A_{k+1,j} - A_{k+1,j+1}\right]$$

$$E_{k,\ell} \le \left(1 - \frac{\ell}{k+1}\right)\sum_{j=\ell}^{k}\left[A_{k+1,j} - A_{k+1,j+1}\right]$$

$$= \left(1 - \frac{\ell}{k+1}\right)\left[A_{k+1,\ell} - A_{k+1,k+1}\right]$$

Hence

70 $$E_{k,\ell} \le \left(1 - \frac{\ell}{k+1}\right)A_{k+1,\ell} \le \left(1 - \frac{\ell}{k+1}\right).$$

Clearly, 70 is the nearest neighbor version of Equation 2.35.

From the above discussion, it should be clear that the nearest neighbor rules are closely related to the Bayes rule. This relationship will be even more apparent in the following section where the performances of these rules are being compared.

3.8. ERROR BOUNDS

The problem we address in this section is that of comparing the nearest neighbor and Bayes decision rules on the basis of their respective performances. As a consequence of the optimality property of the Bayes rule it is clear that $\forall k,\ E_k \ge E^*$. So an interesting question is : may E_k be arbitrary larger than E^*? We shall first answer this question in terms of the 1-NN error rate E_1.

Recall from Equation 2.94, that in a two-class case

71 $$e^*(\underline{x}) = \min\left[\eta_1(\underline{x}), \eta_2(\underline{x})\right].$$

We may therefore write 10 as follows

72 $$e_1(\underline{x}) = 2e^*(\underline{x})\left[1-e^*(\underline{x})\right].$$

By taking expectation with respect to $p(\underline{x})$ we obtain

$$E_1 = \int e_1(\underline{x})p(\underline{x})d\underline{x}$$

$$= 2\int\left[e^*(\underline{x}) - e^*(\underline{x})^2\right]p(\underline{x})d\underline{x}$$

$$= 2E^* - 2E^{*2} - 2\text{var}\left\{e^*(\underline{x})\right\}$$

73 $$\leq 2E^*\left(1-E^*\right) \leq 2E^*,$$

where var{.} designates the variance of {.}. In a problem of c classes, it is about equally easy to show that

74 $$E_1 \leq E^*\left(2 - \frac{c}{c-1} E^*\right).$$

So, under the large-sample assumption, the 1-NN error rate is bounded from above by twice the Bayes rate. This important result provided much of the incentive for the widespread interest in nearest neighbor rules over the last decade. In a sense, it shows that *half of the classification information available in an infinite collection of classified samples is contained in the first nearest neighbor.*

REMARK : We may now fill the gap which we purposely left open in Section 2.10. By inverting the leftmost inequality of 73 we find

75 $$\frac{1}{2}\left[1 - \sqrt{1-2E_1}\right] \leq E^* \leq E_1.$$

Let $\rho(\underline{x}) = \sqrt{\eta_1(\underline{x})\eta_2(\underline{x})}$. Since $\rho(\underline{x}) \leq \frac{1}{2}$, we have

$$\rho(\underline{x}) \geq 2\rho(\underline{x})^2 = e_1(\underline{x}),$$

and

76 $$\int \rho(\underline{x})p(\underline{x})d\underline{x} \geq E_1.$$

We may see that $\rho(\underline{x})$ is the quantity which we used in Equations 2.95-2.97. Besides, the substitution of 76 into 75 yields the lower bound to E^* in terms of the Bhattacharyya coefficient which we claimed without proof in Equation 2.99.

Before returning to our discussion of error bounds with the k-NNR, let us exhibit two very useful formulae. First, by solving 72 for $e^*(\underline{x})$ we obtain

77 $$e^*(\underline{x}) = \frac{1}{2} - \frac{1}{2}\sqrt{1-4\eta_1(\underline{x})\eta_2(\underline{x})},$$

and the MacLaurin expansion of the right hand side of 77 is

$$e^*(\underline{x}) = \sum_{i=1}^{\infty} \frac{1}{i}\binom{2i-2}{i-1}\eta_1(\underline{x})^i\eta_2(\underline{x})^i$$

78 $$= \frac{1}{2}\sum_{i=1}^{\infty} \frac{1}{2i-1}\, a_{2i,s=i}(\underline{x}).$$

A very similar formula holds in terms of the binomial probability distribution. With our notation it reads

79 $$\sum_{j=k'}^{k} \left(1-\frac{j}{k}\right)a_{k,s=j}(\underline{x}) = \frac{1}{2}\sum_{i=1}^{k''} \frac{1}{2i-1}\, a_{2i,s=i}(\underline{x}),$$

and it may be seen that 78 follows from 79 in the limit as $k \to \infty$. The series in 78 is absolutely convergent. Hence, by taking expectations we obtain the two basic formulae

80 $$E^* = \frac{1}{2} \sum_{i=1}^{\infty} \frac{1}{2i-1} A_{2i,s=i}$$

81 $$\sum_{j=k'}^{k} \left(1-\frac{j}{k}\right) A_{k,s=j} = \frac{1}{2} \sum_{i=1}^{k''} \frac{1}{2i-1} A_{2i,s=i}$$

It is easy to show that the acceptance probability $A_{2i,s=i}$ satisfies the following inequality.

82 $$2iA_{2i,s=i} \leq (2i-1)\ A_{2i-2,s=i-1}.$$

With this in mind, let us consider the remainder of the truncated series in 81. We assume k even, hence $k'' = k' = k/2$.

$$\frac{1}{2} \sum_{i=k''+1}^{\infty} \frac{1}{2i-1} A_{2i,s=i} = \frac{1}{2} \sum_{i=k''+1}^{\infty} \left(\frac{2i}{2i-1} A_{2i,s=i} - A_{2i,s=i}\right)$$

$$\leq \frac{1}{2} \sum_{i=k''+1}^{\infty} \left(A_{2i-2,s=i-1} - A_{2i,s=i}\right)$$

$$= \frac{1}{2} A_{k,s=k'}.$$

By using this in 80 we obtain

$$E^* \leq \frac{1}{2} \sum_{i=1}^{k''} \frac{1}{2i-1} A_{2i,s=i} + \frac{1}{2} A_{k,s=k'}$$

83 $$= \sum_{j=k'}^{k} \left(1 - \frac{j}{k}\right) A_{k,s=j} + \frac{1}{2} A_{k,s=k'}.$$

The right hand side of 83 is a decreasing function of k which converges to E^* as $k \to \infty$. On the other hand, the right hand sides of 83 and 66.b are identical except for the substitution of k for k+1. There follows that 83 also reads $E^* \le E_{k-1}$, and for k odd, or k = 2k'-1, E_k is a decreasing function of k which converges to E^* as k grows arbitrarily large. So we have proved the following

84 $$E^* \le \ldots \le E_{2k'+1} \le E_{2k'-1} \le \ldots \le E_3 \le E_1 \le 2E^*.$$

Until now, the case of E_k with k even has been left aside. However it is a very simple matter to verify from 66, 67 and 81 that $E_{2k'-1} = E_{2k'}$. *When the last nearest neighbor is of even rank it does not contribute any additional classification information.* By combining this with 84 we get the following sequence of upper bounds to E^*.

85 $$E^* \le \ldots \le E_{2k'+2} = E_{2k'+1} \le E_{2k'} = E_{2k'-1} \le \ldots = E_3 \le E_2 = E_1 \le 2E^*$$

The derivation of this important series of inequalities is quite satisfying. Still, it leaves two things to be desired. First of all, it does not permit us to invert the inequalities, i.e., to derive lower bounds to E^* in terms of E_k, a very desirable result from the viewpoint of Bayes error estimation. Second, it does not tell us much about the rate of convergence of E_k to E^*. Precise answers to these questions may be obtained in the following way.

Let us assume k odd. By substituting 81 into 66 and using 80 we get

$$E_k = \frac{1}{2} \sum_{i=1}^{k'} \frac{1}{2i-1} A_{2i,s=i} + \frac{1}{2} A_{2k',s=k'}$$

$$\leq \frac{1}{2} \sum_{i=1}^{\infty} \frac{1}{2i-1} A_{2i,s=i} + \frac{1}{2} A_{2k',s=k'}$$

86 $$= E^* + \frac{1}{2} A_{2k',s=k'}.$$

Next, by recursivity, 82 yields

$$A_{2k',s=k'} \leq 2 \frac{k!!}{(k+1)!!} A_{2,s=1}$$

87 $$= 2 \frac{k!!}{(k+1)!!} E_1$$

88 $$\leq 2 \frac{k!!}{(k+1)!!} E^*(1-E^*),$$

where k!! denotes the semi-factorial of k. From 85-88 we conclude

89 $$E_{2k'-1} = E_{2k'} \leq E^* + \frac{(2k'-1)!!}{(2k')!!} E_1$$

90 $$\leq E^* + 2 \frac{(2k'-1)!!}{(2k')!!} E^*(1-E^*).$$

The inequality of 90 can be inverted and it yields a lower bound to E^* in terms of E_k. In order to evaluate the convergence rate in 85 let us invoke the second formula of Wallis. It says that when k is large,

91 $$\frac{(2k'-1)!!}{(2k')!!} \simeq \sqrt{1/k'\pi}.$$

By using 91 in 89 we obtain

92 $$E_k \leq E^* + E_1/\sqrt{k'\pi}.$$

So, the rate of convergence of E_k to E^* is at least of the order of $k^{-1/2}$.

This completed our analysis of error bounds in terms of the k-NNR without reject. In this analysis, we studied the behaviour of E_k with the quorum k as a variable. In the remainder of this section, we shall concentrate on error bounds which are orthogonal to the preceding ones. To this end we shall let k be fixed and study what happens when we consider the majority level ℓ as a variable. Our first step will be to prove that for any k,

93 $$E_{k,k} \leq E_{k,k-1} \leq \cdots \leq E_{k,k'+1} \leq E^* \leq E_k.$$

Among the various (k,ℓ)-NNR *with* k *fixed, the* k-NNR *only has an error rate which exceeds the Bayes rate.* Here, it is important to bear in mind that E^* is the error rate of the Bayes rule with NO reject.

On the ground of what we have acquired so far, the proof of 93 is extremely simple. Actually, all that needs to be proved is the next to last inequality. By 69, we have for any k

$$E_{k,k'+1} = \sum_{j=k'+1}^{k} \left(1 - \frac{j}{k+1}\right) A_{k+1,s=j}$$

94 $$\leq \sum_{j=(k+1)'}^{k+1} \left(1 - \frac{j}{k+1}\right) A_{k+1,s=j}.$$

with equality if k is even. Then, by 81 and 80

$$E_{k,k'+1} \leq \frac{1}{2} \sum_{i=1}^{(k+1)''} \frac{1}{2i-1} A_{2i,s=i}$$

95 $$\leq E^*.$$

The derivation of 94 indicates that the lower bound with $E_{k,k'+1}$ is tighter when k is even. Specifically

$$E_{2k'-1,k'+1} \le E_{2k',k'+1} \le E^*.$$

This is in apparent contradiction with our previous statement that when of even rank, the last NN did not contribute additional classification information. Fortunately it is easy to reconcile these contradictory observations for the reader should have no difficulty in providing a proof that a) for k odd, the mean of the upper and lower bounds E_k and $E_{k,k'+1}$ is still a lower bound to E^*, b) the latter bound is precisely $E_{k+1,k'+1}$. By collecting these findings in a single statement we have

96 $$E_{2k'-1,k'+1} \le \left[E_{2k'-1,k'+1}+E_{2k'-1}\right]/2=E_{2k',k'+1}$$
$$\le E^* \le E_{2k'-1}=E_{2k'}.$$

The difference between the tightest bounds in 96 is $\frac{1}{2} A_{2k',s=k'}$. It converges to zero at a rate which is again of the order of $k^{-1/2}$.

97 The performance of the (k,ℓ)-NNR can also be compared with the performance of the Bayes rule with the reject option. In principle, the comparison can be made very simple if we suppose that the rejection threshold λ_r in the decision rule of Equation 2.15 is chosen in such a way that $A^*(\lambda_r) = A_{k,\ell}$, equivalently $R^*(\lambda_r) = R_{k,\ell}$. Then, by the optimality property of the Bayes rule (cfr. Paragraph 2.28) we must have $E^*(\lambda_r) \le E_{k,\ell}$. Obviously, it is tempting to search an upper bound to $E_{k,\ell}$ in terms of $E^*(\lambda_r)$. However, this appears to be an extremely difficult problem, whose solution has been obtained in

analytical form in the case where $\ell=k$ only. The result, which we will give here without proof, is as follows.

Let λ_r be chosen such that

$$A^*(\lambda_r) = A_{k,k}.$$

Then it can be shown that

98 $$E^*(\lambda_r) \le E_{k,k} \le (1 + k/2)E^*(\lambda_r).$$

99 We shall conclude our discussion of error bounds with the formulation of a conjecture. For the (k,ℓ)- and (q,m)-NNR where $k < q \le \infty$, let k,ℓ,q and m be chosen such that

$$A_{k,\ell} = A_{q,m}.$$

Then, the conjecture is that

100 $$E_{k,\ell+1} \le E_{q,m} \le E_{k,\ell}.$$

3.9. NUMERICAL ILLUSTRATION

In general, even when the underlying distributions are known, the performance of the NNR cannot be calculated because 19 and 24 are too difficult to integrate. There is one notable exception to the rule. It consists of the class of underlying distributions such that the probability distribution of the conditional Bayes risk is uniform on a subinterval of [0,1]. This is the case, for instance, when in a two-class problem

101 $$\Pr\left\{e^*(\underline{x})<\xi\right\} = 2\xi, \qquad 0\le\xi\le 0,5.$$

The reader is rightly entitled to find this definition rather obscure. So, one specific example will be helpful. Let us consider a problem of two classes with $P_1=P_2=1/2$. Let x be unidimensional and with triangular, class-conditional distributions $p(x|\omega_1) = 2-p(x|\omega_2) = 2x$ on the unit interval [0,1]. It is readily verified that 101 is satisfied by these distributions. For the purpose of our discussion let us pose $e^*(\underline{x})=r$.

Under these conditions, the Bayes rate can be calculated as follows.

$$E^* = \int_0^{0,5} rp(r)dr = \int_0^{0,5} 2rdr = 1/4.$$

Likewise, by 72, the 1-NN error rate E_1 is

$$E_1 = \int_0^{0,5} 2r(1-r)p(r)dr = 1/3.$$

For the acceptance and error probabilities $A_{k,s=j}$ and $E_{k,s=j}$ in 19 and 24 we have

102 $$A^i_{k,s=j} = \binom{k}{j}\int_0^{0,5} r^j(1-r)^{k-j}p(r)dr = \frac{1}{k+1},$$

and

103 $$E^i_{k,s=j} = \binom{k}{j}\int_0^{0,5} r^j(1-r)^{k-j+1}p(r)dr = \frac{k-j+1}{(k+1)(k+2)}.$$

Clearly, these fomulae suffice to calculate the performance of any NNR. The calculation of the error rate has been made for

$1 \le k \le 10$, and the results are displayed in Figure 3.8. As predicted by 85, one can see the stepwise convergence from above of E_k to E^*, $(\ell = k')$, according to the formula

104 $$E_{2k'-1} = E_{2k} = \frac{2(k'+1)}{4(2k'+1)} = E^* + \frac{1}{4(2k'+1)}.$$

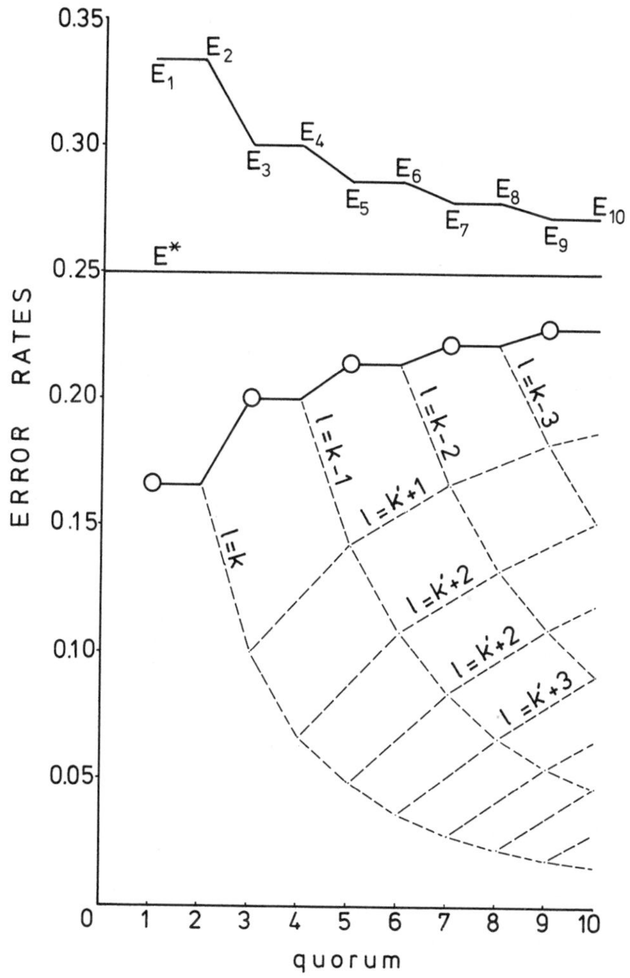

Figure 3.8. Numerical illustration

Likewise $E_{k,k'+1}$ converges to E^* from below according to the formula

105 $$\left[E_{2k'-1,k'+1} + E_{2k'-1}\right]/2 = E_{2k',k'+1} = \frac{2k'}{4(2k'+1)} = E^* - \frac{1}{4(2k'+1)}.$$

In this example problem, the upper and lower bounds of E^* in 96 are symmetrical, and the rate of convergence is of the order of k^{-1}. In Figure 3.8 the leftmost term of 105 is represented by empty circles in order to indicate that they do not correspond to one single rule. Also displayed are the curves corresponding to $k-\ell$ = constant, and $\ell-k'$ = constant. They should help the reader gain some insight into the behaviour of $E_{k,\ell}$ in terms of these parameters.

3.10. FINITE-SAMPLE CONSIDERATIONS

The results we have obtained so far are valid in the limit only as the number of samples goes to infinity. It is useful to recall that the "large-sample assumption" was essentially required to guarantee the convergence to $\underline{x}$ of the k-NN to $\underline{x}$ from S_n. In other words, a classification decision concerning $\underline{x}$ is guaranteed to be based on information gathered in an arbitrary small neighborhood of $\underline{x}$. Unfortunately, in any practical application, the large-sample assumption is not satisfied. So, all of our results hold only approximately. The essential reason is that the k-NN occupy a finite volume which, in general, increases with the ratio k/n. As a matter of principle, the k-NNR should therefore be used only when a very large training set is available and the number k should be small in order that all k-NN to $\underline{x}$ be contained in a small neighborhood of $\underline{x}$.

However, the requirement that S_n be as large as possible makes the rule very demanding in terms of storage space and computational complexity as the complete set must be examined to find the k-NN each time a new pattern is to be classified.

A great many attempts have been made to remedy the situation. For example, fast algorithms for searching nearest neighbors have been devised. As this is a very classical problem in Computer Science, we shall not discuss it here. An alternative approach, one that will be pursued hereafter, consists in *reducing* the number of samples in S_n by selecting a *representative* subset of the initial set. In order to assess representativeness of one sample with respect to the initial sample set we shall require that, with probability nearly equal to one, the classification performance with the reduced set be at least as good as with the complete set. The techniques we shall use for the purpose of selecting a representative subset are known under the names of Editing and Condensing.

3.11. THE EDITING TECHNIQUE

106 Without loss of generality, we consider a two-class problem and we assume k odd. We shall temporarily suppose that the original design set S_n was partitioned into two independent sets S_{n_1} and S_{n_2} where $n_1+n_2=n$ and the ratio n_1/n_2 is bounded away from zero and infinity. Next, let us perform the following preprocessing of the design data.

<u>Step 1</u> : Classify the samples from S_{n_1} using the k-NNR with S_{n_2} as a design set.

<u>Step 2</u> : Edit (discard) from S_{n_1} all the samples that were misclassified at Step 1. Let $S_{n_1'}$ denote the remaining subset.

Subsequently, classification is performed using the 1-NNR with $S_{n_1'}$ as a design set. In the following it is important to bear in mind that the k-NNR is used for editing and the 1-NNR is used for classification.

We shall temporarily disregard the fact that the data in S_{n_2} is not used at the classification stage. However, we may already observe that Step 2 above entails a first reduction in the size of S_{n_1}. We wish to examine the effect of this reduction on the performance of the 1-NNR.

107 An arbitrary sample $(\underline{x},\theta)\epsilon S_{n_1}$ is retained in $S_{n_1'}$ if $\theta=\omega_i$ and $k_i \geq k'$, i=1 or 2. Recalling Section 3.4, this occurs with asymptotic probability $\eta_i(\underline{x})a_k^i(\underline{x})$. For $\underline{x}$ to be discarded, we must have $\theta=\omega_i$ and $k_j > k'$, i,j=1,2, i≠j. This has limiting probability

$$\eta_1(\underline{x})a_k^2(\underline{x}) + \eta_2(\underline{x})a_k^1(\underline{x}) = e_k(\underline{x}).$$

So, on the average, the probability of editing any sample is $E\left\{e_k(\underline{x})\right\} = E_k$ and the preprocessing retains a fraction (close to) $1-E_k$ of the data in S_{n_1}.

To simplify matters, we shall take it for granted that, after editing, the first NN to $\underline{x}$ still converges to $\underline{x}$ as $n \to \infty$. Then, the probability of the first NN $\underline{x}_n'$ to $\underline{x}$ being a class-ω_i neighbor after editing is the ratio of the probability of $\underline{x}_n'$ being retained as a class-ω_i sample over the probability of $\underline{x}'_n$ being retained irrespective of its class. In the limit as $\underline{x}'_n \to \underline{x}$ this probability is given by

108 $$\phi_{k,1}(i|\underline{x}) = \eta_i(\underline{x})a_k^i(\underline{x}) \Big/ \Big[1-e_k(\underline{x})\Big].$$

There follows that the conditional error probability $\varepsilon_{k,1}$ of classifying $\underline{x}$ with the 1-NNR can be calculated as

$$\varepsilon_{k,1}(\underline{x}) = \eta_1(\underline{x})\phi_k(2|\underline{x}) + \eta_2(\underline{x})\phi_k(1|\underline{x})$$

$$= \frac{\eta_1(\underline{x})\eta_2(\underline{x})\Big[a_k^1(\underline{x})+a_k^2(\underline{x})\Big]}{1-e_k(X)}.$$

The term between brackets is equal to unity. So, by using 10 and 72 we obtain

109 $$\varepsilon_{k,1}(\underline{x}) = \frac{e_1(\underline{x})}{2\Big[1-e_k(\underline{x})\Big]} = e^*(\underline{x})\ \frac{1-e^*(\underline{x})}{1-e_k(\underline{x})}.$$

It readily follows that $\varepsilon_{k,1}(\underline{x}) \le e_k(\underline{x})$. So by using editing, we have reduced the number of candidate neighbors to be searched and we have improved the performance over the k-NNR as well. In particular, we observe that when the 1-NN error probability is small (say, $e_1(\underline{x}) \le .05$), so are $e_k(\underline{x})$ and $e^*(\underline{x})$. In this case we conclude from 109

$$\varepsilon_{k,1}(\underline{x}) \cong e_1(\underline{x})/2 \cong e^*(\underline{x}),\ k=1,2,\ \ldots\ .$$

So, when the error probability is small, the 1-NNR with edited data is quasi Bayes-optimal. Indeed, for all practical purposes, the edited 1-NNR could hardly be distinguished from the Bayes rule.

The editing technique appears to be advantageous from both operational and computational viewpoints. Therefore, one may wonder whether the same technique could be applied more than once to reduce the data further, and improve the performance somewhat more ?

Clearly, if we were to repeat the editing procedure in 106 we would soon run out of samples. Devising ways of making effective use of the samples available at the outset is a very general problem we shall discuss at some length in the context of classification-error estimation (Chapter 10). So, for the time being, we shall first examine what would happen with repeated editing under the theoretical provision that an arbitrarily large number of samples is available at any time of the editing process. Next, we shall describe a sample-based procedure which is an effective replicate of the process analyzed theoretically.

3.12. REPEATED EDITING

110 Let us consider editing with 1-NN. As $a_1^i(\underline{x}) = \eta_i(\underline{x})$, we have

$$\phi_1(i|\underline{x}) = \eta_i(\underline{x})^2 \Big/ \left[\eta_1(\underline{x})^2 + \eta_2(\underline{x})^2\right],$$

and

$$\varepsilon_{1,1}(\underline{x}) = e_1(\underline{x})/2\left[1-e_1(\underline{x})\right].$$

Recall that the initial set S_n was drawn from underlying distributions with mixture p.d.f. $p(\underline{x})$ and *a posteriori* probabilities $\eta_i(\underline{x})$, i=1,2. It should be pointed out that these probabilities suffice to specify completely the underlying model.

The effect of editing as explained above can be seen as a

transformation of these actual distributions into new or apparent distributions. We have seen that a given sample is edited with probability $e_1(\underline{x})$. Consequently the apparent mixture p.d.f. after editing is

111 $$p'(\underline{x}) = p(\underline{x}) \frac{1-e_1(\underline{x})}{1-E_1}$$

Likewise, the apparent *a posteriori* probabilities are given by

112 $$\eta_i'(\underline{x}) = \phi_1(i|\underline{x}) = \eta_i(\underline{x})^2 \Big/ \left[\eta_1(\underline{x})^2+\eta_2(\underline{x})^2\right], \quad i=1,2.$$

Suppose now that we were allowed to draw a new sample set from the model specified by 111 and 112. If this set was edited in turn, the asymptotic probability $\phi_{2\times 1}(i|\underline{x})$ of the first neighbor to $\underline{x}$ being a class-ω_i neighbor would be

$$\phi_{2\times 1}(i|\underline{x}) = \eta_i'(\underline{x})^2 \Big/ \left[\eta_1'(\underline{x})^2+\eta_2'(\underline{x})^2\right]$$

$$= \eta_i(\underline{x})^{2^2} \Big/ \left[\eta_1(\underline{x})^{2^2}+\eta_2(\underline{x})^{2^2}\right], \quad i=1,2.$$

If one repeated the sampling-editing cycle M times, one would obtain

113 $$\phi_{M\times 1}(i|\underline{x}) = \eta_i(\underline{x})^{2^M} \Big/ \left[\eta_1(\underline{x})^{2^M}+\eta_2(\underline{x})^{2^M}\right], \quad i=1,2.$$

The asymptotic error probability of classifying a sample $\underline{x}$ drawn from the actual (initial) distributions by using the 1-NNR with the Mth edited subset would be

$$\varepsilon_{M\times 1,1}(\underline{x}) = \eta_1(\underline{x})\phi_{M\times 1}(2|\underline{x})+\eta_2(\underline{x})\phi_{M\times 1}(1|\underline{x})$$

$$= 1- \frac{\eta_1(\underline{x})^{2^M+1}+\eta_2(\underline{x})^{2^M+1}}{\eta_1(\underline{x})^{2^M}+\eta_2(\underline{x})^{2^M}}.$$

At this point it is easy to verify that

114 $$\lim_{M\to\infty} \varepsilon_{M\times 1,1}(\underline{x}) = \min\left[\eta_1(\underline{x}),\eta_2(\underline{x})\right] = e^*(\underline{x}).$$

Thus our somewhat artificial procedure is asymptotically Bayes optimal with respect to the original problem.

Let us now take a more pragmatic viewpoint and see how the above distribution-based analysis can be converted into a sample-based algorithm. It is easy to figure out the fate of an arbitrary point in S_n with such an algorithm. In theory, a class-ω_i sample is retained with probability $\eta_i(\underline{x})\phi_{M\times 1}(i|\underline{x})$. Besides, it follows from 113 that

$$\phi_{M\times 1}(1|\underline{x}) \xrightarrow{M} \begin{matrix} 1 \\ 1/2 \\ 0 \end{matrix} \quad \text{if} \quad \eta_1(\underline{x}) \begin{matrix} > \\ = \\ < \end{matrix} \eta_2(\underline{x}).$$

Consequently, to be ultimately retained, one sample must belong to the Bayes acceptance region corresponding to its own class. In other words, the sample-based algorithm will iteratively tend to edit all samples which do not belong to their own Bayes acceptance region. It goes without saying that some samples which could legitimately be retained will be discarded as well.

From the discussion in Chapter 10 it will be obvious that a careless implementation of a sample-based editing procedure would generate statistical dependence between the samples retained in any subset. As independence was implicitely assumed many times in our analysis, every care must be taken to preserve it at any step of the algorithm. Consequently, the following procedure has been based on the twin paradigms, familiar to cryptographers, of *diffusion* and *confusion* which are known to effectively remove unwanted statistical dependence.

The MULTIEDIT algorithm

Step 1. Diffusion : Make a random partition of the available data S into N subsets $S_1,\ldots,S_N$, $N \geq 3$.

Step 2. Classification : Classify the samples in S_i using the 1-NNR with $S_{(i+1)\text{Mod } N}$ as a training set, $i=1,\ldots,N$.

Step 3. Editing : Discard all the samples that were misclassified at Step 2.

Step 4. Confusion : pool all the remaining data to constitute a new set S.

Step 5. Termination : If the last I iterations produced no editing then exit with the final set S, else go to Step 1.

Subsequently, classification is performed using the 1-NNR with the remaining data as a design set.

It should be obvious to the alert reader that the MULTIEDIT algorithm is a fair sample-based replicate of the procedure we have discussed theoretically. At any iteration, the initial set is regarded as representative of the current underlying distributions, such as specified by 111 and 112. Each subset in Step 1 is regarded as a random sample from these distributions. The rotation of indices in Step 2 is intended to avoid two-way interaction between any two subsets, (still another way to preserve independence). It should also

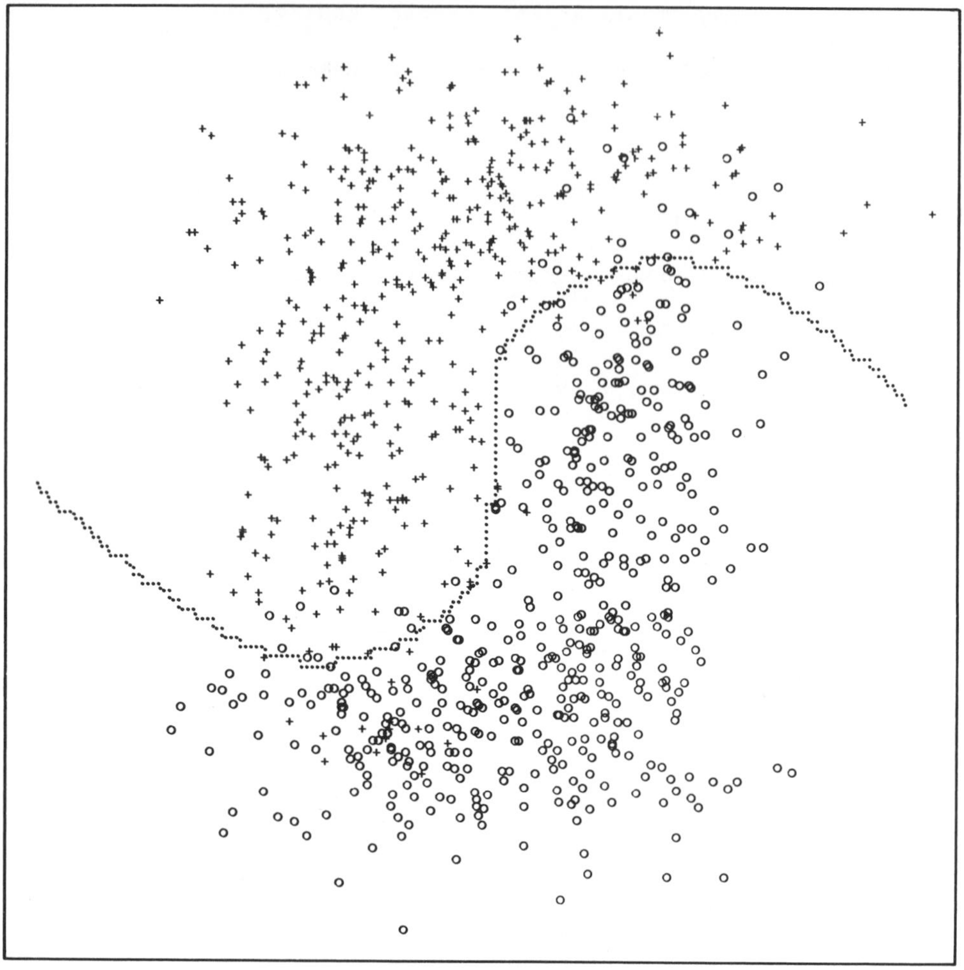

Figure 3.9. Initial, two-dimensional data used to illustrate the performance of the MULTIEDIT algorithm. (The dotted curve shows the Bayes decision boundary).

be noted that owing to randomization, the fact that one iteration produces no editing is no evidence that the current set S is for ever immune to further editing; hence Step 5.

In spite of their close conceptual similarity, the distribution- and sample-based procedures differ in many respects. It cannot be overemphasized that our theoretical argument is no proof that the sample-based algorithm would indeed lead us to a Bayes-optimal decision rule. At best we can hope to be able to approximate the

Bayes rule reasonably well. This appears to be the case for the example problem illustrated by Figures 3.9 through 3.11.

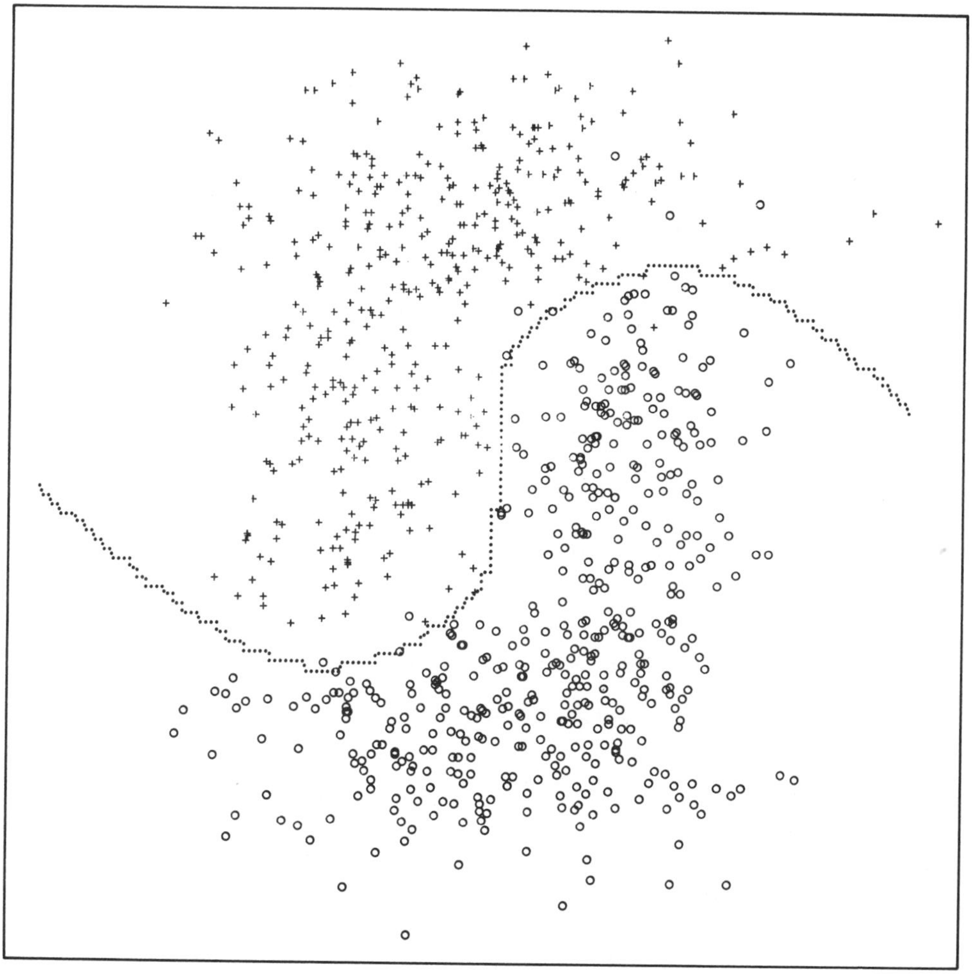

Figure 3.10. Illustration of the performance of the MULTIEDIT algorithm. Data retained after the first iteration.

3.13. COMMENTS

Before turning to the condensing technique, let us pause for a short while and observe that, thus far, we encountered three theoretical possibilities to achieve Bayes optimality by using nearest neighbor techniques.

In the first place, this goal can be achieved, under appropriate assumptions, by k-NN classification or 1-NN classification with k-NN edited data. In both cases, k must be arbitrarily large. These two possibilities are however of little practical avail for, as we commented in Section 3.10, using a large value of k in the finite-sample case is all but advisable.

In the second place, Bayes optimality can also be achieved by the use of repeated editing with the 1-NNR followed by 1-NN classification. This approach exchanges the need for using information from very many neighbors for the need for using information from the first neighbor very many times. So, the latter approach relies on information which is bound to remain more local and it is therefore better suited to the finite-sample case.

The consideration of the editing technique was motivated by our desire to reduce the storage and computational complexity of the NNR. So far, this goal has been achieved to a very limited extent only. In fact, the reader should have little difficulty to verify that the proportion of samples retained by repeated editing is bounded from below by $(1-2E_1)$. Our partial failure at reducing significantly the size of the design set is nonetheless largely compensated for by an improvement of the classification performance. Moreover, the preprocessing with the MULTIEDIT algorithm has casually given the remaining data set the ideal structure for subsequent application of the Condensing technique which is the next, and last, topic to which we now turn.

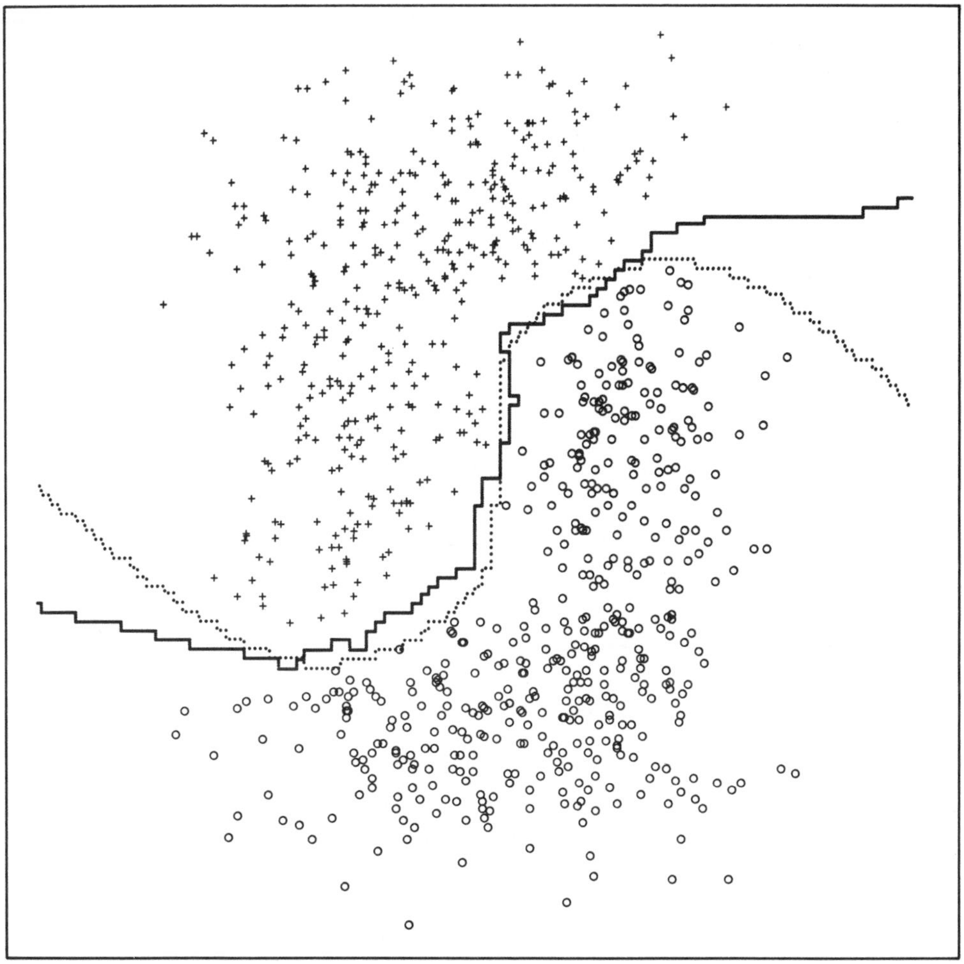

Figure 3.11. Illustration of the performance of the MULTIEDIT algorithm. Data retained after the last iteration. (The solid line shows the 1-NN decision boundary).

3.14. THE CONDENSING TECHNIQUE

The MULTIEDIT algorithm has created homogeneous clusters of samples. Each cluster is spanning the Bayes acceptance region corresponding to its class. The 1-NN classification rule using the edited data implements a piecewise-linear decision boundary which is the sample-based approximation of the Bayes-optimal decision boundary, (Figure 3.11). Loosely speaking, the sample-based decision boundary is defined by a small number of samples belonging to the outer envelopes of the clusters. In other words, those samples which do not contribute to define the boundary, for example those deeply imbedded within the clusters, may be discarded with no effect on the subsequent performance of the 1-NNR. This is the basic idea which is at work in the condensing technique.

Let us reformulate our objective in a somewhat more precise manner. Ideally, we would like to select the minimal subset of the complete data set such that 1-NN classification of any new pattern with the selected subset would be identical to 1-NN classification with the complete set. Although simple to formulate, this problem appears to be of an overwhelming computational complexity when the pattern space has a moderately large number of dimensions. Consequently we shall have to head towards a less ambitious objective.

As an alternative, we could want to select one minimal subset such that the 1-NNR with the selected subset would correctly classify the remaining points in the sample set. Again, asking for a "minimal" subset is computationally unfeasible. However, the following algorithm produces a subset with the desired properties except for the fact that it is not guaranteed to be minimal.

We assume that the sample set produced by MULTIEDIT is arranged in some order. We set up bins called STORE and GRABBAG. The first sample is placed in STORE, all the other samples are placed in GRABBAG. We let n_g designate the current number of samples in GRABBAG whenever Step 1 of the algorithm is entered.

The CONDENSING algorithm

Step 1 : Use the 1-NNR with the current contents of STORE to classify the ith sample from GRABBAG. If classified correctly the sample is returned to GRABBAG, otherwise it is placed in STORE. Repeat this operation for $i=1,\ldots,n_g$.

Step 2 : If one complete pass is made through Step 1 with no transfer from GRABBAG to STORE or the GRABBAG is exhausted then terminate; else go to Step 1.

The final contents of STORE constitute the condensed subset to be used with the 1-NNR. The contents of GRABBAG are discarded.

The result of applying the CONDENSING algorithm to the data in Figure 3.11 is shown in Figure 3.12. The reduction in the number of training samples is presently a very drastic one. As could be expected from the above discussion, condensing entails some further distortion in the approximation of the Bayes decision boundary. It should be clear, however, that preprocessing of the initial data with the MULTIEDIT and CONDENSING algorithms has reduced the computational complexity of the 1-NNR to a point where it compares quite favorably with the simplest possible competing techniques.

3.15. BIBLIOGRAPHICAL COMMENTS

The nearest neighbor rule first appeared in two important reports by Fix and Hodges (1951, 1952) that set the stage for most of the subsequent work in this area. The first proof of the convergence of the nearest neighbor is due to Cover and Hart (1967). Convergence

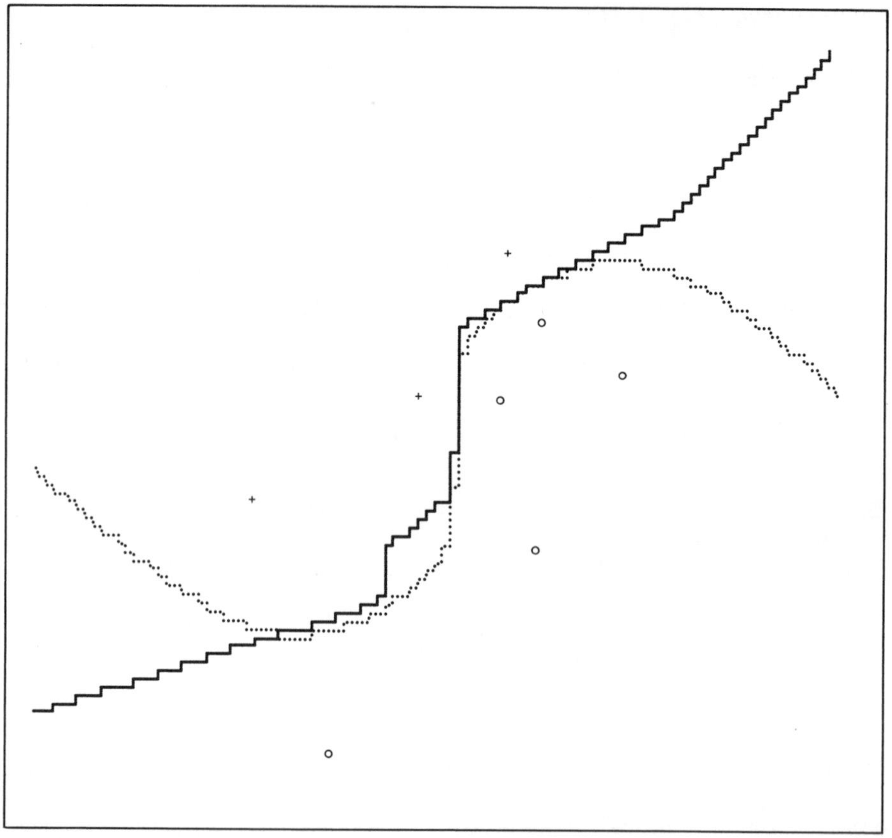

Figure 3.12. Illustration of the performance of the CONDENSING algorithm applied to the data in Figure 3.11.

conditions were substantially relaxed by Stone (1977) and Devroye (1981). These works were concerned with the asymptotic convergence of $\mathbf{E}\{e_1(\underline{x},\underline{x}'_n)\}$ to E_1. Wagner (1971) and Devroye (1981) extended these results by establishing the asymptotic convergence to E_1 of $\mathbf{E}\{e_1(\underline{x})|S_n\}$. Rates of convergence were examined by Cover (1968).

The nearest neighbor rules with a reject option, viz., the (k,ℓ)-NNR, were introduced by Hellman (1970), and extended to the (k,ℓ_i)-NNR by Devijver (1977). Our exposition of acceptance, error, and error-acceptance relationships follows Devijver (1977).

The surprising nearest neighbor error bound is due to Cover and Hart (1967). The k-NN error-bounds in Section 3.8 were given by Devijver (1979). Error-bounds with the (k,ℓ)-NNR were borrowed from Hellman (1970) and Devijver (1979).

The idea of using editing was suggested and investigated by Wilson (1972). Wagner (1973) has given a simple proof of the convergence of the edited nearest neighbor. Wilson's results were criticized by Penrod and Wagner (1977) and the controversy was resolved by Devijver and Kittler (1979) who also suggested the repeated-editing technique.

The simple condensing algorithm we have discussed is due to Hart (1968). Many subsequent attempts at selecting condensed subsets inducing less distortion of the decision boundary are discussed and compared by Chidananda Gowda and Krishna (1979).

Among the various topics which have gone barely mentioned, if at all, both the choice of the distance measure and the algorithmic problem of searching nearest neighbors deserve consideration. A very elegant idea proposed by Short and Fukunaga (1980) is to use a local distance measure that minimizes the difference between asymptotic and finite-sample error-rates. Fukunaga and Narendra (1975) used the Branch and Bound algorithm (which we discuss in Chapter 5) to increase the speed of computing the nearest neighbors. Other algorithms for finding nearest neighbors were suggested by Friedman et al (1975), Yunck (1976), and too many others to be cited here.

3.16 REFERENCES

Chidananda Gowda, K., and Krishna, G.,"The condensed nearest neighbor rule using the concept of mutual nearest neighborhood", *IEEE Trans. Inform. Theory*, Vol. 25, pp. 488-490, July 1979.

Cover, T.M., "Rates of convergence of nearest neighbor decision procedures", *Proc. Hawaii Internat. Conf. on System Sciences*, pp. 413-415, Jan. 1968.

Cover, T.M., and Hart, P.E., "Nearest neighbor pattern classification", *IEEE Trans. Inform. Theory*, Vol. 13, pp. 21-27, Jan. 1967.

Devijver, P.A., Reconnaissance des Formes par la Méthode des Plus Proches Voisins, Doctoral Dissertation, Univ. Paris VI, June 1977.

Devijver, P.A., "New error bounds with the nearest neighbor rule", *IEEE Trans. Inform. Theory*, Vol. 25, pp. 749-753, Nov 1979.

Devijver, P.A., and Kittler, J., "On the edited nearest neighbor rule", *Proc. Fifth Internat. Conf. on Pattern Recognition*, Miami Beach, Fl., pp. 72-80, Dec. 1980.

Devroye, L., "On the inequality of Cover and Hart in nearest neighbor discrimination", *IEEE Trans. Pattern Anal. Machine Intell.*, Vol. 3, pp. 75-78, Jan. 1981.

Fix, E., and Hodges, J.L., "Discriminatory analysis, nonparametric discrimination", USAF School of Aviation Medicine, Randolph Field, Tex. , Project 21-49-004, Rept. 4, Feb. 1951, (Reprinted in *Machine Recognition of Patterns*, A.K.Agrawala Ed., IEEE Press, New York, 1977, pp. 261-279).

Fix, E., and Hodges, J.L., "Discriminatory analysis, small sample performance", USAF School of Aviation Medicine, Randolph Field, Tex., Project 21-49-004, Rept. 11, Aug. 1952, (Reprinted in *Machine Recognition of Patterns*, A.K. Agrawala Ed., IEEE Press, New York, 1977, pp. 280-322).

Friedman, J.H., et. al., "An algorithm for finding nearest neighbors", *IEEE Trans. Comput.*, Vol. 24, pp. 1000-1006, Oct. 1975.

Fukunaga, K., and Narendra, P.M., "A branch and bound algorithm for computing k-nearest neighbors", *IEEE Trans. Comput.*, Vol. 24, pp. 750-753, July 1975.

Hart, P.E., "The condensed nearest neighbor rule", *IEEE Trans. Inform. Theory*, Vol. 14, pp. 515-516, May 1968.

Hellman, M., "The nearest neighbor classification rule with a reject option", *IEEE Trans. Systems Sci. Cybernet.*, Vol. 6, pp. 179-185, July 1970.

Penrod, C.S., and Wagner, T.J., "Another look at the edited nearest neighbor rule", *IEEE Trans. Systems Man Cybernet.*, Vol. 7, pp. 92-94, Feb. 1977.

Short, R.D., and Fukunaga, K., "A new nearest neighbor distance measure", *Proc. Fifth Internat. Conf. on Pattern Recognition*, pp. 81-86, Miami Beach, Fl., Dec. 1980.

Stone, C.J., "Consistent nonparametric regression", *Ann. Statist.*, Vol. 5, pp. 595-645, 1977.

Wagner, T.J., "Convergence of the nearest neighbor rule", *IEEE Trans. Inform. Theory*, Vol. 17, pp. 566-571, 1971.

Wagner, T.J., "Convergence of the edited nearest neighbor", *IEEE Trans. Inform. Theory*, Vol. 19, pp. 696-697, Sept. 1973.

Wilson, D.L., "Asymptotic properties of nearest neighbor rules using edited data", *IEEE Trans. Systems Man Cybernet.*, Vol. 2, pp. 408-420, July 1972.

Yunck, T.P., "A technique to identify nearest neighbors", *IEEE Trans. Systems Man Cybernet.*, Vol. 6, pp. 678-683, Oct. 1976.

3.17 PROBLEMS

1. Let $E_1^{i/j}$ denote the asymptotic probability of substitution error with the 1-NNR. Specifically, $E_1^{i/j}=\Pr\left\{\hat{\omega}_1=\omega_i,\omega=\omega_j\right\}$, $i\neq j$. Show that

$$E_1^{i/j} = E_1^{j/i}.$$

Does this result extend to error probabilities $E_k^{i/j}$ of the k-NNR?

2. Show that, in the finite-sample case, it holds true that for $\ell>k$",

$$A_{k,\ell} \geq A_{k-1,\ell},$$
$$A_{k,\ell} \geq A_{k-1,\ell+1},$$
$$A_{k,\ell} \geq A_{k,\ell+1},$$
$$A_{k,\ell} \geq A_{k+1,\ell+1}.$$

(Note that these are the inequalitites 27-30 which were claimed to hold in the large-sample case.)

3. The error-reject tradeoff for (k,ℓ_i)-NNR was given in the text in two different versions, *viz.*, 59 and 63. Establish three (or more) additional versions and interpret them in terms of the votes cast by the nearest neighbors. Hint : Combine the acceptance theorem or the error theorem with the error-acceptance theorem.

4. Extend the proof of 73, namely $E_1 \le 2E^*(1-E^*)$ to the case when there are more than two classes. In other words, show that

$$E_1 \le E^*\left(2 - \frac{c}{c-1} E^*\right), \quad c=2,3, \ldots .$$

Determine the conditions for the equality to be satisfied.

5. In the two-class case, show that

(a) $E_{2k'-1,s=k'} = 2E_{2k',s=k'} = A_{2k',s=k'}$.

(b) $E_{2k'-1} = E_{2k'}$.

(c) $\left[E_{2k'-1,k'+1} + E_{2k'-1}\right]/2 = E_{2k',k'+1}$.

6. Verify that the conjecture in 99 holds true in the case of the example-problem of Section 3.9. Next, attempt to provide a general proof of the conjecture.

7. (a) Show that

$$2iA_{2i,s=i} \le (2i-1)A_{2i-2,s=i-1}, \quad i=2,3,\ldots .$$

(b) Show that the probability $(1-E_1')$ of an arbitrary sample being retained at the second pass of the repeated editing procedure is bounded from below (with equality) by

$$\frac{2-3E_1}{2-2E_1}.$$

Hint : $E_1' = \int \eta_1'(\underline{x})\eta_2'(\underline{x})p'(\underline{x})d\underline{x}$ where $p'(\underline{x})$ and $\eta_1'(\underline{x})$, $\eta_2'(\underline{x})$ are given by 111 and 112. Next, use (a) in the process of deriving an upper bound to E_1.

(c) Use the result of (b) to establish that the proportion of samples retained by repeated-editing is bounded from below (with equality) by $(1-2E_1)$.

(d) Devise a two-dimensional example where equality is achieved in the bounds of (a), (b) and (c).

Chapter 4

DISCRIMINANT FUNCTIONS

4.1. INTRODUCTION

In Chapter 2, we constantly assumed that the probability distributions of the pattern classes were known, and in some simple cases, we were able to obtain the explicit form of the Bayes classifier. For instance, for two normally distributed pattern classes with identical covariance matrices, the minimum error rate decision boundary was shown to be Anderson's discriminant plane

1 $$\underline{x}^t \Sigma^{-1}\left(\underline{\mu}_1-\underline{\mu}_2\right) = \frac{1}{2}\left(\underline{\mu}_1+\underline{\mu}_2\right)^t \Sigma^{-1}\left(\underline{\mu}_1-\underline{\mu}_2\right) + \log \frac{P_2}{P_1}.$$

We also commented that the optimal decision boundary has so simple a structure in situations which are exceptions rather than the rule.

In Chapter 3, our investigation of editing and condensing was also motivated by our desire to produce a simple approximation of the Bayes decision boundary for minimum error-rate classification. One interesting feature of this approach was that it did not presuppose any particular "shape" for the decision boundary.

In this chapter, we take a radically different approach.

Specifically, we assume that the functional form of the decision boundary is selected *a priori*. In other words, the analytical expression of the decision boundary is given except for the values of a set of parameters. Then, we shall develop methods of using the samples to estimate the parameters of the classifier.

2 For instance, for a given functional form $g(\underline{x})$ and a problem of c classes, one possibility is to have c *discriminant functions* $g_i(\underline{x})$, $i=1,\ldots,c$. Classification of a pattern $\underline{x}$ is performed by forming these c discriminant functions and assigning $\underline{x}$ to the class associated with the largest discriminant function. In the two-class case, it is equivalent to form a single function

$$g(\underline{x}) = g_1(\underline{x}) - g_2(\underline{x})$$

and to assign $\underline{x}$ to class ω_1 if $g(\underline{x})>0$, and to class ω_2 if $g(\underline{x})<0$. Throughout this chapter, we shall focus our attention on this formulation. Clearly, it is very much reminiscent of the theory of Chapter 2 for if we were to take $g_i(\underline{x})$ to be the *a posteriori* probability $P(\omega_i|\underline{x})$ we would obtain the Bayes classifier for minimum error-rate. Thus, the essential distinction lies in the fact that, hereafter, the functional form of $g(\underline{x})$ is not imposed by the underlying distributions.

The approach has the genuine advantage that one may select the functional form of $g(\underline{x})$ as he pleases. For instance, taking $g(\underline{x})$ to be *linear* in $\underline{x}$ results in *linear discriminant functions* which are easily implemented on special-purpose devices. As we just recalled, they can even be optimal if the underlying distributions are very cooperative. When they are not, one might still be willing to trade some performance for the advantage of simplicity. Much of our discussion will be concerned with linear discriminant functions. However, following well established traditions, the theory of linear discriminant functions will be developed in a way which is directly and easily extensible to more general functional forms.

The selection of a suitable functional form for a discriminant function is a problem of crucial importance. Clearly, there is little hope of any good coming from a discriminant function which is not reasonably well matched to the problem at hand. Theoretical guidance relative to this choice will be one of our permanent concerns. It will be seen however that the theory has not yet reached the stage where it can tell us how to "build" an effective discriminant function. At best, it will help us make a proper choice amidst various competing designs. Therefore, as a rule, the theory can be used successfully only when a sizeable amount of *a priori* knowledge about the problem to be dealt with can be properly embodied in the design of the discriminant function.

4.2. LINEAR DISCRIMINANT FUNCTIONS

4.2.1. The Two-Class Case

Let us consider first the family of linear discriminant functions of the form

3
$$g(\underline{x}) = v_1 x_1 + v_2 x_2 + \dots + v_d x_d + v_{d+1} = \underline{v}^t \underline{x} + v_{d+1}.$$

The d-dimensional vector $\underline{v}=\left[v_1,v_2,\ldots,v_d\right]^t$ is called the *weight vector* and v_{d+1} is the *threshold weight*. The decision rule corresponding to the discriminant function $g(\underline{x})$ is to assign $\underline{x}$ to class ω_1 if $g(\underline{x})>0$, and to class ω_2 if $g(\underline{x})<0$. If $g(\underline{x})=0$, the indeterminacy may be resolved as one pleases and we shall leave the classification undefined. The decision boundary is defined by the equation $g(\underline{x})=0$. As $g(\underline{x})$ is linear in $\underline{x}$ the decision surface is a linear surface, thus a *hyperplane* in d-dimensional space. It is given by

4 $$\underline{v}^t\underline{x} = -v_{d+1}.$$

Let us briefly recall some elementary facts about the geometry of hyperplanes. Let $\underline{x}$ and $\underline{x}_1$ be two points on the hyperplane, and $\underline{u}$ be a unit vector, normal to the hyperplane at point $\underline{x}_1$ and directed into the half-space of points $\underline{\xi}$ such that $\underline{v}^t\underline{\xi}>-v_{d+1}$, (see Figure 4.1).

As $\underline{x}$ and $\underline{x}_1$ are both on the hyperplane, we have

5 $$\underline{v}^t\underline{x}_1 + v_{d+1} = \underline{v}^t\underline{x} + v_{d+1} = 0,$$

thus

6 $$\underline{v}^t\left(\underline{x} - \underline{x}_1\right) = 0.$$

On the other hand, as $\underline{u}$ is normal to the hyperplane, we also have

7 $$\underline{u}^t\left(\underline{x} - \underline{x}_1\right) = 0.$$

Comparing 6 and 7, we conclude that $\underline{v}$ is also normal to the hyperplane and

8 $$\underline{u} = \frac{\underline{v}}{\|\underline{v}\|},$$

where $\|\underline{v}\| = \left[\sum_{i=1}^{d} v_i^2\right]^{1/2}$. The vector $\underline{v}$ defines the *orientation* of the hyperplane. The normal Euclidean distance from the origin to the hyperplane is

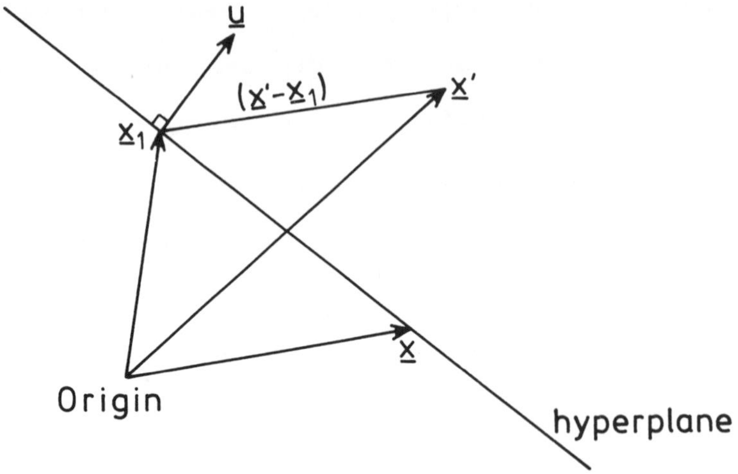

Figure 4.1. The geometry of hyperplanes

9 $$\underline{x}_1^t\underline{u} = \underline{x}_1^t \frac{\underline{v}}{\|\underline{v}\|} = \frac{-v_{d+1}}{\|\underline{v}\|}.$$

With appropriate normalization, the threshold weight defines the *location* of the hyperplane. Clearly, when $v_{d+1} = 0$, the hyperplane passes through the origin. Let δ denote the signed, normal Euclidean distance from an arbitrary point $\underline{x}'$ to the hyperplane, δ being positive if $g(\underline{x}')>0$ and negative if $g(\underline{x}')<0$. Then (see Figure 4.1),

$$\delta = \underline{u}^t\left(\underline{x}'-\underline{x}_1\right) = \frac{\underline{v}^t}{\|\underline{v}\|}\left(\underline{x}'-\underline{x}_1\right)$$

10 $$= \frac{\underline{v}^t\underline{x}'}{\|\underline{v}\|} + \frac{v_{d+1}}{\|\underline{v}\|} = g(\underline{x}')/\|\underline{v}\|.$$

The distance δ is proportional to $g(\underline{x}')$. The point $\underline{x}'$ is said to lie on the positive or the negative side of the hyperplane according as $g(\underline{x}')>0$ or $g(\underline{x}')<0$.

A pattern classifier employing linear discriminant functions is called a *linear machine*. An important special case of a linear machine is a *minimum distance classifier* with respect to points. Suppose we are given two points X_1 and X_2, each X_i being a representative prototype for the class ω_i. A minimum distance classifier with respect to X_1 and X_2 assigns each new pattern $\underline{x}$ to the class which corresponds to the nearest of the prototype points X_1 and X_2. The squared Euclidean distance from $\underline{x}$ to X_i is given by

$$\|\underline{x}-X_i\|^2 = \underline{x}^t\underline{x} - 2\underline{x}^tX_i + X_i^tX_i.$$

As $\underline{x}^t\underline{x}$ is independent of index i, the minimum distance classification can be effected by forming the discriminant functions

11 $$g_i(\underline{x}) = \underline{x}^tX_i - \tfrac{1}{2}X_i^tX_i, \quad i=1,2,$$

which are linear functions of $\underline{x}$. The equation of the decision boundary is

$$g(\underline{x}) = g_1(\underline{x}) - g_2(\underline{x})$$

12 $$= \underline{x}^t\left(X_1-X_2\right) - \tfrac{1}{2}\left(X_1^tX_1-X_2^tX_2\right) = 0.$$

It is of the general form of $g(\underline{x}) = \underline{v}^t\underline{x} + v_{d+1}$ with

$$\underline{v} = X_1 - X_2$$

and

$$v_{d+1} = -\tfrac{1}{2}\left(X_1^tX_1 - X_2^tX_2\right).$$

It is easy to see that this decision boundary is the perpendicular bisector of the line segment joining X_1 and X_2, (see Figure 4.2).

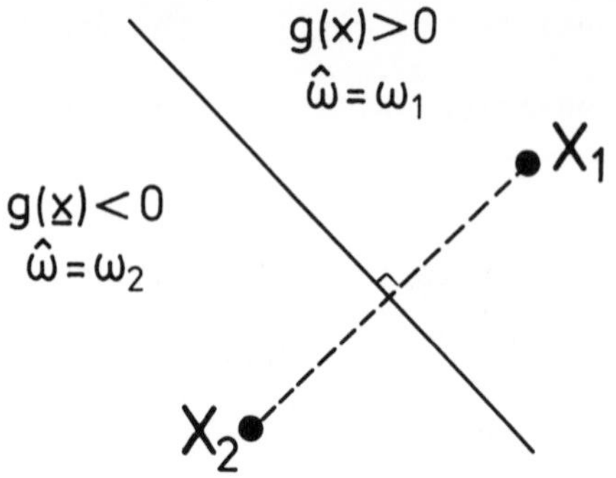

Figure 4.2. Minimum distance classification

4.2.2. Piecewise Linear Discriminant Functions

13 An interesting generalization occurs when there are more than one prototype point per class. One example of such a situation was obtained by the condensing technique of the preceding chapter. Let $X_i^1, \ldots, X_i^{n_i}$ denote the prototype points associated with class ω_i, i=1,2. The ith discriminant function corresponds with the minimum of the distances from $\underline{x}$ to $X_i^1, \ldots, X_i^{n_i}$. By a straightforward extension of the preceding discussion we have

$$g(\underline{x}) = g_1(\underline{x}) - g_2(\underline{x}),$$

where

$$g_i(\underline{x}) = \max_{j=1,\ldots,n_i} \left[g_i^j(\underline{x}) \right],$$

and

$$g_i^j(\underline{x}) = \underline{x}^t X_i^j - \frac{1}{2}\left[X_i^j\right]^t X_i^j.$$

14 This method partitions the space into n_1+n_2 convex, polyhedral regions Ω_i^j, $j=1,\dots,n_i$, $i=1,2$ such that any point in Ω_i^j is closer to X_i^j than to any other prototype point. The set of regions Ω_i^j is known as the *Dirichlet tessellation* of the space with respect to the set of points $X_1^1,\dots,X_1^{n_1}$, $X_2^1,\dots,X_2^{n_2}$. The common boundary of two adjacent regions, say Ω_i^k and Ω_j^l is a portion of the hyperplane

$$g_i^k(\underline{x}) = g_j^l(\underline{x}),$$

and the faces of each polyhedron are plane polygons. The decision region Ω_1 associated with the class ω_1 is the union of regions $\Omega_1^1,\dots,\Omega_1^{n_1}$. It is separated from Ω_2 by portions of hyperplanes. Thus, the minimum distance classifier generates a *piecewise linear decision boundary* as illustrated by Figure 4.3 in the case of a two-dimensional example. In the case where each pattern in the design set is taken as a prototype point, the minimum distance classifier is equivalent to the nearest neighbor decision rule of the preceding chapter.

It should be stressed that, in spite of the close apparent similarity, piecewise linear discriminant functions do not belong to the family of linear discriminant functions. In fact, the methods that will be used hereafter to determine the weights of the latter cannot be extended to the determination of the weights of the former.

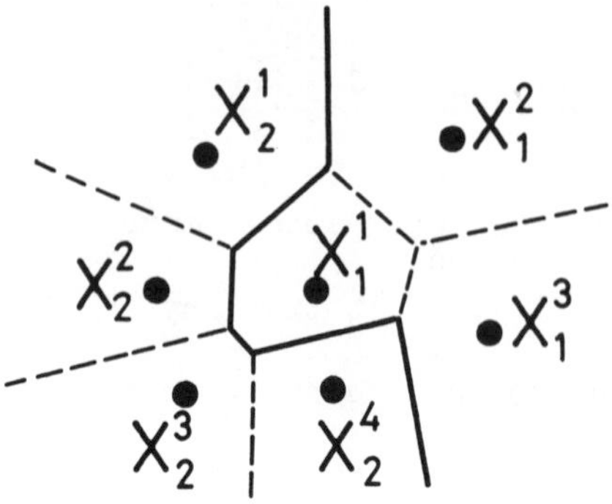

Figure 4.3. The Dirichlet tessellation of the space, and a piecewise linear discriminant function

4.2.3. The Multiclass Case

Many of the concepts we just introduced can be straightforwardly extended to the case when there are more than two classes. This is so, for instance, for the minimum distance classifier. The multiclass case offers however some more possibilities. In counterpart, it raises some additional difficulties. We wish to examine some of them briefly.

15 In the first place, one c-class problem can be converted into c two-class subproblems. Each subproblem amounts to discriminate the samples belonging to, say, class ω_i from those that do not belong to class ω_i. Although intuitively satisfying, this approach has the disadvantage that some future points may be found not to belong to any class or to belong to several classes (up to c-1) simultaneously.

These possibilities are illustrated by Figure 4.4 for a three-class problem.

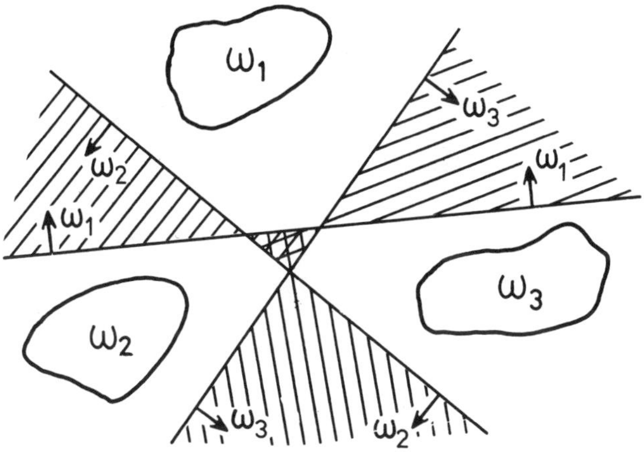

Figure 4.4. Undefined or ambiguous decisions in the multiclass case

16 A second possibility is to convert the c-class problem into c(c-1)/2 two-class subproblems of discriminating each possible pair of classes. The decision rule is then to assign the pattern to the class that scores (c-1) positive answers from the pairwise discriminant functions. In addition to being very costly, this method also has the disadvantage that some decisions may be undefined. This case is illustrated by Figure 4.5.

These difficulties can be easily overcome by returning to our initial formulation in 2. It consisted in defining c linear discriminant functions

17 $$g_i(\underline{x}) = v_{i,1}x_1 + v_{i,2}x_2 + \cdots + v_{i,d}x_d + v_{i,d+1}$$
$$= \underline{v}_i^t\underline{x} + v_{i,d+1}, \qquad i=1,\ldots,c,$$

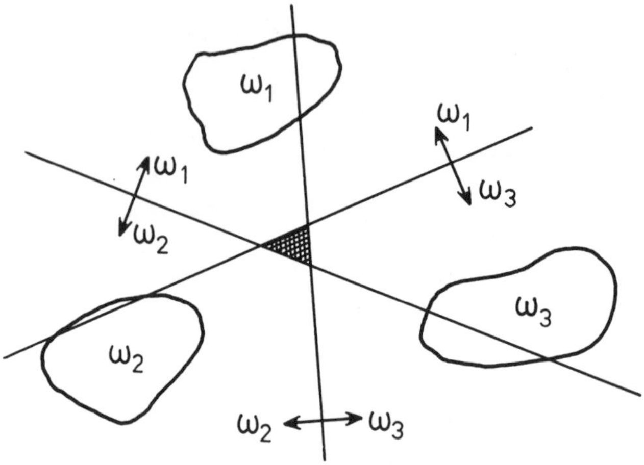

Figure 4.5. Undefined decisions in the multiclass case

and assigning $\underline{x}$ to class ω_i if $g_i(\underline{x})>g_j(\underline{x})$, $\forall j\neq i$. By this method, the space is partitioned into c decision regions Ω_i,

18 $$\Omega_i = \left\{\underline{x}\,|\,g_i(\underline{x})>g_j(\underline{x}),\ j=1,\ldots,c,\ j\neq i\right\}, \quad i=1,\ldots,c.$$

Each region Ω_i may be shown to be a convex polyhedron with at most c-1 polygonal faces which are portions of the hyperplanes defined by the equations

$$g_i(\underline{x}) = g_j(\underline{x}) \qquad j=1,\ldots,c,\ j\neq i.$$

It is apparent that, with this formulation, the classification of any pattern is uniquely defined, except for those on the decision boundaries, (See Figure 4.6).

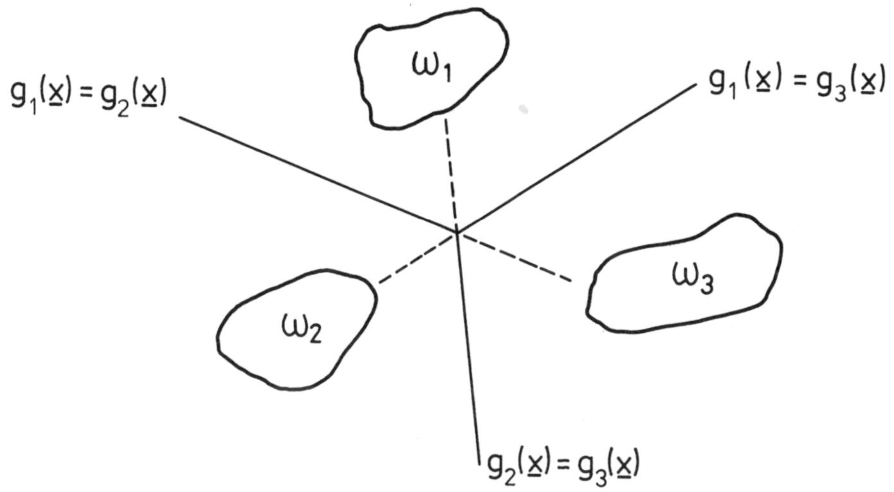

Figure 4.6. Linear decision boundaries with a maximum selector

4.3. GENERALIZED LINEAR DISCRIMINANT FUNCTIONS

Linear discriminant functions are very attractive because of their simplicity. They suffer however severe limitations. In particular they are not suitable when the desired decision regions are either not convex or multiply connected. This point, together with a simple way to remedy the situation can be conveniently illustrated by the simple example depicted by Figure 4.7.

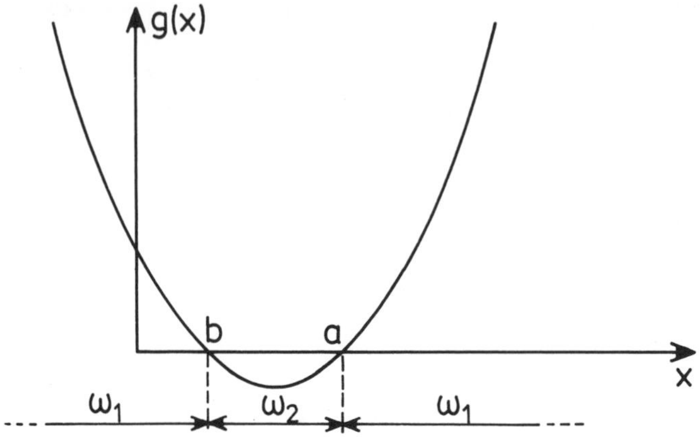

Figure 4.7. Discrimination with a quadratic function of x

Let the pattern x be one-dimensional and suppose that the desired classification is ω_1 if $x<b$ or $x>a$, and ω_2 if $b<x<a$. (So, to avoid trivialities $b \neq a$ is assumed). It is clear that no linear discriminant function of the form $g(x) = v_1 x + v_2$ is able to satisfy our needs. It is also clear that a piecewise linear discriminant function could be easily devised to solve this simple problem. However, it is even more obvious that the simplest solution is to build the *quadratic* discriminant function $g(x) = (x-a)(x-b)$ and to assign x to class ω_1 if $g(x)>0$ and to class ω_2 if $g(x)<0$. The quadratic discriminant function has the general form

19 $$g(x) = v_1 x^2 + v_2 x + v_3,$$

with

$$v_1 = 1, \quad v_2 = -(a+b), \quad v_3 = ab.$$

We shall presently give it the general form of a linear discriminant function by introducing two auxiliary variables $\phi_1(x)=x^2$ and $\phi_2(x)=x$. Thus we can write

20
$$g(x) = v_1\phi_1 + v_2\phi_2 + v_3$$
$$= \underline{v}^t\underline{\Phi} + v_3,$$

where $\underline{\Phi} = \left[\phi_1, \phi_2\right]^t$.

The mapping $x \rightarrow \underline{\Phi}(x)$ establishes a one to one correspondence such that to every x in R^1 there is a unique $\underline{\Phi}$ in R^2. There follows that for every quadratic function of x with the form of 19, there corresponds a unique linear function of $\underline{\Phi}$ with the form of 20. The equation of the decision boundary, namely $g(x)=0$ defines two points in x-space and a straight line in ϕ-space, i.e., the space spanned by the variables ϕ_1 and ϕ_2. This is illustrated by Figure 4.8.

We have thus converted the problem of finding a quadratic discriminant function in the original x-space into that of finding a linear discriminant function in the transformed ϕ-space.

Two comments are in order. First, the above discussion may give the illusory feeling that the choice of an appropriate functional form for $g(x)$ follows straightforwardly from some elementary prior knowledge about the problem at hand. Exactly the contrary ! As we already commented, the question of how to make a good choice will be a permanent concern in the sequel. Second, the mapping $x \rightarrow \underline{\Phi}$ seems to transform the one-dimensional variable x into the two-dimensional variable $\underline{\Phi}$. This, again, is illusory. In fact, the new variable $\underline{\Phi}$ has also an *intrinsic dimensionality* of one. By this we mean that the

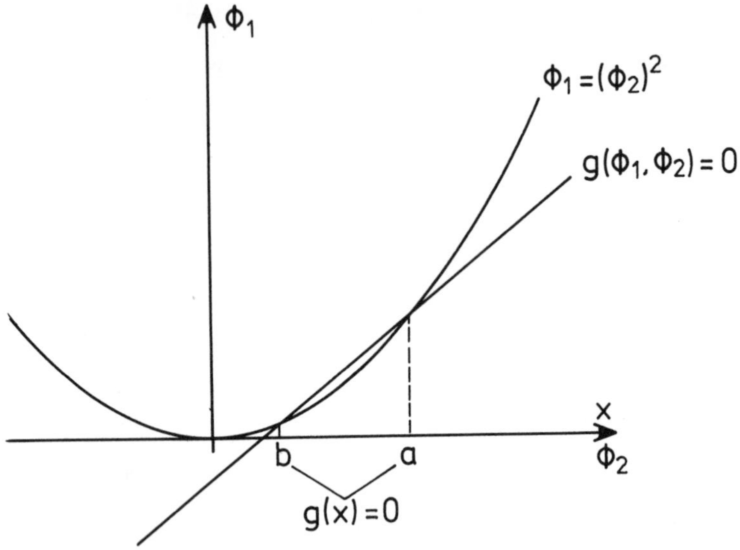

Figure 4.8. An illustration of the mapping $x \to \phi(x)$

points $\underline{\Phi}(x)$ lie on the nonlinear one-dimensional subspace of R^2 defined by the equation $\phi_1 = \left(\phi_2\right)^2$.

An embarrassing consequence of this is that when x has a probability distribution, the mapping $x \to \underline{\Phi}(x)$ induces in R^2 a joint probability distribution $p\left(\phi_1, \phi_2\right)$ which is degenerate : it is zero everywhere except on the curve $\phi_1 = \left(\phi_2\right)^2$ where it is infinite. Fortunately, this does not preclude the existence of the moments of $\underline{\Phi}$ for we have

$$E\left\{\phi_i\right\} = \int \phi_i(x)\, p(x)\, dx$$

and

$$\mathrm{var}\left\{\phi_i\right\} = \int\left[\phi_i(x)\right]^2 p(x)dx - \left[E\left\{\phi_i\right\}\right]^2.$$

Thus, these - and other - moments exist provided only that the corresponding integrals exist.

We may now safely capitalize on the concepts encountered thus far and define the family of *generalized linear discriminant functions.* As before, let the pattern $\underline{x}$ denote a d-dimensional random vector $\underline{x}=\left[x_1,\ldots,x_d\right]^t$. Let $\underline{\Phi}(\underline{x})$ denote a D-dimensional vector-function of $\underline{x}$, $\underline{\Phi}(\underline{x}) = \left[\phi_1(\underline{x}),\phi_2(\underline{x}),\ldots,\phi_D(\underline{x})\right]^t$ where the $\phi_i(\underline{x})$, $i=1,\ldots,D$, are linearly independent, real and single-valued functions of $\underline{x}$. Then, a generalized linear discriminant function $g(\underline{x})$ has the form

$$g(\underline{x}) = v_1\phi_1(\underline{x}) + v_2\phi_2(\underline{x}) + \ldots + v_D\phi_D(\underline{x}) + v_{D+1}$$

21 $$= \underline{v}^t\underline{\Phi}(\underline{x}) + v_{D+1}.$$

Clearly, with this formulation, all the considerations that were, and will be put forth in terms of simple linear discriminant functions are equally applicable to generalized linear discriminant functions.

22 Specific examples of so-called Φ-functions are

- linear functions : $\phi_i(\underline{x}) = x_i$, $i=1,\ldots,D$, $D=d$.
- quadratic functions : $\phi_i(\underline{x}) = x_{k_1}^{\ell_1} x_{k_2}^{\ell_2}$

  for $k_1,k_2 = 1,\ldots,d$, $\ell_1,\ell_2 = 0$ or 1,

  and $i=1,\ldots,D$, $D=(d+1)(d+2)/2$.
- νth order polynomials : $\phi_i(\underline{x}) = x_{k_1}^{\ell_1} x_{k_2}^{\ell_2} \ldots x_{k_\nu}^{\ell_\nu}$

for $k_1, k_2, \ldots, k_\nu = 1, \ldots, d$, $\ell_1, \ell_2, \ldots, \ell_\nu = 0$ or 1,

and $i=1,\ldots,D$, $D=\binom{d+\nu}{\nu}$.

23 These more and more complicated functional forms can be thought of as truncated series expansions of some arbitrary $g(\underline{x})$. In turn, this interpretation suggests the idea of searching a generalized discriminant function that approximates in some sense, the optimum Bayes discriminant function for minimum error rate, $g_i^*(\underline{x}) = P(\omega_i|\underline{x})$. We may note in passing that this idea will be pursued further in the following. Intuitively, one may expect that the highest the degree of the series expansion, the best the approximation and, hopefully, the classification performance. This simple reasoning soon confronts us with the "curse of dimensionality" phenomenon by which the number of terms in the expansion increases at a tremendous rate with the order of the expansion. Now, not only do we have to calculate all these terms, we also have to determine the D+1 weights of the discriminant function $g(\underline{x})$.

As we shall see shortly, these weights are "estimated" from the samples. As with any estimation problem it is natural to require that the number of weights to be estimated be significantly less than the number of samples available. Aside from computational considerations, this requirement sets an upper limit on the admissible complexity of generalized linear discriminant functions.

Before we turn to the consideration of methods to determine the weights of a discriminant function, we wish to introduce a quite useful, and classical notational convention. For any arbitrary D-dimensional Φ-function, let $\underline{y}$ denote the (D+1)-dimensional vector

24 $$\underline{y} = \left[\phi_1, \phi_2, \ldots, \phi_D, 1\right]^t.$$

Likewise, let $\underline{w}$ denote the (D+1)-dimensional weight-vector

25 $$\underline{w} = \left[\frac{\underline{v}}{1}\right]$$

With these notations, any discriminant function has the homogeneous form $g(\underline{x})=\underline{w}^t\underline{y}$. In the case that $\underline{\Phi}(\underline{x})=\underline{x}$, $\underline{y}=[\underline{x}^t,1]^t$ and $\underline{y}$ is said to designate the *augmented pattern vector*.

As far as the following theoretical developments are concerned, it does not really matter whether $\underline{y}$ is either the augmented pattern vector or, so to speak, an augmented Φ-vector. Whichever the case, our problem is to find the corresponding weight vector $\underline{w}$. The determination of $\underline{w}$ will be based on the set S_n of training samples. In fact, we shall use the same symbol S_n to designate the set of design samples in the original space or the corresponding sets of points in Φ-space or in $\underline{y}$-space.

4.4. DETERMINISTIC LEARNING ALGORITHMS

4.4.1. Probability of Linear Separability

We shall presently investigate some nonstatistical methods of determining the weight vector $\underline{w}$ of a discriminant function. In the past, these methods have been regarded as *learning methods*, and have set the stage for many subsequent developments in the field of pattern recognition. Our aim here is not only to pay a tribute to early pioneer work, but also to exhibit some important results whose practical significance will become fully apparent in Chapter 10 only.

26 Suppose we have a set S_n of training samples, $S_n = \{\underline{y}_1, \underline{y}_2, \dots, \underline{y}_n\}$. For the purposes of this section, let us assume that every sample is assigned to one of two classes ω_1 or ω_2 by some random mechanism. One such assignment produces a *dichotomy*. Clearly, there are 2^n possible dichotomies of n samples. If a linear machine, that is a linear discriminant function, can place each sample into its proper class, the dichotomy is said to be *linearly separable*, or to be a *linear dichotomy*. In other words, the dichotomy is linearly separable if there exists a vector $\underline{w}$ such that

$$\underline{w}^t \underline{y} > 0 \qquad \forall \underline{y} \in \omega_1,$$
$$\underline{w}^t \underline{y} < 0 \qquad \forall \underline{y} \in \omega_2.$$

The number of linear dichotomies is a function of n and the dimensionality D of the Φ-space, but under quite mild conditions it is independent of the configuration of the points. For instance the reader should easily satisfy himself that out of the $2^4 = 16$ possible dichotomies of four points in 2-space, 14 are linearly separable provided only that no three of the points are collinear. More generally, under the condition that no subset of D+1 points lies on a (D-1)-dimensional subspace if n>D or no (n-2)-dimensional subspace contains the set of points if n≤D, it can be demonstrated that the number L(n,D) of linearly separable dichotomies is given by

27
$$L(n,D) = 2^n \qquad \text{for } n \le D,$$
$$= 2 \sum_{i=0}^{D} \binom{n-1}{i} \qquad \text{for } n > D.$$

Now, suppose that one particular dichotomy is selected at random from among the 2^n possibilities. The probability $P_{n,D}$ that it is a linear dichotomy is then given by

28 $$P(n,D) = 1 \qquad \text{for } n \le D$$

$$= 2^{1-n} \sum_{i=0}^{D} \binom{n-1}{i} \qquad \text{for } n > D.$$

A plot of the function $P_{n,D}$ versus $n/(D+1)$ appears in Figure 4.9. It shows a marked threshold effect around $n = 2(D+1)$. As $D+1$ is the number of weights of the discriminant function, it is natural to use twice this number to define the *capacity* of the linear discriminant function. When D is moderately large, we can be almost certain of being able to separate linearly any given dichotomy of less than $2(D+1)$ points whereas we can be almost certain to fail to separate linearly any given dichotomy of more than $2(D+1)$ patterns.

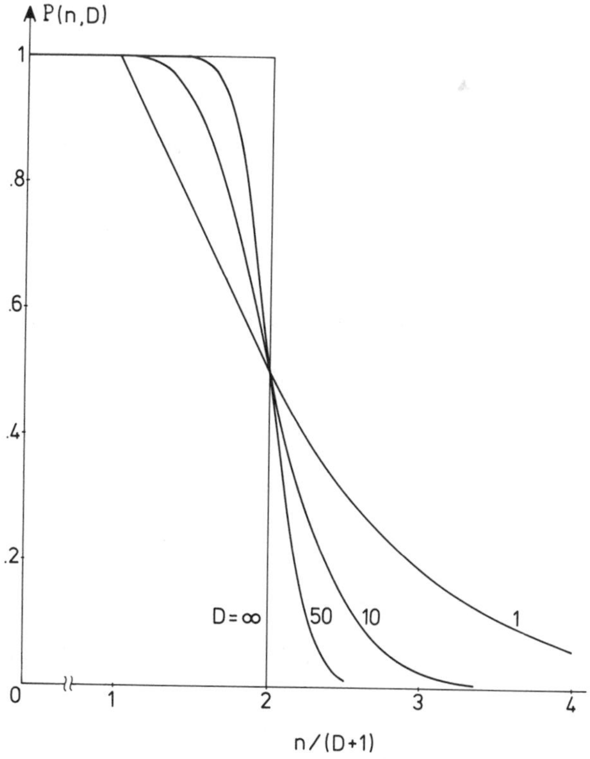

Figure 4.9. Probability of linear separability for a dichotomy of n patterns in D-dimensional space.

4.4.2. The Perceptron Learning Algorithm

Let us consider again the normal situation when we have a finite training set S_n of classified samples, $S_n = \left\{\underline{y}_i, \theta_i\right\}_{i=1}^{n}$ where θ_i is the true class of $\underline{y}_i$. For simplicity, we consider the two-class case only, so S_n is a dichotomy. We also assume that this particular dichotomy is linearly separable. In other words, we assume that there exists a weight vector $\underline{w}$ such that

29 $$g(x_i) = \underline{w}^t \underline{y}_i > 0 \qquad \forall \underline{y}_i \in S_n \text{ with } \theta_i = \omega_1,$$

$$g(x_j) = \underline{w}^t \underline{y}_j < 0 \qquad \forall \underline{y}_j \in S_n \text{ with } \theta_j = \omega_2.$$

Our problem is to find such a vector.

After all, this problem is merely one of solving a set of linear inequalities, and there are various methods for doing this. The one we shall outline hereafter is an iterative procedure that was used to display the "learning capabilities" of the Perceptron, a linear machine invented by Frank Rosenblatt.

Let us first introduce some notation. Let $\underline{w}_k$ denote the weight vector at the kth step of the algorithm, k=1,2,..., and $(\underline{y}^k, \theta^k)$ denote the kth sample obtained by scanning the set S_n sequentially and repeating the scan cyclically, *viz.*, $\underline{y}^k = \underline{y}_i$ if $i \equiv k(\text{mod.}n)$. Let ρ_k designate a sequence of positive scale factors governing the step size, and $\underline{w}_0$ be an arbitrary initial weight-vector. The algorithm is a simple *error-correcting* procedure that can be written as

30.a $$\underline{w}_{k+1} = \underline{w}_k + \rho_k \underline{y}^k \quad \text{if } \underline{w}_k^t \underline{y}^k < 0 \text{ and } \theta^k = \omega_1,$$

30.b $$= \underline{w}_k - \rho_k \underline{y}^k \quad \text{if } \underline{w}_k^t \underline{y}^k > 0 \text{ and } \theta^k = \omega_2,$$

30.c $$= \underline{w}_k \quad \text{otherwise.}$$

The principle of this algorithm is to leave the current weight-vector $\underline{w}_k$ unchanged whenever the linear machine makes a right decision, and to make the new weight-vector $\underline{w}_{k+1}$ "move in the right direction" whenever the linear machine makes a wrong decision. Let us examine the case of an arbitrary class-ω_1 sample $\underline{y}^k$. (The case of a class-ω_2 sample is treated in a like manner).

From 29, we want $\underline{w}_k^t \underline{y}^k > 0$. If this is the case the current weight-vector is left unchanged (see 30.c). If it is not, the new weight vector becomes $\underline{w}_{k+1} = \underline{w}_k + \rho_k \underline{y}^k$, (Equation30.a). It is easy to see that this adjustment tends to rectify the error for

31 $$\underline{w}_{k+1}^t \underline{y}^k = \underline{w}_k^t \underline{y}^k + \rho_k (\underline{y}^k)^t \underline{y}^k > \underline{w}_k^t \underline{y}^k.$$

The extent of the adjustment is controlled by the correction increment ρ_k. For $\rho_k = \rho$, a positive number independent of k, the procedure is called the *fixed-increment rule*. The adjustment in 30.a may or may not actually correct the error for pattern $\underline{y}^k$, but, in any case, it moves $g\left(\underline{x}^k\right)$ towards positive values. A second possibility, the *absolute correction rule*, is to take ρ_k to be the smallest integer that will make the value of $\underline{w}_{k+1}^t \underline{y}^k$ cross the threshold of zero. From 31, it is seen that ρ_k must be the smallest integer greater than $\left|\underline{w}_k^t \underline{y}^k\right| / \left(\underline{y}^k\right)^t \underline{y}^k$. Still another possibility, the *fractional correction rule*, is to set ρ_k at a value which is a certain positive fraction λ

of $|\underline{w}_k^t \underline{y}^k| / (\underline{y}^k)^t \underline{y}^k$. If $\lambda > 1$, the response of the linear machine after the adjustment will anew agree with the desired response.

32 To examine the convergence properties of the error-correcting procedure, it is helpful to think of the weight-vector $\underline{w}$ as a point in (D+1)-dimensional space, or weight-space. The assumption that the dichotomy in S_n is linearly separable is equivalent to the assumption that there exists a solution region Ω_s for $\underline{w}$ in weight-space. Moreover, it is easy to see that any solution region is an open set of points inside a convex polyhedral cone. Now, it can be proved that if Ω_s is not empty, the fixed-increment rule and the absolute correction rule yield a solution vector in a finite number of steps, irrespective of the choice of the initial weight-vector $\underline{w}_0$.

For the fractional correction rule, the convergence properties are somewhat less clear-cut. The convergence is guaranteed for $0<\lambda<2$ and any choice of the initial weight-vector, and the procedure either yields a point belonging to the closure of Ω_s in a finite number of steps or converges (as $k\to\infty$) to a point on the boundary of Ω_s. These convergence results have been proved and re-proved in many different ways and they have been extensively documented in the literature for a number of years. The interested reader will find pertinent references in the bibliographical comments at the end of the chapter.

There is no doubt that the perceptron learning algorithm is one of the simplest ways to determine the weight-vector of a linear machine. Unfortunately its usefulness hinges crucially on the assumption that the given training set is a linear dichotomy. Even when it is, the obtaining of a hyperplane that correctly classifies all the patterns in the training set is no guarantee that the classifier will achieve acceptable performance on new patterns not in the training set. We shall have more to say on this in Chapter 10. When the training set is not a linear dichotomy, it is clear that the above procedures will never terminate. To handle this case, a number of heuristics have been suggested. For instance, one of these heuristics is to let the correction increment ρ_k decrease with k. Intuitively, it is clear that this tends to reduce the disruptive effects due to those "bad" samples that render the training set nonseparable.

A discussion of such refinements would take us too far away from our statistical preoccupations. So we shall proceed with another approach that does not require the linear separability of the training set.

4.5. THE LEAST MEAN-SQUARED-ERROR PROCEDURE

4.5.1. The Least Mean-Squared-Error Design Criterion

33 In this section we seek again linear function of $\underline{y}$, *viz.*, $g(\underline{x})=\underline{w}^t\underline{y}$ which is positive when $\underline{x}$ comes from class ω_1 and negative when $\underline{x}$ comes from class ω_2. One way to do this is to require that for any sample in the training set

$$\underline{w}^t\underline{y} = 1 \qquad \text{if } \underline{x} \text{ is from class } \omega_1$$
$$\underline{w}^t\underline{y} = -1 \qquad \text{if } \underline{x} \text{ is from class } \omega_2.$$

Thus $\underline{w}$ is now the solution to a set of linear equations. As we have n equations in D+1 unknowns, $\underline{w}$ is in general overdetermined and no exact solution exists. However, we can seek a solution vector $\underline{w}$ that minimizes some function of the error between $\underline{w}^t\underline{y}$ and +1 or -1. The function we select to minimize is the sum of squared errors which is a well known and understood criterion function.

So, our problem becomes one of minimizing the quantity

34 $$\frac{1}{n}\left[\sum_{\underline{x}\in\omega_1}\left(\underline{w}^t\underline{y}-1\right)^2 + \sum_{\underline{x}\in\omega_2}\left(\underline{w}^t\underline{y}+1\right)^2\right]$$

$$= \frac{n_1}{n}\cdot\frac{1}{n_1}\sum_{\underline{x}\in\omega_1}\left(\underline{w}^t\underline{y}-1\right)^2 + \frac{n_2}{n}\cdot\frac{1}{n_2}\sum_{\underline{x}\in\omega_2}\left(\underline{w}^t\underline{y}+1\right)^2.$$

For the purpose of simplifying the discussion in some of the following sections, we shall solve this problem under the assumption that an arbitrary large design set is available. By the law of large numbers, as n approaches infinity the quantity in 34 approaches

35 $$J_2(\underline{w}) = P_1\mathcal{E}_1\left\{\left(\underline{w}^t\underline{y}-1\right)^2\right\} + P_2\mathcal{E}_2\left\{\left(\underline{w}^t\underline{y}+1\right)^2\right\},$$

with probability one, where

$$\mathcal{E}_1\left\{\left(\underline{w}^t\underline{y}-1\right)^2\right\} = \int\left(\underline{w}^t\underline{y}-1\right)^2 p\left(\underline{x}|\omega_1\right)d\underline{x}$$

and

$$\mathcal{E}_2\left\{\left(\underline{w}^t\underline{y}+1\right)^2\right\} = \int\left(\underline{w}^t\underline{y}+1\right)^2 p\left(\underline{x}|\omega_2\right)d\underline{x}.$$

In order to find the minimizing $\underline{w}$ we set the gradient of $J_2(\underline{w})$ equal to zero:

36 $$\nabla_{\underline{w}}J_2(\underline{w}) = P_1\mathcal{E}_1\left\{\underline{y}\underline{y}^t\right\}\underline{w} - P_1\mathcal{E}_1\left\{\underline{y}\right\} + P_2\mathcal{E}_2\left\{\underline{y}\underline{y}^t\right\}\underline{w} + P_2\mathcal{E}_2\left\{\underline{y}\right\} = 0.$$

37 Let K_i denote the class-conditional matrix of second-order moments of $\underline{y}$,

$$K_i = \mathcal{E}_i\left\{\underline{y}\underline{y}^t\right\},$$

and $M_i = P_i \underline{\mu}_i^y$ where $\underline{\mu}_i^y$ is the class-conditional mean vector of $\underline{y}$, $i=1,2$. If K denotes the matrix of second-order moments under the mixture distribution we have

$$K = P_1 K_1 + P_2 K_2.$$

As K is the expected value of the direct product $\underline{y}\underline{y}^t$ it is symmetric, hence definite non-negative. We shall also assume that it is nonsingular so that its inverse K^{-1} exists.

Now, 36 can be written

$$\left(P_1 K_1 + P_2 K_2\right)\underline{w} = M_1 - M_2$$

or

$$K\underline{w} = M_1 - M_2,$$

and the solution vector $\underline{w}^*$ to the minimization problem is given by

38
$$\underline{w}^* = K^{-1}\left(M_1 - M_2\right).$$

To be consistent with the design criterion 35 the decision rule is as follows. For any new pattern $\underline{x}$ to classify, we first calculate the corresponding $\underline{y}$ vector. Then, in accordance with 33, the decision will be $\hat{\omega}_{MSE} = \omega_1$ if $\left[g(\underline{x})-1\right]^2 < \left[g(\underline{x})+1\right]^2$ and $\hat{\omega}_{MSE} = \omega_2$ otherwise. An equivalent formulation is

39
$$\hat{\omega}_{MSE} = \omega_1 \quad \text{if } \underline{y}^t K^{-1} M_1 > \underline{y}^t K^{-1} M_2$$

$$\hat{\omega}_{MSE} = \omega_2 \quad \text{if } \underline{y}^t K^{-1} M_1 < \underline{y}^t K^{-1} M_2.$$

Clearly, the equation of the decision boundary is $g(\underline{x}) = 0$, or

$$\underline{y}^t K^{-1} M_1 = \underline{y}^t K^{-1} M_2.$$

40   The approach we just described seems quite reasonable. The simplicity of deriving the solution is also quite satisfying.

However, the derivation thus far does not tell us much about the future classification performance of the decision rule in 39. In particular it gives us no indication as to how the ϕ-functions should be chosen in view of achieving good performance. In fact, considerable scrutiny will be required before such information becomes available (yet, to some limited extent). In this respect, the magnitude of the residual mean-squared-error, *viz.*, $J_2(\underline{w}^*)$ will play a prominent role. It is given by

41 $$J_2(\underline{w}^*) = P_1 E_1\left\{\left(\underline{y}^t K^{-1}(M_1-M_2)-1\right)^2\right\} + P_2 E_2\left\{\left(\underline{y}^t K^{-1}(M_1-M_2)+1\right)^2\right\}$$
$$= 1-(M_1-M_2)^t K^{-1}(M_1-M_2).$$

4.5.2. Linear Discrimination in Pattern Space

42 We wish to examine more closely the implications of the results just obtained. To simplify matters - more precisely, to simplify notation - we shall discuss discrimination in pattern space. So, we assume $\underline{\Phi}(\underline{x}) \equiv \underline{x}$, and $\underline{y}$ is just the augmented pattern vector. It should be noted, however, that this assumption does not reduce the generality of the argument. The results to be obtained hold unchanged when they are interpreted in terms of $\underline{\Phi}(\underline{x})$.

First, we introduce the necessary notation. Let $\underline{\mu}_i$ denote the class-conditional mean vector of $\underline{x}$, and $\underline{\mu} = \sum_i P_i \underline{\mu}_i$ denote the mean vector of the mixture distribution. We have,

43 $$M_i = \begin{bmatrix} P_i \underline{\mu}_i \\ \cdots \\ P_i \end{bmatrix} \qquad i=1,2.$$

For an arbitrary number c of classes, hence also for two classes, let S_b designate the *between-class covariance* (or scatter) *matrix*

44 $$S_b = \sum_{i=1}^{c} P_i(\underline{\mu}_i-\underline{\mu})(\underline{\mu}_i-\underline{\mu})^t.$$

A useful alternative expression for S_b is

$$S_b = \sum_{i \le j}^{c} P_i P_j(\underline{\mu}_i-\underline{\mu}_j)(\underline{\mu}_i-\underline{\mu}_j)^t.$$

Note that for a problem of c classes, S_b has rank at most equal to c-1. So, in the two-class case, S_b has rank one, unless the two classes have identical mean vectors. Let Σ_i be the class-conditional covariance matrix

$$\Sigma_i = \boldsymbol{E}_i\left\{(\underline{x}-\underline{\mu}_i)(\underline{x}-\underline{\mu}_i)^t\right\}, \quad i=1,\dots,c,$$

and S_w be the average class-conditional covariance matrix,

45 $$S_w = \sum_{i=1}^{c} P_i\Sigma_i.$$

Of course, if $\Sigma_1 = \Sigma_2 = \dots = \Sigma_c = \Sigma$, then $S_w = \Sigma$. Finally, let S_T designate the covariance matrix in the mixture population,

$$S_T = \boldsymbol{E}\left\{(\underline{x}-\underline{\mu})(\underline{x}-\underline{\mu})^t\right\}.$$

Note that the matrices S_w and S_T are frequently called the *within-class scatter-matrix*, and the *total scatter-matrix* respectively. A discussion of the concept of scatter can be found in Chapter 6. It is easy to verify that the matrices S_T, S_w and S_b are connected by the simple relationship

46 $$S_T = S_w + S_b.$$

Let us now return to the analysis of the solution to the

minimization problem in the preceding section. It involves the reciprocal of matrix K, which can be expressed in terms of the parameters just defined.

47 $$K = \boldsymbol{E}\left\{\underline{y}\,\underline{y}^t\right\} = \left[\begin{array}{c|c} \boldsymbol{E}\left\{\underline{xx}^t\right\} & \underline{\mu} \\ \hline \underline{\mu}^t & 1 \end{array}\right] = \left[\begin{array}{c|c} S_T + \underline{\mu\,\mu}^t & \underline{\mu} \\ \hline \underline{\mu}^t & 1 \end{array}\right]$$

To calculate K^{-1} we shall make use of the following classical results in matrix algebra:

48 Let us be given a d×d, nonsingular symmetric matrix A. Let A be partitioned into submatrices as follows

$$A = \left[\begin{array}{c|c} A_{1,1} & A_{1,2} \\ \hline A_{1,2}^t & A_{2,2} \end{array}\right]$$

Then, a partitioned form of the reciprocal $R = A^{-1}$ is

$$R_{1,1} = \left(A_{1,1} - A_{1,2}A_{2,2}^{-1}A_{1,2}^t\right)^{-1}$$

$$R_{1,2} = R_{2,1}^t = -A_{1,1}^{-1}A_{1,2}\left(A_{2,2} - A_{1,2}^tA_{1,1}^{-1}A_{1,2}\right)^{-1}$$

$$R_{2,2} = \left(A_{2,2} - A_{1,2}^tA_{1,1}^{-1}A_{1,2}\right)^{-1},$$

provided the submatrices to be inverted are nonsingular. In order to calculate the reciprocal of K by these formulae, we need to know the reciprocal of $\left[S_T + \underline{\mu\,\mu}^t\right]$. As $\underline{\mu\,\mu}^t$ is a direct product, we may use the formula of Sherman-Morisson and Bartlett, *viz.*,

$$\left[S_T + \underline{\mu}\underline{\mu}^t \right]^{-1} = S_T^{-1} - \frac{S_T^{-1} \underline{\mu}\underline{\mu}^t S_T^{-1}}{1 + \underline{\mu}^t S_T^{-1} \underline{\mu}}.$$

By applying these formulae to the expression of matrix K in 47 we obtain

49
$$K^{-1} = \left[\begin{array}{c|c} S_T^{-1} & -S_T^{-1}\underline{\mu} \\ \hline -\underline{\mu}^t S_T^{-1} & 1 + \underline{\mu}^t S_T^{-1}\underline{\mu} \end{array} \right]$$

By substituting 49 in 38 and using 43, we find

50
$$\underline{w}^* = \left[\begin{array}{c|c} S_T^{-1} & -S_T^{-1}\underline{\mu} \\ \hline -\underline{\mu}^t S_T^{-1} & 1 + \underline{\mu}^t S_T^{-1}\underline{\mu} \end{array} \right] \left[\begin{array}{c} P_1\underline{\mu}_1 - P_2\underline{\mu}_2 \\ \hline P_1 - P_2 \end{array} \right]$$

and by straightforward calculation 50 becomes

51
$$\underline{w}^* = \left[\begin{array}{c} 2P_1 P_2 S_T^{-1}\left(\underline{\mu}_1 - \underline{\mu}_2 \right) \\ \hline \left(P_1 - P_2 \right) - 2P_1 P_2 \underline{\mu}^t S_T^{-1}\left(\underline{\mu}_1 - \underline{\mu}_2 \right) \end{array} \right]$$

We know from 46 that $S_T = S_w + S_b$ where S_b is again a direct product, namely $S_b = P_1 P_2 \left(\underline{\mu}_1 - \underline{\mu}_2 \right)\left(\underline{\mu}_1 - \underline{\mu}_2 \right)^t$. Therefore, we may apply again the formula of Sherman-Morisson and Bartlett,

52
$$S_T^{-1} = \left[S_w + S_b \right]^{-1}$$

$$= S_w^{-1} - \frac{P_1 P_2 S_w^{-1}\left(\underline{\mu}_1 - \underline{\mu}_2 \right)\left(\underline{\mu}_1 - \underline{\mu}_2 \right)^t S_w^{-1}}{1 + P_1 P_2 \left(\underline{\mu}_1 - \underline{\mu}_2 \right)^t S_w^{-1}\left(\underline{\mu}_1 - \underline{\mu}_2 \right)}.$$

One should note that the quadratic form $\Delta = \left(\underline{\mu}_1 - \underline{\mu}_2 \right)^t S_w^{-1}\left(\underline{\mu}_1 - \underline{\mu}_2 \right)$ in the denominator of 52 is a close relative to the Mahalanobis distance measure which was introduced in Section 2.5. In fact, *it is* the Mahalanobis distance measure when the two classes have normal distributions with identical covariance matrices, for in this case $S_W=\Sigma_1=\Sigma_2$ and

53 $$\Delta = \left(\underline{\mu}_1-\underline{\mu}_2\right)^t\Sigma^{-1}\left(\underline{\mu}_1-\underline{\mu}_2\right).$$

For the want of a better name, we shall henceforth call Δ the Mahalanobis distance measure when the two classes do not have the same covariance matrix or are even not normally distributed.

The substitution of 52 in 51 yields after some further algebraic manipulations

54 $$\underline{W}^* = \begin{bmatrix} \dfrac{2P_1P_2}{1+P_1P_2\Delta}\, S_W^{-1}\left(\underline{\mu}_1-\underline{\mu}_2\right) \\ \hline \left(P_1-P_2\right) - \dfrac{2P_1P_2}{1+P_1P_2\Delta}\, \underline{\mu}^t S_W^{-1}\left(\underline{\mu}_1-\underline{\mu}_2\right) \end{bmatrix}$$

Recalling that the equation of the decision boundary is $\underline{W}^{*t}\underline{y}=0$, we are now in a position to formulate this equation in terms of the parameters of the underlying distributions. We have

55 $$\frac{2P_1P_2}{1+P_1P_2\Delta}\left(\underline{x}-\underline{\mu}\right)^t S_W^{-1}\left(\underline{\mu}_1-\underline{\mu}_2\right) + \left(P_1-P_2\right) = 0.$$

Equivalently,

56 $$\underline{x}^t S_W^{-1}\left(\underline{\mu}_1-\underline{\mu}_2\right) = \underline{\mu}^t S_W^{-1}\left(\underline{\mu}_1-\underline{\mu}_2\right) - \frac{P_1-P_2}{2P_1P_2}\left(1+P_1P_2\Delta\right).$$

So far, our treatement of the MSE design criterion did not involve very constraining assumptions regarding the underlying distributions. First, it was implicitely assumed that these distributions have first and second order moments. Second, it may be seen that the assumption of nonsingularity of the within-class scatter-matrix S_W suffices, in general, to guarantee the necessary nonsingularity of matrix K. Third, for our derivation to be meaningful, that is for $\underline{w}^*$ to be different from a null vector, we should have $\underline{\mu}_1 \neq \underline{\mu}_2$. Apart from these rather harmless restrictions, the derivation is free of any further regularity conditions on the distribution of $\underline{x}$ or the joint distribution of $(\underline{x}, \omega)$.

With these considerations in mind, it is instructive to compare the equation of the linear decision boundary in 56 with the equation of the Bayes-optimal Anderson discriminant plane in 1, namely,

57 $$\underline{x}^t \Sigma^{-1}\left(\underline{\mu}_1 - \underline{\mu}_2\right) = \frac{1}{2}\left(\underline{\mu}_1 + \underline{\mu}_2\right)^t \Sigma^{-1}\left(\underline{\mu}_1 - \underline{\mu}_2\right) + \log \frac{P_2}{P_1}.$$

If the classes have equal a priori probabilities, the last terms in Equations 56 and 57 vanish and $\frac{1}{2}\left(\underline{\mu}_1 + \underline{\mu}_2\right) = \underline{\mu}$. If, in addition, the class-conditional p.d.f.s have identical covariance matrices, then $\Sigma_1 = \Sigma_2 = S_W = \Sigma$. Under these conditions, 56 and 57 both reduce to

58 $$\left(\underline{x} - \underline{\mu}\right)^t \Sigma^{-1}\left(\underline{\mu}_1 - \underline{\mu}_2\right) = 0$$

So, if we further assume that the classes are normally distributed, we may conclude that the MSE criterion function yields the Bayes-optimal decision boundary. Consequently, the error probability of using the discriminant function in 56 can be calculated by the method discussed in Chapter 2.

We are now quite confident that the MSE discriminant function will perform very well in the most favorable case. Unfortunately, it is definitely impossible to extend the above analysis to more general situations. In those more general cases, the best we will be able to do is to derive an upper-bound on the error probability E_{MSE} associated with the discriminant function in 56.

4.5.3. An Error-Bound

The derivation of the bound involves the residual mean-squared-error $J_2(\underline{w}^*)$ in 41. From 38 and 43, $J_2(\underline{w}^*)$ can be written as

$$59 \quad J_2(\underline{w}^*) = 1-(M_1-M_2)^t \underline{w}^*$$

$$= 1- \left[(P_1\underline{\mu}_1-P_2\underline{\mu}_2)^t \mid (P_1-P_2) \right] \cdot$$

$$\cdot \left[\begin{array}{c} \dfrac{2P_1P_2}{1+P_1P_2\Delta} S_w^{-1}(\underline{\mu}_1-\underline{\mu}_2) \\ \hline (P_1-P_2) - \dfrac{2P_1P_2}{1+P_1P_2\Delta} \underline{\mu}^t S_w^t(\underline{\mu}_1-\underline{\mu}_2) \end{array} \right]$$

$$= 1-(P_1-P_2)^2 - \frac{4P_1^2P_2^2\Delta}{1+P_1P_2\Delta}$$

$$= \frac{4P_1P_2}{1+P_1P_2\Delta}.$$

60   Intuitively, one may expect that the smaller the residual error $J_2(\underline{w}^*)$, equivalently the larger the Mahalanobis distance Δ, the better the discrimination. We shall see, presently, that this is indeed the case. Recall that the decision rule associated with our design

criterion is to decide $\hat{\omega}_{MSE} = \omega_1$ when $g(\underline{x}) = \underline{w}^{*t}\underline{y} \geq 0$, and $\hat{\omega}_{MSE} = \omega_2$ otherwise. For the purposes of this section let us introduce a new random variable z which is defined as follows

61 $$\begin{aligned} z = f(\underline{x}) &= \underline{w}^{*t}\underline{y} \quad \text{if } \underline{x}\epsilon\omega_1, \\ &= -\underline{w}^{*t}\underline{y} \quad \text{if } \underline{x}\epsilon\omega_2. \end{aligned}$$

We now have a simple expression for the average error-rate E_{MSE} of using the MSE discriminant function, namely,

62 $$E_{MSE} = \Pr\{z<0\}.$$

Let μ_z and σ_z^2 denote the mean and variance of z respectively. By invoking the inequality of Chebyshev we may write

63 $$\Pr\left\{\mu_z - \rho\sigma_z^2 \leq z \leq \mu_z + \rho\sigma_z^2\right\} \geq 1-\rho^2,$$

where ρ is an arbitrary positive constant. Let us take $\rho=\mu_z/\sigma_z$. So, without loss of generality, we assume $\mu_z > 0$. The inequality 63 becomes

$$\Pr\{z>0\} \geq 1 - \sigma_z^2/\mu_z^2$$

or

64 $$E_{MSE} \leq \sigma_z^2/\mu_z^2.$$

The reader should have little difficulty to verify that

65 $$\begin{aligned} \mu_z &= \left(M_1-M_2\right)^t S_T^{-1}\left(M_1-M_2\right) \\ &= 1 - J_2(\underline{w}^*). \end{aligned}$$

Moreover, in view of 61, the minimum of the criterion function 34 can be expressed as

66 $$\begin{aligned} J_2(\underline{w}^*) &= \int\left[f(\underline{x})-1\right]^2 p(\underline{x})\,d\underline{x} \\ &= \sigma_z^2 + \left(1-\mu_z\right)^2. \end{aligned}$$

The substitution of $J_2(\underline{w}^*)$ from 66 to 65 yields

$$\sigma_z^2 = \mu_z\left(1-\mu_z\right).$$

Thus

67
$$\frac{\sigma_z^2}{\mu_z^2} = \frac{1-\mu_z}{\mu_z} = \frac{J_2(\underline{w}^*)}{1-J_2(\underline{w}^*)}$$

By using 67 in 64 we obtain

68
$$E_{MSE} \le \frac{J_2(\underline{w}^*)}{1-J_2(\underline{w}^*)}.$$

Finally, in view of 59, the error-bound in 68 can be expressed as

69
$$E_{MSE} \le \frac{4P_1P_2}{\left(1-4P_1P_2\right)+P_1P_2\Delta}.$$

The error-bounds in 68 and 69 confirm our intuitive expectation that a small mean-squared-error $J_2(\underline{w}^*)$, or a large Mahalanobis distance Δ, is synonymous with a small expected error-rate. An interesting property of these bounds is that they are quite general. As a tribute to their generality, they may be not very tight. Indeed, like nearly all results derived from Chebyshev's inequality they must be regarded as theoretical tools rather than practical methods of estimation. However, the full theoretical implication of these bounds will be visible only when we have acquired some more properties of the MSE discriminant function.

4.5.4. Relationship With the Bayes and 1-NN Decision Rules

70 Let us return for a short moment to the consideration of the nearest neighbor decision rule of the preceding chapter. With the

1-NNR, if the first NN $\underline{x}'$ to $\underline{x}$ is from class ω_i, the decision $\hat{\omega}_1 = \omega_i$ is taken without the slightest consideration of the possibility of taking the decision $\hat{\omega}_1 = \omega_j$, $j \neq i$. In other words, the 1-NNR can be viewed as a maximum *a posteriori* probability decision rule with the provision that the true *a posteriori* probability $P\left(\omega_i|\underline{x}\right)$ be approximated by one or zero according as $\underline{x}$ belongs to class ω_i or not. Let $P_{NN}\left(\omega_i|\underline{x}\right)$ denote this 1-NN approximation to $P\left(\omega_i|\underline{x}\right)$, i=1,2.

Under this interpretation the MSE criterion function of 35 can be written as

71 $$J_2(\underline{w}) = P_1 E_1\left\{\left[\underline{w}^t\underline{y}-g_{NN}(\underline{x})\right]^2\right\} + P_2 E_2\left\{\left[\underline{w}^t\underline{y}-g_{NN}(\underline{x})\right]^2\right\}$$

$$= \int \left[\underline{w}^t\underline{y}-g_{NN}(\underline{x})\right]^2 p(\underline{x})\,d\underline{x},$$

where

72 $$g_{NN}(\underline{x}) = P_{NN}(\omega_1|\underline{x}) - P_{NN}(\omega_2|\underline{x}).$$

In turn, the function $g_{NN}(\underline{x})$ can be viewed as a 1-NN approximation to the Bayes discriminant function

73 $$g^*(\underline{x}) = P(\omega_1|\underline{x}) - P(\omega_2|\underline{x}).$$

Let us calculate the mean-squared-error of approximating $g^*(\underline{x})$ with $g_{NN}(\underline{x})$. We have

74 $$\int \left[g^*(\underline{x})-g_{NN}(\underline{x})\right]^2 p(\underline{x})\,d\underline{x}$$

$$= \sum_{i=1}^{2} \int\left[g^*(\underline{x})-g_{NN}(\underline{x})\right]^2 p(\underline{x},\omega_i)\,d\underline{x}.$$

It is easy to verify that

75 $$\int\left[g^*(\underline{x})-g_{NN}(\underline{x})\right]^2 p(\underline{x},\omega_i)\,d\underline{x} = \int\left[4P(\omega_1|\underline{x})P(\omega_2|\underline{x})\right]p(\underline{x}|\omega_j)\,d\underline{x},$$

where i,j=1,2 and i≠j. The substitution of 75 in 72 yields

$$\int\left[g^*(\underline{x})-g_{NN}(\underline{x})\right]^2 p(\underline{x})\,d\underline{x} = \int\left[4P(\omega_1|\underline{x})P(\omega_2|\underline{x})\right]p(\underline{x})\,d\underline{x}.$$

Now, recalling Equation 3.12 where we used the notation $\eta_i(\underline{x})$ for $P(\omega_i|\underline{x})$, we see that

76 $$\int\left[g^*(\underline{x})-g_{NN}(\underline{x})\right]^2 p(\underline{x})\,d\underline{x} = 2E_1,$$

where E_1 designates the 1-NN error rate.

Let us temporarily close this little digression and return to the consideration of criterion function $J_2(\underline{w})$. Presently, we wish to establish the following important property : The minimum mean-squared-error approximation to $g_{NN}(\underline{x})$, that is $\underline{w}^{*t}\underline{y}$, is also the minimum mean-squared-error approximation to the Bayes discriminant function $g^*(\underline{x})$ of 73. In order to demonstrate this, let us write $J_2(\underline{w})$ as follows:

$$J_2(\underline{w}) = \int\left[\underline{w}^t\underline{y}-g^*(\underline{x})+g^*(\underline{x})-g_{NN}(\underline{x})\right]^2 p(\underline{x})\,d\underline{x}$$

$$= \int\left[\underline{w}^t\underline{y}-g^*(\underline{x})\right]^2 p(\underline{x})\,d\underline{x}$$

$$+ 2\int\left[\underline{w}^t\underline{y}-g^*(\underline{x})\right]\left[g^*(\underline{x})-g_{NN}(\underline{x})\right]p(\underline{x})\,d\underline{x}$$

77 $$+ \int\left[g^*(\underline{x})-g_{NN}(\underline{x})\right]^2 p(\underline{x})\,d\underline{x}.$$

The first term in 77 is the mean-squared-error between $\underline{w}^t\underline{y}$ and $g^*(\underline{x})$. Let $Q_2(\underline{w})$ designate this mean-squared-error. The last term was just shown to be equal to twice the 1-NN error-rate. To calculate the middle term, we observe that

$$\int \underline{W}^t \underline{y}\, g^*(\underline{x}) p(\underline{x}) d\underline{x} = \int \underline{W}^t \underline{y}\, g_{NN}(\underline{x}) p(\underline{x}) d\underline{x} = \underline{W}^t (M_1 - M_2),$$

$$\int g^*(\underline{x}) g^*(\underline{x}) p(\underline{x}) d\underline{x} = \int g^*(\underline{x}) g_{NN}(\underline{x}) p(\underline{x}) d\underline{x} = 1-2E_1.$$

There follows that this term is equal to zero whatever be the vector $\underline{W}$. Thus 77 becomes

$$J_2(\underline{W}) = \int \left[\underline{W}^t \underline{y} - g^*(\underline{x})\right]^2 p(\underline{x}) d\underline{x} + 2E_1$$

78 $$= Q_2(\underline{W}) + 2E_1.$$

The last term, $2E_1$, is clearly independent of $\underline{W}$. Hence the vector $\underline{W}$ that minimizes $J_2(\underline{W})$ also minimizes $Q_2(\underline{W})$. We may therefore conclude that the vector $\underline{W}^*$ in 38 or 54 which was obtained by minimizing the criterion function in 35 gives also the best approximation, in the sense of minimum mean-squared-error, to the Bayes discriminant function $g^*(\underline{x})$ in 73.

The mean-squared-error of approximating $g^*(\underline{x})$ by $\underline{W}^{*t}\underline{y}$ can be readily calculated by 41 and 78,

$$Q_2(\underline{W}^*) = J_2(\underline{W}^*) - 2E_1$$

79 $$= 1 - \left(M_1 - M_2\right)^t K^{-1} \left(M_1 - M_2\right) - 2E_1,$$

and for a linear discriminant function in pattern space, we obtain from 59 and 79

80 $$Q_2(\underline{W}^*) = \frac{4P_1P_2}{1+P_1P_2\Delta} - 2E_1.$$

By definition $Q_2(\underline{W}^*) \geq 0$, and $E_1 \geq E^*$, where E^* is the Bayes error-rate. There follows

81 $$\frac{2P_1P_2}{1+P_1P_2\Delta} \geq E_1 \geq E^*.$$

We have here the demonstration of an error-bound that was claimed without a proof in 2.93. On the other hand, suppose that the underlying distributions are such that

82 $$\frac{2P_1P_2}{1+P_1P_2\Delta} = E_1.$$

From 80 we see that this assumption implies $Q_2(\underline{w}^*) = 0$, or, more specifically,

83 $$\int\left[\underline{w}^{*t}\underline{y} - g^*(\underline{x})\right]^2 p(\underline{x})d\underline{x} = 0.$$

84 From this we conclude that, when 82 is satisfied, $\underline{w}^{*t}\underline{y}=g(\underline{x})$ $\forall x$, except possibly on an unimportant subset of the pattern-space where $p(\underline{x})=0$. In other words, we see that 82 is a sufficient condition of Bayes-optimality of the MSE discriminant function. In this case we have $E_{MSE}=E^*$.

4.5.5. Discussion

The above derivations have given us considerable insight into the mean-squared-error procedure. Most of the practical implications of our results pertain to the problem of feature selection, one subject matter which is discussed at length in the subsequent chapters. In fact, this fortuitous circumstance obliges us to anticipate slightly on what follows.

First of all, it should be stressed again that our choice to emphasize linear discrimination in pattern-space was motivated merely by notational convenience. All of our results hold unchanged when they are expressed in terms of arbitrary Φ-functions. For instance, if $J_2^{\Phi}(\underline{W}^*)$ is the minimum mean-squared-error for a given mapping $\underline{x} \rightarrow \underline{\Phi}(\underline{x})$, it holds true that

85 $$\frac{J_2^{\Phi}(\underline{W}^*)}{1-J_2^{\Phi}(\underline{W}^*)} \geq E_{MSE},$$

86 $$J_2^{\Phi}(\underline{W}^*) \geq 2E_1 \geq 2E^*,$$

87 $$J_2^{\Phi}(\underline{W}^*) = 2E_1 \text{ implies } E_{MSE} = E^*.$$

It should be noted that in 85-87, $J_2^{\Phi}(\underline{W}^*)$ and E_{MSE} depend on the distribution induced by the mapping $\underline{x} \rightarrow \underline{\Phi}(\underline{x})$, whereas both E_1 and E^* do not depend on the selected Φ-function and characterize the original distribution of $(\underline{x},\omega)$.

Now, suppose that we have to choose between two possible mappings, say, $\underline{\Phi}$ and $\underline{\Phi}'$. If $J_2^{\Phi}<J_2^{\Phi'}$, $\underline{\Phi}$ should be preferred because, by 85, it yields a least upper bound of the corresponding error-rate E_{MSE}, and, by 78, it permits us to achieve a better approximation to the Bayes discriminant function $g^*(\underline{x})$. This is not enough of an argument however because criterion function J_2 alone cannot tell us whether a Φ-function is well matched to the problem at hand. Clearly, there would be no point in looking for the best mapping when both are poorly matched.

Ideally, one would like to be able to calculate the criterion $Q_2^{\Phi}(\underline{W}^*)$ in order to assess how well the discriminant function $g(\underline{x})$

approximates the Bayes discriminant function $g^*(\underline{x})$. Unfortunately, in most practical situations, this calculation cannot be performed directly because it involves the *a posteriori* probabilities which are generally unknown. On the contrary, both quantities $J_2^\Phi(\underline{W}^*)$ and E_1 can be readily estimated from samples and Equations 79 or 80 can be used to obtain indirectly an estimate of $Q_2^\Phi(\underline{W}^*)$. There follows that our requirement of obtaining a small value for Q_2^Φ is equivalent to the requirement of obtaining a value for J_2^Φ that is not much larger than $2E_1$. When this latter condition is satisfied for a given Φ-function, the Φ-function in question is definitely well matched to the problem at hand.

88 In summary, a good choice for a Φ-function has to fulfill the following two conditions : a) the value of $J_2^\Phi(\underline{W}^*)$ must be small, and b) it must be not much larger than $2E_1$. It would be nice if these conditions could be quantified in a precise manner, and if we knew how to *design* Φ-functions to satisfy these requirements. Unfortunately, as we already commented, the theory has not yet reached the stage where it can answer these important questions.

4.6. MULTICLASS EXTENSIONS

The approach in Sections 4.5.1 and 4.5.4 can be readily extended to the case where there are more than two classes. Suppose that the $g(\underline{x})$ in 33 was defined by $g(\underline{x}) = g_1(\underline{x}) - g_2(\underline{x})$ where it was desired that $g_i(\underline{x})$ takes the value of one when $\underline{x}$ belongs to class ω_i and zero otherwise. The problem would then amount to approximate both $g_1(\underline{x})$

and $g_2(\underline{x})$. It is easy to establish that a MSE procedure based on these new premises would yield the same decision rule as 39. We shall presently extend this formulation in order to handle cases when there are more than two classes.

For a c-class problem, let V_i designate the ith column-vector of a c×c identity matrix, and $g_i(\underline{x})$ be the discriminant function associated with class ω_i,

$$\begin{aligned} g_i(\underline{x}) &= v_{i,1}\phi_1(\underline{x})+v_{i,2}\phi_2(\underline{x})+\ldots+v_{i,D}\phi_D(\underline{x})+v_{i,D+1} \\ &= \underline{w}_i^t\underline{y}, \qquad\qquad i=1,\ldots,c. \end{aligned}$$

Our goal is to find the c-dimensional vector-function

89 $$G(\underline{x}) = \left[g_1(\underline{x}),\ldots,g_c(\underline{x})\right]^t = W^t\underline{y},$$

where W is a (D+1)×c matrix of weights

$$W = \left[\underline{w}_1,\ldots,\underline{w}_c\right]$$

to be determined via the minimization of the following criterion function

90 $$\frac{1}{n}\left[\sum_{\underline{x}\in\omega_1}\|W^t\underline{y}-V_1\|^2 + \sum_{\underline{x}\in\omega_2}\|W^t\underline{y}-V_2\|^2 +\ldots+ \sum_{\underline{x}\in\omega_c}\|W^t\underline{y}-V_c\|^2\right].$$

We shall again invoke the law of large numbers and consider the large-sample expression of criterion function 90, namely

91 $$J_c(W) = \sum_{i=1}^{c} P_i\mathcal{E}_i\left\{\|W^t\underline{y}-V_i\|^2\right\}$$

$$= \sum_{i=1}^{c} P_i \int \|W^t\underline{y}-V_i\|^2 p(\underline{x}|\omega_i)d\underline{x}.$$

To find the minimizing W, we set the gradient of $J_c(W)$ to zero to obtain

92 $$\nabla_W J_c(W) = 2\sum_{i=1}^{c} P_i\mathcal{E}_i\left\{\underline{y}\underline{y}^t\right\}W - 2\sum_{i=1}^{c} P_i\mathcal{E}_i\left\{\underline{y}\right\}V_i^t = [0],$$

where [0] is a (D+1)×c null matrix. From 37, we have $\boldsymbol{E}_i\{\underline{y}\underline{y}^t\}=K_i$, moreover, we see that $\boldsymbol{E}_i\{\underline{y}\}V_i^t$ is a (D+1)×c matrix whose column-vectors are all null-vectors but for the ith one which is $\underline{\mu}_i^y$. Hence, 92 reads

93 $$KW = M,$$

where $K = \sum_{i=1}^{c} P_i K_i$ and $M = \left[M_1,\ldots,M_c\right]$ with $M_i = P_i\underline{\mu}_i^y$. Under the assumption that K is nonsingular, the minimizing W is found to be

94 $$W^* = K^{-1}M,$$

and the residual mean-squared-error is now given by

95 $$J_c(W^*) = 1+\mathrm{tr}\left\{M^tK^{-1}M\right\},$$

where tr{.} denotes the trace of matrix {.}. The associated decision rule is to assign $\underline{x}$ to class ω_i if $\underline{y}^tK^{-1}M_i > \underline{y}^tK^{-1}M_j$, j=1,...,c, j≠i. In the two-class case this decision rule is identical to that obtained in 39.

There is a fairly apparent similarity between the derivations in the two-class problem and the multiclass problem. However, some of the results obtained in the former case do not quite generalize in the latter one.

For instance, in Section 4.5.2, we were able to express the weight-vector $\underline{w}^*$ in terms of the class-conditional mean-vector and covariance matrices. When there are more than two classes, the reasoning may be repeated up to Equation 49. Then by 49 and 94 we obtain the expression for the ith weight-vector $\underline{w}_i^*$ in matrix W^*

$$\underline{w}_i^* = \left[\begin{array}{c|c} S_T^{-1} & -S_T^{-1}\underline{\mu} \\ \hline -\underline{\mu}^tS_T^{-1} & 1+\underline{\mu}^tS_T^{-1}\underline{\mu} \end{array}\right]\left[\begin{array}{c} P_i\underline{\mu}_i \\ \hline P_i \end{array}\right]$$

that is,

96 $$\underline{w}_i^* = \begin{bmatrix} P_i S_T^{-1}(\underline{\mu}_i-\underline{\mu}) \\ \hline P_i[1-\underline{\mu}^t S_T^{-1}(\underline{\mu}_i-\underline{\mu})] \end{bmatrix},$$

where it is useful to recall that S_T designates the covariance matrix in the mixture population. There follows that the linear discriminant function associated with class ω_i is given by

97 $$g_i(\underline{x}) = P_i\left\{(\underline{x}-\underline{\mu})^t S_T^{-1}(\underline{\mu}_i-\underline{\mu})+1\right\}, \quad i=1,\ldots,c.$$

The fact that parameters of the class-conditional distributions are replaced in the multiclass-case by parameters of the mixture distribution sheds light on the limitations of the approach in exploiting all of the structure in an arbitrary set of data. In the same line of thought let it also be mentioned that in the multiclass-case the residual mean-squared-error

$$J_c(W^*) = \sum_{i=1}^{c} P_i^2\left\{1+(\underline{\mu}_i-\underline{\mu})^t S_T^{-1}(\underline{\mu}_i-\underline{\mu})\right\}$$

has not been found to be related in any way to the error-rate E_{MSE} associated with the discriminant function in 97.

A satisfying observation however is that the discriminant function $(W^*)^t\underline{y}$ obtained by minimizing the criterion function 91 retains the essential property of being the best approximation, in the sense of minimum mean-squared-error, to the Bayes discriminant function.

To demonstrate this property, let $V(\underline{x})$ denote the vector of *a posteriori* probabilities,

98 $$V(\underline{x}) = \left[P(\omega_1|\underline{x}),\ldots,P(\omega_c|\underline{x})\right]^t,$$

and recall from Chapter 2 that minimum error-rate classification is achieved by calculating $V(\underline{x})$ and assigning $\underline{x}$ to class ω_i if the ith component of $V(\underline{x})$ is maximum. We shall show that $G(\underline{x}) = (W^*)^t\underline{y}$ is a best approximation to $V(\underline{x})$, in the sense of minimizing the criterion function

99 $$Q_c(W) = \int \|G(\underline{x}) - V(\underline{x})\|^2 p(\underline{x})d\underline{x}.$$

This result could be obtained very rapidly by showing that 99 is minimized by $W = K^{-1}M$. We shall proceed differently however in order to emphasize the relationship connecting $J_c(W)$ and $Q_c(W)$ which will be of interest from the viewpoint of feature selection.

Equation 91 may be transformed as follows

$$J_c(W) = \sum_{i=1}^{c} P_i \mathcal{E}_i\left\{\|W^t\underline{y}-V(\underline{x})+V(\underline{x})-V_i\|^2\right\}.$$

After some easy algebraic manipulations we find

100 $$J_c(W) = \int \|W^t\underline{y}-V(\underline{x})\|^2 p(\underline{x})d\underline{x} - \int \|V(\underline{x})\|^2 p(\underline{x})d\underline{x}$$

$$+ \sum_{i=1}^{c} P_i \int \|V_i\|^2 p(\underline{x}|\omega_i)d\underline{x}$$

$$+ 2\sum_{i=1}^{c} P_i \int \underline{y}^t W[V(\underline{x})-V_i]p(\underline{x}|\omega_i)d\underline{x}.$$

It may be observed that

101 $$\int \|V(\underline{x})\|^2 p(\underline{x})d\underline{x} = 1-E_1,$$

102 $$\sum_{i=1}^{c} P_i \int \|V_i\|^2 p(\underline{x}|\omega_i)d\underline{x} = 1,$$

103 $$\sum_{i=1}^{c} P_i \int \underline{y}^t W\left[V(\underline{x})-V_i\right]p(\underline{x}|\omega_i)d\underline{x} = 0.$$

The proof that 103 holds true for any value of W is as follows

$$\sum_{i=1}^{c} P_i \int \underline{y}^t WV(\underline{x}) p(\underline{x}|\omega_i) d\underline{x} = \int \underline{y}^t WV(\underline{x}) p(\underline{x}) d\underline{x}$$

$$= \sum_{i=1}^{c} \int \underline{y}^t \underline{w}_i p(\underline{x}, \omega_i) d\underline{x}$$

$$= \sum_{i=1}^{c} P_i \int \underline{y}^t WV_i p(\underline{x}, \omega_i) d\underline{x}.$$

By using 99 and 101-103 in 100 we obtain

104 $$J_c(W) = Q_c(W) + E_1,$$

which is the multiclass generalization of 78. As E_1 is independent of W, 104 shows that the matrix W^* that minimizes $J_c(W)$ also minimizes $Q_c(W)$ and this is but an alternative formulation of the property which we set out to prove. In addition, as $Q_c(W) \geq 0$ and $E_1 \geq E^*$ we obtain from 104

105 $$J_c(W^*) \geq E_1 \geq E^*.$$

Besides, equality of $J_c(W^*)$ and E_1 is seen again to be a sufficient condition of Bayes optimality for the MSE discriminant function. Finally, let us note that equation 104 would enable us to repeat most of the comments which were the subject matter of Section 4.5.5. However, the details of the discussion will be left as an exercice for the reader.

4.7. APPROXIMATIONS OF VARIOUS TYPES

106 The mean-squared-error criterion of the preceding sections has attracted much attention because of its mathematical simplicity and ease of implementation. From a classification viewpoint however, it leaves something to be desired. Firstly, it places emphasis on the

approximation error in densely populated regions, that is in regions where $p(\underline{x})$ is large, rather than in regions near the decision boundary. Secondly, it is apparent that the classification error-rate E_{MSE} plays no role in designing the discriminant function. A number of modifications of the MSE criterion function have been put forth to remedy these deficiencies. Two of these modifications are briefly summarized hereafter.

4.7.1. Approximation in the L_r Norm

Let us consider the following modification of the criterion functions 90 and 91:

107 $$\frac{1}{n}\sum_{i=1}^{c}\sum_{\underline{x}\epsilon\omega_i}\left(\|W^t\underline{y} - V_i\|_r\right)^r$$

and

108 $$J_c^r(W) = \sum_{i=1}^{c} P_i \int\left(\|W^t\underline{y}-V_i\|_r\right)^r p\left(\underline{x}|\omega_i\right)d\underline{x},$$

where for any vector $\underline{v}$, $\|\underline{v}\|_r = \left(\sum_i v_i^r\right)^{1/r}$ and r is taken to be an even, positive integer. Clearly, 90 and 91 are identical to 107 and 108 respectively provided that r=2. On the other hand, if r is taken very large, it is known from approximation theory that the minimizing W tends to minimize the maximum of the approximation error $|W^t\underline{y}-V_i|$, thereby outweighing the influence of the density function.

Loosely speaking, training samples that are misclassified by, say, the MSE discriminant function correspond to large approximation errors. Consequently by trying to minimize these large errors we may expect to correct those misclassifications. On the other hand, too large a value for r would render the approach unduly sensitive to the presence of any aberrant sample in the training set. So a good compromise is to use a moderate value of r of, say, a few tens.

The criterion function 108 is a strictly convex function of W, so the solution to the minimization problem exists and is unique. Unfortunately, when $r \neq 2$, it cannot be given in closed form. The problem can be solved however by using an iterative procedure such as the Newton-Raphson method.

Let us first define some notation. Let $\zeta_i(\underline{x}) = 1$ if $\underline{x}$ is from class ω_i and $\zeta_i(\underline{x}) = 0$ otherwise. Then, the criterion function of 108 can be expressed as

109 $$J_c^r(W) = \int \sum_{i=1}^{c} \left[\underline{w}_i^t \underline{y}(\underline{x}) - \zeta_i(\underline{x})\right]^r p(\underline{x}) d\underline{x},$$

where we purposely insist on the dependence on $\underline{x}$. Let $\underline{w}(k)$ denote the weight vector $\underline{w}$ obtained at the kth iteration. Then, the vector $\underline{w}(k+1)$ is found as the sum of $\underline{w}(k)$ and a correction increment $\underline{\tilde{w}}(k)$,

110 $$\underline{w}(k+1) = \underline{w}(k) + \underline{\tilde{w}}(k).$$

Let $\varepsilon_i(\underline{x})$ denote the residual approximation error with the weight vector $\underline{w}(k)$,

$$\varepsilon_i(\underline{x}) = \zeta(\underline{x}) - \underline{w}_i^t(k)\underline{y}(\underline{x}).$$

Then, at the (k+1)th iteration, our problem is that of minimizing the criterion function

$$J_c^r(W) = \sum_{i=1}^{c} \int \left[\underline{w}_i^t(k)\underline{y}(\underline{x}) + \underline{\tilde{w}}_i^t(k)\underline{y}(\underline{x}) - \zeta_i(\underline{x})\right]^r p(\underline{x}) d\underline{x}$$

111 $$= \sum_{i=1}^{c} \int \left[\underline{\tilde{w}}_i^t(k)\underline{y}(\underline{x}) - \varepsilon_i(\underline{x})\right]^r p(\underline{x}) d\underline{x}.$$

The minimization of each integral can be performed independently. So, let $I(\underline{\tilde{w}}_i)$ be given by

$$I(\underline{\tilde{w}}_i) = \int \left[\underline{\tilde{w}}_i^t(k)\underline{y}(\underline{x}) - \varepsilon_i(\underline{x}) \right]^r p(\underline{x})d\underline{x}, \qquad i=1,\ldots,c.$$

Application of the Newton-Raphson procedure for minimizing $I(\underline{\tilde{w}}_i)$ yields the following increment vector $\underline{\tilde{w}}_i(k)$

112 $$\underline{\tilde{w}}_i(k) = -\,[H(I)]^{-1}\nabla I,$$

where H(I) is the Hessian matrix of second derivatives of I

113 $$H(I) = r(r-1)\int \underline{y}(\underline{x})\underline{y}^t(\underline{x})\;\varepsilon_i^{r-2}(\underline{x})p(\underline{x})d\underline{x}$$

and

114 $$\nabla I = r\int \underline{y}(\underline{x})\varepsilon_i^{r-1}(\underline{x})p(\underline{x})d\underline{x}.$$

The results in 112-114 can be given an interesting interpretation. Let $f(\underline{x}) = \varepsilon_i^{r-2}(\underline{x})p(\underline{x})$, so $f(\underline{x}) \geq 0$. Then $\underline{\tilde{w}}_i(k)$ in 112 is also the solution vector to the problem of minimizing the following least-squared-error criterion function

$$\int \left[\underline{\tilde{w}}_i^t\underline{y}(\underline{x}) - \varepsilon_i(\underline{x}) \right]^2 f(\underline{x})d\underline{x}.$$

This formulation has the advantage of illuminating the error-correcting property of the approach, for each increment vector $\underline{\tilde{w}}_i$ can be thought of as resulting from a weighted least-squared-error approximation of the residual error $\varepsilon_i(\underline{x})$ with a weighting function that focuses on regions where the error is large.

The algorithm obtained by substituting 112 in 110 converges to the minimum of $J_c^r(W)$ irrespective of the initial choice of W(0). However, if the algorithm is initialized with a null matrix, W(0)=[0], it follows from 112-114 that, for any $r \geq 2$, $W(1)=K^{-1}M$, which was the solution to the minimization of the mean-squared-error criterion function. Finally, let us note that the procedure involves a significant amount of computation. At each iteration it requires the inversion of one $(D+1)\times(D+1)$ matrix per class.

4.7.2. Minimization of the Classification Error-Rate

In spite of its attractive error-correcting properties, the approach discussed above still fails to ensure minimum error-rate classification. Here and in what follows, it is important to bear in mind that we are concerned with the minimum error-rate that can be achieved with a classifier of a given structure corresponding to the $\underline{\Phi}(\underline{x})$ employed. It should not be confused with the Bayes error-rate E^*. In fact, even a minimum error-rate classifier may prove unacceptable in the case that $\underline{\Phi}(\underline{x})$ was poorly chosen.

115 The first step in our attempt to design a minimum error-rate discriminant function is to express the error-rate as a function $E(\underline{w})$ of the weight vector of $g(\underline{x})=\underline{w}^t\underline{y}$. We focus our attention on the two-class problem. Let the random variable z be defined by

$$z(\underline{x}) = 1 \quad \text{if} \quad \underline{x}\epsilon\omega_1,$$
$$= -1 \quad \text{if} \quad \underline{x}\epsilon\omega_2.$$

The expected value of z conditioned upon $\underline{x}$ is

116 $$E_{z|\underline{x}}\{z(\underline{x})\} = P(\omega_1|\underline{x})-P(\omega_2|\underline{x}) = g^*(\underline{x}).$$

A discriminant function $g(\underline{x}) = \underline{w}^t\underline{y}$ partitions the space into two decision regions Ω_1 and Ω_2 and the error probability corresponding to the partition is given by

$$E(\underline{w}) = \int_{\Omega_2} p(\underline{x},\omega_1)d\underline{x} + \int_{\Omega_1} p(\underline{x},\omega_2)d\underline{x},$$

which can be written as

$$E(\underline{w}) = P_1 - \int_{\Omega_1} g^*(\underline{x})p(\underline{x})d\underline{x}$$

117 $$= P_1 - \int_{\Omega_1} E_{z|\underline{x}}\{z(\underline{x})\}p(\underline{x})d\underline{x}.$$

Next, let $u(\xi)$ be the unit step function $\left(u(\xi) = 1 \text{ if } \xi > 0, \text{ and } u(\xi)=0 \text{ if } \xi < 0\right)$. So, $u(\underline{w}^t\underline{y})$ is the indicator function of decision region Ω_1. Thus,

$$E(\underline{w}) = P_1 - \int E_{z|\underline{x}}\{z(\underline{x})\}u(\underline{w}^t\underline{y})p(\underline{x})d\underline{x},$$

118 $$= P_1 - E_{\underline{x}}\left\{E_{z|\underline{x}}\{z(\underline{x})u(\underline{w}^t\underline{y})\}\right\}.$$

We may now consider minimizing $E(\underline{w})$ by using a gradient descent procedure by which the vector $\underline{w}_{k+1}$ at the (k+1)th step is obtained from $\underline{w}_k$ by the algorithm

119 $$\underline{w}_{k+1} = \underline{w}_k - \rho_k \nabla_{\underline{w}} E(\underline{w}_k),$$

where ρ_k is a positive scale factor that sets the step size.

Using 118, the gradient of $E(\underline{w})$ is given as

120 $$\nabla_{\underline{w}} E(\underline{w}) = -E_{\underline{x}}\left\{E_{z|\underline{x}}\{z(\underline{x})\underline{y}\delta(\underline{w}^t\underline{y})\}\right\},$$

where $\delta(.)$ is the delta Dirac function. Obviously, this expression for the gradient is quite embarrassing since it takes into account points lying on the decision boundary only (and up to now we tacitly assumed that such points occur with probability zero). This shows that $E(\underline{w})$ as given in 118 is not a very convenient objective function to minimize. To overcome the difficulty, we shall build another, more cooperative objective function that can be handled more easily and has the property of being minimized for the same value of $\underline{w}$. This new function is obtained by substituting a "smoothed" version of the step function in 118. For instance, we may use

121 $$u(\xi,\nu) = \int_{-\infty}^{\xi} h(\zeta,\nu)d\zeta,$$

where ν is a real, positive parameter and $h(\zeta,\nu)$ is a well-behaved *window function* satisfying some mild conditions and converging to $\delta(\zeta)$ when $\nu \to 0$. As an example of such a window function, we can take $h(\zeta,\nu) = (2\pi)^{-1/2}\nu^{-1}\exp[-\frac{1}{2}(\zeta/\nu)^2]$, *viz.*, the Gauss- Laplace function.

By using 121 in 118, the new objective function is

122 $$E(\underline{w},\nu) = P_1 - E_{\underline{x}}\left\{E_{z|\underline{x}}\{z(\underline{x})u_\nu(\underline{w}^t\underline{y},\nu)\}\right\},$$

whose gradient is given by

123 $$\begin{aligned}\nabla_{\underline{w}}E(\underline{w},\nu) &= -E_{\underline{x}}\left\{E_{z|\underline{x}}\{z(\underline{x})\,\underline{y}\,h(\underline{w}^t\underline{y},\nu)\}\right\}\\ &= -P_1\int \underline{y}\,h(\underline{w}^t\underline{y},\nu)p(\underline{x}|\omega_1)d\underline{x}\\ &\quad +P_2\int \underline{y}\,h(\underline{w}^t\underline{y},\nu)p(\underline{x}|\omega_2)d\underline{x}.\end{aligned}$$

It is apparent that $\lim_{\nu\to 0} E(\underline{w},\nu) = E(\underline{w})$ and $\lim_{\nu\to 0}\nabla_{\underline{w}}E(\underline{w},\nu) = \nabla_{\underline{w}}E(\underline{w})$. Consequently it may be shown that, under mild conditions, $E(\underline{w})$ can be minimized by using $\nabla_{\underline{w}}E(\underline{w},\nu)$ in 119, and letting ν become arbitrarily small. Thus, the algorithm reads

124 $$\underline{w}_{k+1} = \underline{w}_k - \rho_k\nabla_{\underline{w}}E\left(\underline{w}_k,\nu_k\right),$$

where $\nabla_{\underline{w}}E\left(\underline{w}_k,\nu_k\right)$ is given by 123.

This algorithm can be given a form that bears much resemblance of the Perceptron learning algorithm which we discussed in Section 4.4.2.

Let us first remark that $\nabla_{\underline{w}} E(\underline{w},\nu)$ is the weighted difference of the class-conditional expected values of $\underline{y}h(\underline{w}^t\underline{y},\nu)$. Suppose that in place of the true gradient we substitute the "noisy version" $-\underline{y}h(\underline{w}^t\underline{y},\nu)$ if $\underline{x}$ is from class ω_1 and $\underline{y}h(\underline{w}^t\underline{y},\nu)$ if $\underline{x}$ is from class ω_2. Using the notation of Section 4.4.2, the substitution leads to the algorithm

125
$$\underline{w}_{k+1} = \underline{w}_k + \rho_k \underline{y}^k h\left(\underline{w}_k^t \underline{y}^k, \nu_k\right) \quad \text{if } \theta^k = \omega_1$$
$$= \underline{w}_k - \rho_k \underline{y}^k h\left(\underline{w}_k^t \underline{y}^k, \nu_k\right) \quad \text{if } \theta^k = \omega_2.$$

The primary difference between the algorithms 30 and 125 is that the former is an error-correction rule that reacts on incorrectly classified samples only, whereas the latter focuses on all patterns (misclassified or not) near the current decision boundary via the weighting function $h(\underline{w}^t\underline{y},\nu)$. Here a word of caution is in order.

Recall from Section 4.2.1 that $g(\underline{x})=\underline{w}^t\underline{y}$ is proportional to the distance from $\underline{\Phi}(\underline{x})$ to the hyperplane $\underline{w}^t\underline{y}=0$. Moreover, from the definition of $h(\underline{w}^t\underline{y},\nu)$, it is clear that the window function emphasizes points at short distance from the decision boundary, and the scalar ν serves to scale that distance. So, to preserve the effectiveness of the method, it is indispensible to let $\underline{w}^t\underline{y}$ measure the true distance in question. This imposes the requirement that $\underline{w}_k$ be constantly normalized as in 10.

126 Algorithms such as 124 and 125 belong to the family of stochastic approximation procedures. These procedures are known to converge to the minimum of the objective function or to the zero of its gradient under fairly general conditions. In the case of the algorithms given above these conditions are

$$\rho_k \geq 0, \qquad \nu_k \geq 0, \qquad \lim_{k\to\infty} \nu_k=0,$$

$$\sum_{k=1}^{\infty} \rho_k = \infty, \qquad \sum_{k=1}^{\infty} \rho_k\nu_k < \infty, \qquad \sum_{k=1}^{\infty} \frac{\rho_k^2}{\nu_k} < \infty.$$

Full justification of these conditions is beyond the scope of the present exposition and we must limit ourselves to refer the interested reader to the literature.

4.8. BIBLIOGRAPHICAL COMMENTS

The statistical theory of discriminant analysis finds its origin in the classical paper by R.A. Fisher (1936). Since then, the published literature on discriminant functions has grown to the point where even specialized bibliographies can contain hundreds of references. Therefore, the references that we mention hereafter provide no more than a possible starting point for further study.

The theory of discriminant analysis developed by statisticians is well exemplified by the work of Anderson (1958) who concentrates on multivariate normal data. One of the first systematic account of linear, and generalized linear discriminant functions with application to pattern recognition can be found in the text by Sebestyen (1962).

Following Rosenblatt (1962), Perceptron theorists formulated the problem as the deterministic one of finding the solution to a system of linear inequalities. The probability of linear separability had been well studied by switching theorists, and was developed in the pattern recognition context by Cover (1965). The convergence of the

Perceptron learning algorithm has been proved by too many authors to be cited here. Let us mention, however, the very elegant proof by Novikoff (1963). All these problems are very clearly treated by Nilsson (1965). A more recent, thorough study of the Perceptron can be found in the book by Minsky and Papert (1969).

Our formulation of the least mean-squared-error procedure stems from a variety of sources, especially Wee (1968). The derivation of the error-bound in Section 4.5.3 follows an idea by Yau and Lin (1968). Tighter upper bounds were also developed by Rey (1976). The relationships with the Bayes and 1-NN decision rules are due to Devijver (1973, 1976). Both Wee (1968) and Devijver (1973) discuss the multiclass problem. The idea of using a best approximation in the L_r norm was suggested by Devijver (1971), and the algorithm for minimizing the classification error-rate is a simplified version of an algorithm proposed by Do Tu and Installé (1978).

The techniques discussed in this chapter constitute only a little part of the variety of possible approaches. Many other techniques can be found in e.g., Duda and Hart (1973), Ho and Kashyap (1965), Ho and Agrawala (1968), Kashyap (1970), Sammon (1970), and Warmack and Gonzalez (1973).

4.9. REFERENCES

Anderson, T.W., *An Introduction to Multivariate Statistical Analysis*, John Wiley, New York, 1958.

Cover, T.M., "Geometrical and statistical properties of systems of linear inequalities with applications in pattern recognition", *IEEE Trans. Comput.*, vol. 14, pp. 326-334, June 1965.

Devijver, P.A., "A general order Minkowski metric pattern classifier", in *Artificial Intelligence*, (AGARD Conf. Proc. No.94) Technical Editing and Reproduction Ltd, London, 1971, pp. 18/1-18/11.

Devijver, P.A., "Relationship between statistical risks and the least mean-squared-error design criterion in pattern recognition", *Proc. First Internat. Joint Conf. Pattern Recognition*, Washington, D.C., Nov 1973, pp. 139-148.

Devijver, P.A., "Entropie quadratique et reconnaissance des formes", in *Computer Oriented Learning Processes*, J.C. Simon Ed., Noordhoff, Leyden, 1976, pp. 257-278.

Do Tu, H., and Installé, M., "Learning algorithm for nonparametric solution to the minimum error classification problem", *IEEE Trans. Comput.*, vol. 27, pp. 648-659, July 1978.

Duda, R.O., and Hart, P.E., *Pattern Classification and Scene Analysis*, John Wiley, New York, 1973.

Fisher, R.A., "The use of multiple measurements in taxonomic problems", *Ann. Eugenics*, vol. 7, Part II, pp. 179-188, 1936.

Ho, Y-C., and Kashyap, R.L., "An algorithm for linear inequalities and its applications", *IEEE Trans. Comput.*, vol. 14, pp. 683-688, Oct. 1965.

Ho, Y-C., and Agrawala, A.K., "On pattern classification algorithms : Introduction and Survey", *Proc. IEEE*, vol. 56, pp. 2101-2114, Dec. 1968.

Kashayp, R.L., "Algorithms for pattern classification", in *Adaptive, Learning and Pattern Classification Systems*, J.M. Mendel, and K.S. Fu Eds., Academic Press, New York, 1970, pp. 81-113.

Minsky, M., and Papert, S., *Perceptrons : An Introduction to Computational Geometry*, MIT Press, Cambridge, Mass., 1969.

Nilsson, N.J., *Learning Machines : Foundations of Trainable Pattern Classifying Systems*, McGraw-Hill, New York, 1965.

Novikoff, A.B.J., "On convergence proofs for perceptrons", Tech. Rept., Stanford Research Institute, SRI Project No. 3605, Jan. 1963.

Rey, W.J.J., "On the upper bound of the probability of error, based on Chebyshev's inequality, in two-class linear discrimination", *Proc. IEEE*, (Lett.), vol. 64, pp. 361-362, March 1976.

Rosenblatt, F, *Principles of Neurodynamics : Perceptrons and the Theory of Brain Mechanisms*, Spartan Books, Washington, D.C., 1962.

Sammon, J.W., "An optimal discriminant plane", *IEEE Trans. Comput.*, vol. 19, pp. 826-829, Sept. 1970.

Sebestyen, G., *Decision Making Processes in Pattern Recognition*, Macmillan, New York, 1962.

Warmack, R.E., and Gonzalez, R.C.,"An algorithm for the optimal solution of linear inequalities and its application to pattern recognition", *IEEE Trans. Comput.*, vol. 22, pp. 1065-1075, 1973.

Wee, W.G., "Generalized inverse approach to adaptive multiclass pattern classification", *IEEE Trans. Comput.*, vol. 17, pp. 1157-1164, Dec. 1968.

Yau, S.S., and Lin, T.T., "On the upper bound of the probability of error of a linear pattern classifier for probabilistic pattern classes", *Proc. IEEE* (Lett.), vol. 56, pp.321-322, March 1968.

4.10. PROBLEMS

1. Show that, for a c-class problem, c≥2,

$$\sum_{i=1}^{c} P_i\left(\underline{\mu}_i-\underline{\mu}\right)\left(\underline{\mu}_i-\underline{\mu}\right)^t = \sum_{i=1}^{c}\sum_{j>i}^{c} P_iP_j\left(\underline{\mu}_i-\underline{\mu}_j\right)\left(\underline{\mu}_i-\underline{\mu}_j\right)^t.$$

2. It is easy to see that using a linear discriminant function $g(\underline{x})=\underline{v}^t\underline{x}+v_{d+1}$ is equivalent to projecting pattern $\underline{x}$ onto a line in the direction of vector $\underline{v}$, and comparing the position of the projection with that of the threshold weight v_{d+1}.

   (a) Given a vector $\underline{v}$, verify that, for the projected points, the between- and within-class scatters are given by $s_b=\underline{v}^tS_b\underline{v}$, and $s_w=\underline{v}^tS_w\underline{v}$ respectively.

   (b) Consider a two-class problem and assume that matrix S_w is non-singular. Determine the vector $\underline{v}^*$ for which the *Fisher discriminant ratio*

$$F(\underline{v}) = \frac{\underline{v}^tS_b\underline{v}}{\underline{v}^tS_w\underline{v}}$$

   is maximum. Compare the solution vector with that obtained in Section 4.4.

   (c) Show that

$$\frac{2P_1P_2}{1+F(\underline{v}^*)} \geq E_1,$$

where E_1 is the 1-NN error-rate.

(d) At this point it is clear that the maximization of the Fisher discriminant ratio does not involve the threshold weight v_{d+1}. Show that, when equality is achieved in (c) above, there exists a threshold weight v^*_{d+1} such that $g(\underline{x})=\underline{v}^{*t}\underline{x}+v^*_{d+1}$ is Bayes-optimal.

3. When using the Fisher discriminant ratio, we seek to compute an optimum direction $\underline{v}^*$ such that orthogonally projected samples are maximally discriminated. The approach can be generalized by computing an *optimal discriminant plane*. The first axis of the optimal plane is the Fisher vector $\underline{v}^*$ found in Problem 2. The second axis $\underline{v}'$ is found by maximizing the Fisher discriminant ratio under the constraint that this second vector be orthogonal to $\underline{v}^*$. Verify that the vector $\underline{v}'^*$, for which the objective function

$$\frac{\underline{v}'^t S_b \underline{v}'}{\underline{v}'^t S_w \underline{v}'} - \lambda(\underline{v}'^t \underline{v}^*)$$

is maximum, is given by

$$\underline{v}'^* = k\left\{S_w^{-1} - \frac{\left(\underline{\mu}_1-\underline{\mu}_2\right)^t\left[S_w^{-1}\right]^2\left(\underline{\mu}_1-\underline{\mu}_2\right)}{\left(\underline{\mu}_1-\underline{\mu}_2\right)^t\left[S_w^{-1}\right]^3\left(\underline{\mu}_1-\underline{\mu}_2\right)}\left[S_w^{-1}\right]^2\right\}\left(\underline{\mu}_1-\underline{\mu}_2\right),$$

where λ is a Lagrange multiplier, and k is a normalizing constant.

4. We have seen in Section 4.5.5 that

$$\frac{2P_1P_2}{1+P_1P_2\Delta} = E_1$$

is a sufficient condition of Bayes-optimality of the MSE discriminant function. Verify numerically that this equality is satisfied for the example-problem which we discussed in Section 3.9.

5. In the multiclass case of Section 4.6, the $(D+1)\times c$ matrix W^* that

minimizes the MSE design criterion was given as $W^{*}=K^{-1}M$, where $K=\sum_i K_i$ with $K_i=\boldsymbol{E}_i\left\{\underline{y}\,\underline{y}^t\right\}$, and $M=\left[M_1,\ldots,M_c\right]$ with $M_i=P_i\underline{\mu}_i^y$.

(a) Show that the row-sums of matrix W^{*} are all equal to zero but for the (D+1)th which is equal to one.

(b) Verify that this property is retained at each iteration of the approximation in the L_r norm.

6. Let $\Lambda=\left[\lambda(\omega_i|\omega_j)\right]_{i,j}$, $i,j=1,\ldots,c$ denote a loss matrix. (Recall from Chapter 2 that $\lambda(\omega_i|\omega_j)$ is the loss incurred when assigning to class ω_i a pattern that belongs to class ω_j.) Given $\underline{x}$, let $V(\underline{x})$ be the vector of *a posteriori* probabilities.

(a) Verify that $\Lambda^t V(\underline{x})$ is vector function whose components are the conditional risks defined by Equation 2.3, and re-formulate the Bayes rule in terms of this vector.

(b) Derive the MSE approximation of the Bayes rule for minimum risk by minimizing the criterion function

$$Q_c'(W) = \int \|G(\underline{x}) - \Lambda^t V(\underline{x})\|^2 p(\underline{x})d(\underline{x}),$$

where $G(\underline{x})=W^t\underline{y}$, and determine the corresponding decision rule.

Hint: Use the fact that the MSE approximation of the linear transform of a given function is the same linear transform of the MSE approximation of that function.

Chapter 5

INTRODUCTION TO FEATURE SELECTION AND EXTRACTION

5.1. STATEMENT OF THE PROBLEM

From our experience we know that classification of patterns as performed by humans is based on a very few of the most important attributes. For instance, in the problem of classification of crops we may base our decision entirely on the color of the field. By analogy we attempt to design systems for automatic classification of patterns in any pattern recognition problem on the basis of only a few significant features characterizing the class membership of the patterns, preferably those that would be used for classification purposes by man. Although there is no conceptual justification for limiting the number of pattern descriptors we work with, the main motivation for keeping it to the absolute minimum is to curtail the effect of the "curse of dimensionality" phenomenon on the complexity of the classifier.

If the significant features were known *a priori* then the problem of designing a feature selector would be essentially deterministic amounting to implementation of the required measurements which could be carried out as an integral part of the pattern representation stage design. But in practice we are seldom confronted with pattern recognition problems where the relevant information is sufficiently well defined and understood so as to facilitate the design of an automatic system purely by heuristic methods. Frequently, only indirect observations of properties of elements of classes are available to the designer, in which the discriminatory information is encoded in a very complex manner and it may not be apparent which measurements are important for pattern classification. This situation is usually aggravated through insufficient knowledge of the process by which patterns are generated. Then it becomes essential to use transducers which are capable of retaining as much information about patterns as possible.

It is apparent that often the representation of patterns will have a large number of components which may exceed hundreds or, in the case of images, hundreds of thousands. These patterns will inevitably contain information which is either redundant or irrelevant to the classification task. Moreover, the pattern-generating mechanism and the transducer are likely to introduce, in addition to natural pattern variability, some distortion and noise. It is therefore the fundamental function of the feature selector to extract with appropriate tools the most useful information from the representation vector and present it in a form of a pattern vector of a lower dimensionality whose elements represent only the most significant aspects of the input data.

But the goal of feature selection does not merely lie in the physical reduction of dimensionality as required by feasibility limitations of either a technical or economical nature. Even if no constraints were imposed on the dimensionality of the pattern vector, it might still be beneficial to incorporate a feature selection stage in the pattern recognition system with the aim of removing any redundant and irrelevant information which may have a detrimental effect on the classifier performance.

Finally, as a useful by-product, the feature selection process provides an indication about the discriminatory potential of the features and, consequently, about the highest achievable performance of the decision making system for a given representation space. Thus it can be considered that a further role of the feature selection process is to establish whether it is necessary to seek additional measurements which would contain discriminatory information allowing the improvement of the performance of the classifier.

All mathematical feature selection techniques can be classified into one of two major categories : feature selection in the measurement space and feature selection in a transformed space. Techniques belonging to the first category are appropriate when the acquisition of measurements representing the input pattern is costly. Thus the main objective of feature selection in this case is to accomplish dimensionality reduction by reducing the number of required measurements in order to minimize the overall cost of measurement acquisition. This can be achieved by eliminating those measurements which are redundant or do not contain enough relevant information. Thus the problem of feature selection in the measurement space lies in selecting the best subset X of d features,

1 $$X = \left\{x_i \mid i = 1,2,\ldots,d,\ x_i \in Y\right\}$$

from the set Y,

2 $$Y = \left\{y_j \mid j = 1,2,\ldots,D\right\}$$

of $D > d$ possible measurements representing the pattern. By the best subset we understand the combination of d features which optimizes a criterion function, J(.), ideally the probability of correct classification, with respect to any other combination, $\Xi=\left\{\xi_i \mid i=1,2,\ldots,d\right\}$, of d measurements taken from Y. In other words, X satisfies

3 $$J(X) = \max_{\Xi} J(\Xi).$$

In the following we shall refer to feature selection in the measurement space briefly as *feature selection*.

4 REMARK : The representation of feature patterns as sets of descriptors (i.e., X, Ξ) will be especially useful in a later section of this chapter concerned with search algorithms. However, in the discussion of feature selection criterion functions it will be more convenient to use the conventional vector representation where feature sets X and Ξ are represented by vectors $\underline{x}$ and $\underline{\xi}$ respectively, whose components are the elements of X and Ξ, i.e.

5 $$\underline{x} = \left[x_1,\ x_2,\ldots,\ x_d\right]^t$$

and

6 $$\underline{\xi} = \left[\xi_1,\ \xi_2,\ldots,\ \xi_d\right]^t.$$

Using this notation, the problem of feature selection becomes one of determining vector $\underline{x}$ satisfying

7 $$J(\underline{x}) = \max_{\underline{\xi}} J(\underline{\xi}).$$

In contrast, feature selection techniques in the second category utilize all the information in the pattern representation vector, $\underline{y}$, to yield feature vector $\underline{x}$ of lower dimension. Apart from the general justification of dimensionality reduction given earlier, the need for feature selection in a transformed space may also arise from engineering considerations. For example, if it is necessary to separate the data collection and classification stages of a pattern recognition system, it may be highly desirable to compress the observed information into a lower dimensional space to facilitate its transmission or storage. Here the elimination of the irrelevant information and redundancy is an integral part of the transformation which maps pattern vector $\underline{y}$ from the representation space into a lower dimensional feature space, i.e.

8 $$\underline{x} = W(\underline{y}).$$

Similarly, the mapping, $W(\underline{y})$, is obtained by optimizing a criterion function $J(.)$. More specifically, $W(\underline{y})$, is determined amongst all admissible transformations $\{\widetilde{W}(\underline{y})\}$ as one that satisfies

9 $$J\{W(\underline{y})\} = \max_{\widetilde{W}} J\{\widetilde{W}(\underline{y})\}.$$

In general, the map, $W(\underline{y})$, could be any vector function of $\underline{y}$ but the majority of existing methods of feature selection in the transformed space is restricted to linear mappings, i.e.

10 $$\underline{x} = W^t \underline{y}.$$

where W is a (D×d) matrix of coefficients.

In the following, feature selection in the transformed space will be referred to briefly as *feature extraction*.

5.2. GENERAL COMMENTS ON FEATURE SELECTION AND EXTRACTION

It has been argued in the introductory chapter that, ideally, the problem of feature selection and extraction on the one hand and the classifier design on the other should never be considered independently. Yet often, practical considerations will force us to make the simplifying assumption that the feature selection/extraction and classification stages are mutually independent. Whilst this assumption allows for a considerable simplification of the pattern recognition system design, it is likely that the overall system performance will be adversely affected. In particular, if the feature selection/extraction stage is coupled to a classifier subjected to design constraints, the use of a sophisticated feature evaluation criterion may lead to an overall performance of the pattern recognition system that is inferior to that of the recognizer utilizing a simplistic feature selector. Likewise, even the most sophisticated classifier will be unable to compensate for any information loss incurred by an inadequate feature selector. And since the division of the pattern recognition problem into independent problems of feature evaluation and classification is consistent with our practical design philosophy, every attempt must be made to avoid unsatisfactory matching of the feature selection and decision making stages by a careful selection of the design objectives.

The above remarks are particularly relevant to feature extraction where, in addition to the problem of choosing a suitable feature evaluation measure, we have to consider problems arising from restricting the feature extraction mapping to a particular form.

In the preceding section we mentioned that one of the goals of feature selection and extraction is to achieve good performance of the pattern recognition system. This claim may seem somewhat controversial, for it is well known from statistical decision theory that probability of classification error or risk should decrease when additional measurements are taken into consideration. However, this is generally true only for infinite sample sets for which the errors on estimates of the pattern recognition system parameters can be ignored. In practice, only finite training sets are available and, consequently, estimation errors will no longer be negligible. As a result of estimation errors, the system would be finely tuned to the data used for learning the system parameters. However, its performance could drastically deteriorate on new data; that is, the system would lack generalization ability. Since the number of system parameters and, consequently, associated estimation errors (for training sets of a given size) increase rapidly with dimensionality, it may be advantageous to sacrifice some useful information in order to keep the number of these parameters to a minimum. In summary, feature selection can be seen to be aimed at improving the generalization ability of the recognition system and, therefore, its performance on unknown patterns by trading off error probability for estimation errors. Note, however, that this argument is rather weak in connection with feature extraction methods where, as we shall see later, the mapping itself and its generalization ability may be affected by estimation errors. The beneficial effect of the dimensionality reduction, obtained by feature extraction, on the system's performance will be even more eroded in cases where, by restricting the form or criterion of the mapping, we implicitly assume an oversimplistic model of the pattern recognition system. Such a situation will arise if, for instance, the classes are not linearly separable and we restrict the feature extractor to a linear form. In such cases the decrease in estimation errors would have to be large enough to compensate for the inevitably greater loss of discriminatory information.

5.3. BASIC CONCEPTS OF CLASS SEPARABILITY

5.3.1. Error Probability

The ultimate goal of pattern recognition system design is to achieve a very high system performance which is often synonymous with a low classification error rate. A minimum error probability has been aimed at either directly or indirectly by all the classification methods discussed in the preceding chapters and, likewise, this performance index will serve as the principal design criterion in the context of feature selection and extraction.

Recalling Chapter 2, error probability in the space spanned by random variable $\underline{\xi}$, $E(\Xi)$, is defined as

11 $$E(\Xi) = \int\left[1 - \max_i P(\omega_i|\underline{\xi})\right]p(\underline{\xi})d\underline{\xi}.$$

Although error probability is, from the theoretical viewpoint, an ideal measure of class separability in a given space, unfortunately, as we shall see in Chapter 10, it is very difficult to evaluate, and often other measures of class separability must be resorted to. In this section we shall introduce various concepts of class separability on which alternative feature selection and extraction criteria are based. A detailed discussion of specific criteria of class separability and corresponding feature selection and extraction methods will be deferred to the subsequent chapters.

5.3.2. Interclass Distance

Consider Figure 5.1, where elements of classes ω_1 and ω_2 are represented by circles and crosses respectively. Obviously, the greater the average pairwise distance between patterns of different classes, the better the separability of the two classes. The notion of *interclass distance* is the simplest concept of class separability which can be used to assess discriminatory potential of pattern representations in a given space. Since interclass distance is not defined explicitly via class conditional probability density functions, its estimate based on elements of the training set can be computed directly without prior determination of the probabilistic structure of the classes. This property of the interclass

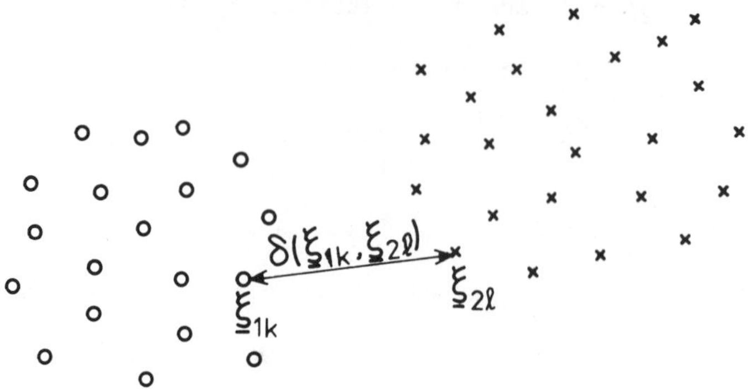

Figure 5.1. The distance between patterns $\underline{\xi}_{1k}$ and $\underline{\xi}_{2\ell}$ as measured with metric δ.

separability measure is particularly attractive from the computational point of view.

Inevitably, up to a certain extent, the probabilistic structure of classes will be reflected in the interclass distance separability measure by virtue of the distance averaging process. However, since detailed information about probabilistic distribution of the classes is not used in defining the interclass distance, separability measures based on this concept cannot serve as true indicators of mutual class overlap.

5.3.3. Probabilistic Distance

To obtain a more realistic picture of the overlap of the subspaces occupied by individual classes, it is essential to introduce a concept of class separability which uses the complete information about the probabilistic structure of classes. Such information is provided, for instance, by the class conditional probability density functions (p.d.f.s), $p(\underline{\xi}|\omega_i)$, $i=1,2,\ldots,c$ and *a priori* class probabilities P_i.

Let us now consider p.d.f.s of classes ω_i, $i = 1, 2$ given in Figure 5.2 and assume that $P_1 = P_2$. The classes will be fully separable if $p(\xi|\omega_1)$ is zero for all ξ such that $p(\xi|\omega_2) \neq 0$ as illustrated in Figure 5.2a. On the other hand, when $p(\xi|\omega_1) = p(\xi|\omega_2)$, $\forall\xi$, as in Figure 5.2b, it is impossible to distinguish elements of class ω_1 from those belonging to ω_2. In other words the classes are completely overlapping.

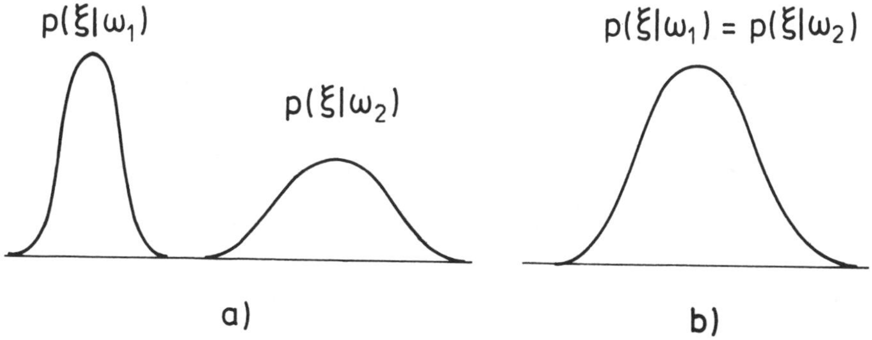

Figure 5.2. Probability density functions of a) two well separated classes and b) two completely overlapping classes.

Intuitively, the overlap of density functions can be assessed by measuring the "distance" between $p(\underline{\xi}|\omega_1)$ and $p(\underline{\xi}|\omega_2)$. In general, any function $J(.)$,

12 $$J(.) = \int g\left[p(\underline{\xi}|\omega_1),\ p(\underline{\xi}|\omega_2),\ P_1,\ P_2\right] d\underline{\xi},$$

satisfying

13 a. $J(.)$ is non-negative, i.e., $J(.) \geq 0$,

14 b. $J(.)$ attains a maximum when the classes in the $\underline{\xi}$ space are disjoint, i.e.,

$J(.) = \max$ if $p(\underline{\xi}|\omega_1) = 0$ when $p(\underline{\xi}|\omega_2) \neq 0$, $\forall \underline{\xi}$,

15 c. $J(.)$ equals zero when p.d.f.s are identical, i.e.,

$$J(.) = 0 \text{ if } p(\underline{\xi}|\omega_1) = p(\underline{\xi}|\omega_2),$$

can be used as a *probabilistic distance measure* of class separability.

5.3.4. Probabilistic Dependence

Alternatively, the problem of measuring the overlap of p.d.f.s can be formulated indirectly as one of assessing *probabilistic dependence* of pattern vectors $\underline{\xi}$ and classes ω_i, $i=1,2$. If the random variables $\underline{\xi}$ and ω_i are independent then the joint probability density $p(\underline{\xi},\omega_i)$ is given as

16 $$p(\underline{\xi},\omega_i) = p(\underline{\xi})P_i,$$

while in general

17 $$p(\underline{\xi},\omega_i) = p(\underline{\xi}|\omega_i)P_i.$$

When $\underline{\xi}$ and ω_i are statistically independent, by observing $\underline{\xi}$ we shall not gain any information about ω_i or, in other words, about the class membership of $\underline{\xi}$. Comparing the right hand sides of 16 and 17 it is apparent that the implication of this special case is that the class conditional p.d.f. $p(\underline{\xi}|\omega_i)$ and the mixture p.d.f., $p(\underline{\xi})$, are identical, i.e.,

$$p(\underline{\xi}|\omega_i) = p(\underline{\xi}).$$

On the other hand, when $\underline{\xi}$ is statistically dependent on ω_i, the i-th class p.d.f. $p(\underline{\xi}|\omega_i)$ will be different from the mixture distribution (see Figure 5.3). It follows that the task of determining probabilistic dependence between patterns and classes leads to the problem of measuring the difference ("distance") between class conditional and mixture p.d.f.s $p(\underline{\xi}|\omega_i)$ and $p(\underline{\xi})$ respectively. Recalling our earlier discussion, any criterion function satisfying conditions 13 - 15 can be used in this context, i.e.,

18 $$J(.) = \int g\left[p(\underline{\xi}|\omega_i),\ p(\underline{\xi}),\ P_i\right]d\underline{\xi}.$$

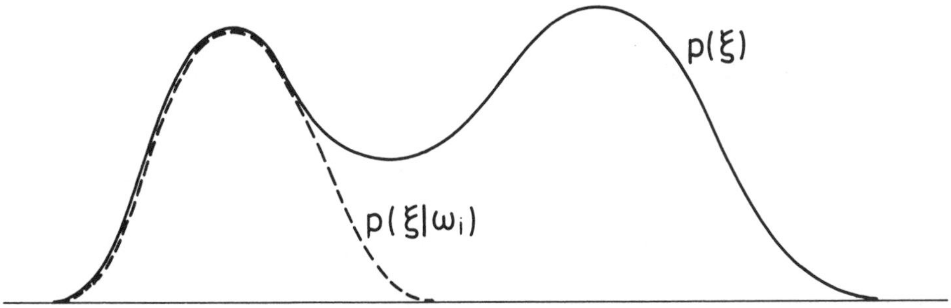

Figure 5.3. Depicting the distinction between the conditional p.d.f. of patterns in class ω_i and the mixture p.d.f.

The greater the magnitude of the distance the greater the dependence between $\underline{\xi}$ and ω_i. Moreover, from Figure 5.3 it is also apparent that a large distance between $p(\underline{\xi}|\omega_i)$ and $p(\underline{\xi})$ implies that the distance between p.d.f.s $p(\underline{\xi}|\omega_i)$ and $p(\underline{\xi}|\omega_j)$ is also large. Hence we can conclude that probabilistic dependence constitutes a natural concept of class separability.

5.3.5. Entropy

Consider *a posteriori* class probability functions $P(\omega_i|\underline{\xi})$, $\forall i$, which together with the mixture p.d.f. $p(\underline{\xi})$ also provide an alternative complete description of the probabilistic structure of classes. From our earlier discussion in Chapter 2 we know that if the *a posteriori* class probabilities, given pattern $\underline{\xi}$, are identical, i.e.,

$$P(\omega_i|\underline{\xi}) = \frac{1}{c} \qquad i=1,2,\ldots,c,$$

then the membership of $\underline{\xi}$ in each class ω_i, i = 1, 2, ..., c is equally likely and $\underline{\xi}$ can be classified quite arbitrarily. Naturally, since

19 $$\sum_{i=1}^{c} P(\omega_i|\underline{\xi}) = 1,$$

the probability, $e(\underline{\xi})$, of $\underline{\xi}$ being misclassified is in this case

$$e(\underline{\xi}) = 1 - \frac{1}{c} = \frac{c-1}{c}.$$

Let us now take another extreme example where $P(\omega_i|\underline{\xi})=1$ and $P(\omega_j|\underline{\xi})=0$, $\forall j \neq i$. In this situation, pattern $\underline{\xi}$ will be assigned to ω_i with absolute certainty, that is the error probability, $e(\underline{\xi})$, will be zero, i.e.,

$$e(\underline{\xi}) = 0.$$

The intuitively justifiable conclusion that we can draw from these two examples is that decision-making in the feature space where the *a posteriori* class probabilities are by and large uniformly distributed will result in a high classification error rate. Conversely, error probability associated with a space where $P(\omega_i|\underline{\xi})$ are unevenly distributed will be relatively small. The practical implication of this observation is that we should be able to assess the discriminatory potential of a set of features simply by measuring the dispersion of magnitudes of $P(\omega_i|\underline{\xi})$ using any suitable criterion function.

<u>REMARK</u> : In order to serve its purpose adequately, the notion of unevenness to be adopted should faithfully reflect discriminatory ability of $\underline{\xi}$. For instance, the degree of "unevenness" of probabilities given in Figure 5.4 must necessarily be greater than that of probabilities in Figure 5.5.

A suitable dispersion measure satisfying the above requirements can be found using the information theoretic approach. First of all, let us formulate the problem of selecting the best features in terms of information theory. Denote by ω a random variable taking values ω_i, $i=1,2,\ldots,c$ with *a priori* probabilities P_i. Further, let the outcome of ω be dependent on random variable $\underline{\xi}$ characterized by probability density function $p(\underline{\xi})$. In other words, given $\underline{\xi}$, the respective probabilities of states ω_i, $i=1,2,\ldots,c$, will be $P(\omega_i|\underline{\xi})$.

We shall now carry out a simple experiment involving the joint observation of variable $\underline{\xi}$ and the corresponding outcome of the

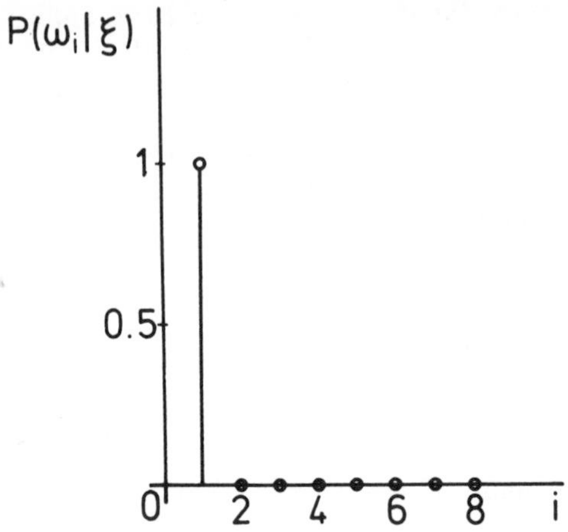

Figure 5.4. Example of an ideal distribution of *a posteriori* class probabilities.

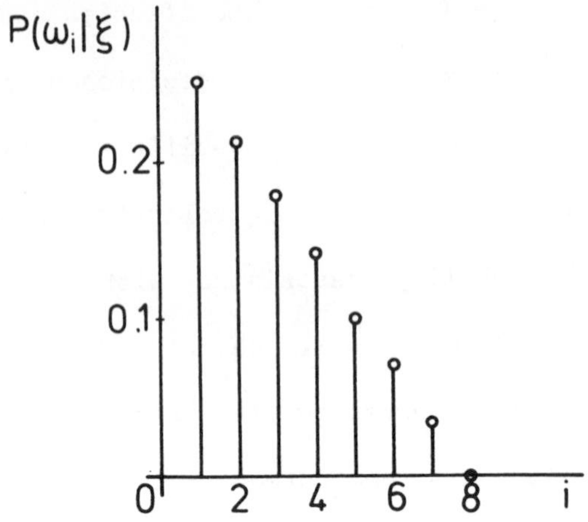

Figure 5.5. Example of a less desirable distribution of *a posteriori* class probabilities.

discrete variable ω. The question we ask here is the following : given $\underline{\xi}$, how much information do we gain from observing the outcome of ω, or, alternatively, what is our uncertainty about ω. Obviously, if for some $\underline{\xi}$, there exists i such that $P(\omega_i|\underline{\xi}) = 1$ and $P(\omega_j|\underline{\xi}) = 0$, $\forall j \neq i$, then the outcome, $\omega = \omega_i$, is certain and we shall receive no information by observing the realization of ω. In contrast, if $P(\omega_i|\underline{\xi}) = \text{const}$, $\forall i$, we can but hazard guesses of the likely outcome of ω and the amount of information gained from learning which of the possible events, ω_i, actually occurred will be nonzero and will correspond to the uncertainty prevailing before the outcome of ω has been observed.

From the above arguments, it is apparent that, in the context of feature evaluation, the smaller the uncertaintv the better the feature vector, $\underline{\xi}$. In information theory, uncertainty is quantified by means of the so called *entropy*, $J_c[P(\omega_1|\underline{\xi}),\ldots,P(\omega_c|\underline{\xi})]$, which is a measure of the information expected from an experiment. As such it must have certain essential properties which are listed in Appendix C.

A family of information measures which possess these properties are the generalized entropies of degree α defined as

20 $$J_c^{\alpha}\left[P(\omega_1|\underline{\xi}),P(\omega_2|\underline{\xi}),\ldots,P(\omega_c|\underline{\xi})\right]=(2^{1-\alpha}-1)^{-1}\left[\sum_{i=1}^{c}P^{\alpha}(\omega_i|\underline{\xi})-1\right],$$

where α is a real, positive parameter with $\alpha \neq 1$.

Let us now return to the problem of feature evaluation. Evidently, in order to assess the discriminatory potential of $\underline{\xi}$, we must inspect the values of the entropy function everywhere in the space. Obviously, if these values are low then this means that for every pattern $\underline{\xi}$, we shall know its most likely classification ω and, further, the probability that $\underline{\xi}$ will belong to any other class will be small. On the other hand, if, in a part of the space, the entropy takes on large values, then in that part of the space the class membership of $\underline{\xi}$ will be uncertain. By implication, in this latter case the classes will be overlapping, while in the former the overlap will be negligible. We can conclude that the expected value of the entropy function,

21 $$J(.) = \boldsymbol{E}\left\{J_c^{\alpha}\left[P(\omega_1|\underline{\xi}),\ldots,P(\omega_c|\underline{\xi})\right]\right\}$$

is an indicator of class separability and it can, therefore, be used as a feature evaluation measure.

COMMENT : Note that some feature extraction methods described in later chapters do not use the above notions of class separability directly. The conceptual bases of the methods which do not conform to the general framework outlined here will be introduced before discussing each of these particular methods.

5.4. SEARCH ALGORITHMS FOR FEATURE SELECTION

Above, we introduced various concepts of class separability, any of which can be used as a basis for assessing the discriminatory power of individual feature sets that have to be evaluated to determine the best combination of d features out of D measurements. Owing to statistical dependence of measurements it is indispensable that, in the course of the feature selection process, all the possible subsets of d out of D attributes be considered to guarantee optimality of the feature set selected. The number, q, of these sets is given by the well known combinatorial formula, i.e.

22 $$q = \binom{D}{d} = \frac{D!}{(D-d)!\ d!}.$$

It is apparent that, even for moderate values of D and d, direct exhaustive search will not be possible. For instance, in a typical pattern recognition problem, we might be selecting ten features out of say a hundred available measurements which would require evaluation of more than 10^{13} feature sets. But, even for relatively simple problems involving selection of say 10 features out of 20 measurements, 184756 feature sets would have to be considered. This represents a problem which is beyond the capabilities of present day computers. Evidently, in practical situations, alternative, computationally feasible procedures will have to be employed. Such search algorithms, both optimal and suboptimal, that obviate the exhaustive search comprise the remainder of this chapter.

REMARK : The search strategy for feature selection is independent of the criterion function used. Hence the following strategies could be used with any of the criterion functions to be discussed in subsequent chapters. This remark does not apply to feature extraction. So feature extraction algorithms will be discussed in conjunction with the particular criterion functions.

In all the search algorithms to be discussed in the sequel, the best feature set is constructed by adding to and/or removing from the current feature set a small number of measurements at a time until the required feature set, X, of cardinality d is obtained. In particular, the starting point can be either an empty set which is then gradually built up or, alternatively, we can start from the complete set of measurements, Y, and successively eliminate superfluous observations. The former approach is known as the "bottom up" method while the latter is referred to as the "top down" search.

More specifically, let Ξ_k be a set containing k elements, ξ_1, $\xi_2,\ldots,\xi_k$, from the set of available measurements, Y, i.e.

23 $$\Xi_k = \left\{\xi_i | i = 1,2,\ldots,k,\ \xi_i \epsilon Y\right\}.$$

Further denote by $\bar{\Xi}_k$ the set of D-k features obtained by removing k attributes $\xi_1, \xi_2, \ldots, \xi_k$, from the complete set of measurements, Y, i.e.

24 $$\bar{\Xi}_k = \left\{ y_i | y_i \in Y,\ 1 \le i \le D,\ y_i \ne \xi_j,\ \forall_j \right\}.$$

Obviously, by choosing different descriptors ξ_j, we shall construct different sets Ξ_k and $\bar{\Xi}_k$ and we shall consider, therefore, Ξ_k and $\bar{\Xi}_k$ as variables.

Now let J(.) be a measure of class separability chosen by the user. Then in the "bottom up" approach the best feature set at the k-th step of an algorithm, X_k, is the one that satisfies

25 $$J(X_k) = \max_{\{\Xi_k\}} J(\Xi_k).$$

Here $\{\Xi_k\}$ is the set of all the candidate sets of k features which depends on the particular algorithm used. As we shall see, $\{\Xi_k\}$ is as a rule determined at the (k-1)th step of the search procedure, Note that initially the feature set is an empty set, i.e.

26 $$X_0 \equiv \Xi_0 \equiv \emptyset$$

and the final feature set, X, is given as

27 $$X \equiv X_d.$$

In contrast, the initial feature set in the "top down" methods, $\bar{X}_0$, is given as

28 $$\bar{X}_0 \equiv \bar{\Xi}_0 \equiv Y.$$

By analogy, successively reduced feature sets $\bar{X}_k$, k=1,2,...,D-d are then constructed so that

29 $$J(\bar{X}_k) = \max_{\{\bar{\Xi}_k\}} J(\bar{\Xi}_k),$$

where $\{\bar{\Xi}_k\}$ is the set of all the candidate combinations of features, $\bar{\Xi}_k$. Here the feature set, X, is defined as

30 $$X = \bar{X}_{D-d}.$$

5.5. OPTIMAL SEARCH

The only optimal search method in which all the possible subsets, Ξ_n, of d out of D attributes are implicitly inspected without the exhaustive search is the *branch and bound algorithm.* It is basically a "top down" search procedure but with a backtracking facility which allows all the possible combinations of features to be examined. The computational efficiency of the method lies in an effective organization of the search process. By virtue of this process, detailed enumeration of many candidate feature sets can be avoided without undermining optimality of the feature selection procedure. This is achieved by using the monotonicity property shared by the majority of feature selection criterion functions, namely that for nested sets of features $\bar{\Xi}_i$, $i = 1,2,\ldots,k$, i.e.

31 $$\bar{\Xi}_1 \supset \bar{\Xi}_2 \supset \ldots \supset \bar{\Xi}_k,$$

the criterion functions, $J(\bar{\Xi}_i)$, satisfy

32 $$J(\bar{\Xi}_1) \geq J(\bar{\Xi}_2) \geq \ldots \geq J(\bar{\Xi}_k).$$

By a straightforward application of this property, many combinations of features can be rejected from the set of candidate feature sets.

In any branch and bound algorithm, the search is organized so that nested sets, $\bar{\Xi}_k$, are constructed at each stage of the algorithm. First a number of $\bar{\Xi}_1$ sets are constructed by removing selected attributes from the complete set of measurements, Y. At the second stage, from each set $\bar{\Xi}_1$, a number of $\bar{\Xi}_2$ sets are acquired in a similar manner and this process is continued until the cardinality of the sets being constructed is reduced to d. In effect, this process amounts to generating a solution tree where at the k-th stage of the algorithm the features removed from each $\bar{\Xi}_{k-1}$ set constitute nodes of the tree at the k-th level. In Figure 5.6 an example of this construction process is illustrated for a case where 2 features out of 6 measurements are to be selected. At most two branches (two successive nodes) are allowed from all the nodes at each stage of the algorithm.

Suppose that some branches of a solution tree have already been explored up to level (D-d) and that the criterion function for the current best feature set, $\bar{\Xi}_{D-d}$, equals B, i.e., $J(\bar{\Xi}_{D-d})=B$. Now consider a node at the k-th level of an unexplored section of the tree where the value of the criterion function is less than threshold B, i.e.

$$J(\bar{\Xi}_k) < B. \tag{33}$$

Then, obviously, it would be pointless to evaluate the feature sets corresponding to the portion of the tree branching from this node since these sets are nested and by virtue of 32 they will be inferior to the current best feature set. Returning to the example in Figure 5.6, if A is such a point, then four candidate sets need not be evaluated. This is the main principle of reducing the computational burden of the exhaustive search.

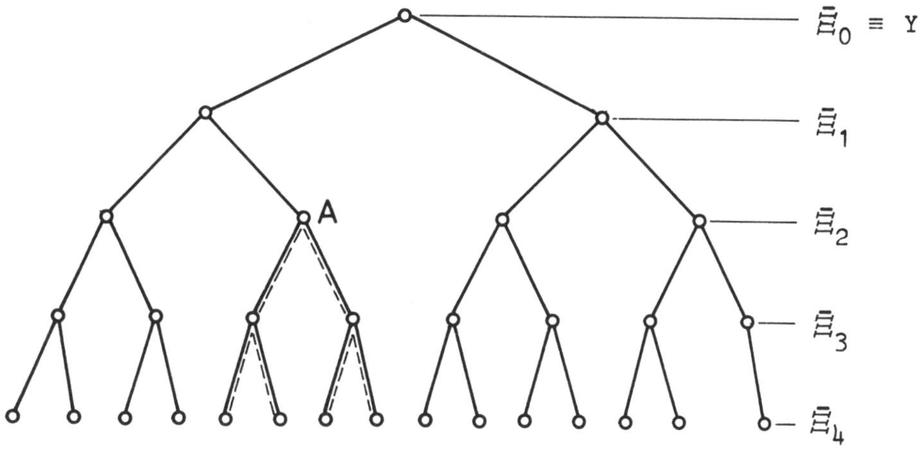

Figure 5.6. Example of a feature set search tree.

Given a pair of numbers (D,d), a large number of different solution trees could, of course, be constructed. However, for a search to be efficient, certain rules should be observed when a solution tree is being generated. First of all, the generating process should be systematic to ensure that the algorithm is easily programmable. Second, the section of a tree branching from a node associated with a low value of the criterion function is more likely to be rejected than the branches originating from a node where the criterion function takes a large value. It is advantageous, therefore, to relate the number of successive nodes to each node to the magnitude of the criterion function at that node. In other words, the tree should be asymmetrical. Third, a tree must have D-d levels to ensure that the cardinality of the candidate feature sets corresponding to the terminal nodes of the tree is d.

A solution tree satisfying the above requirements is shown in Figure 5.7 (for D = 6 and d = 2). Each node has a number of successors depending on the node level and the number of available measurements from which attributes to be discarded can be chosen. For instance, at the zero node, all D measurements are available for selecting the first level nodes but at least D-d-1 (the number of remaining levels) attributes must be retained in the set of available descriptors to allow for completion of the tree to the final level. Thus, here the number of successive nodes to the zero node, q(0), is given as q(0) = D-(D-d-1) = d+1 which in the example illustrated in Figure 5.7 equals 3.

In accordance with our earlier discussion, the actual successors, ξ_i^{k+1}, i = 1,2,...,q(k), to each node at the k-th level are selected so that the feature sets, $\bar{\Xi}_k - \xi_i^{k+1}$, corresponding to these successor nodes satisfy

34 $$J\left(\bar{\Xi}_k - \xi_i^{k+1}\right) < J\left(\bar{\Xi}_k - \xi_j^{k+1}\right),\ \forall i<j,$$

since in this particular solution tree the nodes ξ_i^{k+1} with lower indices have a large number of successors. As a matter of fact it is advantageous to select ξ_i^{k+1}, i = 1,2,...q(k), as those q(k) attributes in the set of available measurements which yield the lowest values of the criterion function, for the lower the criterion function at a node the more probable it is that the node will be rejected. This strategy

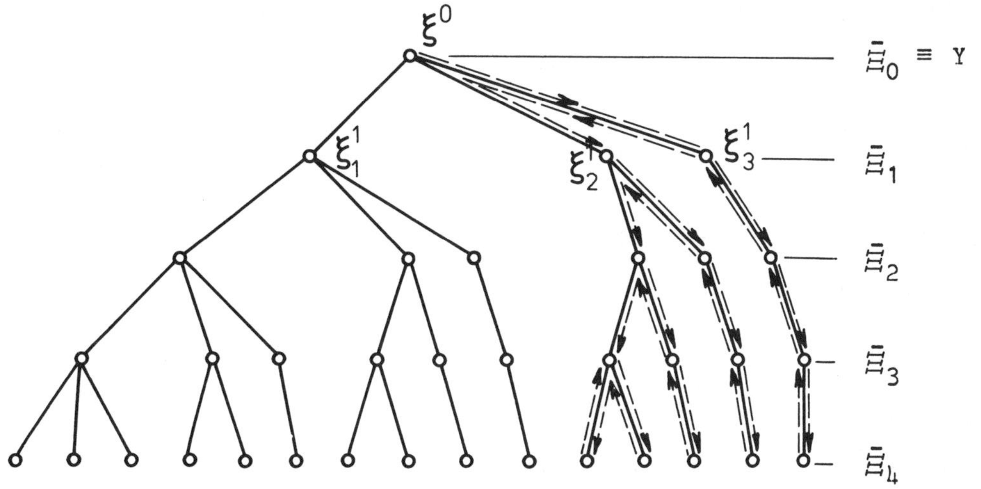

Figure 5.7. Example of the solution tree for the branch and bound algorithm.

may seem paradoxical, since our aim is to find the feature set with the largest possible measure of class separability. However, recalling that we are implicitly inspecting all the possible feature sets anyway, there is no cause for concern.

The solution tree is actually not constructed level by level but from the least dense part of the tree to the part with most branches (from right to left). First the single right-most branch is generated and the magnitude of the separability measure at the terminal node is taken as the current threshold. We then return to the nearest branching node and generate the next right-most branch of the tree. If at any node the criterion function takes on a value that is smaller than the threshold, the search of the section of tree originating from this node is abandoned and the algorithm backtracks to the nearest branching point in a lower level. The next right most branch is then generated. This process is continued until the whole tree is constructed.

If the final level is reached while a branch is being generated, this means that the set of features corresponding to the terminal node of the branch yields a greater value of the criterion function than the current threshold and this feature set must, therefore, be the best set of features found so far. The threshold is then updated and after backtracking to the nearest branching point, the next section of the tree is then generated. The path illustrating this construction process for the solution tree in Figure 5.7 is marked by a dashed line.

We shall now give a formal statement of the algorithm which should clarify any ambiguity of the above informal description of the search procedure. Also it should facilitate software implementation of the algorithm.

The Branch and Bound algorithm

35 Suppose that we are at an arbitrary node at level k. That means that, for all the preceding nodes at levels i = 0,1,2,...,k-1, we have sequences $Q_i = \left(\xi_1^{i+1}, \xi_2^{i+1}, \ldots, \xi_{q(i)}^{i+1}\right)$ of q(i) successor points to these respective nodes. The current feature set after k measurements have been discarded is $\bar{\Xi}_k$. The set of available measurements, $\Psi_k = \bigcup_{i=1}^{k-1} Q_i$, is of cardinality r_k.

Step 1 : Determine the sequence $Q_k=\left(\xi_1^{k+1},\ldots,\xi_{q(k)}^{k+1}\right)$ of q(k) succeeding elements, where q(k) is given as

36 $$q(k) = r_k - (D-d-k-1)$$

and elements ξ_j^{k+1} satisfy

37 $$J\left(\bar{\Xi}_k-\xi_1^{k+1}\right)\le J\left(\bar{\Xi}_k-\xi_2^{k+1}\right)\le\ldots\le J\left(\bar{\Xi}_k-\xi_{q(k)}^{k+1}\right)\le\ldots\le J\left(\bar{\Xi}_k-\xi_{r_k}^{k+1}\right),$$

and $\xi_j^{k+1}\in\Psi_k$. Remove Q_k from Ψ_k and update r_k, i.e.

$$\Psi_{k+1} = \Psi_k - Q_k$$
$$r_{k+1} = r_k - q(k).$$

Step 2 : (Check bound for the candidate successive point $\xi_{q(k)}^{k+1}$). If q(k)=0 then go to Step 4. If $J\left(\bar{\Xi}_k-\xi_{q(k)}^{k+1}\right)<B$ then set $\ell=q(k)$ and go to Step 3. Else, discard $\xi_{q(k)}^{k+1}$ from $\bar{\Xi}_k$ to form a new feature set $\bar{\Xi}_{k+1}$, i.e.,

$$\bar{\Xi}_{k+1} = \bar{\Xi}_k - \xi_{q(k)}^{k+1}.$$

Now if k+1=D-d, then go to Step 5 else set k=k+1 and return to Step 1.

Step 3 : Return $\xi_{q(k)}^{k+1}$ to Ψ_{k+1}, i.e.

$$\Psi_{k+1} = \Psi_{k+1} + \xi_{q(k)}^{k+1}$$

and update r_{k+1} by one, i.e., $r_{k+1}=r_{k+1}+1$. Set $q(k)=\ell$ and $\ell=\ell-1$. If $\ell=0$ then go to Step 2. Otherwise go to Step 3.

Step 4 :(Backtracking) Set k=k-1. If k=-1, terminate the algorithm. Otherwise return $\xi_{q(k)}^{k+1}$ to the current feature set, i.e.

$$\bar{\Xi}_k = \bar{\Xi}_{k+1} + \xi_{q(k)}^{k+1}.$$

Set $r_k=r_{k+1}$, $\Psi_k=\Psi_{k+1}$, $\ell=1$ and return to Step 3.

Step 5 : (Bound updating). Set $B=J\left(\bar{\Xi}_{D-d}\right)$. Store $\bar{\Xi}_{D-d}$ as X_d, i.e.,the current best feature set. Set $\ell=q(k)$ and return to Step 3.

Note that to initialize the algorithm r_0 and Ψ_0 should be set to

$$r_0 = D$$

$$\Psi_0 = Y.$$

The initial feature set $\bar{\Xi}_0$ is, of course, the complete set of measurements Y.

COMMENT : In comparison to the exhaustive search, the branch and bound algorithm affords substantial computational saving. As a rule only a fraction of all the possible candidate feature sets need be enumerated to find the optimal set of features, with the reduction factor of computation costs being most dramatic for $d \cong D/2$. Note, however, that in addition to the sets, $\bar{\Xi}_{D-d}$, which correspond to the terminal nodes of the fully generated branches, all the sets $\bar{X}_{D-d+j}$, $j=1,2,\ldots,D-d$, must also be evaluated. Thus the actual number of inspected sets is somewhat higher. This should be borne in mind when we are deciding whether to use the branch and bound algorithm or opt for the exhaustive search which for very small values of d or values of d approaching D may be less involved.

5.6. SUBOPTIMAL SEARCH

In many pattern recognition problems even the powerful branch and bound search procedure may not be computationally feasible. In such situations we have to resort to suboptimal search methods and by implication trade off optimality for computational efficiency. In the following, various search procedures are discussed in order of their increasing complexity and reliability. Note, however, that algorithm reliability should not be understood here in the true sense of the word but rather in a probabilistic sense. There is no guarantee that the feature set yielded by a sophisticated suboptimal algorithm will not be worse than the feature set obtained using the simplest suboptimal procedure. Nevertheless, the likelihood of obtaining better features when more complicated search schemes are employed springs from two sources : first, the total number of candidate feature sets explored by more sophisticated search methods is greater than that of simplistic procedures; second, a systematic search which uses information on statistical dependences between measurements is likely to lead to a better feature set than a scheme evaluating an identical number of feature sets selected at random.

5.6.1. Best Features

The simplest and, of course, the most unreliable method of constructing a feature set, X, is to select the d individually best measurements in Y. More specifically, let us rank measurements $y_j \in Y$ so that

38 $$J(y_1) \geq J(y_2) \geq \dots \geq J(y_d) \geq \dots J(y_D).$$

Then the feature set, X, is defined as

39 $$X = \{y_i \mid \forall i \leq d\}.$$

The method may lead to a suboptimal feature set even if all the measurements in Y are statistically independent and, consequently, it should be used only if no alternative is feasible. The only situation where this simple feature selection algorithm will retain optimality is when the criterion function $J(\underline{y})$ can be expressed either as

$$J(\underline{y}) = \sum_{i=1}^{D} J(y_i)$$

or as

$$J(\underline{y}) = \prod_{i=1}^{D} J(y_i).$$

As we shall see in Chapter 7, such a situation would arise, for instance, if the Mahalanobis probabilistic distance measure were to be used in a two class problem with normally distributed pattern vectors the components of which are statistically independent.

5.6.2. Sequential Forward Selection (SFS)

SFS is a simple bottom up search procedure where one measurement at a time is added to the current feature set. At each stage, the attribute to be included in the feature set is selected from among the remaining available measurements so that the new enlarged set of features yields a maximum value of the criterion function used.

The SFS algorithm

40 Suppose k features have been selected to form feature set X_k. Rank the elements, ξ_j, of the set of available measurements, $Y-X_k$, so that

$$J\left(X_k + \xi_1\right) \geq J\left(X_k + \xi_2\right) \geq \dots \geq J\left(X_k + \xi_{D-k}\right).$$

Then feature set X_{k+1} is given as

$$X_{k+1} = X_k + \xi_1.$$

The algorithm is initialized by setting $X_0 \equiv \emptyset$.

The SFS algorithm selects successive attributes with reference to the current set of features. By taking into account statistical dependence between measurements, the feature set obtained by this algorithm is likely to be superior to the one yielded by the preceding method. The main drawback of SFS is that, once a measurement is included in the feature set, the method has no mechanism for deleting it from the feature set even if at a later stage when more measurements have been added this feature becomes superfluous. In other words the feature sets X_k, k=1,2,...,d are nested.

5.6.3. Generalized Sequential Forward Selection GSFS(r)

The GSFS(r) algorithm is basically an SFS method but here, instead of adding one measurement at a time, r features are added to the current feature set at each stage of the algorithm.

The GSFS algorithm

41 Suppose k feature sets have been selected to form feature set X_k. Generate all the possible sets, Ξ_{k+r}, by adding to X_k various combinations of r measurements from the set of available measurements $Y - X_k$. Then select as X_{k+r} that set Ξ_{k+r} that maximizes the class separability measure J(.), i.e.

$$J\left(X_{k+r}\right) = \max_{\Xi_{k+r}} J\left(\Xi_{k+r}\right).$$

In the SFS method, by restricting the number of measurements to be added at each step of the algorithm to one, it is impossible to take into consideration the statistical relationship between elements of the set of available measurements. This problem is overcome in the GSFS(r) algorithm which as a result is likely to be more reliable but, of course, also to be more costly to implement, for at each stage $\binom{D-k}{r}$ feature sets Ξ_{k+r} have to be inspected to find set X_{k+r}. Note that, as in the SFS method, nesting of successive feature sets, X_k, is not prevented here.

5.6.4. Sequential Backward Selection (SBS)

The SBS algorithm is the "top down" counterpart of the SFS method. Starting from the complete set of measurements, Y, we discard one feature at a time until D-d measurements have been deleted.

The SBS algorithm

42 Assume that k features have been discarded from $\bar{X}_0 \equiv Y$ to form feature set $\bar{X}_k$. Now to obtain reduced feature set $\bar{X}_{k+1}$, rank the elements ξ_j of set $\bar{X}_k$ so that

$$J\left(\bar{X}_k - \xi_1\right) \geq J\left(\bar{X}_k - \xi_2\right) \geq \ldots \geq J\left(\bar{X}_k - \xi_{D-k}\right).$$

Then

$$\bar{X}_{k+1} = \bar{X}_k - \xi_1.$$

At each stage of the algorithm the element to be removed from the current feature set is determined by investigating statistical dependence of the features in the set. Also, as in the SFS algorithm, the feature sets, $\bar{X}_k$, $k = 0,1,\ldots,D-d$, yielded by the SBS method are nested. However, the main difference between these two methods is that the SBS procedure provides as a by-product a measure of maximum achievable class separability with the given set of measurements, Y. This can be used then to assess the amount of information lost in the feature selection process. Note, however, that SBS is computationally more demanding than the SFS since, in the former case, criterion J(.) is evaluated in spaces of dimensionality greater than or equal to d while, in the latter case, the dimensionality of the inspected feature spaces is at most equal to the cardinality of feature set X.

5.6.5. Generalized Sequential Backward Selection GSBS(r)

By analogy, the GSBS(r) algorithm is essentially the same as the SBS procedure with the exception that more than one feature is discarded at a time.

The GSBS algorithm

43 Suppose k features have been discarded from Y to form feature $\bar{X}_k$. Now form all the possible sets, $\bar{\Xi}_{k+r}$, by removing various combinations of r attributes from $\bar{X}_k$. Then select as $\bar{X}_{k+r}$ the candidate feature set $\bar{\Xi}_{k+r}$ that maximizes the class separability measure J(.), i.e.

$$J\left(\bar{X}_{k+r}\right) = \max_{\bar{\Xi}_{k+r}} J\left(\bar{\Xi}_{k+r}\right).$$

The GSBS(r) algorithm takes into consideration not only statistical dependence of elements in the current feature set, $\bar{X}_k$, but also relationship between the discarded measurements. This greater sophistication of the feature selection procedure is achieved only at the expense of extra computations for at each stage $\binom{D-k}{r}$ sets must be evaluated as compared with the D-k candidate sets in the case of the SBS algorithm. Once again the successive feature sets are nested.

5.6.6. "Plus ℓ-Take Away r" Selection

Nesting of feature sets can be partially avoided simply by allowing a low level backtracking in the feature selection process. In particular, at the k-th stage of the algorithm we first enlarge the current feature set by ℓ features using the SFS method. From the resulting set, r features are then discarded applying the SBS algorithm. In the following discussion the "Plus ℓ-Take Away r" algorithm will be referred to as the (ℓ,r) algorithm.

The $(\ell-r)$ algorithm

44 Suppose k features have been selected to generate set X_k.

<u>Step 1</u> : Using the SFS method add ℓ features, ξ_j, from the set of available measuremens, $Y-X_k$, to X_k, to create feature set $X_{k+\ell}$. Set $k=k+\ell$, $\bar{X}_{D-k}=X_k$.

<u>Step 2</u> : Remove the r worst features, ξ_j, from the set $\bar{X}_{D-k}$ using the SBS procedure to form feature set $\bar{X}_{D-k+r}$. Set $k = k - r$. If $k = d$ then terminate the algorithm. Otherwise set $X_k = \bar{X}_{D-k}$ and return to Step 1.

<u>Initialization</u> : If $\ell>r$ the (ℓ,r) algorithm is a bottom up search method. Commence from Step 1 with k and X_0 set respectively to k=0 and $X_0 \equiv \emptyset$. For $\ell<r$ the (ℓ,r) algorithm is a top down procedure. Set k=D and $X_0 \equiv Y$ and start from Step 2.

Although in the (ℓ,r) algorithm the problem of nesting has been overcome, the search procedure still suffers from other drawbacks of the SFS and SBS algorithms, namely that groups of features are added and removed from the current set irrespective of their mutual relationship. This problem is resolved in the following procedure.

5.6.7. Generalized "Plus ℓ-Take Away r" Selection

At this stage the reader will probably find as no surprise that the only essential difference between the generalized "Plus ℓ-Take Away r" selection method and the (ℓ,r) algorithm is that the former approach employs the GSFS(ℓ) and GSBS(r) algorithms instead of the basic SFS and SBS procedures. However, we shall take the generalization process a step further and allow each number ℓ and r to be composed of several integer components ℓ_i, $i=1,2,\ldots,z_\ell$ and r_j, $j=1,2,\ldots,z_r$ satisfying

45 $$0 \le \ell_i \le \ell \qquad\qquad 0 \le r_j \le r$$

46 $$\sum_{i=1}^{z_\ell} \ell_i = \ell \qquad\qquad \sum_{j=1}^{z_r} r_j = r$$

Now, at each stage of the algorithm, instead of applying GSFS(ℓ) and GSBS(r) methods, we acquire the feature set of appropriate cardinality by applying successively first the GSFS(ℓ_i) procedure for all i and then the GSBS(r_j) procedure for all j. By splitting the forward and backward selections into a number of substeps, we shall be able to curb computational complexity of the algorithm.

In order to give a formal statement of the algorithm, let us designate by Z_ℓ and Z_r the sequences of elements ℓ_i and r_j respectively satisfying conditions 45 and 46, i.e.,

$$Z_\ell = \left(\ell_1, \ell_2, \ldots, \ell_{z_\ell}\right)$$

$$Z_r = \left(r_1, r_2, \ldots, r_{z_r}\right)$$

The set of parameters (Z_ℓ, Z_r) defines the following generalized "Plus ℓ-Take Away r" selection algorithm :

The (Z_ℓ, Z_r) algorithm

47 Suppose k features have been selected to generate set X_k.

Step 1 : Enlarge X_k by successive application of the GSFS(ℓ_i) algorithm for $i = 1,2,\ldots,z_\ell$ where ℓ_i are elements of the sequence Z_ℓ. Set $k = k + \sum_i^{z_\ell} \ell_i$ and $\bar{X}_{D-k} = X_k$.

Step 2 : Reduce $\bar{X}_{D-k}$ by successive application of the GSBS(r_i) algorithm for $j = 1,2,\ldots,z_r$ where r_j are elements of sequence Z_r. Set $k = k - \sum_{j=1}^{z_r} r_j$. If $k = d$ then terminate the algorithm. Otherwise set $X_k = \bar{X}_{D-k}$ and return to Step 1.

Initialization : Initialization of the algorithm is identical to that of the (ℓ, r) algorithm discussed above.

It should be noted that the computational complexity of the (Z_ℓ, Z_r) algorithm rapidly increases with the magnitude of elements of sequences Z_ℓ and Z_r. Perhaps the most important aspect of this algorithm is that it provides a generalization of all the search algorithms discussed earlier. This is apparent from Table 5.1.

Furthermore, the (Z_ℓ, Z_r) algorithm can be viewed as a search method using the dynamic programming principle of optimization with the successive transition states defined by the numbers ℓ_i and r_j of sequences Z_ℓ and Z_r. In this sense this approach can be considered also as a generalization of various dynamic programming search algorithms.

(Z_ℓ, Z_r) algorithm		equivalent algorithms
$Z_\ell = (1)$	$Z_r = (0)$	SFS, (1,0) algorithm
$Z_\ell = (0)$	$Z_r = (1)$	SBS, (0,1) algorithm
$Z_\ell = (n)$	$Z_r = (0)$	exhaustive search
$Z_\ell = (\ell)$	$Z_r = (0)$	GSFS(ℓ)
$Z_\ell = (0)$	$Z_r = (r)$	GSFS(r)
$Z_\ell = (1,1,1,\ldots,1)$	$Z_r = (1,1,\ldots,1)$	(ℓ,r) algorithm

Table 5.1

5.7. COMMENTS

To conclude the discussion of feature set search algorithms, two notes of warning should be issued. The first relates to the suboptimal search strategies and is merely a reiteration of the statement made earlier that the suboptimality of these strategies must be understood in at least two senses. First of all, when using a suboptimal method, we have no guarantee that the best set of features will be found. Second, the more sophisticated suboptimal search strategies do not necessarily yield a better feature set. The validity of the latter statement has not only been demonstrated experimentally but also analytically. For instance, it can be shown that, in the case of two normally distributed classes, for any given ordering of feature sets satisfying the monotonicity condition, it is always possible to find class conditional distributions which will exhibit this ordering whilst the resulting feature set will not be optimal.

The second note concerns the optimal branch and bound algorithm. Even if a criterion function inherently satisfies the monotonicity condition, the monotonicity property may fail to hold when the function values are estimated using a data set of finite size. The caution is particularly applicable in the case of nonparametrically distributed classes where the estimation of class probability densities depends on a number of control parameters (see Appendix A). In such circumstances the branch and bound algorithm will not even guarantee conditional optimality pertaining to a particular data set.

5.8. BIBLIOGRAPHICAL COMMENTS

The pioneering work in the area of mathematical feature selection and extraction is associated with the names of Sebestyen (1962), Lewis (1962), and Marill and Green (1963).

Most of the concepts of class separability, designed to replace the decision-rule-dependent classification error in feature evaluation, were introduced in the early stages of the pattern recognition field development. Sebestyen (1962) was the proponent of the use of interclass distance. An entropy measure was adopted by Lewis (1962). (Our exposition of generalized entropies follows Aczel and Daroczy (1975).) Marill and Green (1963) advocated a probabilistic distance measure. The probabilistic dependence concept was introduced later by

Vilmansen (1973). The concepts of class separability were reviewed in Kittler (1975). Additional references on separability measures can be found in Chapters 6 and 7.

Lewis (1962) and Marill and Green (1963) were also among the first to address the problem of feature set search. To simplify the search problem, Lewis (1962) assumed independence, and selected features on the basis of their individual merits. Elashoff, Elashoff and Goldman (1967) showed that, in order to guarantee optimality of the feature set, even independent features cannot be selected on the single feature basis. Further supporting evidence was provided by Toussaint (1971), and Cover (1974).

The sequential backward selection of features was first suggested by Marill and Green (1963). Whitney (1971) used sequential forward selection, and other simple algorithms were described by Meisel (1972).

A method of preventing nesting of feature sets was put forward by Michael and Lin (1973) in the context of sequential forward selection. The idea was later refined and developed into the plus ℓ - take away r algorithm by Stearns (1976). The basic SFS, SBS and (ℓ-r) algorithms were generalized by Kittler (1978).

The dynamic programming approach to the feature set search problem was pursued by Chang (1973). A discussion of feature selection algorithms for sequential recognition systems, a subject beyond the scope of this book, can be found in Fu (1968).

The potential of any suboptimal feature set search algorithm to select the worst possible set of features was pointed out by Cover and Van Campenhout (1977).

A real breakthrough in optimal feature set search is represented by the branch and bound algorithm due to Narendra and Fukunaga (1977).

For supplementary background reading on feature selection and extraction, the reader is referred to Fukunaga (1962).

5.9. REFERENCES

Aczel, J., and Daroczy, Z., *On Measures of Information and Their Characterization*, Academic Press, New York, 1975.

Chang, C.Y., "Dynamic programming as applied to feature selection in pattern recognition systems", *IEEE Trans. Systems Man and Cybernet.*, vol. 3, pp. 166-171, 1973.

Cover, T.M., "The best two independent measurements are not the two best", *IEEE Trans. Systems Man Cybernet.*, vol. 4, pp. 116-117, 1974.

Cover, T.M., and Van Campenhout, J.M., "On the possible orderings in the measurement selection problem", *IEEE Trans. Systems Man Cybernet.*, vol. 7, pp. 657-661, 1977.

Elashoff, J.D., Elashoff, R.M., and Goldman, G.E., "On the choice of variables in classification problems with dichotomous variables", *Biometrika*, vol. 54, pp. 668-670, 1967.

Fu, K.S., *Sequential Methods in Pattern Recognition and Machine Learning*, Academic Press, New York, 1968.

Fukunaga, K., *Introduction to Statistical Pattern Recognition*, Academic Press, New York, 1972.

Kittler, J., "Mathematical methods of feature selection in pattern recognition", *Internat. J. Man-Mach. Stud.*, vol. 7, pp. 603-637, 1975.

Kittler, J., "Une généralisation de quelques algorithmes sous-optimaux de recherche d'ensembles d'attributs", *Proc. Congrès AFCET/IRIA, Reconnaissance des Formes et Traitement des Images*, Paris, Fév. 1978, pp. 678-686.

Lewis, P.M., "The characteristic selection problem in recognition systems", *IRE Trans. Inform. Theory*, vol. 8, pp. 171-178, 1962.

Marill, T., and Green, D.M., "On the effectiveness of receptors in recognition systems", *IEEE Trans. Inform. Theory*, vol. 9, pp. 11-17, Jan. 1963.

Meisel, W.S., *Computer Oriented Approaches to Pattern Recognition*, Academic Press, New York, 1972.

Michael, M., and Lin, W.C., "Experimental study of information measures and inter-intra class distance ratios on feature selection and ordering", *IEEE Trans. Systems Man Cybernet.*, vol. 3, pp. 172-181, 1973.

Narendra, P.M., and Fukunaga K., "A branch and bound algorithm for feature subset selection", *IEEE Trans. Comput.*, vol. 26, pp. 917-922, Sept. 1977.

Sebestyen G., *Decision Making Processes in Pattern Recognition*, Macmillan, New York, 1962.

Stearns, S.D., "On selecting features for pattern classifiers", *Proc. Third Internat. Conf. Pattern Recognition*, Coronado, Ca, 1976, pp. 71-75.

Toussaint, G.T., "Note on the optimal selection of independent binary features for pattern recognition", *IEEE Trans. Inform. Theory*, vol. 17, p. 618, 1971.

Vilmansen, T.R., "Feature evaluation with measures of probabilistic dependence, *IEEE Trans. Comput.*, vol. 22, pp. 381-388, 1973.

Whitney, A., "A direct method of nonparametric measurement selection", *IEEE Trans. Comput.*, vol. 20, pp. 1100-1103, 1971.

5.10 PROBLEMS

1. Show that the Battacharyya coefficient

$$J_{12} = -\ln \int \left[p(\underline{x}|\omega_1)p(\underline{x}|\omega_2) \right]^{1/2} d\underline{x}$$

is a probabilistic distance measure. Comment on the effect of a nonoverlapping pair of classes on the multiclass criterion

$$J = \sum_i \sum_{j>i} J_{ij}.$$

Suggest an alternative multiclass criterion which curbs the dominance of two, well separated classes.

2. Let $p(\underline{x}|\omega_i) \sim \mathcal{N}(\underline{\mu}_i, \Sigma_i)$, i=1,2. Show that, under the assumption of conditional independence of the components x_j, j=1,...,d, of $\underline{x}$, the feature evaluation measure

$$J = \int \left[p(\underline{x}|\omega_1) - p(\underline{x}|\omega_2) \right] \cdot \ln \frac{p(\underline{x}|\omega_1)}{p(\underline{x}|\omega_2)} d\underline{x}$$

can be expressed as

$$J = \sum_{j=1}^{d} J_j.$$

where J_j is a function of x_j only.

3. Let x_i, i=1,2,3, be conditionally independent binary valued features with $P(x_i=1|\omega_1)=\alpha_i$, and $P(x_i=1|\omega_2)=\beta_i$. Show that under the assumption of equiprobable classes, and α_i, β_i satisfying conditions (a) $\alpha_i<\beta_i$, $\forall i$, (b) $\beta_1-\alpha_1>\beta_2-\alpha_2>\beta_3-\alpha_3$, the minimum error probability $e(x_i)$ when ith feature alone is used satisfies

$$e(x_1) < e(x_2) < e(x_3).$$

4. It can be shown that for the previous problem the error probability of two features used jointly is given by

$$e(x_i,x_j) = \frac{1}{2}\left[e(x_i)+e(x_j)-(\beta_i-\alpha_i)|e(x_j)-\alpha_j|-(\beta_j-\alpha_j)|e(x_i)-\alpha_i|\right].$$

Find the conditions under which $e(x_1,x_2)<e(x_2,x_3)$. Hence, show that the best pair of features does not have to contain the best single feature.

5. Let M_j and Σ_j be j×j symmetric parameter matrices associated with the feature set $\bar{X}_j$, j=0,1,...,D-1. M_j and Σ_j satisfy $|M_j|\geq 0$, and $|\Sigma_j|>0$. Suppose that for nested $\bar{X}_j$ the matrices M_j, Σ_j can be obtained from M_k, Σ_k, j<k, by deleting appropriate rows and columns of M_k and Σ_k.

Now consider the feature selection criterion

$$J(\bar{X}_j) = \mathrm{tr}\left(M_j\Sigma_j^{-1}\right).$$

Show that $J(\bar{X}_j)$ satisfies the set inclusion monotonicity property.

6. Let $p(\underline{x}|\omega_i)$, i=1,2, be uniform p.d.f.s defined on squares $A_iB_iC_iD_i$ where

$A_1=(0,0)$ $B_1=(0,1)$ $C_1=(1,1)$ $D_1=(1,0)$

$A_2=(1,-0.5)$ $B_2=(1,0.5)$ $C_2=(2,0.5)$ $D_2=(2,-0.5)$.

Show that the classification error incurred by the nearest mean decision rule does not satisfy the monotonicity property.

Chapter 6

INTERCLASS DISTANCE MEASURES IN FEATURE SELECTION AND EXTRACTION

6.1. INTRODUCTION

The ability to classify patterns by machine relies on the implied assumption that classes occupy distinct regions in the pattern space. Intuitively, the more distant the classes are from each other, the better the chances of successful recognition of class membership of patterns. It is reasonable, therefore, to select as the feature space that d-dimensional subspace of the pattern representation space in which the classes are maximally separated. More specifically, denote the distance between d-dimensional feature vectors $\underline{\xi}_{ik}$, $\underline{\xi}_{j\ell}$, from classes ω_i and ω_j respectively by $\delta\left(\underline{\xi}_{ik}, \underline{\xi}_{j\ell}\right)$. Then we shall seek as a feature vector, $\underline{x}$, the one that maximizes the average distance between elements of c classes, $J(\underline{\xi})$, defined as

$$J(\underline{\xi}) = \frac{1}{2} \sum_{i=1}^{c} P_i \sum_{j=1}^{c} P_j \frac{1}{n_i n_j} \sum_{k=1}^{n_i} \sum_{\ell=1}^{n_j} \delta\left(\underline{\xi}_{ik}, \underline{\xi}_{j\ell}\right), \tag{1}$$

where n_i denotes the number of training patterns from class ω_i in the design set $\mathcal{S}_n$.

This particular definition of the average distance assumes the knowledge of *a priori* class probabilities P_i. When these probabilities are not known, they can be estimated from the design set by observing the frequency of occurrence of patterns from each class. The estimate $\tilde{P}_i$ of P_i is then given by

2 $$\tilde{P}_i = \frac{n_i}{n},$$

where n is the total number of patterns in the set S_n. In this case the criterion function $J(\underline{\xi})$ in 1 becomes

3 $$J(\underline{\xi}) = \frac{1}{2n^2} \sum_{i=1}^{c} \sum_{j=1}^{c} \sum_{k=1}^{n_i} \sum_{\ell=1}^{n_j} \delta\left(\underline{\xi}_{ik}, \underline{\xi}_{j\ell}\right) = \frac{1}{2n^2} \sum_{k=1}^{n} \sum_{\ell=1}^{n} \delta\left(\underline{\xi}_{k}, \underline{\xi}_{\ell}\right).$$

Comparing criterion functions 1 and 3, it is apparent that, in definition 3 any pair of points in the design set contributes to the average distance on equal basis. In contrast, in expression 1 the average distance is cushioned from the effects of unrepresentative frequency distributions of the design patterns over the possible classes.

The optimal feature vector in the sense of criterion 1 satisfies

4 $$J(\underline{x}) = \max_{\underline{\xi}} J(\underline{\xi}).$$

We have seen in the previous chapter that, in *feature selection* applications, criterion 1 is maximized over the set $\{\underline{\xi}\}$ of all the possible combinations of d features out of D measurements $y_1, y_2, \ldots, y_D$, representing the pattern. Optimization of 1 in the *feature extraction* context is carried out over all possible linear D×d transformations W which define feature vector $\underline{\xi}$, i.e.,

5 $$\underline{\xi} = W^t \underline{y}.$$

Thus the feature extraction problem can be reformulated as

6 $$J(\underline{x}) = \max_{W} J(W^t \underline{y}).$$

The interclass distance criterion function given in 1 is of a general form which must be further specified by choosing a particular metric for measuring the distance between two points, $\delta\left(\underline{\xi}_{ik}, \underline{\xi}_{j\ell}\right)$. In the next section, common metrics will be reviewed. Subsequently we shall turn our attention to criterion functions based on the Euclidean metric, and their role in feature selection. The nonlinear metric criterion function discussed in Section 6.4 not only overcomes some shortcomings of the Euclidean separability measures but also bridges the gap between two conceptually different approaches to feature selection : the heuristic approach based on the notion of interclass distance which is the subject of discussion in this chapter and the more sophisticated probabilistic distance measure methods of the next chapter. The last section of this chapter is then devoted to feature extraction and in particular to the discriminant analysis approach.

6.2. A REVIEW OF METRICS

The distance, $\delta\left(\underline{\xi}_k, \underline{\xi}_\ell\right)$, between two points in a multidimensional space can be measured by any convenient metric. A large number of metrics have been suggested in the pattern recognition literature, each having particular advantages and drawbacks. However, it is not the purpose of this section to provide a complete list of these various measures. It would be an impossible task bearing in mind that every minor modification in scaling and dissemblance evaluation of two variates would yield a new measure. Instead we shall mention only the most important metrics commonly used and also those relevant to our future discussion.

MINKOWSKI METRIC OF ORDER s:

6 $$\delta_M(\underline{\xi}_k,\underline{\xi}_\ell) = \left[\sum_{j=1}^{d} |\xi_{kj} - \xi_{\ell j}|^s\right]^{1/s}$$

CITY BLOCK (a special case of $\delta_M(\underline{\xi}_k,\underline{\xi}_\ell)$ with s=1):

8 $$\delta_C(\underline{\xi}_k,\underline{\xi}_\ell) = \sum_{j=1}^{d} |\xi_{kj} - \xi_{\ell j}|$$

EUCLIDEAN (a special case of $\delta_M(\underline{\xi}_k,\underline{\xi}_\ell)$ with s=2):

9 $$\delta_E(\underline{\xi}_k,\underline{\xi}_\ell) = \left[\sum_{j=1}^{d} (\xi_{kj}-\xi_{\ell j})^2\right]^{1/2} = \left[(\underline{\xi}_k-\underline{\xi}_\ell)^t(\underline{\xi}_k-\underline{\xi}_\ell)\right]^{1/2}$$

CHEBYCHEV:

10 $$\delta_T(\underline{\xi}_k,\underline{\xi}_\ell) = \max_j |\xi_{kj} - \xi_{\ell j}|$$

QUADRATIC

11 $$\delta_Q(\underline{\xi}_k,\underline{\xi}_\ell) = (\underline{\xi}_k - \underline{\xi}_\ell)^t Q(\underline{\xi}_k - \underline{\xi}_\ell)$$

where Q is a positive definite scaling matrix.

NONLINEAR:

12 $$\delta_N(\underline{\xi}_k,\underline{\xi}_\ell) = \begin{cases} H & \delta(\underline{\xi}_k,\underline{\xi}_\ell) > T \\ 0 & \delta(\underline{\xi}_k,\underline{\xi}_\ell) \le T, \end{cases}$$

where H and T are parameters of the metric and δ stands for any of the previously defined distances.

The choice of a particular metric depends on the actual application and in general it is governed by three main characteristics of each metric : computational complexity, analytical tractability and feature evaluation "reliability".

In the next section we shall discuss in detail feature selection measures using the Euclidean metric which allows for both analytical and computational simplifications of the interclass distance criterion.

6.3. EUCLIDEAN DISTANCE MEASURES

Let us first of all introduce the necessary notation. Denote by $\underline{m}_i$ the mean vector of the ith class training patterns, i.e.,

13 $$\underline{m}_i = \frac{1}{n_i} \sum_{k=1}^{n_i} \underline{\xi}_{ik},$$

and let the mixture sample mean be designated by $\underline{m}$, i.e.

14 $$\underline{m} = \sum_{i=1}^{c} P_i \underline{m}_i .$$

Now consider the Euclidean distance or, for convenience, the square of the distance between two points $\underline{\xi}_{ik}$ and $\underline{\xi}_{j\ell}$ from classes ω_i and ω_j respectively

15 $$\delta(\underline{\xi}_{ik}, \underline{\xi}_{j\ell}) = (\underline{\xi}_{ik} - \underline{\xi}_{j\ell})^t (\underline{\xi}_{ik} - \underline{\xi}_{j\ell}).$$

Substituting 15 into criterion 1 and using 13 and 14 it is easy to show that the average distance between points in the training set, $J_1(\underline{\xi})$, is

16 $$J_1(\underline{\xi}) = \sum_{i=1}^{c} P_i \left[\frac{1}{n_i} \sum_{k=1}^{n_i} (\underline{\xi}_{ik} - \underline{m}_i)^t (\underline{\xi}_{ik} - \underline{m}_i) + (\underline{m}_i - \underline{m})^t (\underline{m}_i - \underline{m}) \right].$$

The second term in the brackets represents the (squared Euclidean) distance of the ith class mean vector from the mixture mean $\underline{m}$. Intuitively, it is apparent that the greater the magnitude of this term the greater the distance of vector $\underline{m}_i$ from the means of the other classes. As a matter of fact, it was shown in Chapter 4 that the weighted sum of these terms over all the classes is nothing but the average distance between the class conditional mean vectors, i.e.

17 $$\sum_{i=1}^{c} P_i(\underline{m}_i-\underline{m})^t(\underline{m}_i-\underline{m}) = \frac{1}{2}\sum_{i=1}^{c} P_i \sum_{j=1}^{c} P_j(\underline{m}_i-\underline{m}_j)^t(\underline{m}_i-\underline{m}_j).$$

The first term of 16, on the other hand, represents the average distance of elements belonging to class ω_i from the ith class sample mean vector. In other words, this term signifies the average within-class distance. Its weighted sum over all the classes is then the average within-class distance of the patterns in the mixture training set.

Obviously, we look for a feature space where the interclass distance as represented by the second term of criterion $J_1(\underline{\xi})$ is large and at the same time the intraclass distance is as small as possible. It follows that the magnitude of criterion function 16 would not be a good indicator of class separability. However, before discussing more realistic measures, let us express $J_1(\underline{\xi})$ in an alternative manner in terms of matrices $\tilde{S}_b$ and $\tilde{S}_w$ defined as

18 $$\tilde{S}_b = \sum_{i=1}^{c} P_i(\underline{m}_i-\underline{m})(\underline{m}_i-\underline{m})^t$$

19 $$\tilde{S}_w = \sum_{i=1}^{c} P_i \frac{1}{n_i} \sum_{k=1}^{n_i} (\underline{\xi}_{ik} - \underline{m}_i)(\underline{\xi}_{ik} - \underline{m}_i)^t.$$

Then criterion $J_1(\underline{\xi})$ can be written

20 $$J_1(\underline{\xi}) = \mathrm{tr}\left(\tilde{S}_w + \tilde{S}_b\right).$$

The reader should note that, when introducing the measure of class separability 1, it was natural to define this function for a finite number of points. As a result, the criterion function in 20 is expressed in terms of the sample means $\underline{m}_i$ and sample matrices $\tilde{S}_b$ and $\tilde{S}_w$. However, parameters $\underline{m}_i$, $\tilde{S}_b$ and $\tilde{S}_w$ can be considered as sample-based estimates of, respectively, the class population mean $\underline{\mu}_i$

21 $$\underline{\mu}_i = \boldsymbol{E}_i\{\underline{x}\}$$

and matrices S_b and S_w defined as

22 $$S_b = \sum_{i=1}^{c} P_i(\underline{\mu}_i-\underline{\mu})(\underline{\mu}_i-\underline{\mu})^t$$

23 $$S_w = \sum_{i=1}^{c} P_i\boldsymbol{E}_i\left\{(\underline{\xi}-\underline{\mu}_i)(\underline{\xi}-\underline{\mu}_i)^t\right\},$$

where $\underline{\mu}$ is the mixture population mean, i.e.,

24 $$\underline{\mu} = \boldsymbol{E}\{\underline{x}\} = \sum_{i=1}^{c} P_i\underline{\mu}_i.$$

In the following, rather than using the sample-based quantities $\underline{m}_i$, $\tilde{S}_b$ and $\tilde{S}_w$, it will be more convenient to use the population related equivalents $\underline{\mu}_i$, S_b and S_w. This will enable us to compare directly the criterion functions developed in this chapter with other measures. Needless to say that in practical applications of these criterion functions, the population parameters would be replaced by their sample-based estimates.

Thus, in terms of matrices S_b and S_w, criterion function 20 can be rewritten as

25 $$J_1(\underline{\xi}) = \mathrm{tr}\left(S_w+S_b\right).$$

From our earlier discussion, it follows that a more realistic criterion function which would reflect more closely our intuitive understanding of class separability as based on the notion of interclass distance will be the ratio of the second and first terms in 25. Thus,

26
$$J_2(\underline{\xi}) = \frac{\mathrm{tr}S_b}{\mathrm{tr}S_w}.$$

Although criterion $J_2(\underline{\xi})$ takes into account the within-class variability of patterns, it ignores the effect on the actual separability caused by the correlation of pattern vector components. This shortcoming can be overcome by preprocessing pattern vectors by a suitable transformation U so that the average covariance matrix of the transformed patterns is the identity matrix, i.e.,

27
$$U^t S_w U = I.$$

It is easy to see that matrix

28
$$U = S_w^{-1/2}$$

satisfies condition 27. In the transformed space criterion J_2 becomes

29
$$J_3(\underline{\xi}) = \mathrm{tr}S_w^{-1/2} S_b S_w^{-1/2} = \mathrm{tr}S_w^{-1} S_b = \sum_{k=1}^{d} \tilde{\lambda}_k,$$

where $\tilde{\lambda}_k$, k=1,...,d are the eigenvalues of matrix $S_w^{-1} S_b$.

<u>REMARK</u>: Note that the square of the Euclidean metric 9 is identical to $\delta_Q\left(\underline{\xi}_{ik}, \underline{\xi}_{j\ell}\right)$ with Q = I. By analogy, criterion function 1 using metric 11 could be expressed as

30
$$J(\underline{\xi}) = \mathrm{tr}\left[Q^{1/2} S_w Q^{1/2} + Q^{1/2} S_b Q^{1/2}\right],$$

which, in the particular case when $Q = S_w^{-1}$, simplifies to

31
$$J(\underline{\xi}) = \mathrm{tr}I + \mathrm{tr}S_w^{-1} S_b = d + \mathrm{tr}S_w^{-1} S_b.$$

Thus criterion $J_3(\underline{\xi})$ based on heuristic argument corresponds to separability measure 31 which uses the quadratic metric with the average covariance matrix used as a scaling matrix.

Alternatively the problem of feature selection can be formulated in terms of interclass and intraclass scatters. The *scatter* of a cluster of n points in d-dimensional space around a pivotal point is defined as the sum of the volumes of parallelotopes that can be constructed from each of $\binom{n}{d}$ combinations of d points out of n and the pivotal point. If the pivotal point is the mean of the cluster, then the scatter, s, can be expressed in terms of the covariance matrix C of the data points as

$$s = |C|.$$

In this context the covariance matrix C is called the *scatter matrix.*

If a data set contains several clusters or classes then the scatter of points in each cluster averaged over all the classes, s_w, known as the *within-class scatter*, is given as

32 $$s_w = |S_w|,$$

where S_w, which has been defined in 23, is referred to as the *within-class scatter matrix.* The scatter of the class conditional mean vectors around the mixture population mean, on the other hand, represents the *between class scatter*, s_b, i.e.,

33 $$s_b = |S_b|,$$

where S_b, defined in 22, is referred to as the *between-class scatter matrix.*

Note that the between-class scatter s_b has a geometrical meaning only when the number of classes c exceeds the dimensionality of the space d, for only then shall we be able to construct the respective parallelotopes and, algebraically, the between-class scatter matrix will cease to be rank deficient. Since, in practice, d is likely to be much greater than c, it is convenient to consider the total scatter, s_T, which is the scatter of the points in the mixture set around the mixture mean. Denoting the mixture population covariance matrix by Σ, i.e.,

34 $$\Sigma = \mathcal{E}\left\{(\underline{x}-\underline{\mu})(\underline{x}-\underline{\mu})^t\right\},$$

the total scatter, which is a measure of the volume occupied by the elements of the mixture population, can be expressed as

35 $$s_T = |\Sigma| = |S_w + S_b|.$$

Intuitively, the greater the ratio of the between- and within-class scatters, or more conveniently, of the total- and within-class scatters, the greater the spatial separation of classes. Thus ratio

36 $$J_4(\underline{\xi}) = \frac{|\Sigma|}{|S_w|}$$

is an indicator of class separability that can be used for feature selection purposes.

Let us now consider criterion $J_4(\underline{\xi})$ in a greater detail. Since matrices Σ and S_w are symmetric there exists a matrix U that diagonalizes both Σ and S_w so that

37 $$U^t \Sigma U = \Lambda$$

and

38 $$U^t S_w U = I.$$

From 37 and 38 it follows that criterion $J_4(\underline{\xi})$ can be expressed in terms of the diagonal elements, λ_j, of matrix Λ as

39 $$J_4(\underline{\xi}) = \frac{|U^t \Sigma U|}{|U^t S_w U|} = \prod_{j=1}^{d} \lambda_j .$$

Note also from 37 and 38 that

40 $$S_w^{-1} \Sigma U = U\Lambda .$$

Thus Λ is the matrix of eigenvalues of the product $S_w^{-1}\Sigma$. But since

41 $$S_w^{-1}\Sigma = I + S_w^{-1} S_b ,$$

the eigenvalue problem 31 can be alternatively formulated as

42 $$S_w^{-1} S_b U = U\tilde{\Lambda} .$$

Note that the matrix of eigenvalues $\tilde{\Lambda}$ satisfies

43 $$\tilde{\Lambda} = \Lambda - I .$$

Thus λ_j can be obtained as

44 $$\lambda_j = \tilde{\lambda}_j + 1$$

and consequently criterion $J_4(\underline{\xi})$ can be written as

45 $$J_4(\underline{\xi}) = \prod_{j=1}^{d} \left(1 + \tilde{\lambda}_j\right) .$$

Comparing criteria J_3 and J_4 we can conclude that J_4 is likely to be more reliable for the criterion favors the feature space in which the contributions to the total interclass distance are distributed evenly over all the axes of the coordinate system. Thus, in contrast to criterion J_3, it is unlikely that J_4 would select a set of features allowing good separability between two classes but only at the expense of ability to discriminate between all the other classes. In terms of $\tilde{\lambda}_j$, such a situation would be characterised by the domination of the value of criterion J_3 by a single eigenvalue.

From the point of view of computational requirements, criteria J_1

and J_2 involve only computation of inner products of centralized pattern vectors without the need to store any matrices. In the case of criterion J_3, the matrix inversion can be obviated by the application of the matrix inversion lemma but the storage of at least one $d \times d$ matrix is essential. Evaluation of criterion J_4 in addition involves an eigenanalysis or determinant evaluation.

6.4. NONLINEAR DISTANCE METRIC CRITERION

Despite their relative merits, the main criticism to the above criteria is that they are not closely related to error probability. For instance, the values of criteria J_1 through J_4 will be substantially larger for the classes ω_1, ω_2 illustrated in Figure 6.1 than for classes ω_1, ω_2', although in both cases the classes are well separated and the corresponding probability of misclassification is zero. As a result, classes with overlapping probability density functions may in certain circumstances yield greater values of the criteria than classes completely separable. In particular, in case of pattern classes with equal means shown in Figure 6.2, the criteria will give a misleading result regarding class separability. The core of this drawback is that the Euclidean metric is useful for assessing discriminatory potential only in situations where elements of class sets have equal covariance matrices. In the general case, a more appropriate metric which reflects the local probability structure of the data is required.

Intuitively, it is apparent that once a pattern of one class, say ω_i is distant from each element of all the other classes ω_j, $j \neq i$, by

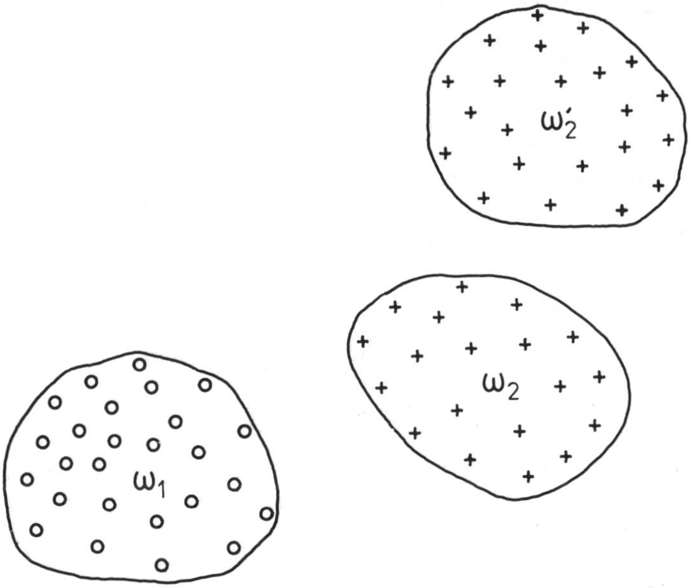

Figure 6.1. Well separated class pairs (ω_1, ω_2) and (ω_1, ω_2') yielding different values for any of the Euclidean distance measures J_1 to J_4

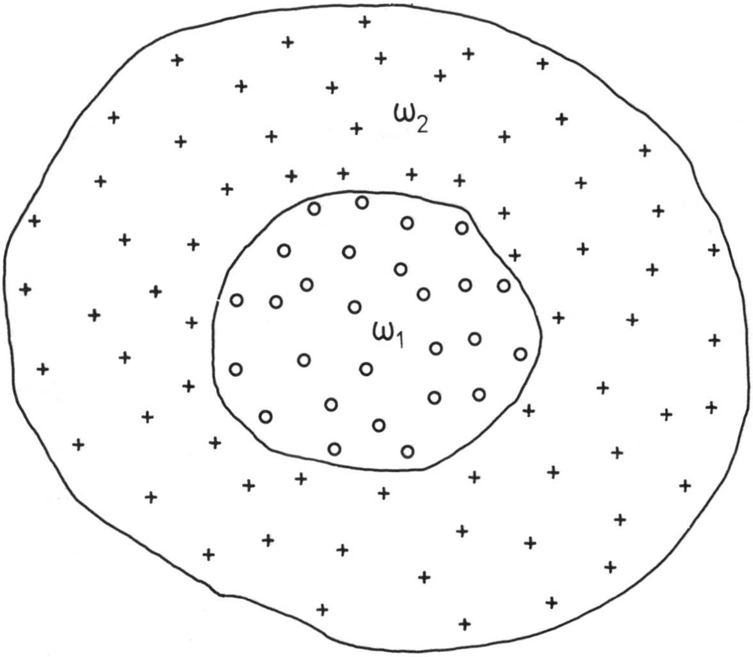

Figure 6.2. Example of two separable classes having identical mean vectors.

at least a "safe distance", T, this point will never be misclassified. Moreover, even if some of the elements of classes ω_j are separated from the pattern under consideration by a Euclidean distance greater than T, the probability of misrecognizing that pattern, which is already zero, cannot, of course, be improved. Consequently, for classification purposes, we can consider that the effective distance between two points $\underline{\xi}_k$, $\underline{\xi}_\ell$ satisfying $\delta_E(\underline{\xi}_k,\underline{\xi}_\ell)>T$ is a constant, H. If, on the other hand, the neighborhood with radius T of a pattern from class ω_i contains elements belonging to the other classes, such a point may produce classification error. Thus, from the point of view of classification, it can be considered to be at zero distance from these neighboring points. We can conclude that a nonlinear distance metric with a threshold T, defined in 12 constitutes a more appropriate basis for a separability measure than the Euclidean metric.

Accordingly we shall now consider as a criterion of feature selection the following separability measure :

46 $$J_5(\underline{\xi}) = \frac{1}{2} \sum_{i=1}^{c} P_i \sum_{j=1}^{c} P_j \frac{1}{n_i n_j} \sum_{k=1}^{n_i} \sum_{\ell=1}^{n_j} \delta_N(\underline{\xi}_{ik},\underline{\xi}_{j\ell}).$$

In order to select a suitable threshold T for the nonlinear distance metric $\delta_N(\underline{\xi}_{ik},\underline{\xi}_{j\ell})$, let us analyze criterion J_5 in more detail. For simplicity we shall consider only the contribution $J_5'(\underline{\xi})$ to $J_5(\underline{\xi})$ due to classes ω_i and ω_j, i.e.

47 $$J_5'(\underline{\xi}) = P_i\ P_j \frac{1}{n_i n_j} \sum_{k=1}^{n_i} \sum_{\ell=1}^{n_j} \delta_N(\underline{\xi}_{ik},\underline{\xi}_{j\ell}).$$

It is apparent that, when the classes are completely separable, then $J_5'(\underline{\xi})$ will attain its maximum, i.e.

48
$$J_5'(\underline{\xi}) = P_i P_j H.$$

This fact suggests an alternative expression for criterion 47 in terms of the hyperspheric kernel $K(\underline{\xi}, \underline{\xi}_{j\ell})$, i.e.,

49
$$J_5'(\underline{\xi}) = P_i \; P_j \left[H - \frac{1}{n_i n_j} \sum_{k=1}^{n_i} \sum_{\ell=1}^{n_j} K(\underline{\xi}_{ik}, \underline{\xi}_{j\ell}) \right],$$

where the kernel $K(\underline{\xi}, \underline{\xi}_{j\ell})$ is defined as

50
$$K(\underline{\xi}, \underline{\xi}_{j\ell}) = \begin{cases} 0 & \text{if } \delta_E(\underline{\xi}, \underline{\xi}_{j\ell}) > T \\ \\ H & \text{if } \delta_E(\underline{\xi}, \underline{\xi}_{j\ell}) \le T. \end{cases}$$

But note that if T satisfies the unbiasedness and consistency conditions of the Parzen estimator (see Appendix A) and, in addition, H is chosen so that

51
$$\int K(\underline{\xi}, \underline{\xi}_{j\ell}) d\underline{\xi} = 1,$$

then criterion 49 can be expressed as

52
$$J_5'(\underline{\xi}) = P_i P_j \left[H - \frac{1}{n_i} \sum_{k=1}^{n_i} \tilde{p}(\underline{\xi}_{ik} | \omega_j) \right],$$

where $\tilde{p}(\underline{\xi}|\omega_j)$ is a Parzen estimate of the conditional probability density function $p(\underline{\xi}|\omega_j)$.

Let us now consider the implications of imposing the above conditions on threshold T. It is well known from the probability density function estimation theory (see Appendix A) that the threshold should decrease as the number of samples in the training set increases. This is quite interesting for, intuitively, we would tend to let the "safe distance" decrease with increasing sample size to ensure that the nonlinear metric is only locally sensitive.

But even more interesting is that the p.d.f. estimation theory agrees with the concept of a "safe distance" in the sense that the absence of points from, e.g., class ω_j in the T-neighborhood of a pattern $\underline{\xi}$ belonging to class ω_i implies that the estimate of p.d.f., $\tilde{p}(\underline{\xi}|\omega_j)$, at this point is zero. Thus, the probability of incorrect decision about the membership of $\underline{\xi}$ is also zero (i.e., $\underline{\xi}$ is safely classified).

When n_j goes to infinity, the estimate $\tilde{p}(\underline{\xi}|\omega_j)$ will approach the true p.d.f. $p(\underline{\xi}|\omega_j)$. Moreover, when n_i also approaches infinity, the summation in 52 becomes the conditional expected value of the p.d.f. $p(\underline{\xi}|\omega_j)$. Consequently, in the limit, criterion 47 can be written as

53 $$\lim_{n_i,n_j\to\infty} J_5'(\underline{\xi}) = P_iP_j\left[H - \int p(\underline{\xi}|\omega_i)p(\underline{\xi}|\omega_j)d\underline{\xi}\right],$$

and, consequently, the multiclass criterion J_5 becomes, after some algebraic manipulations,

54 $$\lim J_5 = \frac{1}{2}\left[H - \int [\sum_{i=1}^{c} P_i p(\underline{\xi}|\omega_i)]^2 d\underline{\xi}\right],$$

which is, of course, identical to

55 $$\lim J_5 = \frac{1}{2}\left[H - \int p^2(\underline{\xi})d\underline{\xi}\right].$$

Note that, for a given sample size, H will be a constant and the maximization of J_5 will amount to minimization of the second term in 55 over all possible feature spaces.

56 REMARK: The second term of 55 can be viewed as a measure of

population entropy, the notion of which is introduced in Chapter 9. In particular, by analogy with Section 7.4, this term can be interpreted as quadratic population entropy. Intuitively, the greater the mixture population entropy (the smaller the absolute value of the quadratic population entropy measure), the more likely it is that the classes will be spatially separated. A low population entropy, on the other hand, corresponds to a large concentration of data which is characteristic of overlapping classes.

By the same argument, a two-class criterion J_6, which is obtained by removing an intraclass contribution from the overall distance measure J_5 and adding constant $\frac{H}{2}$ to ensure that the distance is non-negative, i.e.,

57 $$J_6 = J_5 - \sum_{i=1}^{2} P_i^2 \frac{1}{n_i^2} \sum_{k=1}^{n_i} \sum_{j=1}^{n_i} \delta_N\left(\underline{\xi}_{ik}, \underline{\xi}_{ij}\right) + \frac{H}{2}$$.

can be shown to yield

58 $$\lim_{\substack{n_1 \to \infty \\ n_2 \to \infty}} J_6 = \frac{1}{2} J_p^2,$$

where J_p is the Patrick-Fisher probabilistic distance given in Section 7.2.

Thus, in the limit, maximization of J_6 is equivalent to maximization of the Patrick-Fisher measure which is known to bound the error probability. We can conclude, therefore, that this nonlinear distance feature selection criterion is closely related to classification error. This relationship bridges the conceptual gap between probabilistic separability measures and heuristic interclass distance measures.

6.5. FEATURE EXTRACTION

It has been mentioned in Section 6.1 that the concept of interclass distance can be used not only in feature selection but that it is equally appropriate for formulating the problem of feature extraction. In the latter connection, the separability measure 1 becomes, after substituting for $\underline{\xi}$ from 5,

59 $$J(W) = \frac{1}{2} \sum_{i=1}^{c} P_i \sum_{j=1}^{c} P_j \frac{1}{n_i n_j} \sum_{k=1}^{n_i} \sum_{\ell=1}^{n_j} \delta\left(W^t \underline{y}_{ik}, W^t \underline{y}_{j\ell}\right).$$

In general numerical optimization techniques have to be employed to find the feature extractor W which maximizes the objective function 59. As a rule this involves computation of the gradient of J(W) at each step of the optimum seeking algorithm used. It is apparent that such optimization process is computationally demanding. Moreover, in the case of some of the metrics listed in Section 6.2, the problem is aggravated by the fact that the criterion function is not differentiable. A gradient estimation scheme must then be used to evaluate the gradient of 59. Needless to say, computational considerations seldom allow for this general approach to be used in practice. Instead we have to resort to computationally simpler methods known under the name of *discriminant analysis* which use the Euclidean metric. The next section discusses these methods in detail.

6.6. DISCRIMINANT ANALYSIS

Although Euclidean metric interclass distance measures $J_1(\underline{\xi})$ to $J_4(\underline{\xi})$ discussed in Section 3 can be criticized from the reliability point of view, their simple closed form and the directly related computational simplicity often render these criteria of feature selection the only alternative to more reliable measures. For the same reason, the Euclidean metric plays an important part in feature extraction.

Let us form feature extraction criteria $J_1(W)$ to $J_4(W)$ which correspond to their feature selection counterparts $J_1(\underline{\xi})$ to $J_4(\underline{\xi})$. Recalling 5, 25, 26, 29 and 36 we can readily write

60 $$J_1(W) = \mathrm{tr}\left\{W^t(S_w + S_b)W\right\}$$

61 $$J_2(W) = \frac{\mathrm{tr}W^tS_bW}{\mathrm{tr}W^tS_wW}$$

62 $$J_3(W) = \mathrm{tr}\left\{(W^tS_wW)^{-1}W^tS_bW\right\}$$

63 $$J_4(W) = \frac{|W^t\Sigma W|}{|W^tS_wW|}.$$

Here matrices S_w, S_b and Σ are the D×D scatter matrices of data in the pattern representation space, i.e.

64 $$S_w = \sum_{i=1}^{c} P_i \mathcal{E}\left\{(\underline{y} - \underline{\mu}_i)(\underline{y} - \underline{\mu}_i)^t\right\} = \sum_{i=1}^{c} P_i\Sigma_i$$

65 $$S_b = \sum_{i=1}^{c} P_i(\underline{\mu}_i-\underline{\mu})(\underline{\mu}_i-\underline{\mu})^t$$

66 $$\Sigma = S_w + S_b,$$

where $\underline{\mu}_i$ is the mean vector of patterns, $\underline{y}$, belonging to the ith class, i.e.,

67 $$\underline{\mu}_i = E\{\underline{y}\} \qquad \underline{y}\epsilon\omega_i$$

and $\underline{\mu}$ is the mixture mean, i.e.

68 $$\underline{\mu} = \sum_{i=1}^{c} P_i\underline{\mu}_i.$$

The parametric form of criteria 60 to 63 allows for a considerable simplification of the optimization process by which feature extraction matrix W is determined and in the majority of cases the optimization problem can be solved analytically, yielding an explicit expression for feature extractor W. The following derivations make use of the rules for differentiation of scalar functions of matrix variables given in Appendix B.

6.6.1. Criterion $J_1(W)$

In Section 6.3 it has been pointed out that criterion $J_1(W)$ is the least satisfactory of all Euclidean metric interclass distance measures. The main deficiency of the measure is the unchecked effect of the within-class distance of patterns on the value of the criterion. In feature extraction this shortcoming, however, does not pose a serious problem for the criterion function $J_1(W)$ can be optimized subject to certain constraints so as to minimize any detrimental effects. For example, the influence of the within-class distance can be diminished by restricting W so that

69 $$\mathrm{tr}\left\{W^t S_w W\right\} = \text{constant}.$$

In general, any number k of constraints may be imposed on feature extractor W, i.e.,

70 $$tr\left\{W^tC_jW\right\} = tr\underline{b}_j\underline{b}_j^t \quad j=1,2,\ldots, k,$$

where C_j is a D×D constraint matrix and $\underline{b}_j$ is a d-dimensional vector of constants. For instance, if the j-th constraint on W is that its columns are orthonormal, then C_j and $\underline{b}_j$ must be set respectively to $C_j = I$ and

71 $$\underline{b}_j = [1,1,\ldots,1]^t.$$

The constrained objective function is then given as

72 $$g(W) = J_1(W) - \sum_{j=1}^{k} tr\left\{\Lambda_jW^tC_jW - \Lambda_j\underline{b}_j\underline{b}_j^t\right\},$$

where Λ_j is the d×d diagonal matrix of unknown Lagrange multipliers associated with the j-th constraint. The feature extractor can be found by using a standard optimum seeking algorithm where at each step W and Λ_j, j=1,...,k are updated in the direction of the gradient of function g(W) with respect to W and Λ_j, j=1,...,k.

73 <u>ONE CONSTRAINT</u>: If only one constraint is imposed on the feature extractor, then optimal matrix W can be found analytically. Setting the gradient of g(W) to zero, i.e.,

$$\nabla g(W) = (S_w + S_b)W - CW\Lambda = 0,$$

we find that W can be obtained by solving the eigenvalue problem

74 $$C^{-1}(S_w + S_b)W - W\Lambda = 0.$$

Then the columns of the feature extractor will be eigenvectors of matrix $C^{-1}(S_w + S_b)$.

75 <u>REMARK</u>: From 74 we have

76 $$W^{-1}C^{-1}(S_w + S_b)W = (W^tCW)^{-1}W^t(S_w + S_b)W = \Lambda.$$

Since both matrices $(W^tCW)^{-1}$ and $W^t(S_w + S_b)W$ are symmetric and positive definite, their product can be a diagonal matrix only if W^tCW and $W^t(S_w + S_b)W$ are both diagonal, i.e.,

$$W^t(S_w + S_b)W = \Lambda_\Sigma$$

77

$$W^tCW = \Lambda_C.$$

Scaling the columns of W so that $\Lambda_C = I$, i.e.,

78 $$W^tCW = I,$$

then we get $\Lambda_\Sigma = \Lambda$, i.e.

79 $$W^t(S_w + S_b)W = \Lambda.$$

Using 78, 79 and 76, criterion $J_1(W)$ can be expressed as

80 $$J_1(W) = \mathrm{tr}\{W^tCW\Lambda\} = \mathrm{tr}\Lambda = \sum_{j=1}^{d} \lambda_j.$$

Hence $J_1(W)$ will attain a maximum if eigenvectors of $C^{-1}(S_w + S_b)$ constituting matrix W are selected in the descending order of the corresponding eigenvalues, i.e.

81 $$\lambda_1 \geq \lambda_2 \geq \dots \geq \lambda_d \geq \dots \lambda_D.$$

82 <u>EXAMPLE</u>: Our task is to find the optimal feature extractor W that maximizes the interclass distance while keeping the contributions of the individual axes of the feature space to the within-class distance constant.

In this problem, the constraint matrix C is simply the average within-class covariance matrix S_w. Hence matrix W is the system of d eigenvectors of matrix

83 $$S_w^{-1}(S_w + S_b) = I + S_w^{-1}S_b$$

associated with the largest eigenvalues. Substituting 83 in 74 we get

84 $$S_w^{-1}S_bW - W(\Lambda - I) = S_w^{-1}S_bW - W\tilde{\Lambda} = 0.$$

Since the rank of $S_w^{-1}S_b$ is at most c-1, D-c+1 eigenvalues, $\tilde{\lambda}_j$, of $S_w^{-1}S_b$ will be zero and, therefore, they will not contribute to the interclass distance in the feature space. All relevant information will be conveyed by d=c-1 eigenvectors associated with the nonzero eigenvalues of matrix $S_w^{-1}S_b$ (or eigenvalues of $S_w^{-1}\Sigma$ greater than unity).

6.6.2. Criterion $J_2(W)$

Differentiate $J_2(W)$ to find the stationary point, i.e.

$$\nabla J_2(W) = 2\,\frac{S_bW\mathrm{tr}\{W^tS_wW\} - S_wW\mathrm{tr}\{W^tS_bW\}}{\left[\mathrm{tr}\{W^tS_wW\}\right]^2} = 0.$$

This can be further simplified to

$$S_bW - S_wWJ_2(W) = 0.$$

Hence W is the eigenvector of $S_w^{-1}S_b$ corresponding to the largest eigenvalue, $\tilde{\lambda}_1=J_2(W)$. A complete solution can be induced by considering criterion

85 $$J_2(W) = \frac{\mathrm{tr}\{W^tS_bW\}}{\mathrm{tr}\{\tilde{\Lambda}W^tS_wW\}}.$$

Then matrix W is defined by

86 $$S_bW - S_wW\tilde{\Lambda} = 0.$$

Comparing 84 and 86, it follows that the respective feature spaces are identical.

6.6.3. Criterion $J_3(W)$

By analogy, the stationary point of $J_3(W)$ is defined by

87 $$\nabla J_3(W) = -2\left[S_w W(W^t S_w W)^{-1} W^t S_b W(W^t S_w W)^{-1} - S_b W(W^t S_w W)^{-1}\right] = 0.$$

Let us denote

$$(W^t S_w W)^{-1} W^t S_b W = U\tilde{\Lambda}U^{-1}.$$

Then 87 can be rewritten as

88 $$S_b WU - S_w WU\tilde{\Lambda} = 0.$$

The solution of 88 is again a system of d eigenvectors $V = WU$ of matrix $S_w^{-1}S_b$ and optimal feature extractor W is given as

$$W = VU^{-1}.$$

Note that criterion $J_3(W)$ is invariant to nonsingular transformations. Hence, without affecting the value of $J_3(W)$, we can take as the axes of the feature space directly the d eigenvectors V, of $S_w^{-1}S_b$.

6.6.4. Criterion $J_4(W)$

Differentiation of $J_4(W)$ yields

$$\nabla J_4(W) = 2\,\frac{|W^t\Sigma W W^t S_w W|\,\Sigma W(W^t\Sigma W)^{-1} - |W^t\Sigma W W^t S_w W|\,S_w W(W^t S_w W)^{-1}}{|W^t S_w W|^2} = 0,$$

which simplifies to

$$\Sigma W - S_w W(W^t S_w W)^{-1} W^t \Sigma W = 0.$$

By analogy, denoting

$$(W^t S_w W)^{-1} W^t \Sigma W = U\tilde{\Lambda}U^{-1},$$

we get

$$\Sigma WU - S_w WU\tilde{\Lambda} = 0,$$

or, alternatively,

$$S_w^{-1} S_b WU - WU(\tilde{\Lambda} - I) = 0.$$

Since $J_4(W)$ is also invariant to nonsingular transformations, we find once again that optimal feature extractor W is the system of d eigenvectors of matrix $S_w^{-1} S_b$ associated with the largest (nonzero) eigenvalues of the matrix.

89 REMARK: It is interesting to note that all four criteria $J_1(W)$ to $J_4(W)$ yield an identical feature space although, as we have seen in Section 6.3, in the feature selection context these criteria have different feature evaluation properties.

90 EXAMPLE: Given two classes with equal *a priori* probabilities and

$\underline{\mu}_1=[1,3,-1]^t$, $\underline{\mu}_2=[-1,-1,1]^t$,

$$\Sigma_1 = \begin{bmatrix} 4 & 1 & 0 \\ 1 & 4 & 0 \\ 0 & 0 & 1 \end{bmatrix} \qquad \Sigma_2 = \begin{bmatrix} 2 & 1 & 0 \\ 1 & 2 & 0 \\ 0 & 0 & 1 \end{bmatrix}$$

let us find the optimal feature extractor.

Mixture mean : $\underline{\mu} = \frac{1}{2}[\underline{\mu}_1 + \underline{\mu}_2] = [0,1,0]^t$

Scatter matrices : $S_b = \frac{1}{2}\sum_{i=1}^{2} (\underline{\mu}_i-\underline{\mu})(\underline{\mu}_i-\underline{\mu})^t = (\underline{\mu}_1-\underline{\mu})(\underline{\mu}_1-\underline{\mu})^t$

$$S_w = \frac{1}{2}(\Sigma_1+\Sigma_2) = \begin{bmatrix} 3 & 1 & 0 \\ 1 & 3 & 0 \\ 0 & 0 & 1 \end{bmatrix}$$

Inverse of S_w :

$$S_w^{-1} = \frac{1}{8}\begin{bmatrix} 3 & -1 & 0 \\ -1 & 3 & 0 \\ 0 & 0 & 8 \end{bmatrix}$$

Since the rank of $S_w^{-1}S_b$ is c-1=1, matrix $S_w^{-1}S_b$ will have only one nonzero eigenvalue and W will be a D×1 matrix, i.e., $W=\underline{w}$. Note

91 $$S_w^{-1}S_b\underline{w} - \tilde{\lambda}\underline{w} = S_w^{-1}(\underline{\mu}_1-\underline{\mu})(\underline{\mu}_1-\underline{\mu})^t\underline{w} - \tilde{\lambda}\,\underline{w} = 0.$$

Denoting

$$(\underline{\mu}_1 - \underline{\mu})^t \underline{w} = \tilde{\lambda},$$

we get

$$\underline{w} = S_w^{-1}(\underline{\mu}_1 - \underline{\mu}) = \frac{1}{8}[1,5,-8]^t.$$

6.7. BIBLIOGRAPHICAL COMMENTS

The material in this chapter is based on the interclass distance concept introduced by Sebestyen (1962). Feature selection criterion functions, developed using the Euclidean metric, were used by Michael and Lin (1973), and Kittler (1976).

The use of a nonlinear metric for feature set evaluation was suggested by Meisel (1972), and Kittler (1976). The analysis of the sample-based estimates of probabilistic distance measures in Patrick and Fisher (1969) and Lissack and Fu (1976) demonstrated the superiority of nonlinear metrics over the Euclidean metric in the pattern recognition context.

The techniques resulting from the application of the interclass distance concept to feature extraction are related to discriminant analysis. Its origins are attributed to Fisher (1936). The extension of the discriminant analysis approach to the multiclass case was given by Wilks (1962).

6.8. REFERENCES

Fisher, R.A., "The use of multiple measurements in taxonomic problems", *Ann. Eugenics*, vol. 7, pp. 179-188, 1936.

Friedman, H.P., "On some invariant criteria for grouping data", *J. Amer. Statist. Assoc.*, vol. 62, pp. 1159-1178, 1967.

Fukunaga, K., *Introduction to Statistical Pattern Recognition*, Academic Press, New York, 1972.

Kittler, J., "A nonlinear distance metric criterion for feature selection in the measurement space", *Inform. Sci.*, vol. 9, pp. 359-363, 1976.

Kittler, J., "Methods of feature selection in the measurement space based on interclass distance measures", *Proc. 8th Internat. Congress on Cybernetics*, Namur, pp. 330-342, 1976.

Lissack, T., and Fu, K.S., "Error estimation in pattern recognition via L-distance between posterior density functions", *IEEE Trans. Inform. Theory*, vol. 22, pp. 34-45, 1976.

Michael, M., and Lin, W.C., "Experimental study of information measure and inter-class distance ratios on feature selection and ordering", *IEEE Trans. Systems Man Cybernet.*, vol. 3, pp. 172-181, 1973.

Patrick, E.A., and Fisher, F.P., "Nonparametric feature selection", *IEEE Trans. Inform. Theory*, vol. 15, pp. 577-584, 1969.

Sebestyen, G., *Decision Making Processes in Pattern Recognition*, Macmillan, New York, 1962.

Wilks, S., *Mathematical Statistics*, John Wiley, New York, 1962.

6.9. PROBLEMS

1. Let $\underline{a}$ be a point in a d-dimensional space. Find the volumes of regions of points $\underline{x}$ satisfying a) $\delta_E(\underline{x},\underline{a}) \leq H$, and b) $\delta_T(\underline{x},\underline{a}) \leq H$, where H is an arbitrary constant. Compare these volumes for d=10. Comment on your result.

2. Assuming $\sum_{j=1}^{d} \lambda_j$=const, show that the criterion $J_4(\underline{\xi})$ in 39 attains a maximum when λ_j=const/d, $\forall j$. Comment on the type of spatial configurations of classes favored by this criterion.

3. Consider the interclass distance measure J_5 of 46 for c=2. Suppose $n_1=n_2=n$, and let $\delta_N(\underline{\xi}_k,\underline{\xi}_\ell)$ be defined via the Euclidean metric, with the threshold $T=n^{-1/2d}$ and the constant H equal to one over the volume of a d-dimensional sphere with radius T. Show that,

under the assumption of $n \to \infty$, J_5 is explicitly related to the Patrick-Fisher probabilistic distance measure in 7.5.

4. Find the axis maximizing the Fisher ratio

$$J = \left[\underline{W}^t(\underline{\mu}_1-\underline{\mu}_2)\right]^2 / \underline{W}^t S_w \underline{W},$$

where $\underline{\mu}_i$, i=1,2 is the ith class mean vector and S_w is the within-class scatter matrix.

5. Derive the linear mapping W that maximizes the criterion function $J=|W^tZW|/|W^tS_wW|$, where S_w is the within-class scatter matrix and Z is the mixture population covariance matrix.

6. Suggest a method for optimizing the criterion $J_1(W)$ in 60 subject to the following two constraints : a) $tr\left[W^tS_wW\right]$=const, and b) $W^tW=I$.

Chapter 7

PROBABILISTIC SEPARABILITY MEASURES IN FEATURE SELECTION

7.1. INTRODUCTION

As pointed out in Section 5.3, classification error is an ideal criterion of feature set effectiveness. Often, however this criterion function cannot be used in practical applications because of its computational complexity and we have to resort to other measures of class separability. We already discussed interclass distance measures which, although being somewhat unsophisticated, are, from the computational point of view, very efficient. In this chapter we shall concentrate on probabilistic separability measures which are based on the other concepts of class separability introduced in Chapter 5.

7.2. PROBABILISTIC DISTANCE MEASURES

Let us consider, first of all, the two-class problem. In this case, the following measures have been suggested for evaluating discriminatory information conveyed by a set of features :

<u>CHERNOFF</u>:

1 $$J_C = - \ln \int p^s(\underline{\xi}|\omega_1)p^{1-s}(\underline{\xi}|\omega_2)d\underline{\xi}$$

where s is a parameter from the interval [0,1]. The special case of the Chernoff probabilistic distance measure when s=0.5 is known as the Bhattacharyya distance.

BHATTACHARYYA:

2 $$J_B = -\ln \int \left[p(\underline{\xi}|\omega_1)\ p(\underline{\xi}|\omega_2) \right]^{1/2} d\underline{\xi}$$

MATUSITA:

3 $$J_T = \left\{ \int \left[\sqrt{p(\underline{\xi}|\omega_1)} - \sqrt{p(\underline{\xi}|\omega_2)} \right]^2 d\underline{\xi} \right\}^{1/2}$$

THE DIVERGENCE:

4 $$J_D = \int \left[p(\underline{\xi}|\omega_1) - p(\underline{\xi}|\omega_2) \right] \ln \frac{p(\underline{\xi}|\omega_1)}{p(\underline{\xi}|\omega_2)} d\underline{\xi}$$

PATRICK-FISHER:

5 $$J_P = \left\{ \int \left[p(\underline{\xi}|\omega_1)P_1 - p(\underline{\xi}|\omega_2)P_2 \right]^2 d\underline{\xi} \right\}^{1/2}$$

LISSACK-FU:

6 $$J_L = \int |p(\underline{\xi}|\omega_1)P_1 - p(\underline{\xi}|\omega_2)P_2|^{\alpha} p^{1-\alpha}(\underline{\xi})d\underline{\xi}$$

Note that, in the two-class case considered here, the expression for error probability 5.11 becomes

7 $$E = \frac{1}{2}\left[1 - \int |p(\underline{\xi}|\omega_1)P_1 - p(\underline{\xi}|\omega_2)P_2| d\underline{\xi} \right].$$

The integral in 7 is known as the Kolmogorov variational distance, i.e.

KOLMOGOROV:

8 $$J_K = \int |p(\underline{\xi}|\omega_1)P_1 - p(\underline{\xi}|\omega_2)P_2| d\underline{\xi}$$

It should be noticed that when $\alpha=1$ in 6, $J_L=J_K$.

With the exception of the Kolmogorov variational distance, the expected value of the probability of classification error 7 associated with a feature set cannot be expressed in terms of the above measures. Nevertheless, it is comforting to know that all these measures provide an upper (lower) bound to the error probability. In the case of distances 1-3, 5-6 these bounds can be derived analytically while, for the divergence, the existence of such a bound has been demonstrated experimentally.

The reliability of a separability measure depends, of course, on how tightly it bounds the error probability. Ideally, the designer should consider this merit when choosing a suitable feature selection criterion. However, in practice the choice of a criterion function is based chiefly on computational considerations and we shall not, therefore, attempt to rank the above probabilistic distance measures on the basis of the goodness of the respective error bounds.

A very important aspect of probabilistic distance measures is that a number of these criteria can be analytically simplified in the case when the class conditional p.d.f.s $p(\underline{\xi}|\omega_i)$ belong to a family of parametric p.d.f.s, such as the family of exponential functions. In particular, when the classes are normally distributed, that is $p(\underline{\xi}|\omega_i)$, i = 1,2, is given as

9 $$p(\underline{\xi}|\omega_i) = \left[(2\pi)^d|\Sigma_i|\right]^{-1/2}\exp\left\{-\frac{1}{2}(\underline{\xi}-\underline{\mu}_i)^t\Sigma_i^{-1}(\underline{\xi}-\underline{\mu}_i)\right\},$$

where $\underline{\mu}_i$ and Σ_i are the mean vector and the covariance matrix of the distribution of $\underline{\xi}\epsilon\omega_i$, measures J_C, J_B, J_T, J_D and J_P become

10 $$J_C = \frac{1}{2}\, s(1-s)(\underline{\mu}_2-\underline{\mu}_1)^t\left[(1-s)\Sigma_1 + s\Sigma_2\right]^{-1}(\underline{\mu}_2-\underline{\mu}_1) + \frac{1}{2}\ln \frac{|(1-s)\Sigma_1 + s\Sigma_2|}{|\Sigma_1|^{1-s}\;|\Sigma_2|^{s}}$$

11 $$J_B = \frac{1}{8}(\underline{\mu}_2-\underline{\mu}_1)^t\left[\frac{\Sigma_1 + \Sigma_2}{2}\right]^{-1}(\underline{\mu}_2-\underline{\mu}_1) + \frac{1}{2}\ln \frac{|\frac{1}{2}(\Sigma_1+\Sigma_2)|}{\left[|\Sigma_1|\;|\Sigma_2|\right]^{1/2}}$$

12 $$J_T = \left\{2\left[1 - \exp(-J_B)\right]\right\}^{1/2}$$

13 $$J_D = \frac{1}{2}\left(\underline{\mu}_2-\underline{\mu}_1\right)^t\left(\Sigma_1^{-1}+\Sigma_2^{-1}\right)\left(\underline{\mu}_2-\underline{\mu}_1\right)+\frac{1}{2}\mathrm{tr}\left\{\Sigma_1^{-1}\Sigma_2+\Sigma_2^{-1}\Sigma_1 - 2I\right\}$$

14 $$J_P = \left[(2\pi)^d|2\Sigma_1|\right]^{-1/2} + \left[(2\pi)^d|2\Sigma_2|\right]^{-1/2} - 2\left[(2\pi)^d|\Sigma_1+\Sigma_2|\right]^{-1/2}\exp\left\{-\frac{1}{2}\left(\underline{\mu}_2-\underline{\mu}_1\right)^t\left(\Sigma_1+\Sigma_2\right)^{-1}\left(\underline{\mu}_2-\underline{\mu}_1\right)\right\}.$$

Finally, when $\Sigma_1=\Sigma_2=\Sigma$, the Bhattacharyya distance and the divergence simplify to

15 $$J_M = J_D = 8\,J_B = \left(\underline{\mu}_2-\underline{\mu}_1\right)^t\Sigma^{-1}\left(\underline{\mu}_2-\underline{\mu}_1\right),$$

which is known as the Mahalanobis distance.

Up to now we have considered the discrimination between two classes only. In the case of c classes where c>2, the distance measures 1-6 must be generalized. Unfortunately, there is no obvious way of extending the distance measures into the c-class problem. Nevertheless, we can get a reasonable indication of the class separability by evaluating, for instance, the averaged pairwise distance between classes. Denoting the distance between classes ω_i, ω_j by J_{ij} the generalized distance measure, J, is then defined as

16 $$J = \sum_{i=1}^{c} \sum_{j=1}^{c} P_i P_j J_{ij}.$$

7.3. PROBABILISTIC DEPENDENCE MEASURES

Using the analogy drawn between the concepts of probabilistic distance and dependence in Section 5.3, we can readily write down the following probabilistic dependence measures :

CHERNOFF:

17 $$I_C = \sum_{i=1}^{c} P_i \left\{ -\ln \int p^s(\underline{\xi}|\omega_i) p^{1-s}(\underline{\xi}) d\underline{\xi} \right\}$$

BHATTACHARYYA:

18 $$I_B = \sum_{i=1}^{c} P_i \left\{ -\ln \int \sqrt{p(\underline{\xi}|\omega_i) p(\underline{\xi})} d\underline{\xi} \right\}$$

MATUSITA:

19 $$I_T = \sum_{i=1}^{c} P_i \left\{ \int \left[\sqrt{p(\underline{\xi}|\omega_i)} - \sqrt{p(\underline{\xi})} \right]^2 d\underline{\xi} \right\}^{1/2}$$

JOSHI (derived from the divergence):

20 $$I_D = \sum_{i=1}^{c} P_i \int \left[p(\underline{\xi}|\omega_i) - p(\underline{\xi}) \right] \ln \frac{p(\underline{\xi}|\omega_i)}{p(\underline{\xi})} d\underline{\xi}$$

PATRICK-FISHER:

21 $$I_P = \sum_{i=1}^{c} P_i \left\{ \int \left[p(\underline{\xi}|\omega_i) - p(\underline{\xi}) \right]^2 d\underline{\xi} \right\}^{1/2}$$

LISSACK-FU:

22 $$I_L = \sum_{i=1}^{c} P_i \int |p(\underline{\xi}|\omega_i) - p(\underline{\xi})|^{\alpha} p^{1-\alpha}(\underline{\xi}) d\underline{\xi}$$

Finally, for completeness, the mutual information should be included in the list.

MUTUAL INFORMATION:

23 $$I_I = \sum_{i=1}^{c} P_i \int p(\underline{\xi}|\omega_i)\ln \frac{p(\underline{\xi}|\omega_i)}{p(\underline{\xi})} d\underline{\xi}$$

Two points should be noted regarding probabilistic dependence measures. First of all, they are natural multiclass feature selection criteria. Second, these measures cannot be simplified even if classes ω_i, $\forall i$ are distributed normally, for the mixture p.d.f. $p(\underline{\xi})$ occurring in the expressions will not be Gaussian.

7.4. ENTROPY MEASURES

Substituting for α in 5.20 various positive integer values we obtain specific entropy separability measures.

SHANNON ENTROPY MEASURE (α=1): Using the L'Hospital rule we find

24 $$J_c^1\left[P(\omega_1|\underline{\xi}),\ldots,P(\omega_c|\underline{\xi})\right]=\lim_{\alpha\to 1}(2^{1-\alpha}-1)^{-1}\left[\sum_{i=1}^{c} P^{\alpha}(\omega_i|\underline{\xi})-1\right]$$

$$= -\sum_{i=1}^{c} P(\omega_i|\underline{\xi})\log_2 P(\omega_i|\underline{\xi})$$

which is the well known *Shannon entropy*. The corresponding class separability measure J_S

25 $$J_S = -\int \sum_{i=1}^{c} P(\omega_i|\underline{\xi})\log_2 P(\omega_i|\underline{\xi})p(\underline{\xi})d\underline{\xi}$$

is known under the name of *equivocation*. Note, the optimal feature set must be obtained by minimizing criterion J_S, i.e.,

26 $$J_S(\underline{x}) = \min_{\underline{\xi}} J_S(\underline{\xi})$$

QUADRATIC ENTROPY (α=2): Substituting α=2 into 5.20 we get

27 $$J_c^2\left[P(\omega_1|\underline{\xi}),\ldots,P(\omega_c|\underline{\xi})\right] = 2\left[1 - \sum_{i=1}^{c} P^2(\omega_i|\underline{\xi})\right].$$

Note that J_c^2 will be always less than 2 and the entropy will be minimum when the membership of $\underline{\xi}$ is certain. Thus instead of minimizing the expected value of 27 we can maximize $\sum_{i=1}^{c} P^2(\omega_i|\underline{\xi})$. The corresponding feature selection criterion is then

28 $$J_Q = \int \sum_{i=1}^{c} P^2(\omega_i|\underline{\xi})p(\underline{\xi})d\underline{\xi}.$$

This measure is referred to as the *Bayesian distance.*

7.5. COMMENTS ON FEATURE SELECTION CRITERIA

A few comments on the members of the extensive (but not exhaustive) list of probabilistic separability measures given in the preceding sections are necessary in order to provide some guidance in selecting a suitable feature selection criterion. First of all, it should be mentioned that a number of these measures have been included for completeness rather than because of their practical potential. However, we shall adopt a rather more positive approach here and point out the measures that are important in specific situations and by implication expose the measures of no practical significance.

Let us first consider pattern recognition problems with nonparametrically distributed classes. Recalling Sections 7.2-7.4 it is apparent that in this particular case all the measures involve not only numerical integration but also estimation of probability density functions. But, most importantly, none of these measures is simpler than the error probability criterion, which, moreover, is the most reliable measure of class separability of all. Thus in problems with nonparametric class conditional p.d.f.s, the obvious choice of a feature selection criterion, irrespective of the number of classes involved, is measure 5.11.

When the classes are distributed normally, the situation is somewhat different, for the parametric probabilistic distance measures will be much easier to evaluate than criterion 5.11 especially in two-class problems. Moreover, even in problems with classes having nonparametric distributions, it may be advantageous, not only from the computational point of view, to use the parametric measures. For sample sets of a fixed finite size, the estimation errors on parameters of the Gaussian distribution approximating the true nonparametric probability distribution are bound to be considerably smaller than the errors on estimates of the nonparametric p.d.f.s. If the difference in estimation errors is large enough to compensate for any approximation errors thus incurred, the use of parametric measures will be more than justified.

We shall see in the next chapter that the general form of the Patrick-Fisher probabilistic distance and dependence measures play an important role in feature extraction.

Finally, the quadratic entropy appears to be particularly important in the context of the nearest neighbor decision rule since the bound to the expected error probability in terms of this measure is identical with the error bound on the classification error attainable by this classifier.

7.6. RECURSIVE CALCULATION OF PARAMETRIC SEPARABILITY MEASURES

The common characteristic of all search algorithms discussed in Chapter 5 is that the feature sets to be evaluated at the k-th stage of an algorithm are constructed from an appropriate feature set, Ξ_{k-1}, obtained at the (k-1)th step of the algorithm by adding (or subtracting) a small number of features to this set. Since we already know the value of the criterion function corresponding to the set Ξ_{k-1}, the question we are going to consider now is whether the separability measure could be evaluated for the updated set of features by modifying $J(\Xi_{k-1})$ instead of computing its value from the definition.

It is apparent that any possibility of being able to exploit the knowledge of the discriminatory potential of features in set Ξ_{k-1} gained by means of evaluating $J(\Xi_{k-1})$ extends only to parametric measures discussed in Section 7.2 and we shall now consider these measures in more detail.

A close inspection of parametric measures 10-14 reveals their following general form :

29 $$J = \sum_i f_i\left(\mathrm{tr}\{U_i B_i^{-1}\}\right) + \sum_i g_i\left(|B_i|\right) + \sum_i h_i\left(\underline{z}_i^t B_i^{-1} \underline{z}_i\right),$$

where symmetric definite matrices U_i, B_i and vector $\underline{z}_i$ represent parameters of the measures and $f_i(.)$, $g_i(.)$ and $h_i(.)$ are appropriate functions.

Suppose that U_i, B_i and $\underline{z}_i$ are parameters corresponding to a k-dimensional feature vector $\underline{\xi}$ (a set Ξ_k of k features ξ_j, j=1,2,...,k) that is U_i and B_i, $\forall i$ are (k×k) matrices and $\underline{z}_i$ is a k-dimensional vector. If we now remove the k-th element of $\underline{\xi}$ to form the (k-1) dimensional feature vector $\tilde{\underline{\xi}}$ then, by analogy, the criterion function corresponding to $\tilde{\underline{\xi}}$ will be

30 $$\tilde{J} = \sum_i f_i\left(\mathrm{tr}\left\{\tilde{U}_i\tilde{B}_i^{-1}\right\}\right) + \sum_i g_i\left(|\tilde{B}_i|\right) + \sum_i h_i\left(\tilde{\underline{z}}_i^t\tilde{B}_i^{-1}\tilde{\underline{z}}_i\right),$$

where the (k-1)×(k-1) matrices $\tilde{U}_i$ and $\tilde{B}_i$ are the submatrices of U_i and B_i respectively, obtained by deleting the k-th column and row from of U_i and B_i. Similarly, $\tilde{\underline{z}}_i$ has identical elements to the first k-1 components of $\underline{z}_i$. Since $f_i(.)$, $g_i(.)$ and $h_i(.)$ are elementary functions, we can conclude that it must be possible to compute $\tilde{J}$ from J provided simple relationships exist between the arguments of $f_i(.)$, $g_i(.)$ and $h_i(.)$, $\forall i$, in the (k-1)-dimensional space and those in the k-space. We shall now give a theorem establishing such relationships.

31 <u>THEOREM</u>: Let U and $B=\left[\underline{b}_1,\underline{b}_2,\ldots,\underline{b}_k\right]$ be real (k×k) symmetric definite matrices and denote by $\tilde{U}$ and $\tilde{B}$ the submatrices of U and B obtained by deleting the k-th row and column of U and B respectively. Further, let $\underline{z}=\left[z_1,z_2,\ldots,z_k\right]^t$ be a real k-dimensional vector and designate by $\tilde{\underline{z}}$ the (k-1)-dimensional vector obtained from $\underline{z}$ by deleting its k-th element, z_k. Designate

32 $$B^{-1} = \left[\underline{\beta}_1,\underline{\beta}_2,\ldots,\underline{\beta}_k\right] = \begin{bmatrix}\beta_{11} & \beta_{1k}\\ \beta_{k1} & \beta_{kk}\end{bmatrix}$$

33 $$\underline{\tilde{\beta}}_i = \left[\beta_{1i}, \beta_{2i}, \ldots, \beta_{(k-1)i}\right]^t$$

34 $$V = \left[\underline{\tilde{\beta}}_1, \underline{\tilde{\beta}}_2, \ldots, \underline{\tilde{\beta}}_{k-1}\right]$$

35 $$B = \begin{bmatrix} b_{11}, b_{12}, \ldots, b_{1k} \\ b_{k1}, \qquad , b_{kk} \end{bmatrix}$$

36 $$\underline{\tilde{b}}_i = \left[b_{1i}, \ldots, b_{(k-1)i}\right]^t$$

Then the following relationships hold :

37 $$\tilde{B}^{-1} = V - \frac{\underline{\tilde{\beta}}_k \underline{\tilde{\beta}}_k^t}{\beta_{kk}}$$

38 $$|\tilde{B}| = \beta_{kk} |B|$$

39 $$\mathrm{tr}\left\{\tilde{U}\tilde{B}^{-1}\right\} = \mathrm{tr}\left\{UB^{-1}\right\} - \frac{1}{\beta_{kk}} \underline{\beta}_k^t U \underline{\beta}_k$$

40 $$\underline{\tilde{z}}^t \tilde{B}^{-1} \underline{\tilde{z}} = \underline{z}^t B^{-1} \underline{z} - \frac{1}{\beta_{kk}} \left[\underline{\beta}_k^t \underline{z}\right]^2$$

41 $$\beta_{kk} = \left[b_{kk} - \underline{\tilde{b}}_k^t \tilde{B}^{-1} \underline{\tilde{b}}_k\right]^{-1}$$

42 $$B^{-1} = \left[\begin{array}{c|c} \tilde{B}^{-1} + \beta_{kk} \tilde{B}^{-1} \underline{\tilde{b}}_k \underline{\tilde{b}}_k^t \tilde{B}^{-1} & - \beta_{kk} \tilde{B}^{-1} \underline{\tilde{b}}_k \\ \hline - \beta_{kk} \underline{b}_k^t \tilde{B}^{-1} & \beta_{kk} \end{array}\right]$$

We can see from the theorem that, given U, B and $\underline{z}$ and the values of the appropriate functions of these parameters, we can easily obtain the corresponding functions of $\tilde{U}$, $\tilde{B}$ and $\underline{\tilde{z}}$. Conversely, given $\tilde{U}$, $\tilde{B}$ and

$\tilde{\underline{z}}$ we can determine the functions involving parameters U, B and $\underline{z}$. If more than one feature is added to or removed from a feature set then this theorem can be applied repeatedly.

The theorem enables us to compute parametric feature selection criterion functions recursively in both bottom up and top down search algorithms. Note that, in the "top down" calculation of separability measures, the above result is valid regardless of which of the features ξ_j, j=1,2,...,k, is being discarded since the columns and rows of matrices U and B can be interchanged without affecting the argument.

43 EXAMPLE: We shall determine the recursive expression for the "top down" calculation of the divergence of nested feature sets.

First let us introduce the following notation for the elements of the inverse of matrices Σ_1 and Σ_2 in the k-dimensional space

44 $$\Sigma_i^{-1} = \left[\underline{\theta}_{i1},\dots,\underline{\theta}_{ik}\right] = \begin{bmatrix} \theta_{i11}, & ,\dots,\theta_{i1k} \\ \vdots & \\ \theta_{ik1}, & ,\dots,\theta_{ikk} \end{bmatrix}.$$

Rewriting J_D in 13 in terms of the trace operation, i.e.

45 $$J_D = \frac{1}{2}\,\mathrm{tr}\left\{(M+\Sigma_2)\Sigma_1^{-1} + (M+\Sigma_1)\Sigma_2^{-1}\right\},$$

where

46 $$M = (\underline{\mu}_2-\underline{\mu}_1)(\underline{\mu}_2-\underline{\mu}_1)^t,$$

we find that by a direct application of the theorem the divergence $\mathcal{J}_D$ in the (k-1)-dimensional space (assuming that the j-th feature has been deleted) is

47 $$\mathcal{J}_D = J_D - \frac{1}{2\theta_{1jj}}\left[\underline{\theta}_{1j}^t(M+\Sigma_2)\underline{\theta}_{1j}\right] - \frac{1}{2\theta_{2jj}}\left[\underline{\theta}_{2j}^t(M+\Sigma_1)\underline{\theta}_{2j}\right].$$

The covariance matrices $\tilde{\Sigma}_i^{-1}$, i=1,2, in the reduced space are given as

48 $$\tilde{\Sigma}_i^{-1} = V_i - \frac{\tilde{\underline{\theta}}_{ij}\tilde{\underline{\theta}}_{ij}^t}{\theta_{ijj}},$$

where $\tilde{\underline{\theta}}_{ij}$ is the j-th column of Σ_i^{-1} with the j-th element θ_{ijj} deleted, i.e.

$$\tilde{\underline{\theta}}_{ij} = \left[\theta_{i1j}, \theta_{i2j}, \ldots, \theta_{i(j-1)j}, \theta_{i(j+1)j}, \ldots, \theta_{ikj}\right]^t$$

and

$$V_i = \left[\tilde{\underline{\theta}}_{i1}, \ldots, \tilde{\underline{\theta}}_{i(j-1)}, \tilde{\underline{\theta}}_{i(j+1)}, \ldots, \tilde{\underline{\theta}}_{ik}\right].$$

Matrices $\tilde{M}$, $\tilde{\Sigma}_i$, $\forall i$, can, of course, be obtained by deleting the appropriate row and column from M and Σ_i.

49 COMMENT: Note that to evaluate $\tilde{J}_D$ we do not need to know $\tilde{\Sigma}_i^{-1}$, i=1,2. Deferring the calculation of $\tilde{\Sigma}_i^{-1}$ until it is quite clear from the subsequent investigation of candidate feature sets whether the j-th feature will be permanently removed from the feature set, further saving in computer time can be achieved.

7.7. BIBLIOGRAPHICAL COMMENTS

Probabilistic separability measures have a long history which pre-dates the beginnings of pattern recognition by several decades. Before being adopted by the pattern recognition community, the widely used measures in statistics were the Mahalanobis (1936), Bhattacharyya (1943), Chernoff (1952) and Matusita (1955) probabilistic distances. The divergence was originally proposed by Jeffreys (1946) and later popularized by Kullback (1959). The Kolmogorov variational distance is given in Adhikari and Joshi (1956). Pattern recognition specialists contributed with the probabilistic distance measures of Patrick and Fisher (1969), and Lissack and Fu (1976).

The seminal work of Shannon (1948) on information theory inspired the development of entropy measures. In the pattern recognition context, Vajda (1969) is credited with the quadratic entropy, and Chen (1976) proposed the cubic entropy. The Bayesian distance of Devijver (1974) can be shown to be related to the quadratic entropy. The Bayesian distance was generalized by Boekee and Van Der Lubbe (1979).

Mutual information, another information-theoretic measure, was used by Vilmansen (1973) as a model for a family of probabilistic dependence measures. The Bhattacharyya dependence and the Matusita dependence are due to Vilmansen. However, the first mention of dependence measures can be found in Hoeffding (1942) who used the Kolmogorov dependence. The Joshi dependence measure dates from 1964. The Patrick-Fisher and Lissack-Fu dependence measures are given by Kittler (1975).

Other, less known measures can be found in Kailath (1967), Toussaint (1974), Chen (1976), and Boekee and Van Der Lubbe (1979).

Although the subject of error bounds in terms of probabilistic separability measures has been a center of attention in the pattern recognition research for a very long time, its exposition in this book is limited to the discussion in Chapter 2. For additional material on this topic, the reader is referred to the papers of Kailath (1967), Toussaint (1974), and Lissack and Fu (1976). The significance of error bounds was put in the perspective by Boekee and Van Der Lubbe (1979) who showed that almost any measure can be considered as a special case of either the f-divergence or the general mean (Bayesian) distance.

The recursive calculation of parametric measures was proposed by Kittler (1977), and Narendra and Fukunaga (1977).

Studies of small-sample properties of probabilistic separability measures are generally lacking and inconclusive. The first step in this direction was taken by Jain (1976).

7.8. REFERENCES

Adhikari, B.P., and Joshi, D.D., "Distance, discrimination et resume exhaustif", *Publs. Inst. Statist.*, vol. 5, pp. 57-74, 1956.

Bhattacharyya, A., "On a measure of divergence between two statistical populations defined by their probability distributions", *Bull. Calcutta Math. Soc.*, vol. 35, pp. 99-109, 1943.

Boekee, D.E., and Van Der Lubbe, J.C.A., "Some aspects of error bounds in feature selection", *Pattern Recognition*, vol. 11, pp. 353-360, 1979.

Chen, C.H., "On information and distance measures, error bounds, and feature selection", *Inform. Sci.*, vol. 10, pp. 159-171, 1976.

Chen, C.H., *Statistical Pattern Recognition*, Hayden Book Co., Rochelle Park, New Jersey, 1973.

Chernoff, H., "A measure of asymptotic efficiency for tests of a hypothesis based on a sum of observations", *Ann. Math. Statist.*, vol. 23, pp. 493-507, 1952.

Devijver, P.A., "On a new class of bounds on Bayes risk in multihypothesis pattern recognition", *IEEE Trans. Comput.*, vol. 23, pp. 70-80, 1974.

Fukunaga, K., *Introduction to Statistical Pattern Recognition*, Academic Press, New York, 1972.

Hoeffding, W., "Stochastische abhangigkeir und funktionaler zusammenhang", *Skand. Aktuarietidskr*, vol. 25, pp. 200-227, 1942.

Jain, A.K., "On an estimate of the Bhattacharyya distance", *IEEE Trans. Systems Man Cybernet.*, vol. 6, pp. 763-766, 1976.

Jeffreys, H., "An invariant form for the prior probability in estimation problems", *Proc. Roy. Soc. A*, vol. 186, pp. 453-461, 1946.

Joshi, A.K., "A note on a certain theorem stated by Kullback", *IEEE Trans. Inform. Theory*, vol. 10, pp. 93-94, 1964.

Kailath, T., "The divergence and Bhattacharyya distance measures in signal selection", *IEEE Trans. Commun. Technol.*, vol. 15, pp. 52-60, Feb. 1967.

Kittler, J., "Mathematical methods of feature selection in pattern recognition", *Internat. J. Man-Machine Stud.*, vol. 7, pp. 603-637, 1975.

Kittler, J., "A fast method of evaluating parametric probabilistic distance measures for the top-down search of feature sets", *Proc. IEEE Conf. Pattern Recognition and Image Processing*, Troy, NY, 1977, pp. 350-354.

Kullback, S., *Information Theory and Statistics*, John Wiley, New York, 1959.

Lissack, T., and Fu, K.S., "Error estimation in pattern recognition via L-distance between posterior density functions", *IEEE Trans. Inform. Theory*, vol. 22, pp. 34-45, 1976.

Mahalanobis, P.C., "On the generalized distance in statistics", *Proc. National Inst. Sci. (India)*, vol. 12, pp. 49-55, 1936.

Matusita, K., "Decision rules based on the distance for problems of fit, two samples and estimation", *Ann. Math. Statist.*, vol. 26, pp. 631-640, 1955.

Narendra, P.M., and Fukunaga, K., "A branch and bound algorithm for feature subset selection", *IEEE Trans. Comput.*, vol. 26, pp. 917-922, 1977.

Patrick, E.A., and Fisher, F.P., "Nonparametric feature selection", *IEEE Trans. Inform. Theory*, vol. 15, pp. 577-584, 1969.

Shannon, C.E., "A mathematical theory of communication", *Bell Syst. Tech. J.*, vol. 27, pp. 379-423 and 623-656, 1948.

Toussaint, G.T., "On the divergence between two distributions and the probability of misclassification of several decision rules", *Proc. Second Internat. Conf. Pattern Recognition*, Copenhagen, 1974, pp. 27-34.

Vajda, I., "A contribution to the informational analysis of patterns", in *Methodologies of Pattern Recognition*, S. Watanabe Ed., Academic Press, New York, 1969, pp. 509-519.

Vilmansen, T.R., "Feature evaluation with measures of probability dependence", *IEEE Trans. Comput.*, vol. 22, pp. 381-388, 1973.

7.9. PROBLEMS

1. Show that the Joshi dependence I_D and the generalized divergence

$$J = \sum_{i=1}^{c} P_i \sum_{j>i}^{c} P_j J_{ij},$$

where J_{ij} is the pairwise divergence of classes ω_i, ω_j, are equivalent.

2 Derive the parametric form of the divergence for normally distributed classes with the mean vector $\underline{\mu}_i$ and covariance matrix Σ_i, i=1,2.

3. Derive an explicit formula for the Bhattacharyya coefficient for the special case of multinomial distributions, i.e.,

$$p(\underline{x}|\omega_i) = \sum_{j=1}^{N} p_j^i \delta_{xj}$$

where p_j^i is the conditional probability that pattern x will assume value j and δ_{xj} is the Kronecker delta symbol.

4. It can be shown that the upper bound to the Bayes error probability E^* in terms of the average f-divergence

$$J_F = \int f\left(\frac{P(\omega_1|\underline{x})}{P(\omega_2|\underline{x})}\right) P(\omega_2|\underline{x}) p(\underline{x}) d\underline{x}$$

is given as

$$E^* \leq \frac{f(0)P_2 + f(\infty)P_1 - J_F}{f(0) + f(\infty) - f(1)}.$$

$f(u)$ is a convex function satisfying :

$$f(0) = \lim_{u \to 0} f(u), \qquad 0 \cdot f(\tfrac{0}{0}) = 0,$$

$$0 \cdot f\left(\frac{a}{0}\right) = \lim_{s \to 0} s \cdot f\left(\frac{a}{s}\right) = a \cdot \lim_{u \to \infty} \frac{f(u)}{u} = a \cdot f(\infty), \qquad 0<a<\infty.$$

Find the convex function $f(u)$ such that the average f-divergence becomes equivalent to the average Matusita distance

$$J_T = \left[\int |P^{1/r}(\omega_1|\underline{x}) - P^{1/r}(\omega_2|\underline{x})|^r p(\underline{x})d\underline{x}\right]^{1/r}.$$

Hence, or otherwise, determine the upper bound to E^* in terms of J_T.

5 It can be shown that for $R>1$, $S>0$ and $R \cdot S \geq 1+S$, the general mean distance

$$J_{S,R} = \int \left[\sum_{i=1}^{c} P^R(\omega_i|\underline{x})\right]^S p(\underline{x})d\underline{x}$$

bounds the Bayes error probability from above as $E^* \leq 1-J_{S,R}$. Find an explicit relationship between $J_{S,R}$ and the cubic entropy, J_G, obtained by substituting $\alpha=3$ in the expression 5.20. Hence, or otherwise, determine the upper bound to E^* in terms of J_G.

6. Let B be a $d \times d$ symmetric positive definite matrix. Let $\tilde{B}$ denote the $(d-1)\times(d-1)$ matrix obtained from B by deleting the dth column and row. Show that

$$|\tilde{B}| = \beta_{dd}|B|$$

where β_{dd} is the dth diagonal element of matrix B^{-1}. Hence find a recursive formula for calculating the Bhattacharyya coefficient in the case of normally distributed classes with identical mean vectors.

Chapter 8

FEATURE EXTRACTION METHODS BASED ON PROBABILISTIC SEPARABILITY MEASURES

8.1. INTRODUCTION

Any probabilistic separability measure discussed in the previous chapter in the feature selection context can, in principle, be used for determining a feature extraction mapping, $W(\underline{y})$. Recalling Chapter 5, the main goal of this mapping is to reduce the dimensionality of the pattern representation vector $\underline{y}$. In general, a nonlinear transformation would have to be employed to find the minimum number of features for a given level of information loss. However, the computational complexity of nonlinear problems entails that in the majority of pattern recognition applications the feature extractor must be restricted to a linear form. In addition to this practical consideration, the linear mapping is also highly commendable on the grounds of mathematical tractability. Accordingly, we shall restrict the feature extractors discussed in this chapter to linear transformations only. More specifically we shall seek as the optimal feature extractor a $D \times d$ matrix W,

1 $$W = \begin{bmatrix} w_{11},\ldots,w_{1d} \\ w_{D1},\ldots,w_{Dd} \end{bmatrix} = [\underline{w}_1, \underline{w}_2, \ldots, \underline{w}_d]$$

which optimizes a probabilistic criterion of class separability. The feature vector $\underline{x}$ is thus defined as

2 $$\underline{x} = W^t \, \underline{y}.$$

In other words, each element x_j of the feature vector is generated as a linear combination of the components y_k, k=1,...,D, of the pattern representation vector $\underline{y}$, i.e.,

3 $$x_j = \underline{w}_j^t \underline{y} = \sum_{k=1}^{D} w_{kj} y_k.$$

Let us reformulate the general feature extraction problem given in 5.9 for the particular case considered here, namely for the case of linear feature extractors obtained by optimizing a probabilistic criterion of feature effectiveness. Since all probabilistic separability measures are functions of class conditional probability density functions and class *a priori* probabilities, in general, our task will be to find the W that maximizes criterion function

4 $$J(W) = \max_{\boldsymbol{W}} \sum_{i=1}^{c} \sum_{j=1}^{c} G\left\{\int g\left[p(\boldsymbol{W}^t \underline{y}|\omega_i), p(\boldsymbol{W}^t \underline{y}|\omega_j), P_i, P_j, p(\underline{y})\right] d\underline{y}\right\}.$$

In theory, the general objective function in 4 could be optimized numerically. Note, however, that at each step of a search algorithm the optimization process would involve estimation of p.d.f.s, differentiation of functions G{.} and g[.] and, finally, numerical integration. It is apparent that such a complex numerical problem will, in general, be impracticable. However, since the main obstacle here is posed by the numerical integration we shall, in the following, consider some special cases where this problem can be obviated. In particular, we shall concentrate on criteria of class separability that can be considerably simplified by analytical integration.

8.2. GENERAL PROBABILITY DENSITY FUNCTIONS : TWO-CLASS PROBLEM

8.2.1. Preliminaries

In the majority of pattern recognition problems, the class conditional p.d.f.s will be of a general form and it will be necessary to employ nonparametric p.d.f. estimators in order to determine the underlying probability structure of the classes. Inspecting the p.d.f. estimators summarized in Appendix A it is evident that the only estimator that is likely to be analytically tractable if used in conjunction with probabilistic separability measures is the Parzen estimator $\hat{p}(\underline{y})$ with the Gaussian kernel, i.e.,

5 $$\hat{p}(W^t\underline{y})=\left[\rho^d(2\pi)^{d/2}|\Sigma|^{1/2}n\right]^{-1}\sum_{i=1}^{n}\exp\left\{\frac{-1}{2\rho^2}\left(\underline{y}-\underline{y}_i\right)^t W\Sigma^{-1}W^t\left(\underline{y}-\underline{y}_i\right)\right\},$$

where scalar ρ and matrix Σ are parameters of the estimator and vector $\underline{y}_i$ is the ith element of a training set containing n patterns.

Moreover, it is not difficult to see that, among all the probabilistic separability measures listed in Chapter 7, the only criteria which will allow for analytical simplification are the Patrick-Fisher probabilistic distance and dependence measures. Since in this section we are dealing with the two-class problem, the Patrick-Fisher probabilistic distance measure 7.5

6 $$J(W) = \left\{\int\left[P_1p(W^t\underline{y}|\omega_1) - P_2p(W^t\underline{y}|\omega_2)\right]^2d\underline{y}\right\}^{1/2}$$

is more appropriate. As we shall see in Section 8.3, measure 7.21 will be more convenient in the context of multiclass pattern recognition problems.

8.2.2. Patrick-Fisher Probabilistic Distance Measure

Substituting for the class conditional probability density functions in the Patrick-Fisher probabilistic separability measure given in 6 their Parzen estimate with $\Sigma=I$ and expanding we obtain

7

$$
\begin{aligned}
J(W) = \Bigg\{ & \left[\frac{P_1}{(2\pi)^{d/2}\rho^d n_1}\right]^2 \sum_{k=1}^{n_1}\sum_{\ell=1}^{n_1}\int \exp\left\{\frac{-1}{2\rho^2}\cdot\right. \\
& \left.\cdot\left[\left(\underline{y}-\underline{y}_k^1\right)^t WW^t\left(\underline{y}-\underline{y}_k^1\right) + \left(\underline{y}-\underline{y}_\ell^1\right)^t WW^t\left(\underline{y}-\underline{y}_\ell^1\right)\right]\right\} d\underline{y} \\
& -2\,\frac{P_1P_2}{n_1n_2(2\pi)^d\rho^{2d}} \sum_{k=1}^{n_1}\sum_{\ell=1}^{n_2}\int \exp\left\{\frac{-1}{2\rho^2}\cdot\right. \\
& \left.\cdot\left[\left(\underline{y}-\underline{y}_k^1\right)^t WW^t\left(\underline{y}-\underline{y}_k^1\right) + \left(\underline{y}-\underline{y}_\ell^2\right)^t WW^t\left(\underline{y}-\underline{y}_\ell^2\right)\right]\right\} d\underline{y} \\
& + \left[\frac{P_2}{(2\pi)^{d/2}\rho^d n_2}\right]^2 \sum_{k=1}^{n_2}\sum_{\ell=1}^{n_2}\int \exp\left\{\frac{-1}{2\rho^2}\cdot\right. \\
& \left.\cdot\left[\left(\underline{y}-\underline{y}_k^2\right)^t WW^t\left(\underline{y}-\underline{y}_k^2\right) + \left(\underline{y}-\underline{y}_\ell^2\right)^t WW^t\left(\underline{y}-\underline{y}_\ell^2\right)\right]\right\} d\underline{y}\Bigg\}^{1/2},
\end{aligned}
$$

where $\underline{y}_k^i$ denotes the kth pattern vector from the ith class training set, i.e., $\underline{y}_k^i \epsilon \omega_i$.

Let us consider one general term, $I_{k\ell}^{ij}$, of 7 i.e.,

8

$$
\begin{aligned}
I_{k\ell}^{ij} = & \frac{P_iP_j}{(2\pi\rho^2)^d n_i n_j}\int \exp\left\{\frac{-1}{2\rho^2}\cdot\right. \\
& \left.\cdot\left[\left(\underline{y}-\underline{y}_k^i\right)^t WW^t\left(\underline{y}-\underline{y}_k^i\right) + \left(\underline{y}-\underline{y}_\ell^j\right)^t WW^t\left(\underline{y}-\underline{y}_\ell^j\right)\right]\right\} d\underline{y}.
\end{aligned}
$$

Completing the square in the exponent we can rewrite 8 as

9 $$I_{k\ell}^{ij} = \frac{P_iP_j}{(2\pi\rho^2)^d n_i n_j} \int \exp\left\{\frac{-1}{2\rho^2}\left[2\left\{\underline{y}-\frac{1}{2}\left(\underline{y}_k^i+\underline{y}_\ell^j\right)\right\}^t WW^t \bullet \right.\right.$$
$$\left.\left.\bullet\left\{\underline{y}-\frac{1}{2}\left(\underline{y}_k^i+\underline{y}_\ell^j\right)\right\}+\frac{1}{2}\left(\underline{y}_k^i-\underline{y}_\ell^j\right)^t WW^t\left(\underline{y}_k^i-\underline{y}_\ell^j\right)\right]\right\}d\underline{y}.$$

Note that, since the second term of the exponent in 9 is independent of $\underline{y}$, it can be taken out of the integral. Moreover, apart from a multiplicative constant, the exponential function defined by the first term of the exponent is simply the Gaussian p.d.f. with the mean $\frac{1}{2}W^t\left(\underline{y}_k^i+\underline{y}_\ell^j\right)$ and the covariance matrix $\frac{1}{2}\rho^2 I$. The integral is $(2\rho\sqrt{\pi})^d$. Thus 9 simplifies to

10 $$I_{k\ell}^{ij} = \frac{P_iP_j}{(2\rho\sqrt{\pi})^d n_1 n_2} \exp\left\{\frac{-1}{4\rho^2}\left(\underline{y}_k^i-\underline{y}_\ell^j\right)^t WW^t\left(\underline{y}_k^i-\underline{y}_\ell^j\right)\right\}.$$

In terms of the trace operation, an alternative expression is

11 $$I_{k\ell}^{ij} = \frac{P_iP_j}{(2\rho\sqrt{\pi})^d n_1 n_2} \exp\left\{\frac{-1}{4\rho^2}\operatorname{tr}\left[W^t\left(\underline{y}_k^i-\underline{y}_\ell^j\right)\left(\underline{y}_k^i-\underline{y}_\ell^j\right)^t W\right]\right\}.$$

Using this partial result, criterion 7 becomes

12 $$J(.) = \left\{\frac{1}{(2\rho\sqrt{\pi})^d}\sum_{i=1}^{2}\sum_{j=1}^{2}\sum_{k=1}^{n_i}\sum_{\ell=1}^{n_j}(-1)^{i+j}\frac{P_iP_j}{n_in_j}\bullet\right.$$
$$\left.\bullet\exp\left\{\frac{-1}{4\rho^2}\operatorname{tr}\left[W^t\left(\underline{y}_k^i-\underline{y}_\ell^j\right)\left(\underline{y}_k^i-\underline{y}_\ell^j\right)^t W\right]\right\}\right\}^{1/2}.$$

Since feature extraction measure 12 is a highly nonlinear function of matrix W, its optimization will have to be carried out using an iterative method involving evaluation of first derivative of 12, i.e.

13 $$J'(.) = \frac{1}{2J(.)(2\rho\sqrt{\pi})^d}\sum_{i=1}^{2}\sum_{j=1}^{2}\sum_{k=1}^{n_i}\sum_{\ell=1}^{n_j}(-1)^{i+j}\frac{P_iP_j}{n_in_j}\bullet$$
$$\bullet\exp\left\{\frac{-1}{4\rho^2}\operatorname{tr}\left[W^t\left(\underline{y}_k^i-\underline{y}_\ell^j\right)\left(\underline{y}_k^i-\underline{y}_\ell^j\right)^t W\right]\right\}\left[\frac{-1}{4\rho^2}\left(\underline{y}_k^i-\underline{y}_\ell^j\right)\left(\underline{y}_k^i-\underline{y}_\ell^j\right)^t W\right]$$

at each step of the optimization algorithm.

COMMENT: Criterion function 12 will be maximum when the negative terms of the summation approach zero. These terms will be negligible when the exponent which represents the distance between patterns of different classes in the feature space is very large. Thus, in a way, this method is related to discriminant analysis feature extraction methods discussed in Chapter 6 which also maximize the interclass distance. The present technique, however, is more locally sensitive, since the points which are already sufficiently well separated do not contribute to the value of the criterion function. This can be observed from gradient function 13 where the exponential acts as a weighting function moderating the influence of the well separated points on the best direction of search at the current step of the optimization procedure.

8.3. GENERAL PROBABILITY DENSITY FUNCTIONS : MULTICLASS PROBLEM

In multiclass feature extraction problems where classes have nonparametric probability distributions, we could use the multiclass generalization of the Patrick-Fisher probabilistic distance measure defined in 7.16. However, since this approach involves evaluation of all $c(c-1)/2$ pairwise distances, it is, from the computational point of view, advantageous to use the Patrick-Fisher probabilistic dependence 7.21, i.e.,

14 $$J(W) = \sum_{i=1}^{c} J_i(W) = \sum_{i=1}^{c} P_i\left[\int\left\{p(W^t\underline{y}|\omega_i)-p(W^t\underline{y})\right\}^2 d\underline{y}\right]^{1/2}$$

instead. By analogy, the gradient of 14 can be expressed as

$$
\begin{aligned}
J'(W) = \frac{1}{(2\rho\sqrt{\pi})^d} \sum_{i=1}^{c} P_i \frac{1}{2J_i(W)} \Bigg[& \sum_{k=1}^{n_i} \sum_{\ell=1}^{n_i} \frac{1}{n_i^2} \cdot \\
& \cdot \exp\left\{\frac{-1}{4\rho^2}\left(\underline{y}_k^i-\underline{y}_\ell^i\right)^t WW^t \left(\underline{y}_k^i-\underline{y}_\ell^i\right)\right\}\left\{\frac{-1}{4\rho^2}\left(\underline{y}_k^i-\underline{y}_\ell^i\right)\left(\underline{y}_k^i-\underline{y}_\ell^i\right)^t\right\} \\
& - 2\sum_{k=1}^{n_i} \sum_{\ell=1}^{n} \frac{1}{n_i n} \exp\left\{\frac{-1}{4\rho^2}\left(\underline{y}_k^i-\underline{y}_\ell\right)^t WW^t \left(\underline{y}_k^i-\underline{y}_\ell\right)\right\} \cdot \\
& \cdot \left\{\frac{-1}{4\rho^2}\left(\underline{y}_k^i-\underline{y}_\ell\right)\left(\underline{y}_k^i-\underline{y}_\ell\right)^t\right\} + \sum_{k=1}^{n} \sum_{\ell=1}^{n} \frac{1}{n^2} \exp\left\{\frac{-1}{4\rho^2} \cdot \right. \\
& \left. \cdot \left(\underline{y}_k-\underline{y}_\ell\right)^t WW^t \left(\underline{y}_k-\underline{y}_\ell\right)\right\}\left\{\frac{-1}{4\rho^2}\left(\underline{y}_k-\underline{y}_\ell\right)\left(\underline{y}_k-\underline{y}_\ell\right)^t\right\} \Bigg].
\end{aligned}
\tag{15}
$$

The reader should bear in mind that in 15, $\underline{y}_k^i$ denotes a class-ω_i pattern, while $\underline{y}_k$ denotes an element of the mixture training set of cardinality n.

Using criterion 14 rather than 6, the computational requirements will be reduced by a factor of (c-1)/2 which, in the case of a large number of classes, will represent a considerable saving.

8.4. GAUSSIAN PROBABILITY DENSITY FUNCTIONS : TWO-CLASS PROBLEM

We have seen in Chapter 7 that for normally distributed classes a number of probabilistic separability measures, in particular the divergence and the probabilistic distance measures of Chernoff, Matusita, Mahalanobis and Patrick-Fisher, can be expressed in terms of the distribution parameters, that is the class mean vectors and covariance matrices. Referring to our discussion in Section 8.1, since these measures do not involve numerical integration, they are suitable as practical feature extraction criteria.

Expressing the class conditional mean vectors and covariance matrices in the feature space in terms of the corresponding parameters of the distributions in the representation space, $\underline{\mu}_i$, Σ_i, i=1,2, the relevant separability measures can be written down as follows :

CHERNOFF DISTANCE:

16 $$J_C(W) = \frac{1}{2}s(1-s)(\underline{\mu}_2-\underline{\mu}_1)^t W\left[(1-s)W^t\Sigma_1 W+sW^t\Sigma_2 W\right]^{-1}W(\underline{\mu}_2-\underline{\mu}_1) + \frac{1}{2}\ln\frac{|(1-s)W^t\Sigma_1 W + sW^t\Sigma_2 W|}{|W^t\Sigma_1 W|^{1-s}\;|W^t\Sigma_2 W|^s}$$

DIVERGENCE:

17 $$J_D(W) = \frac{1}{2}(\underline{\mu}_2-\underline{\mu}_1)^t W\left[(W^t\Sigma_1 W)^{-1}+(W^t\Sigma_2 W)^{-1}\right]W(\underline{\mu}_2-\underline{\mu}_1) + \frac{1}{2}\mathrm{tr}\left[(W^t\Sigma_1 W)^{-1}W^t\Sigma_2 W+(W^t\Sigma_2 W)^{-1}W^t\Sigma_1 W-2I\right]$$

MATUSITA DISTANCE:

18 $$J_T(W) = \left\{2\left[1 - \exp\{-J_B(W)\}\right]\right\}^{1/2}$$

where the Bhattacharyya probabilistic distance measure, $J_B(W)$, is the Chernoff distance with parameter s equal to 0.5.

MAHALANOBIS DISTANCE:

19 $$J_M(W) = (\underline{\mu}_2-\underline{\mu}_1)^t W(W^t\Sigma W)^{-1}W^t(\underline{\mu}_2-\underline{\mu}_1)$$

PATRICK-FISHER DISTANCE:

20 $$J_P(W) = \left\{\frac{P_1^2}{\sqrt{(2\pi)^d|2W^t\Sigma_1 W|}} + \frac{P_2^2}{\sqrt{(2\pi)^d|2W^t\Sigma_2 W|}} - \frac{2P_1P_2}{\sqrt{(2\pi)^d|W^t(\Sigma_1+\Sigma_2)W|}}\bullet \exp\left\{-\frac{1}{2}(\underline{\mu}_2-\underline{\mu}_1)^t W\left[W^t(\Sigma_1+\Sigma_2)W\right]^{-1}W^t(\underline{\mu}_2-\underline{\mu}_1)\right\}\right\}^{1/2}$$

Since the Matusita distance is closely related to the Chernoff separability measure and, further, the Mahalanobis distance can be viewed as a special case of the divergence, we shall concentrate in our following discussion on criteria 16, 17 and 20.

8.4.1. Chernoff Probabilistic Distance Measure in Feature Extraction

Let us rewrite criterion 16 in terms of the trace operation, i.e.

21
$$J_C(W) = \frac{1}{2}s(1-s)\,\mathrm{tr}\left\{W^tMW\left[(1-s)W^t\Sigma_1W + sW^t\Sigma_2W\right]^{-1}\right\} + \frac{1}{2}\ln|(1-s)W^t\Sigma_1W + sW^t\Sigma_2W| - \frac{1}{2}(1-s)\ln|W^t\Sigma_1W| - \frac{1}{2}s\ \ln|W^t\Sigma_2W|,$$

where for brevity M denotes

22
$$M = (\underline{\mu}_2-\underline{\mu}_1)(\underline{\mu}_2-\underline{\mu}_1)^t.$$

Differentiating 21 with respect to W in order to find the optimal transformation matrix we get

23
$$J'_C(W) = s(1-s)\left\{MW\left[(1-s)W^t\Sigma_1W+sW^t\Sigma_2W\right]^{-1}-\left[(1-s)\Sigma_1W+s\Sigma_2W\right]\bullet \bullet\left[(1-s)W^t\Sigma_1W+sW^t\Sigma_2W\right]^{-1}W^tMW\left[(1-s)W^t\Sigma_1W+sW^t\Sigma_2W\right]^{-1}\right\} +\left[(1-s)\Sigma_1W+s\Sigma_2W\right]\left[(1-s)W^t\Sigma_1W+sW^t\Sigma_2W\right]^{-1} -(1-s)\Sigma_1W(W^t\Sigma_1W)^{-1}-s\Sigma_2W(W^t\Sigma_1W)^{-1}.$$

The stationary point of the criterion function is defined by setting the first derivative 23 to zero. Thus, provided $\left[(1-s)W^t\Sigma_1W+sW^t\Sigma_2W\right]$ is nonzero, matrix W at the stationary point must satisfy

24
$$MW-\left[(1-s)\Sigma_1W+s\Sigma_2W\right]\left[(1-s)W^t\Sigma_1W+sW^t\Sigma_2W\right]^{-1}W^tMW + \frac{1}{s(1-s)}\left[(1-s)\Sigma_1W+s\Sigma_2W\right] - \frac{1}{s}\Sigma_1W\left[(1-s)I+s(W^t\Sigma_1W)^{-1}W^t\Sigma_2W\right] - \frac{1}{1-s}\Sigma_2W\left[(W^t\Sigma_2W)^{-1}W^t\Sigma_1W+sI\right] = 0.$$

The condition 24 can be further simplified to

25
$$MW-\left[(1-s)\Sigma_1W+s\Sigma_2W\right]\left[(1-s)W^t\Sigma_1W+sW^t\Sigma_2W\right]^{-1}W^tMW+\Sigma_1W\bullet \bullet\left[I-(W^t\Sigma_1W)^{-1}W^t\Sigma_2W\right]+\Sigma_2W\left[I-(W^t\Sigma_2W)^{-1}W^t\Sigma_1W\right] = 0.$$

We can see immediately that, owing to the high nonlinearity in W of the expression on the left hand side of the equation, 25 cannot be solved directly. In order to find the optimal feature extractor W we would have to resort to numerical optimization methods as in Section 8.2. However, in the following special cases 25 can be solved analytically.

8.4.1.1. Equal covariance matrices

26 Consider, for instance, the situation where class conditional covariance matrices Σ_1, Σ_2 satisfy

27 $$\Sigma_1 = \Sigma_2 = \Sigma.$$

Then Equation 25 simplifies to

28 $$MW - \Sigma W(W^t \Sigma W)^{-1} W^t MW = 0.$$

Expressing $(W^t \Sigma W)^{-1} W^t MW$ in terms of its eigenvector and eigenvalue matrices U and Λ respectively, i.e.,

29 $$(W^t \Sigma W)^{-1} W^t MW = U \Lambda U^{-1},$$

Equation 28 can be written as

30 $$\Sigma^{-1} MWU - WU\Lambda = 0.$$

This equation will be satisfied if V=WU is the matrix of eigenvectors, of matrix $\Sigma^{-1}M$. Then optimal transformation W is given as

31 $$W = VU^{-1}.$$

It should be noted that the Chernoff probabilistic distance measure is invariant under any nonsingular transformation. Thus we can postmultiply 31 by the nonsingular matrix U without affecting the optimality of $J_C(W)$. The columns of W will then be identical with eigenvectors $\underline{v}$ of $\Sigma^{-1}M$. Note also that, since matrix M has rank unity, the eigenvalue matrix Λ will have only one nonzero diagonal element. Substituting for W^tMW in 21 from 29 we get

32 $$J_C(W) = \frac{1}{2}s(1-s)\mathrm{tr}\Lambda.$$

It follows that the columns of W corresponding to eigenvectors of $\Sigma^{-1}M$, which are associated with zero eigenvalues, do not contribute to the magnitude of the distance measure and they can, therefore, be discarded. Thus we can conclude that the transformation W which optimizes $J_C(W)$ is a single column matrix defined as the eigenvector of $\Sigma^{-1}M$ associated with the only nonzero eigenvalue, i.e.

33 $$W = \underline{v}_1.$$

In this special case it is not necessary to solve the eigenvalue problem 30 to find eigenvector $\underline{v}_1$. By inspection it can be deduced from 30 that $\underline{v}_1$ is given as

34 $$\underline{v}_1 = \Sigma^{-1}(\underline{\mu}_2-\underline{\mu}_1).$$

8.4.1.2. Equal mean vectors

35 Another interesting case is when the class mean vectors are identical, i.e.,

36 $$\underline{\mu}_1 = \underline{\mu}_2.$$

Then the Chernoff probabilistic distance becomes

37 $$J_C(W) = \frac{1}{2}\ln \frac{|(1-s)W^t\Sigma_1W + sW^t\Sigma_2W|}{|W^t\Sigma_1W|^{1-s}|W^t\Sigma_2W|^s}$$

and referring to 24 its first derivative is

38 $$J_C'(W) = \Sigma_1W\left[I-(W^t\Sigma_1W)^{-1}W^t\Sigma_2W)\right]+\Sigma_2W\left[I-(W^t\Sigma_2W)^{-1}W^t\Sigma_1W\right].$$

Setting the gradient to zero and rearranging we obtain

39 $$\left[\Sigma_2^{-1}\Sigma_1W-W(W^t\Sigma_2W)(W^t\Sigma_1W)^{-1}\right]\left[I-(W^t\Sigma_1W)^{-1}W^t\Sigma_2W\right] = 0.$$

Under the assumption that $\left[I-(W^t\Sigma_1 W)^{-1}W^t\Sigma_2 W\right]$ is nonzero, Equation 39 will be satisfied if the first term in 39 is zero. Expressing the product of the bracketted terms in 39 using the eigenvector and eigenvalue matrices as

40 $$(W^t\Sigma_2 W)^{-1}W^t\Sigma_1 W = U\Lambda U^{-1},$$

it becomes apparent that 39 leads to an eigenvalue problem, i.e.,

41 $$\Sigma_2^{-1}\Sigma_1 WU - WU\Lambda = 0.$$

Thus V=WU is a (D×d) matrix of d eigenvectors of $\Sigma_2^{-1}\Sigma_1$.

By analogy with the above discussion the implied transformation of W by the nonsingular matrix U can be ignored because of the invariance property of the Chernoff measure. The optimal coordinate system W can then be formed directly by d eigenvectors of matrix $\Sigma_2^{-1}\Sigma_1$.

It now remains to determine which d eigenvectors should be selected from the complete set of eigenvectors of $\Sigma_2^{-1}\Sigma_1$ so that the criterion of feature extraction, 37, is maximized. Substituting for $W^t\Sigma_1 W$ in 37 from 40 we get

42 $$J_C(W) = \frac{1}{2}\ln\frac{|(1-s)W^t\Sigma_2 WU\Lambda U^{-1}+sW^t\Sigma_2 W|}{|W^t\Sigma_2 WU\Lambda U^{-1}|^{1-s}|W^t\Sigma_2 W|^s}$$

$$= \frac{1}{2}\ln\frac{|(1-s)U\Lambda U^{-1}+sI|}{|U\Lambda U^{-1}|^{1-s}} = \frac{1}{2}\ln\frac{|(1-s)\Lambda+sI|}{|\Lambda|^{1-s}}.$$

Since both the matrix in the denominator and the one in the numerator of 42 are diagonal, the determinants can be expressed as a product of the diagonal elements, i.e.,

43 $$J_C(W) = \frac{1}{2}\ln\prod_{j=1}^{d}\left[(1-s)\lambda_j^s+s\lambda_j^{s-1}\right] = \frac{1}{2}\sum_{j=1}^{d}\ln\left[(1-s)\lambda_j^s+s\lambda_j^{s-1}\right].$$

Inspecting 43, criterion $J_C(W)$ will attain a maximum if the columns of mapping W are the eigenvectors of $\Sigma_2^{-1}\Sigma_1$ associated with d eigenvalues of the matrix, λ_j, j=1,...,d satisfying

44 $$(1-s)\lambda_1^s+s\lambda_1^{s-1} \geq (1-s)\lambda_2^s+s\lambda_2^{s-1} \geq \ldots \geq (1-s)\lambda_d^s+s\lambda_d^{s-1} \geq \ldots \geq (1-s)\lambda_D^s+s\lambda_D^{s-1}.$$

45 COMMENT: Note that for different values of s we could obtain different orderings of eigenvectors $\underline{v}_j$ of $\Sigma_2^{-1}\Sigma_1$. Since the ultimate goal is to maximize 37, we can first set s = 0.5 and find the optimal axes $\underline{v}_j$, j=1,...,d. For these axes we can then determine the optimal value of parameter s. The ordering of eigenvectors will have to be checked then for this new parameter value and if there are any discrepancies a new set of axes will have to be selected and the inspection procedure repeated. This process must be carried out until a stable set of eigenvectors is acquired.

8.4.1.3. Suboptimal solution

46 In order to avoid numerical optimization when $\underline{\mu}_1 \neq \underline{\mu}_2$ and $\Sigma_1 \neq \Sigma_2$, a suboptimal feature extractor can be constructed using the results of 26 and 35 by considering separately the contributions of the discriminatory power due to differences in the class means and covariance matrices respectively.

47 METHOD 1: Use as the candidate axes for the feature extractor W the system of eigenvectors of matrix $\Sigma_2^{-1}\Sigma_1$ defined in 41. Here, however, the eigenvectors constituting columns of W should be selected by

taking into account the discriminatory information contained not only in the covariance matrices but also in the class mean vectors.

Note from 40 that

48 $$V^t \Sigma_2 V = I$$

49 $$V^t \Sigma_1 V = \Lambda.$$

Substituting 48 and 49 into 21 we get

50 $$J_C(W) = \frac{1}{2}\sum_{j=1}^{d} \left\{ s(1-s)\left[\underline{v}_j^t(\underline{\mu}_2-\underline{\mu}_1)\right]^2\left[(1-s)\lambda_j+s\right]^{-1}+\ln\left[(1-s)\lambda_j^s+s_j^{s-1}\right]\right\}.$$

Thus, in contrast to 35, matrix W should be formed by the first d eigenvectors $\underline{v}_i$, i=1,...,d of $\Sigma_2^{-1}\Sigma_1$ arranged so that the corresponding eigenvalues satisfy

51 $$\begin{aligned} & s(1-s)\left[\underline{v}_1^t(\underline{\mu}_2-\underline{\mu}_1)\right]^2\left[(1-s)\lambda_1+s\right]^{-1}+\ln\left[(1-s)\lambda_1^s+s\lambda_1^{s-1}\right] \geq \cdots \\ & \geq s(1-s)\left[\underline{v}_d^t(\underline{\mu}_2-\underline{\mu}_1)\right]^2\left[(1-s)\lambda_d+s\right]^{-1}+\ln\left[(1-s)\lambda_d^s+s\lambda_d^{s-1}\right] \geq \cdots \\ & \geq s(1-s)\left[\underline{v}_D^t(\underline{\mu}_2-\underline{\mu}_1)\right]^2\left[(1-s)\lambda_D+s\right]^{-1}+\ln\left[(1-s)\lambda_D^s+s\lambda_D^{s-1}\right] \end{aligned}$$

i.e.

52 $$W = \left[\underline{v}_1,\ldots,\underline{v}_d\right].$$

53 <u>METHOD 2</u>: Alternatively matrix W can be constructed from d-1 eigenvectors selected as in 35, i.e.,

54 $$\underline{w}_i = \underline{v}_i \qquad i=1,\ldots,d-1,$$

augmented by the best direction for representing the discriminatory information contained in the class means. By analogy to 26 this direction can be readily expressed, by replacing Σ in 34 with $\left[(1-s)\Sigma_1+s\Sigma_2\right]$ as

55 $$\tilde{\underline{w}}_d = \left[(1-s)\Sigma_1 + s\Sigma_2\right]^{-1}(\underline{\mu}_2-\underline{\mu}_1).$$

Note that features yielded by Method 2 are not additive.

8.4.2. Divergence

Using the notation in 22 the divergence criterion function can be rewritten as

56 $$J_D(W) = \frac{1}{2}\Big[\mathrm{tr}W^tMW\Big\{\big(W^t\Sigma_1W\big)^{-1}+\big(W^t\Sigma_2W\big)^{-1}\Big\} + \mathrm{tr}\Big\{\big(W^t\Sigma_1W\big)^{-1}W^t\Sigma_2W+\big(W^t\Sigma_2W\big)^{-1}W^t\Sigma_1W-2I\Big\}\Big].$$

Differentiating 56 to find the stationary point we obtain

57 $$\begin{aligned}J_D'(W) = {} & MW\Big\{\big(W^t\Sigma_1W\big)^{-1}+\big(W^t\Sigma_2W\big)^{-1}\Big\}-\Sigma_1W\big(W^t\Sigma_1W\big)^{-1}W^tMW\big(W^t\Sigma_1W\big)^{-1}\\ & -\Sigma_2W\big(W^t\Sigma_2W\big)^{-1}W^tMW\big(W^t\Sigma_2W\big)^{-1}-\Sigma_1W\big(W^t\Sigma_1W\big)^{-1}\\ & \cdot W^t\Sigma_2W\big(W^t\Sigma_1W\big)^{-1}+\Sigma_2W\big(W^t\Sigma_1W\big)^{-1}+\Sigma_1W\big(W^t\Sigma_2W\big)^{-1}\\ & -\Sigma_2W\big(W^t\Sigma_2W\big)^{-1}W^t\Sigma_1W\big(W^t\Sigma_2W\big)^{-1} = 0.\end{aligned}$$

Once again the gradient 57 is too complicated to allow for determining an explicit solution for W by analytical methods and the optimum matrix will have to be found numerically. However, as in the previous section, the solution for W can be obtained analytically for the following special cases.

8.4.2.1. Equal covariance matrices

When class-conditional covariance matrices Σ_1 and Σ_2 are identical, the divergence, apart from a multiplicative constant, equals the Chernoff probabilistic distance measure. The optimum feature extractor yielded by the divergence is, therefore, the same as that obtained by optimizing 21 as described in 26.

8.4.2.2. Equal mean vectors

58 When M = 0, condition 57 simplifies to

59 $$\begin{aligned}&\Sigma_1W\big(W^t\Sigma_1W\big)^{-1}W^t\Sigma_2W\big(W^t\Sigma_1W\big)^{-1}\big(W^t\Sigma_2W\big)-\Sigma_2W\big(W^t\Sigma_1W\big)^{-1}W^t\Sigma_2W+\\ &\Sigma_2W\big(W^t\Sigma_2W\big)^{-1}W^t\Sigma_1W-\Sigma_1W = 0.\end{aligned}$$

Denoting

60 $$\left(W^t\Sigma_1 W\right)^{-1} W^t\Sigma_2 W = U\Lambda U^{-1},$$

Equation 59 can be simplified, after some algebraic manipulations, to

$$\Sigma_1 WU - \Sigma_1 WU\Lambda^2 + \Sigma_2 WU\Lambda - \Sigma_2 WU\Lambda^{-1} = 0$$

or, alternatively, to

61 $$\Sigma_1 WU - \Sigma_2 WU\Lambda^{-1} - \left[\Sigma_1 WU - \Sigma_2 WU\Lambda^{-1}\right]\Lambda^2 = 0.$$

Note that 61 will be satisfied if

62 $$\Sigma_1 WU - \Sigma_2 WU\Lambda^{-1} = 0.$$

But the solution of 62 is a system of d eigenvectors $\underline{v}_i$, i=1,2,...,d of matrix $\Sigma_2^{-1}\Sigma_1$, associated with eigenvalues λ_i^{-1}, i=1,2,...,d, i.e.

63 $$\Lambda^{-1} = \begin{bmatrix} \lambda_1^{-1} & 0 \\ 0 & \lambda_d^{-1} \end{bmatrix}.$$

By analogy with 26, since the criterion function 56 is invariant under nonsingular transformations, we can ignore matrix U and take as an optimum solution for W the system of eigenvectors V, i.e.,

64 $$W = V = \left[\underline{v}_1, \ldots, \underline{v}_d\right].$$

Recalling our discussion in 6.66, the feature extraction matrix in Equation 64 must satisfy

65 $$W^t\Sigma_2 W = I, \qquad W^t\Sigma_1 W = \Lambda^{-1}.$$

Substituting from 65 into the divergence we get

66 $$J_D(W) = \frac{1}{2}\mathrm{tr}\left(\Lambda + \Lambda^{-1} - 2I\right) = \frac{1}{2}\sum_{i=1}^{d}\left(\lambda_i + \frac{1}{\lambda_i} - 2\right).$$

It follows that 66 will attain a maximum if the eigenvectors $\underline{v}_i$ generating matrix W are selected so that the corresponding eigenvalues satisfy

67 $$\lambda_1 + \frac{1}{\lambda_1} \geq \lambda_2 + \frac{1}{\lambda_2} \geq \cdots \geq \lambda_d + \frac{1}{\lambda_d} \geq \cdots \geq \lambda_D + \frac{1}{\lambda_D}.$$

Note that matrix W will be identical to the feature extractor 44 for s=0.5 (optimum feature extractor in the sense of the Bhattacharyya probabilistic distance measure).

8.4.2.3. Suboptimal solution

We have already mentioned that, in general, when $\underline{\mu}_1 \neq \underline{\mu}_2$ and $\Sigma_1 \neq \Sigma_2$, the optimum feature extractor can be found only using a search technique. However, if we are content with a suboptimal solution, one of the following strategies can be used to construct feature extractor W.

68 METHOD 1: As in 58, the eigenvectors of the product $\Sigma_2^{-1}\Sigma_1$ are used as the columns of matrix W. But here, since $M \neq 0$, the discriminatory information contained in the class mean vectors, which is represented by the first term of the divergence, must be considered. Substituting for $W^t\Sigma_1 W$ and $W^t\Sigma_2 W$ in 56 from 65 we get

69
$$J_D(W) = \frac{1}{2}\mathrm{tr}\left\{W^t MW[\Lambda+I]+\Lambda+\Lambda^{-1}-2I\right\}$$
$$= \frac{1}{2}\sum_{i=1}^{d} \left\{\left[\underline{w}_i^t(\underline{\mu}_2-\underline{\mu}_1)\right]^2(\lambda_i+1)+\lambda_i+\frac{1}{\lambda_i} - 2\right\}.$$

Thus, in this case, the eigenvectors, $\underline{v}_i$, defining W, i.e.,

70
$$\underline{w}_i = \underline{v}_i,$$

must be selected so that the corresponding eigenvalues satisfy

71
$$\left[\underline{v}_1^t(\underline{\mu}_2-\underline{\mu}_1)\right]^2(\lambda_1+1)+\lambda_1+\frac{1}{\lambda_1} \geq \left[\underline{v}_2^t(\underline{\mu}_2-\underline{\mu}_1)\right]^2(\lambda_2+1)$$
$$+\lambda_2+\frac{1}{\lambda_2} \geq \dots \geq \left[\underline{v}_d^t(\underline{\mu}_2-\underline{\mu}_1)\right]^2(\lambda_d+1)+\lambda_d+\frac{1}{\lambda_d} \geq \dots \geq$$
$$\geq \left[\underline{v}_D^t(\underline{\mu}_2-\underline{\mu}_1)\right]^2 (\lambda_D+1)+\lambda_D+\frac{1}{\lambda_D}.$$

72 METHOD 2: Alternatively, we can select axes defining the feature space by maximizing each term of 56 independently. The simplest way of finding the optimum directions in the representation space for representing the discriminatory information contained in the class mean vectors is to expand the inverse of the product of matrices $\left(W^t\Sigma_1 W\right)^{-1}$ and $\left(W^t\Sigma_2 W\right)^{-1}$ in 56. Note that since W is a (D×d) matrix we have to work with its generalized inverse W^*

73 $$W^* = \left(W^t W\right)^{-1} W^t.$$

Hence criterion 56 becomes

74 $$\begin{aligned} J_D(W) &= \frac{1}{2}\mathrm{tr}\left\{W^t M W\left(W^t W\right)^{-1} W^t\left[\Sigma_1^{-1}+\Sigma_2^{-1}\right]W\left(W^t W\right)^{-1}\right\} \\ &= \frac{1}{2}\mathrm{tr}\left\{W^t M W\left[W^t\left(\Sigma_1^{-1}+\Sigma_2^{-1}\right)W\right]^{-1}\right\}. \end{aligned}$$

The form of criterion 74 is now identical to the first term of measure 21 and we can, therefore, conclude that the optimization of 74 leads to an eigenvalue problem. More specifically, W will be the system of eigenvectors of matrix $\left(\Sigma_1^{-1}+\Sigma_2^{-1}\right)M$ and moreover, since the rank of M is unity, the eigenvector $\underline{v}_1$ associated with the only nonzero eigenvalue of $\left(\Sigma_1^{-1}+\Sigma_2^{-1}\right)M$ will be sufficient to transform all the discriminatory information under consideration into the feature space. By analogy to 34 the eigenvector $\underline{v}_1$ is given as

75 $$\underline{w}_1 = \underline{v}_1 = \left(\Sigma_1^{-1}+\Sigma_2^{-1}\right)\left(\underline{\mu}_2-\underline{\mu}_1\right).$$

Thus the overall feature extractor will be composed of the above eigenvector, $\underline{v}_1$, and the remaining d-1 columns will be formed by the most significant axes for representing the discriminatory information due to the differences of covariance matrices defined in 68.

8.4.3. Patrick-Fisher Probabilistic Distance Measure

From the first derivative of 20 with respect to W, i.e.

76

$$J_P'(W) = \frac{1}{2(2\pi)^{d/2} J_P(W)} \Big\{ - \frac{P_1^2}{2\sqrt{2|W^t\Sigma_1 W|}} \Sigma_1 W\left(W^t\Sigma_1 W\right)^{-1} - \frac{P_2^2}{2\sqrt{2|W^t\Sigma_2 W|}} \Sigma_2 W\left(W^t\Sigma_2 W\right)^{-1} + \frac{P_1P_2}{2\sqrt{|W^t\Sigma_1 W + W^t\Sigma_2 W|}} \cdot$$
$$\cdot \exp\Big\{-\tfrac{1}{2}\mathrm{tr} W^t M W\left[W^t(\Sigma_1+\Sigma_2)W\right]^{-1}\Big\}\Big[MW\left[W^t(\Sigma_1+\Sigma_2)W\right]^{-1} + (\Sigma_1+\Sigma_2)W\left[W^t(\Sigma_1+\Sigma_2)W\right]^{-1} + (\Sigma_1+\Sigma_2)W \cdot$$
$$\cdot \left[W^t(\Sigma_1+\Sigma_2)W\right]^{-1} W^t M W \left[W^t(\Sigma_1+\Sigma_2)W\right]^{-1}\Big]\Big\}$$

it is apparent that we shall not be able to obtain a solution for W analytically even for the special cases of equal covariance matrices or class mean vectors. Since the bound to the probability of error afforded by the Patrick-Fisher criterion is not superior to those of the parametric measures discussed in the preceding sections we shall not pursue this separability measure any further.

8.5. GAUSSIAN PROBABILITY DENSITY FUNCTIONS : MULTICLASS PROBLEM

8.5.1. Parametric Probabilistic Distances Measures

Let $J_{ij}(W)$ be a parametric class pairwise separability measure chosen by the designer. Then, in multiclass pattern recognition problems, we shall seek as an optimum feature extractor matrix W that maximizes the generalized criterion of class separability

77

$$J(W) = \sum_{i=1}^{c}\sum_{j=1}^{c} J_{ij}(W).$$

It is apparent that, whereas in the two-class case we had a reasonable chance to find matrix W analytically, objective function 77 will have to be optimized numerically. Although no numerical integration is involved, this optimization problem will be a very time consuming task owing to the large number of pairwise criteria that need be considered. We shall therefore adopt here a different approach which not only avoids the tedious numerical optimization but uses directly the results obtained in Section 8.4.

Consider the optimum direction, say in the sense of measure 21, for representing the discriminatory information contained in the class mean vectors $\underline{\mu}_i$, $\underline{\mu}_j$, which is given in 34. This axis will obviously be very important for discriminating between classes ω_i and ω_j but, in addition, it is also bound to convey some information about all the other classes. It is reasonable to argue, therefore, that by selecting a number of directions important for differentiating between some class pairs, hopefully these axes will also project into the feature space the information essential for discriminating between all the other classes.

The problem we have to address now is which axes should be used for constructing the multiclass feature extractor. First of all, let us generate a set of candidate axes $\{\underline{v}\}$. Obviously, the set should include the optimum directions for discriminating between each of the class pairs as based on the information contained in the class means. In addition, it should contain the directions reflecting the discriminatory power due to differences of the covariance matrices and, perhaps, other axes such as those yielded by the discriminant analysis discussed in Chapter 6.

78 EXAMPLE: Let us construct a set of candidate axes using the divergence as a measure of class separability. Then the following axes should be considered for possible inclusion :

a. $\underline{v} = \left(\Sigma_i^{-1}+\Sigma_j^{-1}\right)\left(\underline{\mu}_j-\underline{\mu}_i\right)$

b. eigenvectors of $\Sigma_j^{-1}\Sigma_i$ (see 58)

In addition it is always useful to include

c. eigenvectors of $\Sigma^{-1}M$ where M and Σ are defined respectively in 6.56, and 6.57.

79 COMMENT: Note that in general the measure of class separability used to generate a set of candidate axes can be different from the criterion employed to assess the potential of these axes for multiclass feature extraction.

Let us now assume that the set of candidate axes contains D_c members $\underline{v}_i$, i = 1,2,...,D_c each yielding a feature ξ_i, i.e.

80 $$\xi_i = \underline{v}_i^t\underline{y}.$$

Then the task of determining the feature extractor W can be reformulated as a feature selection problem. In particular, we shall seek a combination of d features out of D_c candidates ξ_i that maximizes criterion function 77. Any search algorithm discussed in Chapter 5 can be applied to this problem. The axes $\underline{v}_j$, j=1,...,d, that correspond to features ξ_j, j=1,...,d in the best set define the columns of feature extractor W, i.e.,

81 $$W = \left[\underline{v}_1, \underline{v}_2,\ldots,\underline{v}_d\right].$$

8.5.2. Minimum Error Probability

If the optimality of the feature extractor takes priority over computational considerations then matrix W can be obtained by minimizing error probability 5.11. Let us denote by Y_i the region in the representation space such that for any $\underline{y} \in Y_i$ we have

82 $$P_i p\left(W^t \underline{y} | \omega_i\right) = \max_j P_j p\left(W^t \underline{y} | \omega_j\right).$$

Then 5.11 can be alternatively expressed as

83 $$E = 1 - \sum_{i=1}^{c} \int_{Y_i} P_i p\left(W^t \underline{y} | \omega_i\right) d\underline{y}.$$

Feature extractor W minimizing E can be found by maximizing the second term of 83. Substituting for $p\left(W^t \underline{y} | \omega_i\right)$ from 7.9 we get

84 $$J(W) = \sum_{i=1}^{c} P_i \int_{Y_i} \left[(2\pi)^d |W^t \Sigma_1 W|\right]^{-1/2} \exp\left\{-\frac{1}{2}(\underline{y}-\underline{\mu}_i)^t \cdot \right.$$
$$\left. \cdot W(W^t \Sigma_1 W)^{-1} W^t (\underline{y}-\underline{\mu}_i)\right\} d\underline{y}.$$

Differentiating with respect to W we obtain

$$J'(W) = \sum_{i=1}^{c} \frac{P_i}{\sqrt{(2\pi)^d}} \int_{Y_i} \left[\frac{-|W^t \Sigma_1 W|}{2|W^t \Sigma_1 W|^{3/2}} \Sigma_i W (W^t \Sigma_i W)^{-1}\right.$$

85 $$- \frac{1}{2|W^t \Sigma_1 W|^{1/2}} (\underline{y}-\underline{\mu}_i)(\underline{y}-\underline{\mu}_i)^t W (W^t \Sigma_i W)^{-1} + \frac{1}{2|W^t \Sigma_i W|^{1/2}} \cdot$$
$$\left. \cdot \Sigma_1 W (W^t \Sigma_i W)^{-1} W^t (\underline{y}-\underline{\mu}_i)(\underline{y}-\underline{\mu}_i)^t W (W^t \Sigma_1 W)^{-1}\right] \exp\{.\} d\underline{y}.$$

Let us introduce the following notation

86 $$\Theta_i = \int_{Y_i} (\underline{y}-\underline{\mu}_i)(\underline{y}-\underline{\mu}_i)^t p(\underline{y} | \omega_i) d\underline{y}$$

87 $$\gamma_i = \int_{Y_i} p(\underline{y} | \omega_i) d\underline{y}.$$

Using 86 and 87, 85 simplifies to

88 $$J'(W) = \frac{1}{2}\sum_{i=1}^{c} P_i\left[\gamma_i\Sigma_i+\theta_i-\Sigma_i W(W^t\Sigma_i W)^{-1}W^t\theta_i\right]W(W^t\Sigma_i W)^{-1}$$

The optimum of 88 will have to be found using a search algorithm. Note that θ_i and γ_i appearing in the gradient function, which is required for the optimization process, will be difficult to estimate. However, as a suitable substitute, we can use their approximations defined as

89 $$\hat{\theta}_i = \frac{1}{n_i}\sum_j(\underline{y}_j-\underline{\mu}_i)(\underline{y}_j-\underline{\mu}_i)^t \quad \forall j \text{ s.t. } \underline{y}_j\epsilon\omega_i,\ \underline{y}_j\epsilon Y_i$$

90 $$\hat{\gamma}_i = \frac{1}{n_i}\sum_j 1 \quad \forall j \text{ s.t. } \underline{y}_j\epsilon\omega_i,\ \underline{y}_j\epsilon Y_i.$$

It is interesting to note that $\hat{\theta}_i$ can be expressed in terms of Σ_i as

91 $$\hat{\theta}_i = \Sigma_i - \frac{1}{n_i}\sum_j(\underline{y}_j-\underline{\mu}_i)(\underline{y}_j-\underline{\mu}_i)^t \quad \forall j \text{ s.t. } \underline{y}_j\epsilon\omega_i,\ \underline{y}_j\notin Y_i,$$

that is $\hat{\theta}_i$ is basically the ith class covariance matrix modified by the term due to observations from the ith class training set which, for the current value of the feature extractor, are misclassified by the Bayesian decision rule.

8.6. COMMENTS ON OPTIMIZATION

If a solution for W is not unique, it may be advantageous to constrain the feature extractor by additional requirements of, for instance, the norm of W being constant, i.e.,

92 $$\text{tr}\left\{W^tW\right\} = \text{const.}$$

It may also be desirable that the columns of W be orthogonal.

The former constraint can be satisfied by optimizing the Lagrangian

93 $$\tilde{J}(W) = J(W) - \lambda\left\{\text{tr}(W^tW)-\text{const}\right\}$$

instead of criterion function J(W). The optimal value of the Lagrange multiplier λ can be computed iteratively by updating λ at each step of the search algorithm.

The condition of orthogonality can be satisfied by applying the Gram-Schmidt orthogonalization procedure.

8.7. BIBLIOGRAPHICAL COMMENTS

Using the divergence as a criterion of optimality, Tou and Heydorn (1967) derived the optimal feature extractor under the assumptions of normally distributed classes with equal class mean vectors and equal covariance matrices respectively. Kadota and Shepp (1967) treated the same problems in the context of the Bhattacharyya coefficient. Henderson and Lainiotis (1969), and Fukunaga and Krill (1969) considered the Bhattacharyya coefficient and the divergence in the case of normal distributions with different means and covariance matrices and suggested suboptimal solutions to these problems.

The use of parametric measures in the multiclass problem is discussed by Ichino and Hiramatsu (1974). de Figueiredo, and de Figueiredo *et al.* proposed an algorithm for obtaining a multiclass feature extractor that minimizes classification error.

The feature extraction problem in the general case of nonparametric distributions was considered by Patrick and Fisher (1969), and Kittler (1977).

8.8. REFERENCES

de Figueiredo, R.J.P., Pau, K.C., Sagar, A.D., Starks, S.A., and Van Rooy, D.L., "An algorithm for extraction of more than one optimal feature from several Gaussian pattern classes", *Proc. Third Internat. Conf. Pattern Recognition*, Coronado, Ca., Nov. 1976, pp. 793-796.

de Figueiredo, R.J.P., "Optimal linear and nonlinear feature extraction based on the minimization of the increased risk of misclassification", Institute for Computer Services and Applications, Rice Univ., Tech. Rept. 275-025-014, June 1974.

Fukunaga, K., *Introduction to Statistical Pattern Recognition*, Academic Press, New York, 1972.

Fukunaga, K., and Krill, T.F., "Calculation of Bayes recognition errors for two multivariate Gaussian distributions", *IEEE Trans. Comput.*, vol. 18, pp. 220-229, 1969.

Henderson, T.L., and Lainiotis, D.G., "Comments on linear feature extraction", *IEEE Trans. Inform. Theory*, vol. 15, pp. 729-730, 1969.

Ichino, M., and Hiramatsu, K., "Suboptimal linear feature selection in multiclass problems", *IEEE Trans. Systems Man Cybernet.*, vol. 4, pp. 28-33, 1974.

Kadota, T.T., and Shepp, L.A., "On the best set of linear observables for discriminating two Gaussian signals", *IEEE Trans. Inform. Theory*, vol. 13, pp. 278-284, 1967.

Kittler, J., "Mathematical methods of feature selection in pattern recognition", *Internat. J. Man Mach. Stud.*, vol. 7, pp. 609-637, 1975.

Kittler, J., "A review of feature extraction methods based on probabilistic distance measures", *Proc. SITEL-ULG Seminar on Pattern Recognition*, Liège, Belgium, Nov. 1977, pp. 2.2/1-2.2/10.

Patrick, E.A., and Fisher, F.P., "Nonparametric feature selection", *IEEE Trans. Inform. Theory*, vol. 15, pp. 557-584, 1969.

Tou, J.T., and Heydorn, R.P., "Some approaches to optimum feature extraction", in *Computer and Information Sciences*, J.T. Tou Ed., Academic Press, New York, 1967, pp. 57-89.

8.9. PROBLEMS

1. Derive a parametric form of the Patrick-Fisher distance given in Equation 8.6, for the case of two normally distributed classes.

2. Find an explicit or implicit expression for the stationary points of the parametric criterion function derived in Problem 1.

3. Find the linear transformation that simultaneously diagonalizes two symmetric matrices.

4. Show that the Chernoff distance given in the expression 8.16 is invariant under nonsingular transformations.

5. Let $p(\underline{y}|\omega_i) \sim N(\underline{\mu}_i, \Sigma_i)$, i=1,2. Derive an expression for the Chernoff distance in the feature space spanned by the first d eigenvectors of the matrix $\Sigma_2^{-1}\Sigma_1$.

6. Let the mean vectors and covariance matrices of three normally distributed classes be given as :

$$\underline{\mu}_1 = \begin{bmatrix} 2 \\ 3 \\ 3 \\ -2 \end{bmatrix} \quad \underline{\mu}_2 = \begin{bmatrix} -1 \\ 2 \\ 1 \\ -6 \end{bmatrix} \quad \underline{\mu}_3 = \begin{bmatrix} 0 \\ 1 \\ -1 \\ 2 \end{bmatrix} \quad \Sigma_1 = \Sigma_2 = \Sigma_3 = \begin{bmatrix} 4 & 1 & -3 & 0 \\ 1 & 2 & -1 & 0 \\ -3 & -1 & 3 & 0 \\ 0 & 0 & 0 & 3 \end{bmatrix}$$

Following the method of Section 8.5.1 find the best direction (in the sense of a suitable criterion) for discriminating between the three classes, under the assumption that $P_1=P_2=P_3$.

Chapter 9

FEATURE EXTRACTION BASED ON THE KARHUNEN-LOEVE EXPANSION

9.1. INTRODUCTION

In Chapters 6 and 8 we have discussed feature extraction methods based on various criteria of class separability. The common denominator of these methods is that the optimal transformation matrix is obtained by maximization of an appropriate separability measure in the feature space. In this chapter, we shall focus our attention on a conceptually different approach to the problem of feature extraction, the basis of which is the Karhunen-Loeve expansion. Here the discriminatory information compression is achieved indirectly by approximating the representation pattern vector by a small number of terms of the expansion. In the following, we shall see that, for any given number of terms, the mean square error (MSE) between the approximation and the original pattern is minimal in comparison with the error incurred by truncating any other orthogonal expansion of $\underline{y}$. This implies that most of the information about pattern $\underline{y}$, including the discriminatory information which is of main interest to us in the present context, is compressed into a few terms of the Karhunen-Loeve

(K-L) expansion. It is reasonable, therefore, to adopt the K-L basis vectors used in the MSE approximation as constituent axes of the feature space.

The problem of determining a K-L feature extractor is the subject of our discussion in the following sections. First, we shall derive the Karhunen-Loeve coordinate system and discuss its properties. Subsequently, a number of feature extraction methods based on the K-L expansion will be described.

9.2. THE KARHUNEN-LOEVE EXPANSION

9.2.1. Preliminaries

Consider an infinite set of D-dimensional pattern vectors $\{\underline{y}\}$. It is, of course, always possible to expand every element $\underline{y}$ of the set into an arbitrary but complete system of orthonormal deterministic vectors $\underline{u}_j$, $j=1,\ldots,\infty$,

1 $$\underline{u}_j = \left[u_{j1}, u_{j2}, \ldots, u_{jD}\right]^t,$$

without incurring any information loss as

2 $$\underline{y} = \sum_{j=1}^{\infty} x_j \underline{u}_j,$$

where x_j designates the expansion coefficient associated with basis vector $\underline{u}_j$. The system of basis vectors used in expansion 2 is usually prespecified to meet the needs of a particular application. In the present case, vectors $\underline{u}_j$ should be such that the mean square error ε,

3 $$\varepsilon = E\left\{(\underline{y}-\hat{\underline{y}})^t(\underline{y}-\hat{\underline{y}})\right\},$$

between the pattern vector $\underline{y}$ and its approximation $\hat{\underline{y}}$ obtained by taking a finite number d of terms in expansion 2, i.e.

4 $$\underline{\hat{y}} = \sum_{j=1}^{d} x_j \underline{u}_j,$$

is minimized.

Let us determine the system of discrete expansion functions satisfying the above requirement. Substituting for $(\underline{y}-\underline{\hat{y}})$ in 3 from 2 and 4 and using the orthonormality condition imposed on vectors $\underline{u}_j$, i.e.,

5 $$\underline{u}_j^T \underline{u}_i = \delta_{ij},$$

where δ_{ij} is the Kronecker δ-function, the expression for the approximation error simplifies to

6 $$\varepsilon = \boldsymbol{E}\left\{ \sum_{j=d+1}^{\infty} x_j^2 \right\}.$$

Note that an explicit expression for expansion coefficient x_j can be acquired by multiplying both sides of 2 by $\underline{u}_j^t$. Then, by virtue of the orthonormality condition 5, we get

7 $$x_j = \underline{u}_j^t \underline{y}.$$

Using this relationship, x_j can be eliminated from 6 thus yielding

$$\varepsilon = \boldsymbol{E}\left\{ \sum_{j=d+1}^{\infty} \underline{u}_j^t \underline{y}\,\underline{y}^t \underline{u}_j \right\}.$$

Since $\underline{u}_j$ are deterministic vectors, the order of summation and expectation operations can be interchanged, i.e.,

$$\varepsilon = \sum_{j=d+1}^{\infty} \underline{u}_j^t \left[\boldsymbol{E}\{\underline{y}\,\underline{y}^t\} \right] \underline{u}_j.$$

Now denoting the term in the square brackets by Ψ, i.e.,

8 $$\Psi = \boldsymbol{E}\{\underline{y}\,\underline{y}^t\},$$

the approximation error can be finally expressed as

9 $$\varepsilon = \sum_{j=d+1}^{\infty} \underline{u}_j^t \Psi \underline{u}_j.$$

The coordinate system which minimizes error ε subject to the orthonormality condition 5 can now be found using the method of Lagrange multipliers. The constrained function $g(\underline{u}_j)$ is given as

10 $$g(\underline{u}_j) = \sum_{j=d+1}^{\infty} \underline{u}_j^t \Psi \underline{u}_j - \sum_{j=d+1}^{\infty} \lambda_j \left[\underline{u}_j^t \underline{u}_j - 1\right].$$

Differentiating 10 with respect to $\underline{u}_j$, we get the following condition for the stationary point :

11 $$(\Psi - \lambda_j I)\underline{u}_j = 0.$$

It follows that the optimal coordinate vectors $\underline{u}_j$, known as the *Karhunen-Loeve coordinate axes*, are the eigenvectors of the matrix Ψ, while λ_j are the corresponding eigenvalues. Since Ψ is a $D \times D$ matrix the eigenvalue problem 11 will have only D distinct solutions. In other words, Ψ will have only D linearly independent eigenvectors and, therefore, expansion 2 will consists of D terms only, i.e.,

12 $$\underline{y} = \sum_{j=1}^{D} x_j \underline{u}_j.$$

9.2.2. Minimum MSE Approximation

We shall now determine which d vectors $\underline{u}_j$ in the complete set of eigenvectors $U=\left[\underline{u}_1, \underline{u}_2, \ldots, \underline{u}_D\right]$ of matrix Ψ should be used for approximating pattern vector $\underline{y}$. Since our objective is to minimize the approximation error, let us consider once again expression 9. Substituting for $\Psi \underline{u}_j$ from 11 we get

13 $$\varepsilon = \sum_{j=d+1}^{D} \lambda_j.$$

It is apparent that the error will be minimum if λ_j, $j=d+1,\ldots,D$ are the smallest eigenvalues of matrix Ψ. This result implies that the MSE approximation of $\underline{y}$ should be constructed from the eigenvectors of Ψ asssociated with the d largest eigenvalues of the matrix, i.e.

$$\hat{\underline{y}} = \sum_{j=1}^{d} x_j \underline{u}_j,$$

where eigenvalues λ_j corresponding to vectors $\underline{u}_j$ satisfy

14 $$\lambda_1 \geq \lambda_2 \geq \ldots \geq \lambda_d \geq \ldots \geq \lambda_D.$$

To conclude, the approximation error, ε_v, incurred by truncating an expansion of $\underline{y}$ into any other system of orthonormal basis vectors $\underline{v}_j$, $j=1,\ldots,D$, will be greater than error 13 of the truncated K-L expansion. Designating the contribution to error due to omitting axis $\underline{v}_j$ by ρ_j, i.e.

15 $$\rho_j = \underline{v}_j^t \Psi \underline{v}_j,$$

then, by analogy, the approximation error in the general case can be written as

16 $$\varepsilon_v = \sum_{j=d+1}^{D} \rho_j$$

and for any d, errors 13 and 16 will satisfy

17 $$\varepsilon \leq \varepsilon_v.$$

In addition to the minimum approximation error property of the Karhunen-Loeve coordinate system, the expansion has the following interesting properties : coefficients x_j of the expansion are uncorrelated; it is related to the Discrete Fourier Transform; it minimizes both representation and population entropies. These aspects of the K-L expansion will be discussed in the subsequent section. The reader who is not interested in the mathematical detail can, without any loss of continuity, proceed to Section 9.4 where all these properties are summarized.

9.3. PROPERTIES OF THE K-L EXPANSION

9.3.1. Expansion Coefficients

A very interesting property of the K-L expansion is that coefficients x_j of the expansion are uncorrelated. This can be shown by considering the expected value of the product of two coefficients, $E\{x_k x_j\}$. Using 7, 8 and 11, this expectation can be written as

18 $$E\{x_k x_j\} = E\{\underline{u}_k^t \underline{y}\underline{y}^t \underline{u}_j\} = \lambda_j \underline{u}_k^t \underline{u}_j = \lambda_j \delta_{kj}.$$

Note that the variance of x_j is equivalent to the eigenvalue λ_j of matrix Ψ.

By analogy, the second order moments matrix of vector $\underline{x}$ can be written as

19 $$E\{\underline{x}\underline{x}^t\} = U^t \Psi U = \Lambda,$$

where Λ is the diagonal matrix of eigenvalues of Ψ, i.e.

20 $$\Lambda = \begin{bmatrix} \lambda_1 & & 0 \\ & \lambda_2 & \\ 0 & & \lambda_D \end{bmatrix}$$

It is apparent from 19 that the K-L coordinate system U diagonalizes matrix Ψ. This result suggests another physical interpretation of the information compression ability of the K-L expansion, namely that the compression is achieved by decorrelating the components of vector $\underline{y}$

and, subsequently, by removing the axes which do not convey much information. The essence of the K-L expansion can be best illustrated by the example in Figure 9.1. In the original coordinate system, two coordinates, y_1, y_2 are required for adequate representation of patterns, while, in the K-L coordinate system $\underline{u}_1$, $\underline{u}_2$, one axis alone, $\underline{u}_1$, contains most of the information about $\underline{y}$ and axis $\underline{u}_2$ could be discarded.

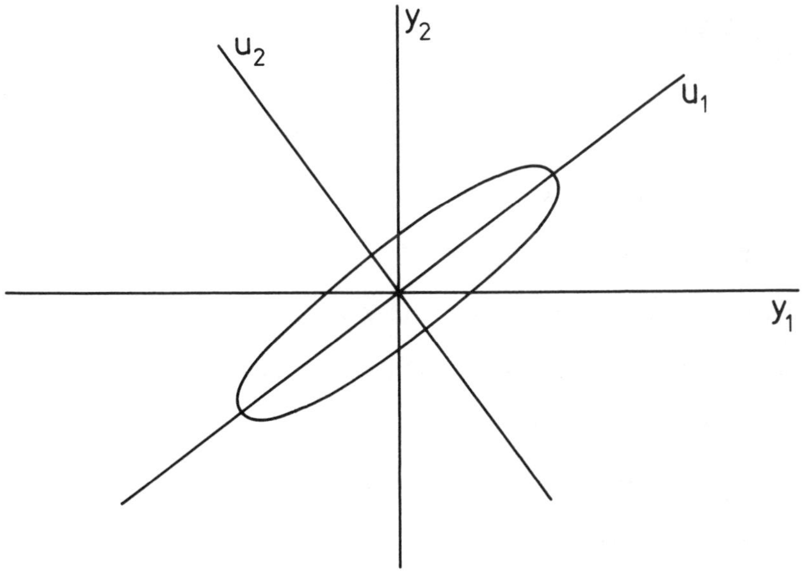

Figure 9.1. Example of the effect of the K-L expansion for one distribution.

9.3.2. Representation Entropy

We have seen in Section 9.2 that, in order to obtain the minimum MSE approximation, $\hat{\underline{y}}$, of pattern vector $\underline{y}$, consisting of d terms of expansion 12, $\hat{\underline{y}}$ should be constructed from the eigenvectors associated with the d largest eigenvalues of matrix Ψ. In the preceding subsection, we have noted that the eigenvalues represent the variance of expansion coefficients. It is evident that the greater the variance of x_j, the more information about $\underline{y}$ is contained in the jth coefficient. Ideally, we would, of course, like to see most of the information about $\underline{y}$ compressed into a very few terms of the expansion, for the information conveyed by the remaining coefficients could then be neglected.

In formal terms, a greater information compression will be achieved if matrix Ψ has a very few eigenvalues of large magnitudes and all the other eigenvalues small, than if the eigenvalues are distributed uniformly over the axes of the K-L coordinate system.

In order to assess the degree of information compressibility of the K-L coordinate system, or of any other system of axes for that matter, it is essential to define an information compression indicator. Since, in effect, it is required to measure the dispersion of information over the axes of a coordinate system as represented by the variance of the expansion coefficients then, recalling Section 5.5.3, an obvious candidate for carrying out this task is an entropy function such as, for instance, the logarithmic entropy function defined in Section 7.4 with probabilities replaced by eigenvalues. Note, however, that in order to assume the role of probabilities, the magnitudes of the eigenvalues should be less than or equal to unity. First of all it is necessary, therefore, to normalize λ_j.

Consider the sequence of components of vector $\underline{y}$ as a discrete signal with energy $\underline{y}^t\underline{y}$. Assuming that both the number of samples of the signal and their values are finite, the average energy of the ensemble of signals,

21 $$K = E\left\{\underline{y}^t\underline{y}\right\}$$

will be finite. Substituting for $\underline{y}$ from 12 and by virtue of the orthonormality conditions 5 and 18, we get

22 $$K = \sum_{j=1}^{D} E\left\{x_j^2\right\} = \sum_{j=1}^{D} \lambda_j.$$

Let us now define a new variable , $\tilde{\lambda}_j$

23 $$\tilde{\lambda}_j = \frac{\lambda_j}{K}.$$

Then $\tilde{\lambda}_j$, $j=1,\ldots,D$ satisfy

24 $$0 \leq \tilde{\lambda}_j \leq 1$$

and

25 $$\sum_{j=1}^{D} \tilde{\lambda}_j = 1.$$

Thus $\tilde{\lambda}_j$ have similar properties to probabilities in 5.20 and the use of the entropy function

26 $$H_R = -\sum_{j=1}^{D} \tilde{\lambda}_j \log \tilde{\lambda}_j$$

obtained by taking the limit in 5.20 for $\alpha \to 1$ becomes justified.

Recalling Section 5.3, criterion function 26 will attain a maximum when all λ_j are identical. In this particular case, the approximation of $\underline{y}$ by d terms of the K-L expansion will be associated with the largest error, or, in different words, with the greatest uncertainty about the true vector $\underline{y}$. On the other hand, zero entropy implies that all the information about $\underline{y}$ is contained in one term of the expansion.

Evidently, the magnitude of the entropy function reflects our uncertainties about pattern $\underline{y}$ if instead of $\underline{y}$ we work only with its representation $\hat{\underline{y}}$. The criterion, H_R, can be considered, therefore, as a measure of representation uncertainties and we shall call it *representation entropy*.

It is interesting to note that both the K-L coordinate system and representation entropy associated with the system are functions of the data set. In general, each data set will lead to a distinct K-L coordinate system and a corresponding representation entropy. But, by the same argument, we can have identical K-L coordinate axes for two distinct data sets yet with different representation entropies. This particular situation highlights the characteristic role of representation entropy as a measure of compressibility of information in a given coordinate system.

The above concept of representation entropy has been developed with reference to the K-L coordinate axes. As a matter of fact, this concept is quite general, that is we can use criterion H_R for assessing representation entropy of data in any coordinate system, $\underline{v}_j$, $j=1,\dots,D$. Naturally, eigenvalues $\tilde{\lambda}_j$ in 26 must be replaced by the normalized variances $\tilde{\rho}_j$ of the x_j of the pattern vector in that coordinate system, i.e.,

27 $$\tilde{\rho}_j = \frac{\rho_j}{K} = \frac{\boldsymbol{E}\left\{x_j^2\right\}}{K} = \left[\underline{v}_j^t \Psi \underline{v}_j\right]\frac{1}{K}.$$

Since the average energy of an ensemble of signals is invariant to any orthonormal transformation, the normalizing constant

$$K = \sum_{j=1}^{D} \rho_j$$

in 27 is identical with the normalizing constant defined in 22.

It is not difficult to show that, as could be expected, the representation entropy associated with the K-L coordinate system is minimum in comparison with that of any other system of basis vectors. A meaningful comparison of representation entropies can, of course, be made only under the assumption that the ordering of axes in both coordinate system $\underline{v}_j$, $\forall j$ and the K-L system is based on the same philosophy, i.e. that the corresponding variances ρ_j satisfy

28 $$\rho_1 \geq \rho_2 \geq \dots \geq \rho_d \geq \dots \geq \rho_D.$$

Let us now consider the representation entropy associated with the arbitrary coordinate system $\underline{v}_j$, j=1,...,D, i.e.,

29 $$H_R = -\sum_{j=1}^{D} \tilde{\rho}_j \log \tilde{\rho}_j.$$

To show that 29 is minimum for the K-L coordinate axes, that is when

$$\underline{v}_j = \underline{u}_j,$$

define a new variable θ_j

$$\theta_j = \sum_{k=1}^{j} \tilde{\rho}_k$$

which satisfies

$$\theta_0 = 0 \qquad \theta_D = 1.$$

Using this new variable, the representation entropy can be expressed as

$$H_R = -\sum_{j=1}^{D} \left(\theta_j - \theta_{j-1}\right) \log\left(\theta_j - \theta_{j-1}\right).$$

Differentiating with respect to θ_j to find the minimum, we obtain

30 $$\frac{\partial H_R}{\partial \theta_j} = \log \frac{\theta_{j+1} - \theta_j}{\theta_j - \theta_{j-1}}.$$

From 28 it follows that the fraction on the right hand side of 30 is less than or equal to one, and, consequently, its logarithm will always be negative or zero. Thus the greater θ_j, the smaller $\partial H_R/\partial\theta_j$ and therefore the greater the rate the representation entropy function will approach the stationary point. Note from 17 that θ_j, $\forall j$ will be largest for the Karhunen-Loeve coordinate system since, after dividing both sides of the inequality by (-K) and adding 1, we have

31 $$\sum_{j=1}^{d} \tilde{\lambda}_j \geq \sum_{j=1}^{d} \tilde{\rho}.$$

Now the left and right hand side of inequality 31 are variables $\bar{\Xi}_d$ and θ_d for the K-L coordinate system and the system of axes $\underline{v}_j$ respectively. Thus we have

$$\bar{\Xi}_d \geq \theta_d \qquad \forall d$$

and consequently the representation entropy associated with the K-L coordinate system will always be smaller than that of any other system.

To conclude, the representation-entropy-measure is ideally suited for assessing the information compression which is achieved. It appears to function at two levels. First, its value is minimized by transforming the data into the K-L system of basis vectors. The value of this minimum then characterizes in absolute terms the compressibility of the information about elements of the data set.

9.3.3. Discrete Fourier Transform

Suppose for the moment that pattern vector $\underline{y}$ is composed of an infinite number of components and, for convenience, let us view these components of vector $\underline{y}$ as consecutive samples of an infinite time series. Then under the assumption of stationarity of the series, the elements ψ_{ij} of matrix Ψ in 8 can be calculated as

32 $$\psi_{ij} = E\{y_i y_j\} = \lim_{D\to\infty} \frac{1}{2D}\sum_{k=-D}^{D} y_{k+i} y_{k-j} = \psi_{i-j}.$$

Let us consider once again the eigenvalue problem given in 11 which can be alternatively written as the following system of equations :

33 $$\sum_{j=-\infty}^{\infty} \psi_{ij} u_{\ell j} = \lambda_\ell u_{\ell i} \qquad \forall i.$$

Here $u_{\ell j}$ denotes the jth element of the ℓ-th basis vector $\underline{u}_\ell$. Since ψ_{ij} in this special case can be replaced by ψ_{i-j}, we get

34 $$\sum_{j=-\infty}^{\infty} \psi_{i-j} u_{\ell j} = \lambda_\ell u_{\ell i} \qquad \forall i.$$

Note that the left hand side of 34 is the convolution of series ψ_{ij} (the ith row of matrix Ψ) and $u_{\ell j}$, $\forall j$. Taking the discrete Fourier Transform (DFT) of both sides of the equation yields

35 $$R_j \eta_{\ell j} = \lambda_\ell \eta_{\ell j} \qquad \forall j,$$

where R_j and $\eta_{\ell j}$ are the jth components of the DFT of series ψ_{ij} and $u_{\ell j}$ respectively. The K-L coordinate system $\underline{u}_\ell$, $\forall \ell$ can therefore be obtained by solving equation 35 which is the frequency domain equivalent of 34. The trivial solution,

$$R_j = \lambda_\ell \qquad \forall j,$$

is not possible, for eigenvalue λ_ℓ is a constant while R_j takes different values for each j. It follows that the only reasonable solution of 35 is in terms of the Dirac delta function, $\delta(j-\ell)$, i.e.,

$$R_j \delta(j-\ell) = \lambda_\ell \delta(j-\ell)$$

and λ_ℓ is given as

36 $$\lambda_\ell = R_\ell.$$

Since $\delta(j-\ell)$ is the DFT of the sinusoidal function

37 $$u_{\ell j} = e^{-i2\pi\ell j},$$

we can conclude that the eigenvectors of matrix Ψ in this case are the complex sinusoids.

38 <u>REMARK</u>: Note that ψ_{i-j} is the autocorrelation function of series y_i. From the Wiener theorem, R_ℓ, $\forall\ell$ is the power spectrum of y_i and eigenvalues λ_ℓ are components of the spectrum R_ℓ.

When the number of pattern vector components is finite, this unique relationship between the DFT and the K-L expansion will not hold, for the stationarity assumption relating to y_i will no longer be satisfied. However, for pattern vectors of reasonable dimensionality, discrete sinusoids will afford a good approximation to the optimal basis vectors.

From the sampling theorem, it follows that for, D-dimensional pattern vectors, the highest determinable frequency of complex sinusoids corresponds to $\ell = \pm D/2$. Note that the total number of complex sinusoids corresponding to both the positive and negative values of index ℓ is D, which agrees with the number of distinct solutions of the eigenvalue problem 11 we would obtain by a direct eigenvalue analysis of $D \times D$ matrix Ψ.

In conclusion, whenever the assumption of stationarity of elements of $\underline{y}$ is satisfied, the K-L coordinate system will be a system of discrete sinusoidal functions and, with the exception of eigenvalues λ_ℓ, the solution of the eigenvalue problem 11 will be known *a priori*.

Moreover, the eigenvalues of matrix Ψ can be obtained very efficiently using the Fast Fourier Transform. Consequently, in this special case the computationally demanding eigenvalue analysis required for determining the K-L coordinate system can be avoided.

9.3.4. Population Entropy

The mean vectors of individual classes usually contain most of the discriminatory information. But this information cannot be fully used if the deviations of pattern vectors from their class mean is large, causing the subspaces occupied by individual classes to overlap. It seems reasonable therefore, to select features so that some measure of uncertainty about the membership of patterns in their classes represented by the mean vectors is minimized. Such a measure is, for instance, the population entropy, H_p, defined as

$$H_p = - \mathcal{E}\{\log p(\underline{x})\}.$$

The relevance of this measure can be verified by considering two extreme examples of class probability density function $p(\underline{x})$, namely $p(\underline{x})=\delta(\underline{x}-\underline{\mu})$ and $p(\underline{x})=1/\boldsymbol{v}$ where $\boldsymbol{v}$ is the volume taken by the membership class of $\underline{x}$. In the case of the delta function, the population entropy will be $-\infty$ and, in the second example, the population entropy equals $\log \boldsymbol{v}$. The greater the volume occupied by a class, the greater the population entropy.

Our task then will be to determine a $D\times d$ matrix W which would map pattern vectors from the representation space into the transformed space so as to reduce the volume occupied by the class. More specifically we have to find matrix W which minimizes the population entropy

39 $$H_p(W) = -E\left\{\log p(W^t\underline{y})\right\}.$$

In the case of a general probability density function, in order to obtain optimal matrix W we would have to employ optimum-seeking methods. However, to simplify the matter, we shall approximate any general probability density function $p(W^t\underline{y})$ by a normal p.d.f., $p_s(W^t\underline{y})$ with the covariance matrix equal to that of the true distribution as sketched in Figure 9.2. This corresponds to representing the deviations of pattern $\underline{y}$ from its mean value by the scatter of the population. Assuming, without any loss of generality, that the mean of the population is zero, and denoting the covariance matrix of $\underline{y}$ by Σ, i.e.

40 $$\Sigma = E\left\{\underline{y}\underline{y}^t\right\},$$

then $p_s(W^t\underline{y})$ replacing the true p.d.f. in 39 is given as

41 $$p_s(W^t\underline{y}) = (2\pi)^{-d/2}|W^t\Sigma W|^{-1/2}\exp\left\{-\tfrac{1}{2}\underline{y}^tW(W^t\Sigma W)^{-1}W^t\underline{y}\right\}.$$

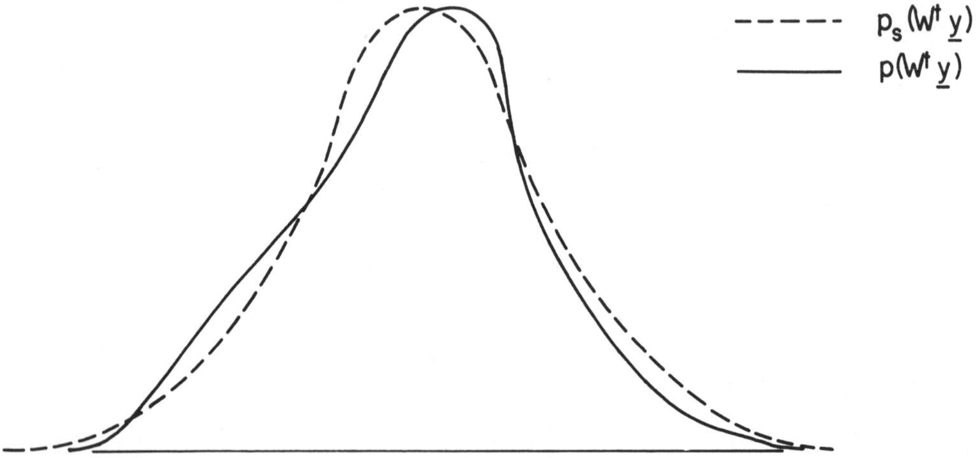

Figure 9.2. Example of the normal p.d.f. $p_s(W^t\underline{y})$ approximating an actual p.d.f. $p(W^t\underline{y})$.

Integration of 39, with p(.) replaced by $p_s(.)$, then yields

$$H_p(W) = \log\left[(2\pi)^d |W^t \Sigma W|\right]^{1/2} + \frac{1}{2}tr\left[(W^t \Sigma W)^{-1}(W^t \Sigma W)\right]$$

and this can be finally written as

42 $$H_p(W) = \frac{1}{2}\log|W^t \Sigma W| + \text{const}.$$

Let us find the stationary point of 42. For convenience, we shall assume that matrix W can be expressed in terms of the D×D matrix of eigenvectors U of matrix Σ and some unknown D×d matrix $B=\left[\underline{b}_1,\ldots,\underline{b}_d\right]$, i.e.,

43 $$W = UB.$$

Then the stationary point of 42 can be found by differentiating with respect to B. Now let it be required that

44 $$W^t W = I.$$

Then the constrained function to be differentiated is

45 $$H_p(B) = \frac{1}{2}\log|B^t U^t \Sigma UB| + \text{const} - \frac{1}{2}tr\left[\tilde{\Lambda}(B^t U^t UB-I)\right],$$

with d×d diagonal matrix $\tilde{\Lambda}$ denoting the unknown Lagrange multipliers. Since $U^t \Sigma U=\Lambda$, where Λ is the diagonal matrix of eigenvalues of Σ, and further recalling that $U^t U=I$, 45 can be simplified to

$$H_p(B) = \frac{1}{2}\log|B^t \Lambda B| + \text{const} - \frac{1}{2}tr[\tilde{\Lambda}(B^t B - I)].$$

Differentiating with respect to B now yields

$$\frac{dH_p(B)}{dB} = \frac{1}{2}\Lambda B(B^t \Lambda B)^{-1} - \frac{1}{2}B\tilde{\Lambda}.$$

Matrix B can be obtained by solving the matrix equation

46 $$\Lambda B(B^t \Lambda B)^{-1} - B\tilde{\Lambda} = 0.$$

Premultiplying 46 by B^t we get

$$\tilde{\Lambda} = I.$$

Postmultiplying 46 with $B^t \Lambda B$ results in

47 $$\Lambda B - BB^t \Lambda B = 0.$$

Equation 47 will be satisfied if either $BB^t=I$ or

$$BB^t = \begin{array}{c} \\ d \\ \\ \end{array}\overset{\displaystyle d}{\begin{bmatrix} I & 0 \\ & \\ 0 & 0 \end{bmatrix}} .$$

The former solution is not possible since matrix B can have only d linearly independent rows and this implies that some of the off-diagonal elements of BB^t would be non-zero. The second solution suggests that matrix B has D-d rows containing zeros, i.e.

$$B = \begin{array}{r} d \\ \\ D-d \end{array}\overset{\displaystyle d}{\begin{bmatrix} B_1 \\ \\ 0 \end{bmatrix}} .$$

Note that matrix B_1 in 48 can be quite arbitrary provided it satisfies $B_1B_1^t=I$. This result is not surprising since both the population entropy of a cluster projected into a subspace of lower dimensionality and the probability density function in this subspace will be invariant under any rotation of the coordinate system of the subspace. Rotation of the axes does not, of course, alter the shape of the probability density function.

Since the columns of matrix B_1 can be quite arbitrary subject to condition $B_1B_1^t=I$, we can choose $\underline{b}_j$ for simplicity as

$$\underline{b}_j = \begin{bmatrix} b_{j1} \\ \cdot \\ \cdot \\ b_{jj} \\ \cdot \\ \cdot \\ b_{jd} \\ b_{j(d+1)} \\ \cdot \\ \cdot \\ b_{jD} \end{bmatrix} = \begin{bmatrix} 0 \\ \cdot \\ \cdot \\ 1 \\ \cdot \\ \cdot \\ 0 \\ 0 \\ \cdot \\ \cdot \\ 0 \end{bmatrix} .$$

Then matrix W becomes

49 $$W = UB = \left[\underline{u}_1, \ldots, \underline{u}_d\right],$$

where $\underline{u}_j$, $j=1,\ldots,d$ are the columns of the matrix of eigenvectors, U.

Substituting for W in 42 from 49, we get

$$H_p(W) = \frac{1}{2}\log|\Lambda_W| + \text{const},$$

where Λ_W is the diagonal matrix of eigenvalues λ_j associated with eigenvectors $\underline{u}_j$, $j=1,\ldots,d$, i.e.

$$\Lambda_W = \begin{bmatrix} \lambda_1 & & 0 \\ & & \\ 0 & & \lambda_d \end{bmatrix}.$$

Expressing the determinant of Λ_W as a product of eigenvalues λ_j, it becomes apparent that the population entropy $H_p(W)$ will be minimized if the d eigenvectors $\underline{u}_j$ constituting the mapping W are selected so that the corresponding eigenvalues λ_j satisfy

$$\lambda_1 \le \lambda_2 \le \ldots \le \lambda_d \le \ldots \le \lambda_D.$$

This result is very interesting. First of all note that axes $\underline{u}_j, \forall j$ are the K-L coordinate axes for the ensemble of pattern vectors $\{\underline{y}\}$. Recalling Section 9.2.2, the best coordinate system for approximating $\underline{y}$ with minimum MSE is defined by d eigenvectors associated with the *largest* eigenvalues of matrix Σ. In contrast, the basis vectors minimizing population entropy are constituted by eigenvectors of Σ associated with the *smallest* eigenvalues. Despite this apparent contradiction, both systems can be used for feature selection purposes as we shall see later in this chapter.

9.4. A SUMMARY OF THE PROPERTIES OF THE K-L EXPANSION

We shall now briefly review the properties of the K-L expansion derived above. We have seen that the K-L expansion provides a method for decomposing the pattern into a number of mutually uncorrelated components and for reducing the number of these components necessary for approximating the pattern to any specified accuracy. Since the K-L coordinate system, which is the basis of the expansion, is deterministic, these components or coefficients contain all the information needed for reconstruction of the pattern. It has been shown that the MSE between the pattern and its approximation is minimized by selecting coefficients with the largest variances. Clearly, these coefficients must contain most of the information about pattern vectors, $\underline{y}$. On the other hand, the coefficients with small variance convey a negligible amount of information. Thus the process of transforming pattern vectors $\underline{y}$ into the K-L coordinate system can be viewed as information compression.

Once determined, the K-L coordinate system is identical for patterns from all the classes. Consequently, all the discriminatory information must be carried by the coefficients x_j of the expansion. But since most of the information is compressed into a small number of these coefficients, it is apparent that it will be less complex computationally to carry out the subsequent decision-making in a lower dimensional feature space.

It has been emphasized that the concepts of representation entropy and information compression are closely related since both these measures are functions of dispersion of eigenvalues λ_j. The greater the dispersion, the smaller the representation entropy (smaller uncertainty associated with the coordinate system) and also the greater the information compression. Conversely, a uniform distribution of variances of the coefficients over the axes of the K-L coordinate system implies association of a greater uncertainty with each axis of the coordinate system. In physical terms, this means that the observation of one coefficient of the K-L expansion in the case of uniformly distributed eigenvalues reduces the uncertainty (entropy) about the pattern only very little, i.e., very little information is gained by observing just one coefficient. This also becomes apparent by recalling that the sum of variances of the coefficients of a complete system of basis functions is constant. When the distribution of the variances is uniform, the acquisition of one term of the expansion reduces the uncertainty about the pattern by factor 1/D where D is the dimensionality of the coordinate system.

In the case of dispersed variances, the observation of the expansion coefficient associated with the largest eigenvalue, λ_1, yields information gain of $\lambda_1 / \sum_{j=1}^{D} \lambda_j$, which will be greater than 1/D. In the extreme case, when $\lambda_j = 0$, $\forall j > 1$, all the information about the pattern is compressed into one coefficient only. By observing this one coefficient alone, we gain complete knowledge about the pattern.

50 <u>REMARK</u>: We can choose the number of terms in 4 so that the approximation error is less than a prespecified fraction α of the total sum of eigenvalues, i.e.,

$$d = \min\left\{ r \mid r = 1, \ldots, D, \text{ s.t. } \sum_{j=1}^{r} \lambda_j \geq \alpha K \right\}.$$

The intuitively appealing information-compression property of the

K-L expansion has been the main motivation for development of a number of feature extraction methods based on this expansion. However, despite the common basis, the various K-L feature extraction methods differ considerably in the way the information-compression potential of the expansion has been used. In the following sections we shall be concerned with these methods, their differences, advantages and shortcomings. First of all, however, we shall comment on matrices of second order statistical moments which define K-L basis vectors.

9.5. K-L COORDINATE SYSTEM GENERATING MATRICES

In the discussion of theoretical properties of the K-L expansion above, we have seen that the K-L coordinate system associated with a data set $\{\underline{y}\}$ is defined solely by second order statistics of the data. In the absence of any information about the class membership of the elements of the data set, an obvious way of defining the matrix of second order moments which generates the K-L coordinate axes is as in 8. Alternatively, as the mean $\underline{\mu}$ of a set of unlabeled patterns is often of no significance, it is even more appropriate to use as a K-L coordinate system generating matrix the covariance matrix of the data, i.e.,

51 $$\Sigma = E\left\{(\underline{y}-\underline{\mu})(\underline{y}-\underline{\mu})^t\right\}.$$

If, however, the patterns in the data set are labeled, then second order statistical moments can be calculated in a number of ways leading to different K-L coordinate systems. For instance, in the pattern recognition context, $\{\underline{y}\}$ will be a mixture set containing elements of classes ω_i, $i=1,\ldots,c$ each occurring with *a priori* probability P_i and being characterized by the mean vector $\underline{\mu}_i$ and the class covariance matrix Σ_i. Then, in addition to 51, other options open. For instance, we can define the K-L coordinate system generating matrix as the average class conditional covariance matrix S_w.

52 $$S_w = \sum_{i=1}^{c} P_i \Sigma_i,$$

where

53 $$\Sigma_i = E\left\{(\underline{y}-\underline{\mu}_i)(\underline{y}-\underline{\mu}_i)^t\right\} \quad \underline{y}\epsilon\omega_i.$$

Alternatively, we could consider only one class at a time. The ith class K-L coordinate axes would then be defined as the system of eigenvectors of matrix Σ_i or, if the ith class mean is to be taken into consideration, then the generating matrix would be Φ_i

54 $$\Phi_i = E\left\{(\underline{y}-\underline{\mu})(\underline{y}-\underline{\mu})^t\right\} \quad \underline{y}\epsilon\omega_i.$$

Note that the differences between the K-L basis vectors defined by these matrices of second order statistical moments reflect the differences in the information content of the moments. In particular, the K-L coordinate system based on 51 will be optimal for compressing information conveyed by $\underline{y}$ irrespective of the class membership of the pattern. In the case of matrix S_w, the optimality of the K-L axes will apply only to the information contained in the class centralized vectors

55 $$\underline{z} = \underline{y}-\underline{\mu}_i \quad \underline{z}\epsilon\omega_i.$$

By analogy, the information compression properties of the K-L axes associated with either matrix Σ_i or Φ_i will only be class conditional.

The methods of feature extraction discussed in the following sections differ from each other depending on the type of discriminatory information they are designed to extract and consequently on the particular K-L coordinate systems employed by these methods. Additional factors determining a feature extractor are both the manner the information projected onto the axes of the coordinate systems is used and also on the particular property of the K-L axes being exploited.

9.6. EXTRACTION OF DISCRIMINATORY INFORMATION CONTAINED IN THE CLASS MEANS

In the majority of pattern recognition problems, the most significant information for classification purposes is contained in class conditional mean vectors $\underline{\mu}_i$, $\forall i$. Intuitively, it is apparent that the components of the mean vectors in the feature space should retain as much of this discriminatory information as possible. From our earlier discussion, we know that the discriminatory power of a feature is proportional to the magnitude of projection of the class mean vectors from the representation space onto the feature axis. However, it has been argued that the true potential of the feature depends also on its variance and the correlation with other variables. It seems reasonable, therefore, that to allow for simple assesment of goodness of individual features, the feature space should be constructed from coordinate axes which decorrelate variates of the centralized pattern vectors.

Recalling Sections 9.3 and 9.5, the coordinate system which decorrelates components of vectors $\underline{z}$ in 55 is the system of K-L basis vectors $U = \underline{u}_1, \ldots, \underline{u}_D]$ defined through matrix S_W in 52 as

56 $$S_w U - U\Lambda = 0.$$

Note that the jth diagonal element of Λ, λ_j, represents the average variance of feature $x_j = \underline{u}_j^t \underline{y}$. In the K-L coordinate system, the amount of discriminatory information, $J(x_j)$, conveyed by the jth feature is now given simply as

57 $$J(x_j) = \frac{\underline{u}_j^t S_b \underline{u}_j}{\lambda_j},$$

where S_b is the scatter matrix of class conditional mean vectors defined in Equation 6.16. Thus to retain maximum discriminatory information, the feature extractor $W = \left[\underline{w}_1, \ldots, \underline{w}_d\right]$ should be constructed from the first d K-L coordinate axes $\underline{u}_j$ arranged in the descending order of magnitudes of criterion $J(x_j)$, i.e.,

58 $$W = \left[\underline{u}_1, \ldots, \underline{u}_d\right],$$

where $\underline{u}_j$, j=1,...,d satisfy

59 $$J(x_1) \geq J(x_2) \geq \ldots \geq J(x_d) \geq \ldots \geq J(x_D).$$

60 <u>EXAMPLE</u>: Given $P_1 = P_2 = 0.5$, $\underline{\mu}_1 = [4,2]^t$, $\underline{\mu}_2 = [-4,-2]^t$,

$$\Sigma_1 = \begin{bmatrix} 3 & 1 \\ 1 & 3 \end{bmatrix} \qquad \Sigma_2 = \begin{bmatrix} 4 & 2 \\ 2 & 4 \end{bmatrix},$$

let us find the optimum 2×1 feature extractor W defined in 58.

Solving 56 where $S_w = 0.5\Sigma_1 + 0.5\Sigma_2$, we find the K-L coordinate axes $U = \left[\underline{u}_1, \underline{u}_2\right]$ and eigenvalues λ_1, λ_2, i.e. $\lambda_1 = 5$, $\lambda_2 = 2$

$$U = \begin{bmatrix} 0.707 & 0.707 \\ 0.707 & -0.707 \end{bmatrix}.$$

Matrix S_b needed for assessing discriminatory potential of each feature is given as

$$S_b = \sum_{i=1}^{2} P_i(\underline{\mu}_i - \underline{\mu})(\underline{\mu}_i - \underline{\mu})^t = \begin{bmatrix} 16 & 8 \\ 8 & 4 \end{bmatrix}.$$

Thus

$$J(x_1) = \frac{\underline{u}_1^t \, S_b \, \underline{u}_1}{\lambda_1} = 3.6$$

and

$$J(x_2) = 1$$

and since $J(x_1) > J(x_2)$ we finally get

$$W = \begin{bmatrix} 0.707 \\ 0.707 \end{bmatrix}.$$

The example is illustrated in Figure 9.3

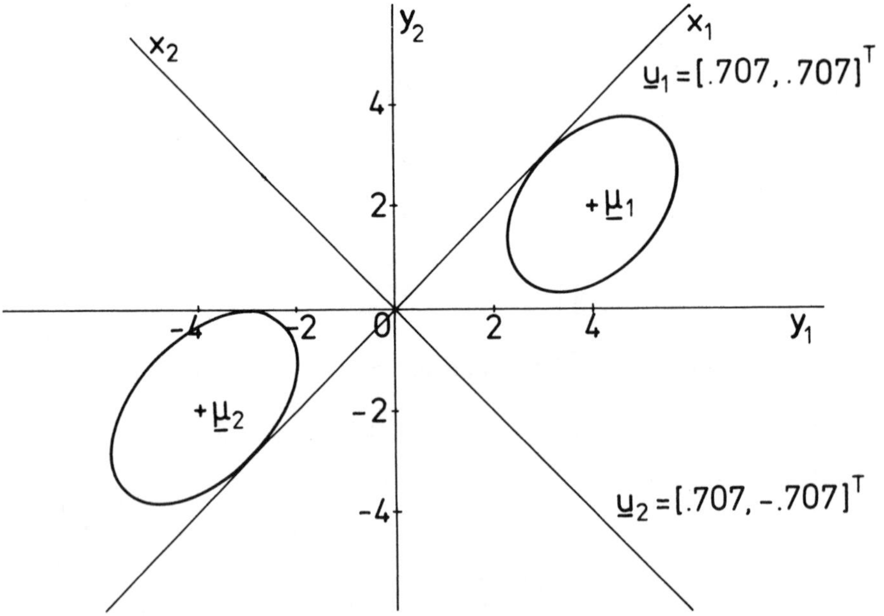

Figure 9.3. The K-L coordinate axes for the example in 9.60.

61 REMARK: Some saving of computation time could be achieved by constructing feature extractor W from axes $\underline{u}_j$, j=1,...,d, associated with the smallest eigenvalues λ_j of matrix S_w, i.e.,

62 $$\lambda_1 \le \lambda_2 \le \dots \le \lambda_d \le \dots \le \lambda_D.$$

The reliability of the resulting minimum population entropy feature extractor, however, would depend on the cumulative magnitude of the projections of the class mean vectors onto the axes of the feature space.

63 EXAMPLE: Let us determine the 2×1 minimum population entropy feature extractor for the problem given in the example in 60.

Since $\lambda_2<\lambda_1$, the minimum population entropy feature extractor will be the axis $\underline{u}_2$ (see Figure 9.3), i.e.

$$W = \begin{bmatrix} 0.707 \\ -0.707 \end{bmatrix}.$$

Note that this method leads to a suboptimal solution in the sense of criterion 59.

9.7. OPTIMAL COMPRESSION OF THE DISCRIMINATORY INFORMATION CONTAINED IN THE CLASS MEANS

The feature extraction method described in the previous section is very simple. However, its main shortcoming is that the discriminatory information contained in class conditional mean vectors $\underline{\mu}_i$ will, in general, be spread over all axes of the K-L coordinate system defined in Equation 56. It is possible, therefore, that if a large dimensionality reduction is required, i.e. d≪D, a significant amount of this information may be lost in the feature extraction process.

Let us consider again the basic problem of compressing the information content of the mean vectors. In the c-class problem, the space spanned by the class mean vectors is at most (c-1)-dimensional. It is therefore, plausible to hypothesize that a more efficient dimensionality reduction can be achieved.

Although the problem of determining the subspace spanned by a set of vectors is relatively simple, the search for an efficient feature extractor is constrained here by the requirement that the dimensionality-reducing transformation yields uncorrelated features.

Suppose for the moment that the average class conditional covariance matrix S_w of a mixture data set is an identity matrix. In this special case, S_w will be invariant under any orthonormal transformation and consequently the variates of the data transformed into the space defined by the class mean vectors will remain uncorrelated. In general, S_w will not be an identity matrix. Nevertheless, since S_w is symmetric positive definite, there exists a matrix B such that

64
$$B^t S_w B = I.$$

In physical terms, this prewhitening transformation implies that the pattern vector components are first decorrelated by the K-L transformation U in 56 and subsequently the variances of the decorrelated variates are normalized to unity, i.e.,

$$B = U\Lambda^{-1/2},$$

where Λ is the matrix of eigenvalues of S_w.

The prewhitening transformation B will, of course, affect not only the class centralized vectors, $\underline{z}$, but also the class mean vectors.

After the transformation, the scatter matrix of the mean vectors, S_b', will be

65
$$S_b' = B^t S_b B.$$

We can now compress the information contained in the class mean vectors transformed by prewhitening transformation B using the K-L expansion without affecting the covariance matrix of the transformed vectors $\underline{y}$. The optimal coordinate system $V=\left[\underline{v}_1,\ldots,\underline{v}_D\right]$ for representing this information is given as

66
$$S_b'V - V\tilde{\Lambda} = 0,$$

where $\tilde{\Lambda}$ is the diagonal matrix of eigenvalues $\tilde{\lambda}_j$, j=1,...,D of matrix S_b'.

Note that since the rank of S_b' is at most d = c-1, the matrix will have only d nonzero eigenvalues. This means that all the relevant information is compressed into d eigenvectors associated with the non-zero eigenvalues of S_b'. Denoting the system of these eigenvectors by V', i.e.,

67
$$V' = \left[\underline{v}_1,\ldots,\underline{v}_d\right],$$

it follows that the optimal feature extractor, W, which compresses all the information contained in the class mean vectors into a minimum number of features, is given as

68
$$W = U\Lambda^{-1/2}V'.$$

69 EXAMPLE: For the pattern recognition problem of the example in 60, find the optimum 2×1 feature extractor W as defined in 68.

First obtain the prewhitening transformation, B :

$$B = \begin{bmatrix} 0.707 & 0.707 \\ 0.707 & -0.707 \end{bmatrix} \begin{bmatrix} 0.447 & 0 \\ 0 & 0.707 \end{bmatrix} = \begin{bmatrix} 0.316 & 0.5 \\ 0.316 & -0.5 \end{bmatrix}$$

The transformed scatter matrix of the class mean vectors is then given as

$$S_b' = B^t S_b B = \begin{bmatrix} 3.6 & 1.897 \\ 1.897 & 1 \end{bmatrix}.$$

Solving eigenvalue problem 66 we get $\tilde{\lambda}_1=4.6$, $\tilde{\lambda}_2=0$,

$$V = \begin{bmatrix} 0.884 & -0.466 \\ 0.466 & 0.884 \end{bmatrix}.$$

The optimal feature extractor is thus

$$W = B\underline{v}_1 = \begin{bmatrix} 0.512 \\ 0.033 \end{bmatrix}.$$

Figure 9.4 shows individual stages of the feature extraction transformation and its effect on the data of the example.

70 <u>REMARK</u>: It is interesting to note that the feature extractor derived in this section is identical with that yielded by the discriminant analysis approach discussed in Chapter 6. This can be readily seen by considering equation 66. Expressing S_b' in terms of matrix S_b and using the relationship 64 we get

71 $$B^t S_b BV - B^t S_w BV\tilde{\Lambda} = 0.$$

Since B is nonsingular, 71 will be satisfied only if

$$|S_w^{-1} S_b BV - BV\tilde{\Lambda}| = 0.$$

Thus $\tilde{\lambda}_j$ and $B\underline{v}_j$, $\forall j$ are respectively the eigenvalues and eigenvectors of the product $S_w^{-1} S_b$ as in 6.86. Although the feature extractors 68

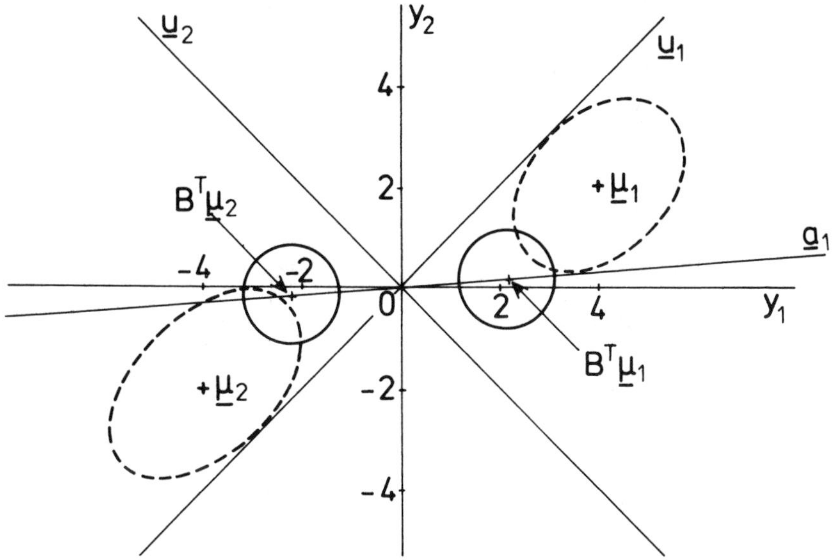

Figure 9.4. The stages of the optimal feature extraction transformation for the example in 9.69.

and 6.86 are identical, it is computationally easier to obtain W via two K-L expansions as described in this section. Each involves eigenvalue analysis of a symmetric matrix in contrast to the matrix product and the subsequent eigenvalue analysis of a nonsymmetric matrix required by the discriminant analysis approach. But even more important, as we have seen in Section 9.3, in the special case when class-centralized vectors, $\underline{z}$, are stationary, the K-L expansion in the first stage of the feature extractor design can be approximated by the discrete Fourier Transform which leads to further computational saving.

9.8. EXTRACTION OF THE DISCRIMINATORY INFORMATION CONTAINED IN CLASS-CENTRALIZED VECTORS

The feature extractors described in the preceding two sections ignore completely any discriminatory information that may be conveyed by the class-centralized vectors. Looking at Figure 9.5, it is apparent that, although in this particular case the classes have an identical mean, both the probability density functions $p(y|\omega_i)$, $i=1,2$ and, therefore, the class conditional variances $E\{y^2|y\epsilon\omega_i\}$ are different, reflecting the fact that up to a certain extent it is possible to differentiate between these two classes.

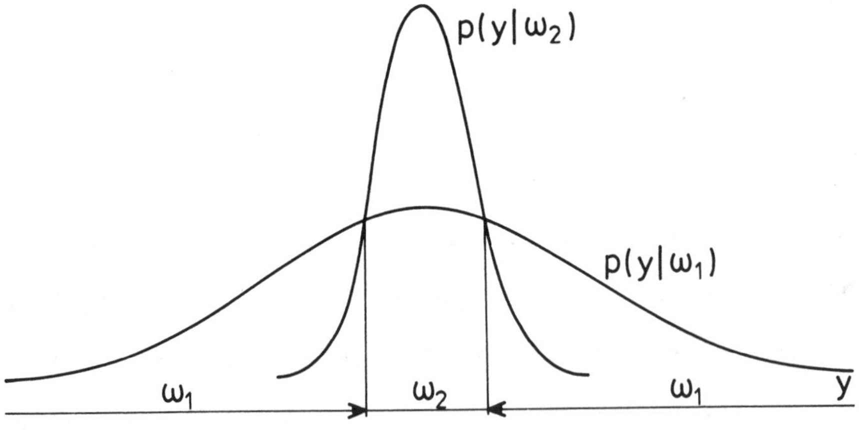

Figure 9.5. Example of the p.d.f.s of patterns in two partially separable classes having identical class means.

The ability to discriminate between elements of different classes seldom depends purely on the information contained in the class-centralized vectors but often this information plays a significant role in the design of low error-rate classification systems. The purpose of this section is to demonstrate how this information can be extracted.

Any function exposing differences between class-conditional variances of a feature can serve as a reliable indicator of its discriminatory information content only if the feature is uncorrelated with other variates. It follows that the system of candidate axes for the feature extractor W should be once again the K-L coordinate system U defined in 56. In order to allow for assessing the significance of each individual candidate basis vector $\underline{u}_j$ and consequently, whether this axis should be included in the feature extractor, it is essential to define a measure of discriminatory power of the jth feature.

Let us denote the variance of the jth feature in the ith class by γ_{ij}. It is intuitively apparent that, if the magnitudes of the class conditional variances (weighted by the *a priori* probability of occurence of classes, P_i) are identical, for all the classes the jth feature will have no discriminatory potential. On the other hand, different magnitudes of γ_{ij} indicate that the feature contains useful discriminatory information. The merit of a feature can be assessed by measuring the dispersion of its class-conditional variances. Recalling Section 9.3, as a suitable measure of dispersion we can use once again the logarithmic entropy function.

Let us define the normalized variance $\tilde{\gamma}_{ij}$ as

72 $$\tilde{\gamma}_{ij} = P_i \frac{\gamma_{ij}}{\lambda_j},$$

where λ_j is the total variance of the jth feature (the jth eigenvalue of matrix S_w), i.e.,

73 $$\lambda_j = \sum_i P_i \gamma_{ij}.$$

Then the entropy criterion of discriminatory power, $J(x_j)$ of feature x_j is given as

74 $$J(x_j) = -\sum_{i=1}^{c} \tilde{\gamma}_{ij} \log \tilde{\gamma}_{ij}.$$

Feature x_j can then be ignored if criterion function $J(x_j)$ approaches its maximum, log c, that is when $\tilde{\gamma}_{ij}$ are identical.

Alternatively, we can define the criterion of discriminatory information content as

75 $$J(x_j) = \prod_{i=1}^{c} \tilde{\gamma}_{ij}.$$

It is easy to show that this function also attains its maximum, $(1/c)^c$ when $\tilde{\gamma}_{ij}$ are identical for all i. Thus, features for which this criterion function reaches this maximum value can be discarded.

It follows that feature extractor W should be constructed from the first d K-L axes $\underline{u}_j$ arranged in the ascending order of magnitudes of the criterion $J(x_j)$ in 74 or 75, i.e.,

76 $$W = \left[\underline{u}_1, \ldots, \underline{u}_d\right]$$

such that

77 $$J(x_1) \leq J(x_2) \leq \ldots \leq J(x_d) \leq \ldots \leq J(x_D).$$

The method introduced in this section is optimal only if class-conditional covariance matrices Σ_i in 52 are identical. In general, when $\Sigma_i \neq \Sigma_j$ determination of the optimal feature extractor should be based on more sophisticated methods such as those discussed in Chapter 8. We have seen, however, that, from the point of view of computational complexity, these methods are very demanding especially in multiclass pattern recognition problems. Thus, in situations where computational efficiency is the decisive factor, the present method often becomes the only possible alternative.

78 EXAMPLE: For the problem given in the example in 60, find the optimal 2×1 matrix W for projecting discriminatory information contained in the class-centralized vectors into the feature space.

In the K-L space the class-conditional covariance matrices $U^t\Sigma_1U$ and $U^t\Sigma_2U$ are given respectively as

$$U^t\Sigma_1U = \begin{bmatrix} 4 & 0 \\ 0 & 2 \end{bmatrix} \qquad U^t\Sigma_2U = \begin{bmatrix} 6 & 0 \\ 0 & 2 \end{bmatrix}.$$

Then, substituting into 72, we find that

$$\tilde{\gamma}_{11} = 0.5\,\frac{4}{5} = 0.4 \qquad \tilde{\gamma}_{12} = 0.5$$
$$\tilde{\gamma}_{21} = 0.5\,\frac{6}{5} = 0.6 \qquad \tilde{\gamma}_{22} = 0.5.$$

Applying criterion 75 we get

$$J(x_1) = 0.24 \qquad J(x_2) = 0.25.$$

Thus, feature x_1 conveys more discriminatory information than feature x_2 and, therefore, axis $\underline{u}_1$ will be the optimal feature extractor W, i.e.,

$$W = \begin{bmatrix} 0.707 \\ 0.707 \end{bmatrix}.$$

9.9. FEATURE EXTRACTOR FOR UNSUPERVISED PATTERN RECOGNITION PROBLEMS

In unsupervised pattern recognition problems, the design of a decision-making system is based entirely on a training set of unlabeled patterns. The absence of the information regarding class membership of the training patterns implies that the class-conditional parameters, Σ_i and $\underline{\mu}_i$ cannot be inferred from the data and, as a result, none of the feature extraction methods discussed thus far will be applicable. In such a situation the only sensible approach to feature extraction is to take advantage of the general information-compression properties of the K-L expansion. More specifically, the feature extractor W should be constructed from the K-L coordinate axes, $\underline{u}_j$, j=1,...,D, satisfying

79 $$\Sigma\underline{u}_j - \lambda_j\underline{u}_j = 0,$$

where Σ is the mixture set covariance matrix defined in 51.

Recalling Section 9.2, to retain most of the information in $\underline{y}$, vectors $\underline{u}_j$, j=1,...,d, which form the columns of the feature extractor

80 $$W = \left[\underline{u}_1, \ldots, \underline{u}_d\right]$$

must be selected in the descending order of magnitudes of their corresponding eigenvalues, i.e.

81 $$\lambda_1 \geq \lambda_2 \geq \ldots \geq \lambda_d \geq \ldots \lambda_D.$$

82 <u>EXAMPLE</u>: Given a training set of unlabeled patterns with mixture mean $\underline{\mu} = [0,\ 0]^t$ and covariance matrix

$$\Sigma = \begin{bmatrix} 19.5 & 9.5 \\ 9.5 & 7.5 \end{bmatrix}.$$

let us find the optimum 2×1 feature extractor W.

Solving eigenvalue problem 79 we find that $\lambda_1 = 24.736$, $\lambda_2 = 2.263$ and

$$U = \left[\underline{u}_1,\ \underline{u}_2\right] = \begin{bmatrix} 0.875 & -0.482 \\ 0.482 & 0.875 \end{bmatrix}.$$

Since $\lambda_1 > \lambda_2$ the optimal feature extractor for this unsupervised pattern recognition problem is

$$W = \begin{bmatrix} 0.875 \\ 0.482 \end{bmatrix}.$$

The pattern recognition problem of the example in 82 is structurally identical with that of 60. Note that the matrix Σ generating the K-L axes satisfies

83 $$\Sigma = S_w + S_b.$$

Thus, if information about class membership of training patterns is not available, the resulting K-L coordinate system aims at a compromise between the optimal compression of the information contained in class-centralized vectors and the class mean vectors.

9.10. DISCUSSION AND COMMENTS

Recalling Section 9.3.3, under the assumption of stationarity of centralized pattern vectors, $\underline{z}$, the K-L coordinate axes U defined in 56 which are essential for determining feature extractors 58, 61, 68 and 76 can be approximated by the discrete sine and cosine functions, i.e.,

84 $$U = \left[\underline{u}_1, \ldots, \underline{u}_D\right] = \sqrt{\frac{2}{D}}\left[\underline{u}_{S1}, \underline{u}_{C1}, \ldots, \underline{u}_{S,D/2}, \underline{u}_{C,D/2}\right]$$

where

$$\underline{u}_{Sk} = \left[\sin\frac{2\pi k}{D}, \sin\frac{2\pi k2}{D}, \ldots, \sin\frac{2\pi kD}{D}\right]^t$$

$$k = 1, 2, \ldots, \left(\frac{D}{2} - 1\right)$$

$$\underline{u}_{Ck} = \left[\cos\frac{2\pi k}{D}, \cos\frac{2\pi k2}{D}, \ldots, \cos\frac{2\pi kD}{D}\right]^t$$

$$k = 1, 2, \ldots, \frac{D}{2}$$

and

$$\underline{u}_{S,D/2} = \frac{1}{\sqrt{2}}\,\underline{u}_{C,0}.$$

The constant $\sqrt{2/D}$ in 84 ensures that the discrete eigenfunctions satisfy the condition of orthonormality 5. The associated eigenvalues can be determined by calculating the expected value of the power spectrum of the pattern vector $\underline{y}$ at an appropriate frequency, i.e.

85 $$\lambda_k = \sum_{i=1}^{c} P_i \boldsymbol{E}\left\{\left[(\underline{y}-\underline{\mu}_i)^t \underline{u}_k\right]^2\right\}.$$

Note that, by virtue of this approximation, not only the tedious eigenanalysis of matrix S_W is obviated but, in addition, there is no need to compute this average within-class covariance matrix. As a result, the approximation leads to considerable computational simplification.

The simplest way of checking whether the stationarity assumption regarding vectors $\underline{z}$ is satisfied is to examine matrix

$$\sum_{i=1}^{c} P_i \boldsymbol{E}\left\{W^t(\underline{y}-\underline{\mu}_i)(\underline{y}-\underline{\mu}_i)^t W\right\}$$

obtained under the hypothesis that the series of successive elements of centralized pattern vectors is stationary. Since this matrix has only d^2 terms, it can be computed and inspected very rapidly. Now if this matrix is dominantly diagonal, then the Discrete Fourier Transform can be considered as an adequate approximation of the exact solution. The opposite case indicates that the assumption of stationarity is not justified and the method is not applicable.

In general, it will not be possible to approximate the eigenvectors of matrix Σ in 51 by the Discrete Fourier Transform, for pattern vectors $\underline{y}$ which define this matrix include class-conditional mean vectors and, therefore, they will not satisfy the stationarity assumption.

The problems of compressing discriminatory information contained in class-conditional mean vectors and in centralized vectors have been separately treated in this chapter. Consequently, a distinct feature-extraction mapping has been obtained for each of these specific problems. In practical situations, however, a feature extractor should be capable of extracting as much discriminatory information as possible regardless of its type. This could, of course, be achieved by devising an overall feature extraction criterion function which would take both these sources of discriminatory potential of a feature into consideration. Needless to say, such a complex criterion would be difficult to define and no doubt even more difficult to optimize. We shall be content here, therefore, with a suboptimal solution obtained by combining feature extractors of Sections 9.6 and 9.7 with that of Section 9.8. In particular, let the required dimensionality of the feature space, d, satisfy $d>c-1$. Then one possibility would be to augment the feature extractor given in 68 which contains all discriminatory information in the class means by $d-c+1$ columns of matrix W in 76.

Finally, the feature extractor of Section 9.9 should be used only for dimensionality reduction in unsupervised pattern recognition problems.

9.11. BIBLIOGRAPHICAL COMMENTS

The K-L expansion was introduced to pattern recognition by Watanabe (1965). Its ability to minimize both the representation entropy and the population entropy was shown respectively by Watanabe (1969), and

Tou and Heydorn (1967). The relationship of the K-L expansion and the Fourier transform was pointed out by Grenander and Szego (1958) and Fukunaga (1972). The generalized form of the K-L expansion is due to Chien and Fu (1967).

The feature extraction method of Section 9.9, known under the acronym of SELFIC, was proposed by Watanabe *et al.* (1967). The approach to feature extraction based on the minimum-population-entropy property of the K-L expansion was suggested by Tou and Heydorn (1967). The methods of Sections 9.7 and 9.8 are due to Kittler and Young (1973). An extension of these methods to high-dimensional problems is discussed in Kittler (1974 and 1975).

9.12. REFERENCES

Chien, Y.T., and Fu, K.S., "On the generalized Karhunen-Loeve expansion", *IEEE Trans. Inform. Theory*, vol.13, pp. 518-520, 1967.

Fukunaga, K., *Introduction to Statistical Pattern Recognition*, Academic Press, New York, 1972.

Grenander, U., and Szego, G., *Toeplitz Forms and Their Applications*, University of California Press, Berkeley and Los Angeles, 1958.

Kittler, J., "A method of feature selection for high dimensional pattern recognition problems", *Proc. Second Internat. Conf. on Pattern Recognition*, Copenhagen, 1974, pp. 41-48.

Kittler, J., "Practical aspects of the Karhunen-Loeve feature selection procedure for high dimensional pattern recognition problems, *Proc. Internat. Comput. Symposium*, Taipei, 1975, pp. 429-433.

Kittler, J., "Mathematical methods of feature selection in pattern recognition, *Internat, J. Man Mach. Stud.*, vol. 7, pp. 609-637, 1975.

Kittler, J., and Young, P.C., "A new approach to feature selection based on the Karhunen-Loeve expansion", *Pattern Recognition*, vol. 5, pp. 335-352, 1973.

Kittler, J., "Feature selection methods based on the Karhunen-Loeve expansion", in *Pattern Recognition Theory and Application*, K.S. Fu and A.B. Whinston Eds., Noordhoff, Leyden, 1977, pp. 61-74.

Tou, J.T., and Heydorn, R.P., "Some approaches to optimum feature extraction", in *Computer and Information Sciences II*, J.T. Tou Ed., Academic Press, New York, 1967, pp. 57-89.

Watanabe, S., "Karhunen-Loeve expansion and factor analysis", *Trans. Fourth Prague Conf. on Information Theory*, 1965.

Watanabe, S., Lambert, P.S., Kulikowski, C.A., Buxton, J.L., and Walker, R., "Evaluation and selection of variables in pattern recognition", in *Computer and Information Sciences II*, J.T. Tou Ed., Academic Press, New York, 1967, pp. 91-112.

Watanabe, S., *Knowing and Guessing*, John Wiley, New York, 1969.

9.13. PROBLEMS

1. Find the system of orthonormal axes W that decorrelate the components of pattern vector $\underline{y}$. Show that W is the K-L coordinate system.

2. Let ε_s be the realization at an instant s of a normally distributed random variable with a zero mean and a finite variance. Show that the autoregressive process $z_s=\phi\cdot z_{s-1}+\varepsilon_s$, where $|\phi|<1$ and ε_s is independent of z_s, is stationary with a zero mean. Suppose that pattern vector $\underline{y}$ is formed by taking for its components D consecutive samples of the time series z_s. Comment on the K-L coordinate system of an ensemble of such vectors.

3. Let $p(\underline{y})\sim\mathcal{N}(0,\Sigma)$ in a d-dimensional space. Find a parametric form for the population entropy $H_p = \int p(\underline{y})\log p(\underline{y})d\underline{y}$.

4. Let Σ_i and P_i be respectively the covariance matrix and the *a priori* probability of class ω_i, i=1,2. Suppose that the data is subjected to a prewhitening transformation B such that $B^tS_wB=I$, where $S_w=\sum_i P_i\Sigma_i$. Show that the K-L coordinate axes generated by matrices $P_1B^t\Sigma_1B$ and $P_2B^t\Sigma_2B$ are identical. Denote by Λ_i the matrix of eigenvalues of $P_iB^t\Sigma_iB$. Show that $\Lambda_1=I-\Lambda_2$.

5. Apply the method of Section 9.7 to find the best feature extractor for mapping the data in Problem 6 of Chapter 8 into a unidimensional space.

6. Find the extrema of the function $f = \prod_{i=1}^{d} \sigma_i$ in the domain $0 \leq \sigma_i \leq 1$, $\forall i$, subject to the constraint $\sum_{i=1}^{d} \sigma_i = 1$.

Chapter 10

PERFORMANCE ESTIMATION

10.1. INTRODUCTION

If the search for informative features and the design of an effective classifier are essential steps in pattern recognition system design, the prediction of future classification performance is by no means a less important one.

1 The first idea that comes to mind is to calculate the performance index, for example the average probability of misclassification, by using methods as in Chapter 2. Unfortunately, as we already commented, this is in general an impossible task, and even in the rare cases where the calculation can be performed, it may yield results which are not very realistic.

2 An obvious alternative is to test the classifier experimentally and to use the result of the test as an estimate of future performance. As an historical comment, let us remark that variations on this theme have constituted the essential segment of early research work on performance evaluation.

3 More recent techniques have evolved from the theory of the

error-reject tradeoff which we discussed in Chapters 2 and 3. Here, the basic idea is to estimate, say, the probability of misclassification for each test sample, and to average the estimate over a set of test samples. Estimation methods belonging to this group have also been extended to the problem of nonparametric estimation of feature selection criterion functions.

Clearly, the last two groups of methods rely in a very direct way on the available samples. As we proceed throughout this chapter, it will become more and more apparent that samples used to design the classifier and samples used to test it should be statistically independent. Hence, the minimum requirement is that they are *different*. The imperative need for different data presents the designer with an embarrassing dilemma. In practice, the amount of available data is always *finite*, and, for various reasons, it is frequently smaller than one would like. If he reserves most of his data for designing the classifier, he will have little confidence in the test. On the other hand, if he reserves most of his data for testing the classifier, he will not have a good design.

A consequence of this dilemma is that the need to use different samples for design and test is in fact frequently overlooked in practice. Therefore it may be worthwile to start our discussion by examining the perils involved.

10.2. THE PERILS OF RESUBSTITUTION

The practice that consists in using the same set of samples to design a classifier and to test it is known - for obvious reasons - as the *resubstitution* method. Let us briefly examine two deceiving examples of the use of the resubstitution method.

4 In one particular experiment, let the design set S_n consist of n samples from two classes ω_1 and ω_2 which, for the purposes of the present discussion, have equal *a priori* probabilities and identical class-conditional distributions. Such an experiment is called the *no-information experiment*. We shall assume that the designer is not aware that he is dealing with a no-information experiment. Let us suppose that he wants to use the Perceptron learning algorithm of Section 4.4.2 to design a linear discriminant function. If the number n of samples is not larger than twice the dimensionality d of the pattern space, we know from Section 4.4.1 that with probability very close to one, a hyperplane exists that separates the samples perfectly. So, let us suppose that such a hyperplane is found. Then, while testing the classifier with the design data, the designer would observe no classification error. On the basis of this result he might be tempted to conclude that a useful set of features and an excellent decision rule have been selected whereas, in effect, a class has been perfectly distinguished from itself! In other words, in this experiment, the empirical error-count with the resubstitution method gives an over-optimistic result of zero when the actual probability of misclassification *for future patterns* is precisely 1/2.

5 As a second glaring illustration of the possible pathological behavior of the resubstitution error-count, let us simply observe that when classification is done with the nearest neighbor rule, it yields again an over-optimistic result of zero *for all problems* provided only that no two or more design samples coincide.

These extreme cases are not intended to demonstrate that resubstitution is a uniformly poor method. Actually it has some merits which we shall discuss in due time. It must be kept in mind however that, if handled without care, it may produce quite misleading results.

10.3. THE COMPARISON OF COMPETING DESIGNS

One of the possible reasons for wanting to know the performance of a classifier is to allow the comparison of two or more competing designs. It is frequently very difficult to determine which design is best. Therefore, it is of interest to examine how this problem can be treated.

Suppose first that we are *given* a classifier, i.e., one decision rule $\hat{\omega}(\underline{x})$ and one set S of samples $S = \left\{\underline{x}_i, \theta_i\right\}_{i=1}^{n}$ where θ_i is the true class of $\underline{x}_i$. Let E denote the actual but unknown error probability of the classifier in question.

6 Let the random variable ζ be defined as follows

$$\zeta(\underline{x}_i) = 0 \quad \text{if} \quad \hat{\omega}(\underline{x}_i) = \theta_i,$$
$$= 1 \quad \text{if} \quad \hat{\omega}(\underline{x}_i) \neq \theta_i.$$

Then, for an arbitrary $\underline{x}$, $\zeta(\underline{x})$ is (to a very high degree of approximation) a Bernoulli random variable that takes value 1 with probability E and value 0 with probability 1-E. Let $\tau = \sum_{i=1}^{n} \zeta(\underline{x}_i)$ denote the number of samples from S that are misclassified by $\hat{\omega}$. Clearly τ has a binomial distribution,

$$\Pr\{\tau = \nu | E\} = \binom{n}{\nu} E^{\nu} (1-E)^{n-\nu}, \quad \nu = 0, 1, \ldots, n.$$

The fraction τ/n of misclassified samples is therefore the *maximum likelihood estimate* $\hat{E}$ of E. The properties of this estimate are well known. As

$$\boldsymbol{E}\{\tau\} = \sum_{\nu=0}^{n} \nu \Pr\{\tau=\nu|E\} = nE,$$

and

$$\sigma^2\{\tau\} = \sum_{\nu=0}^{n} \nu^2 \Pr\{\tau=\nu|E\} - [\boldsymbol{E}\{\tau\}]^2 = nE(1-E),$$

we have

$$\boldsymbol{E}\{\hat{E}\} = E, \text{ and } \sigma^2\{\hat{E}\} = E(1-E)/n.$$

The estimator is *unbiased* and *consistent.*

The *point estimate* $\hat{E}=\tau/n$ provides us quite useful information. Yet, it leaves something to be desired. As E may be any real number, it is clear that, in general $\Pr\{\hat{E}=E\}=0$. Therefore, it is desirable that the estimator be accompanied by some measure of the possible estimation error.

In fact, instead of making the inference of estimating the true value of E to be a point, we might want to make the inference of estimating that, with some measure of assurance, the true value of E is contained in some interval. Classical statistics provides us with the appropriate tools in the form of *confidence intervals.* In view of the practical importance of the subject matter, simple ways of obtaining confidence intervals are outlined hereafter.

As τ is binomially distributed, the asymptotic distribution of $\hat{E}=\tau/n$ is approximately normal with mean E and variance $E(1-E)/n$. Thus, by the De Moivre-Laplace limit theorem, an approximate 100γ percent confidence interval for E is obtained by inverting the inequalities in

$$\Pr\left\{-z < \frac{\hat{E}-E}{[E(1-E)/n]^{1/2}} < z\right\} \cong \gamma,$$

where z is the $[(1+\gamma)/2]$th quantile point of the standard normal distribution. So z is given by $\Phi(z)-\Phi(-z) = \gamma$ where

$$\Phi(z) = \frac{1}{\sqrt{2\pi}} \int_{-\infty}^{z} \exp\left[-y^2/2\right] dy.$$

Inversion of the above inequalities yields

$$\Pr\left\{\frac{2n\hat{E}+z^2-z\sqrt{4n\hat{E}+z^2-4n\hat{E}^2}}{2(n+z^2)} < E < \frac{2n\hat{E}+z^2+z\sqrt{4n\hat{E}+z^2-4n\hat{E}^2}}{2(n+z^2)}\right\} \cong \gamma.$$

For large n, this can be simplified without unduly affecting the accuracy of the approximation. In particular

7 $$\Pr\left\{\hat{E}-z\sqrt{\frac{\hat{E}(1-\hat{E})}{n}} < E < \hat{E} + z\sqrt{\frac{\hat{E}(1-\hat{E})}{n}}\right\} \cong \gamma$$

gives an approximate 100γ percent confidence interval for E. We note that $\sqrt{\hat{E}(1-\hat{E})/n}$ is the sample-based estimate $\hat{\sigma}\{\hat{E}\}$ of the standard deviation $\sigma\{\hat{E}\}$. Thus the inequalities 7 readily convert to give

8 $$\Pr\left\{\hat{E}-z\hat{\sigma}\{\hat{E}\} < E < \hat{E} + z\hat{\sigma}\{\hat{E}\}\right\} \cong \gamma.$$

In particular, for $z=1.960$ we find in the table of the cumulative normal distribution that $2[1-\Phi(z)]=0.05$. Therefore,

9 $$\Pr\left\{\hat{E} - 1.96\hat{\sigma}\{\hat{E}\} < E < \hat{E} + 1.96\hat{\sigma}\{\hat{E}\}\right\} \cong 0.95$$

gives an approximate 95 percent confidence interval for E.

Let us now return to our initial preoccupation of comparing the performance of two, or more, competing designs. We wish to illustrate the situation with a simple numerical example.

10 Suppose that we are given two classifiers with unknown error

probabilities E_1 and E_2, and a test set consisting of, say, 100 samples. Suppose also that the number of classification errors are $\tau_1=10$ with the first classifier, and $\tau_2=13$ with the second one. By using 9, we find that 95 percent confidence intervals are (0.04,0.16) for E_1 and (0.06,0.20) for E_2. Clearly, all we can conclude from the experiment is that we are not in a position to decide that one classifier is definitely better than the other. In fact, with the same empirical frequencies of misclassifications, it is not until we have tested a few thousand samples that we could decide with some measure of assurance that the first classifier is indeed superior to the other one.

It should be noted that, to obtain the inequalities 8, many simplifying assumptions were made. More accurate limits of the confidence interval can be found either by referring to statistical tables, or by making use of the so-called *inverse sine transform*. The latter is based on the fact that if τ has a binomial distribution with mean E,

$$T = \sin^{-1}\sqrt{\frac{\tau}{n+1}} + \sin^{-1}\sqrt{\frac{\tau+1}{n+1}}$$

has an asymptotically normal distribution with mean $2\sin^{-1}\sqrt{E}$ and variance $\sigma^2\{T\}=(n+1)^{-1}$. (To assess the accuracy of the approximation in 8 above, note that for $n=100$, $\tau=10$ and $\gamma=0.95$, statistical tables give the interval (0.04, 0.17)).

10.4. COMMENTS

The discussion thus far was merely intended to demonstrate that the estimation of future classification performance based on a finite amount of data may be a very critical problem indeed. Quite often, the amount of available data is actually too small to enable one to predict the future performance with a reasonable accuracy. When sufficient data is available, one may still wonder how to use it most efficiently. Moreover, it should be clear from Section 10.2 that the estimation technique itself may be responsible for the estimate being quite off the target. And even when the technique cannot be questioned, the *quality* - or the *reliability* - of the estimate as a *predictor* of future performance must in any case be carefully assessed.

It is with these principles in mind that we shall turn in the following sections to the consideration of actual probability of error estimation schemes. Fortunately enough, many of these schemes can be considered without reference to the specific classification procedure used.

A natural, but extremely difficult question arising at this point is : how large should be a large enough design set ? From our investigation of the probability of linear separability in Chapter 4 and our discussion of the no-information experiment in Section 10.2 above, it should be apparent that this question cannot be answered without regard to the dimensionality of the pattern space. Another important factor that should be taken into account is the amount of prior knowledge about the underlying probability structure : the less is known about the underlying structure, the larger is the ratio of sample-size to dimensionality that should be needed. Unfortunately, apart from a few qualitative statements and rules of thumb, the important question of sample-size and dimensionality remains a largely unsolved problem. We shall therefore limit ourselves to refer the interested reader to a few relevant works at the end of this chapter.

10.5. THE APPARENT ERROR-RATE

Very much in the spirit of Chapter 2, let us assume that our design approach consists in estimating the underlying distributions from the available samples and using a decision rule which is Bayes-optimal with respect to the estimated distributions. Let us consider a two-class case and let $\hat{P}_i$ and $\hat{p}(\underline{x}|\omega_i)$ be the sample-based estimates of the *a priori* probability P_i and the class-conditional p.d.f. $p(\underline{x}|\omega_i)$ respectively, i=1,2. The sample-based, minimum error-rate decision rule is given by

11 $$\hat{\omega}(\underline{x}) = \omega_1 \quad \text{if } \hat{P}_1\hat{p}(\underline{x}|\omega_1) > \hat{P}_2\hat{p}(\underline{x}|\omega_2), \qquad = \omega_2 \quad \text{otherwise.}$$

One method of estimating the error probability E of the rule 11 is to substitute $\hat{P}_i$ and $\hat{p}(\underline{x}|\omega_i)$ for P_i and $p(\underline{x}|\omega_i)$ in the expression of the Bayes error probability. The estimate so obtained is called the *apparent* error probability. It is given by

12 $$\hat{E} = 1 - \int \max_{i=1,2} \hat{P}(\omega_i|\underline{x})\hat{p}(\underline{x})dx.$$

At this point an ambiguity arises because it is not clear whether $\hat{E}$ in 12 should be regarded as an estimate of the Bayes error-rate E^* relative to the true underlying model or as an estimate of the future error-rate E of the sample-based decision rule. It is clear that $E^* \leq E$, and the apparent error-rate $\hat{E}$ may be greater or less than E^* and E.

However, it has a definite tendency to be optimistically biased. A detailed analysis indicates that this tendency arises from the fact that the expectation of the maximum of several random variables exceeds the maximum of their expectations.

We already pointed out that the calculation of the integral in 12 may be extremely difficult if not impossible to perform, the notable exception being the multivariate normal case with different mean vectors $\underline{\mu}_1$ and $\underline{\mu}_2$, and common covariance matrix Σ. Recalling Section 2.5 and assuming equal *a priori* probabilities, the error probability E^* is given by

13 $$E^* = \frac{1}{\sqrt{2\pi}} \int_{\Delta/2}^{\infty} e^{-y^2/2}\, dy,$$

where $\Delta^2 = (\underline{\mu}_1-\underline{\mu}_2)^t \Sigma^{-1} (\underline{\mu}_1-\underline{\mu}_2)$ is the Mahalanobis distance. When the parameters $\underline{\mu}_1$, $\underline{\mu}_2$ and Σ are not known, the sample mean vectors $\hat{\underline{\mu}}_1$ and $\hat{\underline{\mu}}_2$ and the sample covariance matrix $\hat{\Sigma}$ are substituted for μ_1, μ_2 and Σ respectively with

14 $$\hat{\underline{\mu}}_i = \frac{1}{n_i} \sum_{\underline{x}_j \epsilon \omega_i} \underline{x}_j, \qquad i=1,2,$$

15 $$\hat{\Sigma} = \frac{1}{n-2} \left\{ \sum_{x_j \epsilon \omega_1} (\underline{x}_j-\underline{\mu}_1)(\underline{x}_j-\underline{\mu}_1)^t + \sum_{x_\ell \epsilon \omega_2} (\underline{x}_\ell-\underline{\mu}_2)(\underline{x}_\ell-\underline{\mu}_2)^t \right\},$$

where n_i is the number of class-ω_i samples, and 15 reflects the assumption that both classes have identical covariance matrix. The substitution in 13 of the sample-based Mahalanobis distance computed with 14 and 15 yields an estimate of the apparent error-rate.

16 The behavior of the estimate so obtained has received considerable attention and to do justice to the subject matter would

require much more space and effort than can be accommodated in this book. Theoretical aspects of the problem involve the distribution of the classification statistic, *viz.*, the Anderson discriminant plane, on the one hand, and the convergence properties of the estimator on the other. The estimate is known to be optimistically biased. Suitable correction terms have been suggested to adjust either the estimate of Δ^2 or the estimate of E^*. However they are rather complicated and their robustness when encountering departures from normality is questionable. On the other hand, as one should always suspect the validity of an assumed parametric model, we shall concentrate hereafter on methods that do not require parametric assumptions.

10.6. ERROR-COUNTING METHODS OF ERROR ESTIMATION

In the early days of pattern recognition, much of the research on error-counting methods of error estimation arose from recurrent dissatisfaction with simple schemes, such as the resubstitution method, in the small-sample case. The evolution that took place and the results obtained along the way are probably better appreciated when placed in the proper historical perspective.

10.6.1. The Resubstitution Estimate

When pattern recognition as a field of study was still in its infancy, a substantial segment of the research work was concerned with Perceptron-like learning algorithms. Recall that one essential property of the Perceptron learning algorithm is that it does converge to one hyperplane that correctly classifies all the training samples provided only that one such hyperplane exists. Variations on this theme were addressing the nonseparable case and were often aimed at minimizing the number of misclassifications on the learning data. In other words, the design criterion was the empirical error-count obtained by resubstitution. It was soon realized that, in experiments involving small to moderate sample-sizes, the nice performance figures on the design sets did not extend to independent test sets. Consequently, researchers were left with no other choice but to find better ways of using the available data.

17 One should note however that when a large design set is available, the resubstitution error-count is probably as good an estimator as any other one. For instance, it may be shown that, in a problem of two classes with equal *a priori* probabilities and multivariate normal data with identical covariance matrices, both the bias and the variance of the resubstitution error-count approach zero as the size of the design set increases without bound. Hence, in this case, the resubstitution estimate is a *consistent* estimator.

10.6.2. The Holdout Estimate

The most obvious alternative to the resubstitution scheme is to partition the data into two mutually exclusive subsets and to use one subset for designing the classifier and the other one to test it. This scheme is known as the *holdout* method. It is obvious that this approach makes poor use of the data since a classifier designed on the entire data set will, on the average, perform better than a classifier designed on only a portion of the data. In case a designer is satisfied with the holdout result, he will normally re-design the classifier based on all the samples and evaluation of the performance of the final design must use again the resubstitution method.

18 For small to moderate sample-sizes, very significant discrepancies between the resubstitution and holdout estimates may be observed. The latter one being an order of magnitude larger than the former is all but exceptional. As it turns out the holdout method has a definite tendency to over-estimate the actual error-rate. In a Bayesian framework, this behavior of the holdout estimate can be explained as follows.

19 Let P denote a global specification of the probability structure of a given problem. In general, the probability of error is a function of two arguments

$$E = E(P_d, P_t),$$

where P_d and P_t represent the specifications of the distributions associated with the design and test sets respectively. When the classifier is the Bayes decision rule, it is clear that

$$E^{\star} = E(P,P) \le E(P',P), \quad \forall P' \neq P.$$

When our knowledge $\hat{P}_d$ and $\hat{P}_t$ of P_d and P_t is inferred from finite sets of n_d and n_t design and test samples, $\hat{P}_d$ is a random variable and

$$E(P,P) \le E(\hat{P}_d, P).$$

Thus

$$E(P,P) \le \boldsymbol{E}\left\{E(\hat{P}_d, P)\right\}.$$

Therefore, if a large test set is available and if $\hat{P}_t \to P$ as $n_t \to \infty$, the holdout estimate is a biased estimate of $E^{\star}$. The bias is such that the expected value is an upper bound on $E^{\star}$.

So, the holdout method is uneconomical in its way of using the data and gives pessimistic error estimates. The next method to which we now turn goes a long way towards making efficient use of the available data and reducing the bias of the error estimate.

10.6.3. The Leave-One-Out Estimate

The so-called *leave-one-out* or *deleted* estimate is formed in the following manner. Remove *one* sample, say $(\underline{x}_i, \theta_i)$, from the design set S_n. Design the classifier using S_{n-1} and test it with $(\underline{x}_i, \theta_i)$. Return $(\underline{x}_i, \theta_i)$ to the design set and repeat these operations for $i=1,\ldots,n$. The empirical frequency of classification error is the leave-one-out estimate of E. Clearly, with this method, virtually all samples are used in each design, and all samples are ultimately used in the tests, though each design and test sets may be regarded as independent.

20 The leave-one-out error estimate has been found experimentally to be approximately unbiased, whatever be the classifier and the underlying distributions. Referring to our discussion in 19 above, the unbiasedness can be explained by the fact that, although independence is preserved, the "models" $\hat{P}_d$ and $\hat{P}_t$ of the distributions underlying design and test sets are essentially identical.

In counterpart, the leave-one-out method suffers from at least two disadvantages. Firstly, it has been established that bias reduction is achieved at the expense of an increase in the variance of the estimator. Secondly, it is quite clear that the method may involve excessive computation as n design sessions are required. However, in the cases when the major computational burden consists in inverting a matrix, say a covariance matrix (for instance in the calculations of the Anderson discriminant plane, cf. 2.54, or the MSE linear discriminant function, cf. 4.56), the additional computation may be greatly reduced by repeated use of the formula of Sherman - Morisson and Bartlett which we encountered in Equation 4.48. The details of the calculations are left as an exercise for the reader.

10.6.4. The Rotation Estimate

The next and last error-counting method which we shall examine is a compromise between the holdout and leave-one-out methods. Let the integer ν be a divisor of n and let the training set be partitioned into n/ν disjoint subsets. Then, remove the ith subset from the design set, design the classifier with the remaining data and test it on the ith subset, return the subset in question to the design set, and repeat the operation for $i=1,\ldots,n/\nu$. The *rotation* estimate is the average frequency of misclassification over the n/ν test sessions.

21 It is clear that when $\nu=1$, the rotation method reduces to the leave-one-out method, whereas when $\nu=n/2$ it reduces essentially to the holdout method where the roles of design and test sets are interchanged. The technique that consists in interchanging design and test data is known in statistical circles as *cross-validation in both directions*. The rotation method reduces both the bias inherent to the holdout method and, to some extent, the computational burden associated with the leave-one-out method.

10.7. AN ALTERNATIVE TO THE ERROR-COUNTING APPROACH

The error-counting methods we just described may be viewed as the *first generation* of nonparametric error estimators. Some of these estimators have been further improved and refined in a number of ways, sometimes at the cost of an overwhelming increase in computational complexity. However, we shall not pursue this topic further. As usual, some useful references may be found at the end of this chapter.

Chronologically, interest in error-counting estimators was followed by work on a *second generation* of error estimators based on the theory of the error-reject tradeoff which we discussed at some length in Chapter 2 in the framework of the Bayes decision theory, and in Chapter 3 in the nearest neighbor framework.

That the error-reject or error-acceptance relationships may prove useful in obtaining error estimators should come as no surprise. For example, let us recall Equation 3.69, *viz.*,

22 $$E_{k,\ell} = \sum_{j=\ell}^{k} \left(1 - \frac{j}{k+1}\right) A_{k+1,s=j},$$

where $E_{k,\ell}$ is the error-rate with the (k,ℓ)-NNR and $A_{k+1,s=j}$ is the acceptance rate with the $(k+1)$-NNR and a score of j out of $(k+1)$ votes. A simple *plug-in* estimator of $E_{k,\ell}$ is formed by substituting estimators of acceptance rates in Equation 22. We shall see hereafter the same principle at work in a number of instances.

Estimators of this type have two advantages over error-counting estimators. Firstly, they are intrinsically designed to have a smaller variance for reasons that we shall uncover in a moment.

Secondly, they permit to use *unclassified samples* as test samples, one fact which we already mentioned in connection with Equation 3.62. Indeed, acceptance-rates may be estimated without regard to the true class of the samples being classified. Clearly, the use of unclassified test samples may be of great economic importance when the labeling of test samples is difficult and expensive, and when it can be an additional source of error as may be found in almost every kind of application.

10.8. RISK AVERAGING METHODS OF ERROR ESTIMATION

10.8.1. Introduction

23 Let us consider first a very simple problem of two pattern classes where we assume that the underlying distributions are known, and we have a set S of independent, identically distributed, unclassified samples $S = \left\{x_j\right\}_{j=1}^{n}$ drawn from the mixture density $p(\underline{x})$. The conditional probability of error when an arbitrary sample $\underline{x}$ is classified according to the Bayes rule is (cf. 2.4)

24 $$e^*(\underline{x}) = \min\left\{P(\omega_1|\underline{x}), P(\omega_2|\underline{x})\right\},$$

and the average Bayes risk is

25 $$E^* = \int e^*(\underline{x})p(\underline{x})d\underline{x}.$$

As we know $e^*(\underline{x})$ as a function of $\underline{x}$, the Bayes error E^* can be estimated by the sample mean of $e^*\left(\underline{x}_j\right)$ for the n samples.

26 $$\hat{E} = \frac{1}{n}\sum_{j=1}^{n} e^*\left(\underline{x}_j\right).$$

By taking expectation we find

$$\mathbf{E}\{\hat{E}\} = \frac{1}{n}\sum_{j=1}^{n} \mathbf{E}\left\{e^{\star}(\underline{x}_j)\right\} = E^{\star}.$$

So, the estimate is unbiased. Moreover, since $0 \le e^{\star}(\underline{x}) \le 1/2$, $\forall \underline{x}$, we have $\left[e^{\star}(\underline{x})\right]^2 \le e^{\star}(\underline{x})/2$. There follows

$$\sigma^2\{e^{\star}(\underline{x}_j)\} = \mathbf{E}\left\{\left[e^{\star}(\underline{x}_j)\right]^2\right\} - (E^{\star})^2$$
$$\le \frac{1}{2}E^{\star} - (E^{\star})^2 = E^{\star}(1-E^{\star}) - \frac{1}{2}E^{\star}.$$

Therefore, the variance of $\hat{E}$ in 26 is bounded by

27 $$\sigma^2\{\hat{E}\} \le \frac{E^{\star}(1-E^{\star})}{n} - \frac{1}{2n}E^{\star}.$$

Note that, in the above analysis, the class assignments of the $\underline{x}_j$ were not needed.

On the other hand, if the class assignments of the $\underline{x}_j$ was available and an error-count was made, the theory of Section 10.3 would be applicable. The error-count estimator, say $\hat{E}'$ would also be unbiased and would have a variance

28 $$\sigma^2\{\hat{E}'\} = \frac{E^{\star}(1-E^{\star})}{n}.$$

Comparison of 27 and 28 shows that the first estimator achieves a reduction in variance of at least $E^{\star}/2n$. The reduction in variance must be attributed to the fact that the error-count estimate uses a (0,1) quantization of the error on a test sample, while $e^{\star}(\underline{x}_j)$ in 26 assigns a real value from the interval [0,1/2].

This simple reasoning shows that the estimator in 26 exhibits both the interesting properties which we announced in the previous section. Unfortunately, in most instances the exact value of $e^{\star}(\underline{x}_j)$ is not known, and we are left with no other choice but to estimate $e^{\star}(\underline{x}_j)$ first. This can be done with the classical tools of nonparametric estimation. In what follows, however, we shall concentrate on the k-NN estimation method for the purpose of simplifying the exposition with the aid of the results derived in Chapter 3.

10.8.2. Direct k-NN Estimate of the Bayes Error-Rate

29 Let us consider a more realistic situation where we have a design set S_d of n_d classified samples, and a test set S_t of n_t possibly unclassified test samples. Here we shall use the representation of the classes ω_1 and ω_2 in the k-NN to the test sample $\underline{x}$ from the design set S_d to estimate the conditional probability of error $e^*(\underline{x})$ in 24. For fixed k, and under the assumption of absolute continuity of the class-conditional probability densities it can be shown using standard nonparametric estimation techniques that one maximum likelihood estimate of $P(\omega_i|\underline{x})$ is k_i/k where k_i is the number of class-ω_i neighbors among the k-NN to $\underline{x}$ from S_d, i=1,2.

Hence, one maximum likelihood estimate of the conditional Bayes risk is

30 $$\hat{e}(\underline{x}_j) = \min\left\{\frac{k_1}{k}, \frac{k_2}{k}\right\},$$

and by using this estimate in 26 we obtain

31 $$\hat{E} = \frac{1}{n_t} \sum_{\underline{x}_j \in S_t} \min\left\{\frac{k_1}{k}, \frac{k_2}{k}\right\}.$$

To calculate the expected value of $\hat{e}$ in 30, we have to invoke the large-sample assumption for S_d. For the sake of simplicity but without loss of generality, let us assume k odd. Consequently the possible values of $\hat{e}(\underline{x})$ are $\left(1 - \frac{q}{k}\right)$, q=k',...,k with k'=⌈k/2⌉ as in

Equation 3.14. Moreover, a little thought indicates that $\hat{e}(\underline{x})$ takes any of these values with a probability $\sum_{i=1}^{2} a^{i}_{k,s=q}(\underline{x})$ where $a^{i}_{k,s=q}(\underline{x})$ is the conditional acceptance probability given in Equation 3.17. Hence the conditional expected value of $\hat{e}(\underline{x})$, given that $\underline{x} = \underline{x}_j$, is given as

32 $$E_{\hat{e}|\underline{x}_j}\{\hat{e}(\underline{x})\} = \sum_{q=k'}^{k} \left(1 - \frac{q}{k}\right) a_{k,s=q}\left(\underline{x}_j\right).$$

Now, by using 32 in 31, the expected value of the estimate $\hat{E}$ with respect to the mixture distribution of $\underline{x}_j$ is found to be

$$E\{\hat{E}\} = \frac{1}{n_t} \sum_{\underline{x}_j \in S_t} E\left\{ \sum_{q=k'}^{k} \left(1 - \frac{q}{k}\right) a_{k,s=q}\left(\underline{x}_j\right)\right\}$$

33 $$= \sum_{q=k'}^{k} \left(1 - \frac{q}{k}\right) A_{k,s=q}.$$

The comparison of the right hand sides of 22 and 33 provides a precise interpretation for the expected value of the estimator $\hat{E}$, namely

34 $$E\{\hat{E}\} = E_{k-1,k'} \leq E^{*}$$

where $E_{k-1,k'}$ is the error-rate with the (k-1,k')-NNR, and we have used the bound given in Equation 3.95. We see from 34 that the estimate is optimistically biased and yields a lower bound on E^{*}. However, as we commented in Chapter 3, the bound is usually very tight.

Clearly, the same error-bound could be estimated from classified test samples by employing an unbiased error-counting estimator with the (k-1,k')-NNR. Under the large-sample assumption for the design set, the variance of this estimator is $E_{k-1,k'}\left(1-E_{k-1,k'}\right)/n_t$. Now, the use of the sample risk $e^*(\underline{x}_j)$ was shown in Section 10.8.1 to provide a reduction in variance in comparison with the error-counting technique. By using the k-NN estimate of $e^*(\underline{x})$ given by 30, this advantage is retained. The variance is given by

$$\sigma^2\{\hat{e}\} = \boldsymbol{E}\left\{\boldsymbol{E}_{\hat{e}|\underline{x}_j}\{\hat{e}(\underline{x})^2\}\right\} - \hat{E}^2_{k-1,k'}$$

$$= \boldsymbol{E}\left\{\sum_{q=0}^{k''}\left(\frac{q}{k}\right)^2\binom{k}{q}\left[\eta_1^q\eta_2^{k-q} + \eta_1^{k-q}\eta_2^q\right]\right\} - \hat{E}^2_{k-1,k'}$$

where we have used η_i as a shorthand notation for $P(\omega_i|\underline{x}_j)$. By using the fact that

$$(k/2)-|q-(k/2)| = q \qquad \text{for } 0 \le q \le k''$$

$$= k-q \qquad \text{for } k' \le q \le k,$$

we can write

$$\sigma^2\{\hat{e}\} = \boldsymbol{E}\left\{\sum_{q=0}^{k}\left(\frac{1}{k}\right)^2\left[\frac{k}{2} - |q - \frac{k}{2}|\right]^2\binom{k}{q}\eta_1^q\eta_2^{k-q}\right\} - \hat{E}^2_{k-1,k'}$$

35 $$= \boldsymbol{E}\left\{\sum_{q=0}^{k}\left[\frac{1}{k}\left(\frac{k}{2} - |q - \frac{k}{2}|\right) + \left(\frac{q}{k}\right)^2 - \frac{q}{k}\right]\binom{k}{q}\eta_1^q\eta_2^{k-q}\right\} - \hat{E}^2_{k-1,k'}.$$

We also have

$$\sum_{q=0}^{k}\left(\frac{1}{k}\right)\left[\frac{k}{2} - |q - \frac{k}{2}|\right]\binom{k}{q}\eta_1^q\eta_2^{k-q} = e_{k-1,k'}(\underline{x}_j),$$

$$\sum_{q=0}^{k}\left(\frac{q}{k}\right)^2\binom{k}{q}\eta_1^q\eta_2^{k-q} = \frac{1}{k}\left[\eta_1 + (k-1)\eta_1^2\right],$$

$$\sum_{q=0}^{k}\left(\frac{q}{k}\right)\binom{k}{q}\eta_1^q\eta_2^{k-q} = \eta_1.$$

By substituting this in 35 and using the fact that $e_1(\underline{x}_j) = 2\eta_1\eta_2$, we obtain

$$\sigma^2\{\hat{e}\} = E\left\{e_{k-1,k'}\left(\underline{x}_j\right) - \frac{k-1}{2k}\, e_1\left(\underline{x}_j\right)\right\} - \hat{E}^2_{k-1,k'}$$
$$= E_{k-1,k'}\left(1-E_{k-1,k'}\right) - \frac{k-1}{2k}\, E_1.$$

For the variance of $\hat{E}$, we have

36 $$\sigma^2\{\hat{E}\} = \frac{E_{k-1,k'}\left(1-E_{k-1,k'}\right)}{n_t} - \frac{(k-1)E_1}{2kn_t}.$$

Equation 36 exhibits the variance-reducing property for the k-NN estimate of 30. The same property was seen in 27, when the function $e^*(\underline{x}_j)$ was assumed to be known.

The lower bound on E^* obtained by using the estimator 31 can be complemented, with little additional computational cost, by an equally tight upper bound corresponding to the estimation of the (k-1)-NNR error-rate E_{k-1}. By using the error-acceptance relationship 3.67 the reader should have little difficulty to satisfy himself that this is accomplished by defining the estimate as follows :

37 $$\hat{E} = \frac{1}{n_t} \sum_{\underline{x}_j \in S_t} \hat{e}(\underline{x}_j),$$

where

38 $$\hat{e}(\underline{x}_j) = \min\left\{\frac{k_1}{k}, \frac{k_2}{k}\right\} \qquad \text{if } \min\left\{k_1,k_2\right\} < k'';$$
$$= \frac{3k'-2}{4k'+2} \qquad \text{if } \min\left\{k_1,k_2\right\} = k'.$$

Then, $E\{\hat{E}\} = E_{k-1} \geq E^*$.

As an introduction to the method we shall describe next, let us remark that the estimators 30-31 and 37-38 may also be implemented by the plug-in technique suggested in Section 10.7. For instance, let $\hat{A}_{k,s=q}$ denote the empirical frequencies of the event $\left[\min\left\{k_1,k_2\right\}=k-q\right]$ for q=k',...,k over the n_t test samples. Then, the plug-in version of estimator 31 is

39 $$\hat{E} = \sum_{q=k'}^{k} \left(1 - \frac{q}{k}\right)\hat{A}_{k,s=q}.$$

The latter estimator is equivalent to the estimator 31.

10.8.3. Bayes Error Estimation Using Ordered Nearest Neighbor Sample Sets

In this section we wish to exhibit still another plug-in method of estimating the same error-bounds $E_{k-1,k'}$ and E_k arrived at in the previous section. Our goal is essentially to introduce, by way of an example, a powerful method of nonparametric estimation which can be applied to the estimation of a wide variety of feature evaluation criteria, (cf. Section 10.10). The approach consists merely of analytical steps. Statistical aspects are relegated to the very last step of the method.

We have seen in Equation 3.73 that the MacLaurin expansion of the function $e^*(\underline{x})$ can be written as

40 $$e^*(\underline{x}) = \frac{1}{2}\sum_{i=1}^{\infty} \frac{1}{2i-1}\binom{2i}{i}\left[P\left(\omega_1|\underline{x}\right)P\left(\omega_2|\underline{x}\right)\right]^i.$$

By truncating the series and bounding the remainder we obtained the bounds (k odd)

$$\frac{1}{2}\sum_{i=1}^{k''} \frac{1}{2i-1}\binom{2i}{i}\left[P\left(\omega_1|\underline{x}\right)P\left(\omega_2|\underline{x}\right)\right]^i \le e^*(\underline{x})$$

$$\le \frac{1}{2}\sum_{i=1}^{k''} \frac{1}{2i-1}\binom{2i}{i}\left[P\left(\omega_1|\underline{x}\right)P\left(\omega_2|\underline{x}\right)\right]^i + \frac{1}{2}\binom{k-1}{k''}\left[P\left(\omega_1|\underline{x}\right)P\left(\omega_2|\underline{x}\right)\right]^{k''}.$$

The lower bound is increasing in k, the upper one is decreasing in k.

As the expansion is uniformly convergent, we may take expectation with respect to the mixture density $p(\underline{x})$. By observing that

$$E\left\{\binom{2i}{i}\left[P\left(\omega_1|\underline{x}\right)P\left(\omega_2|\underline{x}\right)\right]^i\right\} = A_{2i,s=i},$$

we obtain

41 $$\frac{1}{2}\sum_{i=1}^{k''}\frac{1}{2i-1}A_{2i,s=i} \le E^* \le \frac{1}{2}\sum_{i=1}^{k''}\frac{1}{2i-1}A_{2i,s=i} + \frac{1}{2}A_{k-1,s=k''},$$

where $A_{2i,s=i}$ must be interpreted as the overall, asymptotic probability of a tie occurring in the votes of the 2i-NN. We are now ready to apply the plug-in technique of 39. By observing the empirical frequencies of tied votes in the sets of 2,4,...,2k" NN over the n_t test samples, estimates $\hat{A}_{2i,s=i}$ of $A_{2i,s=i}$ are formed and the substitution in 41 yields estimated bounds of E^*. From Equations 3.83 and 3.94, it can be verified that the bounds in 41 correspond again to $E_{k-1,k'}$ and E_k. Another example of application of this method will be outlined in Section 10.10.

10.8.4. Error Estimation For an Arbitrary Classifier

Thus far, our discussion of the method based on averaging estimates of the conditional probability of error has focused on estimating the Bayes error-rate. It is not obvious however, how the method can be extended to the case when we do not have an analytical expression for the conditional risk with the classifier employed.

Before considering this additional problem, it is worthwile to examine the reason why the k-NN estimator defined by 30 and 31 is optimistically biased. It appears that the reason is essentially the same as that which causes the resubstitution estimate to be optimistically biased. However, in the present situation, the resubstitution phenomenon operates in a much more subtle way, as is shown hereafter.

42 Let us consider the following scheme. Suppose that the samples from S_t are classified using the k-NNR with S_d, and for each sample, the conditional probability of error is estimated by $\min\left\{\frac{k_1}{k}, \frac{k_2}{k}\right\}$. It will become clear in a moment that this is a legitimate way of estimating E_k. It is apparent that we would obtain exactly the same estimate $\hat{E}$ as given by 31. However, with this scheme, *the same information, viz.,* k_1 and k_2, *is used for both purposes of decision making and error estimation.* In spite of the fact that the class assignments for test samples are not used, this is but a subtly disguised version of the major criticism we voiced about the resubstitution scheme; and the natural conclusion is $\mathbf{E}\{\hat{E}\} \le E^*$, and $\mathbf{E}\{\hat{E}\} \le E_k$.

In principle, this difficulty can be easily overcome. However, from a practical viewpoint, the solution implies the dramatic requirement of still another set of classified samples.

43 Thus, let the classified samples be partitioned in two disjoint subsets S_d and S_r of sizes n_d and n_r. We call S_d and S_r the *design* and *reference* subsets respectively. Let S_d be used to design the classifier, whatever that classifier may be, and $e(\underline{x})$ and E denote respectively the unknown, conditional and average error probabilities with the classifier in question. For any test sample $\underline{x}_j$, let k_1 and k_2 be the numbers of class ω_1 and ω_2 neighbors among the k-NN to $\underline{x}_j$

from the *reference* set S_r. Suppose that the classifier's decision is to assign $\underline{x}_j$ to class ω_i and let $\kappa = k - k_i$. Thus κ denotes the number of votes that do not concur with the decision being made. The conditional probability of error for that particular decision is $e\left(\underline{x}_j\right) = 1 - P\left(\omega_1 | \underline{x}_j\right)$. On the other hand, under the large-sample assumption for the reference set, the conditional expected value of κ/k, given that $\underline{x} = \underline{x}_j$, is $E_{\kappa/k|\underline{x}_j}\{\kappa/k\} = 1 - P(\omega_i|\underline{x}_j)$. So, κ/k is an asymptotically unbiased estimate of $e(\underline{x}_j)$. Correspondingly, a formal definition of the estimator is as follows :

44 $$\kappa = k - k_i, \qquad \text{if } \hat{\omega}(\underline{x}_j) = \omega_i, \quad i = 1 \text{ or } 2,$$

45 $$\hat{e}(\underline{x}_j) = \frac{\kappa}{k},$$

46 $$\hat{E} = \frac{1}{n_t} \sum_{\underline{x}_j \in S_t} \hat{e}(\underline{x}_j).$$

As a consequence of the unbiasedness of $\hat{e}$ in 45 we have

47 $$\boldsymbol{E}\{\hat{E}\} = \frac{1}{n_t} \sum_{\underline{x}_j \in S_t} \boldsymbol{E}\left\{\hat{e}(\underline{x}_j)\right\} = E.$$

The estimator is unbiased. Furthermore, it is a simple matter to show that the variance of $\hat{E}$ is given by

48 $$\sigma^2\{\hat{E}\} = \frac{E(1-E)}{kn_t} + \frac{(k-1)\sigma^2\{e\}}{kn_t}$$
$$\leq \frac{E(1-E)}{n_t} - \frac{(k-\tilde{\kappa})(k-1)}{k^2 n_t} E,$$

where $\tilde{\kappa}$ denotes the maximum value that may be assumed by κ.

As our reasoning is independent of the classifier used, it may be applied to the estimation of the Bayes error-rate, in which case $E = E^*$, $\boldsymbol{E}\{\tilde{\kappa}\} \leq \frac{k}{2}$, and

49 $$\sigma^2\{\hat{E}\} \leq \frac{E^*(1-E^*)}{n_t} - \frac{k-1}{2kn_t} E^*.$$

The use of both design and reference sets gives the method the flavor of a holdout estimate. By contrast, if the classifier was the (k-1)-NNR, and the reference set was taken to be the same as the design set, we would obtain the scheme outlined in 42 with its definite flavor of resubstitution.

10.9. AN ESTIMATOR THAT COMBINES ERROR-COUNTING AND RISK-AVERAGING

The estimates we were concerned with in Section 8 have the advantage of a lower variance despite the fact that they do not require the information conveyed by the class assignments of test samples. In cases where the class labels of test samples are available, this leads to the paradox that a better estimate can be obtained by ignoring them and raises the question of how to use them to further improve the estimate. Presently, we shall answer this question in the general framework of Section 10.8.4. Specifically, we assume that we are given a classifier and two sets S_r and S_t of independent, identically distributed, classified reference and test samples from the distribution of $(\underline{x},\omega)$.

Without further ado, let us consider the following estimator

50 $$\hat{e}(\underline{x}_j) = \frac{\kappa(\underline{x}_j)+\zeta(\underline{x}_j)}{k+1}$$

51 $$\hat{E} = \frac{1}{n} \sum_{\underline{x}_j \in S_t} \hat{e}(\underline{x}_j),$$

where the dependence on $\underline{x}_j$ is emphasized for reasons that will appear shortly, κ is defined by 44, ζ is the error-indicator defined in 6, and n stands for n_t. Clearly, the estimator so defined is a combination of error-counting via ζ, and risk averaging via κ.

Invoking again the large-sample assumption for the reference set, we have $E_{\kappa|\underline{x}_j}\{\kappa(\underline{x})\} = ke(\underline{x}_j)$, and $E_{\zeta|\underline{x}_j}\{\zeta(\underline{x})\} = e(\underline{x}_j)$. Hence, $E_{\hat{e}|\underline{x}_j}\{\hat{e}(\underline{x})\} = e(\underline{x}_j)$ and the estimator is asymptotically unbiased. Therefore, so is $\hat{E}$ in 51.

To determine the variance of $\hat{E}$, let us consider first the conditional variance given the test set S_t.

$$\begin{aligned}\sigma^2\{\hat{E}|S_t\} &= E\left\{\left[\frac{1}{n}\sum_j \frac{\kappa(\underline{x}_j)+\zeta(\underline{x}_j)}{k+1} - E\right]^2\middle|S_t\right\}\\ &= \frac{1}{(k+1)^2n^2}E\left\{\sum_j\sum_{\ell\neq j}\left[\kappa(\underline{x}_j)\kappa(\underline{x}_\ell)+\kappa(\underline{x}_j)\zeta(\underline{x}_\ell)+\zeta(\underline{x}_j)\zeta(\underline{x}_\ell)\right]\right.\\ &\quad \left.+\sum_j\left[\kappa^2(\underline{x}_j)+\kappa(\underline{x}_j)\zeta(\underline{x}_j)+\zeta^2(\underline{x}_j)\right]\middle|S_t\right\}\\ &\quad -\frac{2E}{(k+1)n}E\left\{\sum_j\left[\kappa(\underline{x}_j)+\zeta(\underline{x}_j)\right]\middle|S_t\right\}+E^2,\end{aligned} \tag{52}$$

where all summations extend from 1 to n. By using the independence assumption, we have

$$\begin{aligned}E\left\{\kappa(\underline{x}_j)\kappa(\underline{x}_\ell)|S_t\right\} &= E\left\{\kappa(\underline{x}_j)\kappa(\underline{x}_\ell)|\underline{x}_j,\underline{x}_\ell\right\}\\ &= E\left\{\kappa(\underline{x}_j)|\underline{x}_j\right\}E\left\{\kappa(\underline{x}_\ell)|\underline{x}_\ell\right\}\\ &= k^2e(\underline{x}_j)e(\underline{x}_\ell).\end{aligned}$$

By proceeding in a like manner for terms involving $\kappa(\underline{x}_j)\zeta(\underline{x}_\ell)$, and $\zeta(\underline{x}_j)\zeta(\underline{x}_\ell)$ and using

$$E\left\{\kappa^2(\underline{x}_j)|S_t\right\} = k\left[e(\underline{x}_j)+(k-1)e^2(\underline{x}_j)\right],$$

equation 52 becomes after some elementary manipulations

$$\sigma^2\left\{\hat{E}|S_t\right\} = \frac{1}{(k+1)^2n^2}\left[(k^2+2k+1)\sum_j\sum_\ell e(\underline{x}_j)e(\underline{x}_\ell)\right.$$

$$\left. + \sum_j(k^2+k)e^2(\underline{x}_j) + \sum_j(k+1)e(\underline{x}_j)\right] - \frac{2E}{n}\sum_j e(\underline{x}_j) + E^2 .$$

Finally, by taking expectation with respect to the mixture density $p(\underline{x})$ we obtain

$$\sigma^2\{\hat{E}\} = \boldsymbol{E}\left\{\sigma^2\{\hat{E}|S_t\}\right\}$$

$$= \frac{1}{(k+1)^2n^2}\left[(k+1)^2n(n-1)E^2+(k+1)nE+k(k+1)n(\sigma^2\{e\}+E^2)\right]-E^2$$

53
$$= \frac{E(1-E)}{(k+1)n} + \frac{k\sigma^2\{e\}}{(k+1)n}$$

$$\leq \frac{E(1-E)}{n} - \frac{(k-\tilde{\kappa})E}{(k+1)n} .$$

By comparing 53 and 48, we conclude that the variance of the estimator that uses the class assignments of test samples in combination with an estimate of the conditional risk is lower by a factor close to $k/(k+1)$ than the estimator that ignores these class assignments. For small values of k, this represents a significant improvement.

10.10. NONPARAMETRIC ESTIMATION OF FEATURE EVALUATION CRITERIA

The discussion thus far has focused on estimation of the error probability which is, after all, the most important performance criterion. In the preceding two chapters, however, we have been concerned with other feature evaluation criterion functions which were easier to manipulate than the probability of error in the multivariate normal case. Here, we wish to indicate briefly how some of the concepts and methods encountered in our analysis of error estimation can be used to estimate these feature evaluation criterion functions.

54 In the parametric case, the point can be quickly made. Recalling Equations 10-15 in Chapter 7, the probabilistic distance measures considered there may be expressed in closed-forms involving the mean vectors and covariance matrices of the class-conditional, multivariate normal distributions involved. Therefore, substitution of sample mean vectors and sample covariance matrices provides, so to speak, *apparent* estimates of these distance measures. One should note, however, that the finite-sample behavior of the estimates so obtained is much less known than in the case of the apparent error-estimate of Section 10.4.

The nonparametric case can be handled with very much the same tools that we used to estimate the error probability in Section 10.8. Here, we do not intend to develop an exhaustive discussion. Instead, we wish to illustrate the point by considering a typical example problem.

Let us consider the problem of estimating the average conditional entropy (Shannon entropy) or equivocation. In a two-class case, the equivocation H is given by

55 $$H = E\{h(\underline{x})\}$$

with

$$h(\underline{x}) = -\sum_{i=1}^{2} P(\omega_i|\underline{x})\log P(\omega_i|\underline{x}),$$

where, for convenience in later developments, natural logarithms are used.

Recalling Section 10.8.2, an obvious estimation method is to use

56 $$\hat{h}(\underline{x}_j) = -\sum_{i=1}^{2} \frac{k_i}{k}\log\frac{k_i}{k}$$

57 $$\hat{H} = \frac{1}{n_t} \sum_{\underline{x}_j \in S_t} \hat{h}(\underline{x}_j).$$

This naive estimator can be shown to be consistent and asymptotically normal. Unfortunately, it gives a grossly optimistic estimate of H especially when k is small. One may accordingly opt for another appealing estimator based on the observation that the conditional p.d.f. of $P(\omega_i|\underline{x})$ given k_1 and k_2 is a beta distribution with expected value $(k_i+1)/(k+2)$. Hence the estimator

58 $$\hat{h}(\underline{x}_j) = - \sum_{i=1}^{2} \frac{k_i+1}{k+2} \log \frac{k_i+1}{k+2}.$$

This, in turn, appears to give a rather pessimistic estimate.

Experimental evidence and some theoretical justification support the conjecture that the bias of the estimator 56-57 is nearly proportional to $H/(k-1)$. Thus an approximately unbiased estimator is

59 $$\hat{h}(\underline{x}_j) = - \sum_{i=1}^{2} \frac{k_i}{k-1} \log \frac{k_i}{k}.$$

This short enumeration of estimators could suffice to impart the assurance that quantities such as H are in no way easier to estimate than was the error probability.

If one wants to try one's hand at writing down k-NN estimates of, say, the Bhattacharyya coefficient (cf. 7.2) or the divergence measure (cf. 7.4) one will soon notice that many difficult problems arise and that there is scant hope that asymptotic properties of such estimators will ever be derived.

One alternative is offered by the method of ordered nearest neighbor sample sets which we briefly described in Section 10.8.3.

Another example of how to use that method will presently be outlined in order to establish estimators of upper and lower bounds of the equivocation H while application of the same method to the estimation of bounds of the Bhattacharyya coefficient or the divergence measure will be left as exercises.

The MacLaurin expansion of the function $h(\underline{x})$ in 55 can be written as

$$h(\underline{x}) = \sum_{j=1}^{\infty} \frac{1}{j}\left[(P(\omega_i|\underline{x})P(\omega_2|\underline{x})^j + P(\omega_1|\underline{x})^j P(\omega_2|\underline{x})\right]$$

60 $$= 1 - \sum_{j=2}^{\infty} \frac{1}{j(j-1)} \left[P(\omega_1|\underline{x})^j + P(\omega_2|\underline{x})^j\right].$$

The series in 60 converges to $h(\underline{x})$ from above. So by truncation we obtain

$$h(\underline{x}) \le 1 - \sum_{j=2}^{k} \frac{1}{j(j-1)} q_j(\underline{x}),$$

where $q_j(\underline{x})$ stands for $\left[P(\omega_1|\underline{x})^j + P(\omega_2|\underline{x})^j\right]$. As $q_j(\underline{x}) \ge q_{j'}(\underline{x})$ for $j<j'$, the remainder can be bounded as follows

$$\sum_{j=k+1}^{\infty} \frac{1}{j(j+1)} q_j(\underline{x}) \le q_k(\underline{x}) \sum_{j=k+1}^{\infty} \frac{1}{j(j-1)}$$

$$= q_k(\underline{x})/k.$$

So, we obtain the following bounds

61 $$1 - \sum_{j=2}^{k} \frac{q_j(\underline{x})}{j(j-1)} - \frac{q_k(\underline{x})}{k} \le h(\underline{x}) \le 1 - \sum_{j=2}^{k} \frac{q_j(\underline{x})}{j(j-1)}.$$

The series in 60 is uniformly convergent, so we may take expectations which yields

62 $$1 - \sum_{j=2}^{k} \frac{Q_j}{j(j-1)} - \frac{Q_k}{k} \le H \le 1 - \sum_{j=2}^{k} \frac{Q_j}{j(j-1)},$$

where

$$Q_j = E\left\{q_j(\underline{x})\right\} = E\left\{P(\omega_1|\underline{x})^j\right\} + E\left\{P(\omega_2|\underline{x})^j\right\}.$$

Now, the analytical form of $q_j(\underline{x})$ may be interpreted as the probability of occurrence of the event [all j-NN to $\underline{x}$ belong to the same class, (be it ω_1 or ω_2)], and Q_j is the overall probability of occurrence of that event. Consequently, returning to a more traditional notation we have

63 $$1 - \sum_{j=2}^{k} \frac{A_{j,s=j}}{j(j-1)} - \frac{A_{k,s=k}}{k} \le H \le 1 - \sum_{j=2}^{k} \frac{A_{j,s=j}}{j(j-1)}.$$

Eventually, the upper and lower bounds on H can be estimated by substituting for $A_{j,s=j}$ the empirical frequencies of unanimous votes in the sets of 2,3,...,k-NN over a set of test samples.

From the two examples we have given, it should be clear that the key to a successful application of the method of ordered nearest neighbor sample sets is to give the terms in the series expansion a form which can be interpreted in terms of sequences of votes cast by the k-NN.

10.11. BIBLIOGRAPHICAL COMMENTS

Estimation of classification error rate was first a matter of concern for statisticians interested in the classification of normal data. The complexity of the problem is well exemplified by the work of John (1961) on the estimation of the apparent error-rate for a two-class problem with known, equal covariance matrices.

In the pattern recognition literature, the first analysis of the holdout method is due to Highleyman (1962) who indicated methods of obtaining confidence intervals, and presented graphs showing how the data should be partitioned between design and test sets for the purpose of minimizing the variance of the error estimate.

Lachenbruch (see Lachenbruch and Mickey (1968)) is usually credited with the leave-one-out method. However, according to Toussaint (1974), substantially the same method was introduced, somewhat earlier, in the russian literature. In the multivariate normal case, Fukunaga and Kessel (1971) have shown that the leave-one-out method involves little extra computation.

The literature up to 1973 has been compiled in the extensive bibliography of Toussaint (1974). For those interested in error-counting techniques, the papers by Hills (1966) and Foley (1972), and Section VI of Kanal (1974) are highly recommended readings.

Risk-averaging methods of error estimation have been developed by Fukunaga and his coworkers : Fukunaga and Kessel (1972, 1973), Fukunaga and Hostetler (1975). An interesting modification of it was proposed by Glick (1978). For normal data, the bias of the estimate was studied by Ganesalingam and McLachlan (1980).

The idea of estimating the Bayes error-rate with ordered nearest neighbor sample sets was proposed by Garnett and Yau (1977). Our exposition of error estimation for an arbitrary classifier follows Kittler and Devijver (1981). In the same paper, it was shown how to combine risk-averaging and error-counting.

In Section 7.7, we commented already that the problem of estimating general feature evaluation criteria is in a far less advanced stage. In this context, the potential of the method of nearest neighbor sample sets was demonstrated by Devijver (1978, b), and a general review of nonparametric estimators can be found in Devijver (1978, a).

10.12. REFERENCES

Devijver, P.A., "Nonparametric estimation of feature evaluation criteria", in *Pattern Recognition and Signal Processing*, C.H. Chen Ed., Sijthoff & Noordhoff, Alphen aan den Rijn, 1978, (a), pp. 61-82.

Devijver, P.A., "Nonparametric estimation by the method of ordered nearest neighbor sample sets", in *Proc. Fourth Internat. Conf. Pattern Recognition*, Kyoto, Japan, 1978, (b), pp. 217-223.

Foley, D.H., "Considerations of sample and feature size", *IEEE Trans. Inform. Theory*, vol. 18, pp. 618-626, Sept. 1972.

Fukunaga, K., and Kessel, D.L., "Estimation of classification error", *IEEE Trans. Comput.*, vol. 20, pp. 1521-1527, Dec. 1971.

Fukunaga, K., and Kessel, D.L., "Application of optimum error-reject functions", *IEEE Trans. Inform. Theory*, vol. 18, pp. 814-817, 1972.

Fukunaga, K., and Kessel, D.L., "Nonparametric Bayes error estimation using unclassified samples", *IEEE Trans. Inform. Theory*, vol. 19, pp. 434-440, July 1973.

Fukunaga, K., and Hostetler, L.D., "k-nearest neighbor Bayes risk estimation", *IEEE Trans. Inform. Theory*, vol. 21, pp. 285-293, May 1975.

Ganesalingam, S., and McLachlan, G.J., "Error rate estimation on the basis of posterior probabilities", *Pattern Recognition*, vol. 12, pp. 405-413, 1980.

Garnett, J.M.III, and Yau, S.S., "Nonparametric estimation of the Bayes error of feature extractors using ordered nearest neighbor sets", *IEEE Trans. Comput.*, vol. 26, pp. 46-54, Jan. 1977.

Glick, N., "Adaptive estimators for probabilities of correct classification", *Pattern Recognition*, vol. 10, pp. 211-222, 1978.

Highleyman, W.H., "The design and analysis of pattern recognition experiments", *Bell Syst. Tech. J.*, vol. 41, pp. 723-744, March 1962.

Hills, M., "Allocation rules and their error rates", *J. Roy. Statist. Soc.* Series B, no 28, pp. 1-31, 1966.

John, S., "Errors in discrimination", *Ann. Math. Statist.*, vol. 32, pp. 1125-1144, 1961.

Kanal, L.N., "Patterns in pattern recognition : 1968-1974", *IEEE Trans. Inform. Theory*, vol. 20, pp. 697-722, Nov. 1974.

Kittler, J., and Devijver, P.A., "An efficient estimator of pattern recognition system error probability", *Pattern Recognition*, vol. 13, pp. 245-249, 1981.

Lachenbruch, P.A., and Mickey, R.M., "Estimation of error rates in discriminant analysis", *Technometrics*, vol. 10, pp. 1-11, 1968.

Toussaint, G.T., "Bibliography on estimation of misclassification", *IEEE Trans. Inform. Theory*, vol. 20, pp. 472-479, July 1974.

10.13. PROBLEMS

1. We have seen in Section 10.3 that, when a classifier is given, the error-count τ has a binomial distribution with mean nE and variance nE(1-E). Suppose you are given a set $S=\left\{\underline{x}_i\right\}_{i=1}^{n}$ of unclassified samples. So τ cannot be observed. On the other hand, you are given the conditional error probabilities $e(\underline{x}_i)$, $i=1,\ldots,n$. Thus τ corresponds to an observation drawn from each of n different populations with probabilities $e(\underline{x}_1),\ldots,e(\underline{x}_n)$ of classification error.

   (a) Determine the distribution of τ, and verify that it has the same mean nE as the binomial distribution in Section 10.3.

   (b) Show that the variance of that distribution is less than that of the binomial distribution by an amount equal to n times the variance of $e(\underline{x})$.

2. Let A denote a nonsingular square matrix and let $B=\underline{x}\underline{x}^t$ (with the same dimensions as A). Show that

$$(A + B)^{-1} = A^{-1} - \frac{A^{-1}\underline{x}\underline{x}^t A^{-1}}{1+\underline{x}^t A^{-1}\underline{x}}$$

Note that this is a simplified version of the formula of Sherman-Morisson and Bartlett which was used many times in the text.

3. Suppose that you are given n_1 and n_2 design samples from two classes with multivariate normal distributions, different mean vectors $\underline{\mu}_1$ and $\underline{\mu}_2$, and identical covariance matrix Σ. Let us assume that you contemplate designing the Anderson discriminant plane for classification, and using the leave-one-out method for error estimation.

(a) Write down the sample-based expression of the discriminant function in terms of the maximum likelihood estimates of the "parameters" P_i, $\underline{\mu}_i$, $i=1,2$, and Σ^{-1} obtained by using all $n=n_1+n_2$ design samples.

(b) The leave-one-out method requires designing the discriminant function n times. Computationally, this amounts essentially to n matrix inversions. For large n, crude application of the method may be too laborious. As an alternative, derive computationally simple procedures for updating the estimates obtained in (a) in order to account for the deletion of one arbitrary design sample. Use the result of Problem 2 for updating the estimate of the inverse of the covariance matrix. Comment on the computational saving.

4. Extend the results of Problem 3 to the case when the class-conditional distributions have different covariance matrices Σ_1 and Σ_2, and the classifier is that obtained in Problem 2 of Chapter 2. Note that this involves updating quadratic terms and determinant terms.

Hint : Updating of the determinant terms can be simplified by using the formula

$$|A + B| = |A|(1 + \underline{x}^t A^{-1} \underline{x}),$$

where A, B, and $\underline{x}$ are as in Problem 2.

5. By using the error-acceptance relationship in Equation 3.67, show that the estimator defined by 38, *viz.*,

$$\hat{E} = \frac{1}{n_t} \sum_{\underline{x}_j \in S_t} \hat{e}(\underline{x}_j),$$

where

$$\hat{e}(\underline{x}_j) = \min\left\{\frac{k_1}{k}, \frac{k_2}{k}\right\} \qquad \text{if } \min\left\{k_1, k_2\right\} < k'';$$

$$= \frac{3k'-2}{4k'+2} \qquad \text{if } \min\left\{k_1, k_2\right\} = k',$$

is an unbiased estimator of the error-rate E_{k-1} of the (k-1)NNR.

6. The purpose of this problem is to derive a nonparametric estimate of the Bhattacharyya distance measure, based on the method of ordered nearest neighbor sample sets, (two-class case). Rather than estimating the Bhattacharyya distance itself, we shall estimate directly the quantity

$$J' = \left[P_1 P_2\right]^{1/2} \int \left[p(\underline{x}|\omega_1)p(\underline{x}|\omega_2)\right]^{1/2} d\underline{x}$$

which we used in obtaining the error bound in Equation 2.96.

(a) Show that J' is also given by

$$J' = \frac{1}{2}\boldsymbol{E}\left\{\left[1-\left(P(\omega_1|\underline{x})-P(\omega_2|\underline{x})\right)^2\right]^{1/2}\right\}.$$

(b) Verify that J' can be expressed as an infinite series expansion, *viz.*,

$$J' = \frac{1}{2}\left[1-\sum_{j=1}^{\infty}\alpha_{2j}\boldsymbol{E}\left\{\left(P(\omega_1|\underline{x})-P(\omega_2|\underline{x})\right)^{2j}\right\}\right],$$

where $\alpha_{2j}=(2j-3)!!/(2j)!!$, and k!! denotes the semi-factorial of k.

(c) Show that $S_{2j}=\boldsymbol{E}\left\{\left[P(\omega_1|\underline{x})-P(\omega_2|\underline{x})\right]^{2j}\right\}$ can be interpreted as the difference between the average probabilities that the 2j-NN (to an arbitrary $\underline{x}$) cast even or odd numbers of votes for either class.

(d) Show that

$$\frac{1}{2}\left\{1-\sum_{j=1}^{k-1}\alpha_{2j}(S_{2j}-S_{2k})-S_{2k}\right\} \le J' \le \frac{1}{2}\left\{1-\sum_{j=1}^{k}\alpha_{2j}S_{2j}\right\},$$

and suggest a practical scheme for estimating the bounds of J'.

7. Consider the slightly generalized version of the divergence which we introduced in Equation 2.104, *viz.*,

$$J_D' = \boldsymbol{E}\left\{ \sum_{i=1}^{2} P(\omega_i|\underline{x}) \ln \frac{P(\omega_i|\underline{x})}{1-P(\omega_i|\underline{x})} \right\}.$$

In order to apply the method of ordered nearest neighbor sample sets, let $Q_j = \boldsymbol{E}\{q_j(\underline{x})\}$, where $q_j(\underline{x})$ is the probability of occurrence of the event [all j NN to $\underline{x}$ belong to the same class]. Then, show that

$$J_D' = -1 + \sum_{j=2}^{\infty} \frac{j+1}{j(j-1)} Q_j,$$

and suggest a practical scheme for estimating a lower bound of J_D'.

Chapter 11

NONSUPERVISED LEARNING PATTERN CLASSIFICATION

11.1. INTRODUCTION

The various approaches to the pattern recognition system design discussed in the preceding chapters are based on the assumption that we have available a design set of labeled pattern vectors. Using this design set, the underlying probability structure of individual classes can be inferred. In some applications, however, information on the class membership of the design patterns is not provided. Such problems are often encountered in medicine, remote sensing, social science, geology and other areas of scientific and engineering activities. The reason for the class labels being unavailable may be the lack of knowledge of the pattern-generating process or it may simply be the impracticability of the pattern labeling. In such circumstances, the only alternative is to study the inherent structure of the data and assign class labels to patterns on the basis of interpattern relationships.

As a specific example, we can consider the task of identifying distinct classes in colour photographs of agricultural scenes taken by

Landsat. Although it would be possible to relate every pixel of an analysed image to the corresponding point in the scene it represents in order to acquire the appropriate class labels, such an approach would certainly be very tedious if not impracticable. An analysis of the relationship between pixels, however, should reveal the similarities of pixels representing one particular type of vegetation. This information can then be used to designate homogeneous groups of picture points which hopefully belong to the same class.

In terms of the statistical model of a pattern recognition system, the nonsupervised learning pattern recognition problem can be formulated as a problem of decomposing the mixture probability density function, $p(\underline{y})$, (see Figure 11.1) into a number of class conditional components $f(\underline{y}|\omega_i)$, i.e.,

1 $$p(\underline{y}) = \sum_{i=1}^{c} P_i p(\underline{y}|\omega_i) = \sum_{i=1}^{c} f(\underline{y}|\omega_i).$$

Note that $p(\underline{y})$ is the only characteristic that can be inferred from unlabeled data.

When the class-conditional distributions are parameteric of a known form, the unknown parameters of the distributions can be estimated from the data by well-known mixture decomposition techniques. Here we shall concentrate on the general case where no *a priori* knowledge about class-conditional distributions is available. Then, instead of recovering the actual conditional densities, we can only hope to be able to partition the pattern space into a minimum number of regions S_i, $i=1,2,\ldots,c$ over which the mixture density is unimodal, as depicted in Figure 11.2. For brevity, we shall refer to these regions

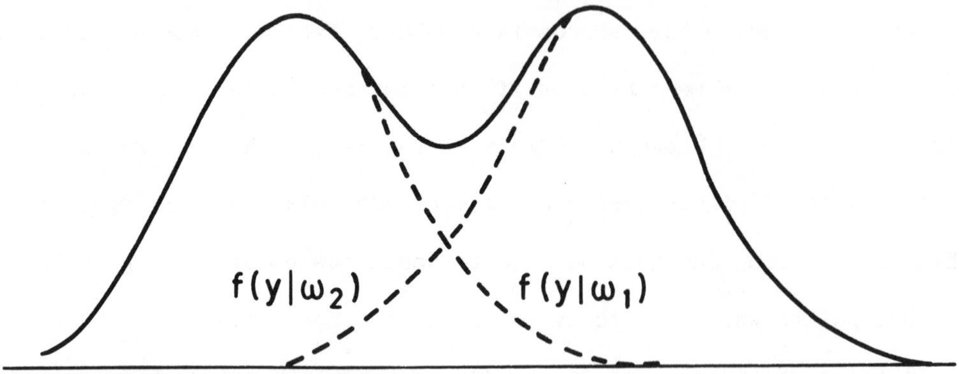

Figure 11.1. Ideal mixture decomposition.

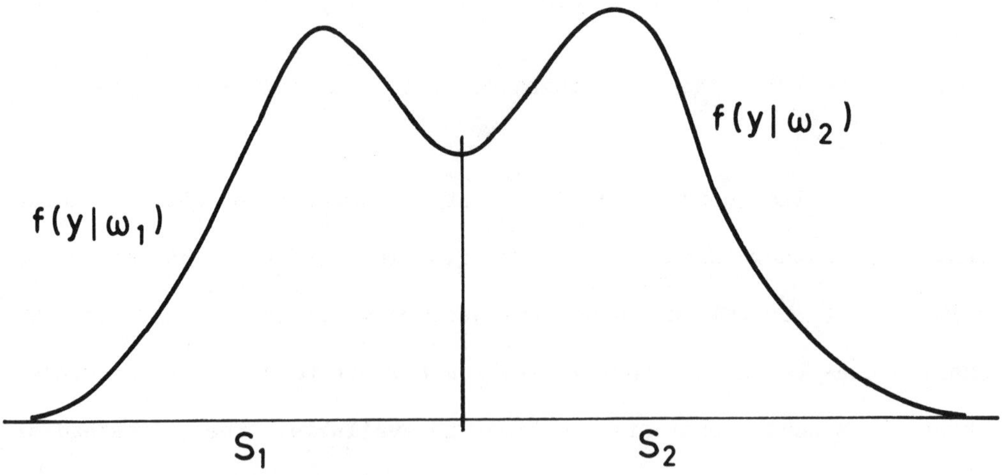

Figure 11.2. Partitioning of the domain of a mixture distribution into unimodal regions.

as unimodal. Each unimodal region S_i will then be associated with a distinct class, ω_i.

In many situations it is more convenient to partition the analyzed data rather than the observation space. The task is then to determine the minimum number of subsets Y_i of the data set, $Y = \{\underline{y}_j | j=1,2,\ldots n\}$, each giving rise to a mode in the mixture p.d.f., $p(\underline{y})$, or its estimate. Again, for simplicity, sets Y_i, $i=1,2,\ldots,c$, will be called unimodal.

Intuitively, function $p(\underline{y})$ will have large values in the densely populated regions while, in sparsely populated regions, the p.d.f. values will be low. The problem of partitioning a data set into unimodal subsets can be considered, therefore, as one of detecting clusters of data points in the observation space.

Once a data set is partitioned into unimodal subsets, the latter can be used as sets of labeled training patterns for the pattern recognition system design. Note that the unimodal regions, S_i, could be used directly to classify new observations according to the following rule :

$$\text{assign } \underline{y} \text{ to } \omega_i \text{ if } \underline{y} \epsilon S_i$$

But often it will be advantageous to find subsequently a more efficient representation of regions S_i and the corresponding decision rule using the supervised learning pattern classification techniques described earlier.

In the following section, various methods of p.d.f. mode separation will be described. Subsequently a number of iterative and non-iterative indirect approaches to mode separation will be discussed.

11.2. MODE SEPARATION METHODS

11.2.1. Projection Method

Suppose there exists a system of coordinate axes $\underline{u}_j$, j=1,2,...,D such that the probabilistic structure of data can be faithfully represented therein by the marginal probability density functions. Then the complex problem of mode separation in a multidimensional space reduces to a considerably simpler task of analyzing probability density functions in uni-dimensional space. In particular, let $\underline{u}_i$ be the ith axis of the coordinate system and denote by $\underline{y}$ an element of data set to be analyzed. Then the ith component, v_i, of the transformed pattern vector, $\underline{v}$, is given as

3 $$v_i = \underline{u}_i^t \underline{y}.$$

If any of the marginal p.d.f., $p(v_i)$, of the projected data is multimodal then the data contains several clusters which can be separated by hyperplanes normal to the appropriate projection axes and intersecting the axes at the points of minima of the univariate probability density functions.

The marginal p.d.f.'s can be estimated from the available data using any p.d.f. estimation method. But since we are dealing with uni-variate functions and, therefore, the feasibility limitations no longer apply, the most convenient and simplest will be the histogram approach (see Appendix A) which provides a p.d.f. estimate at any point of the interval in consideration and consequently allows for a rapid analysis of the function for local minima.

The p.d.f. estimation and the subsequent search for minima of the function are best facilitated by ordering the samples v_i according to their magnitude. The elements of the resulting n order statistics $\{v_i(\ell)\}_n$ satisfy

4 $$v_i(\ell) \le v_i(\ell+j) \qquad \forall\ \ell, j > 0,\ \ell+j \le n.$$

The histogram is constructed from bins of length ρ. Parameter ρ depends on the number of data points, n, and their spread. It is convenient to define ρ as the smallest distance between the ℓth and $(\ell+k)$th points in $\{v_i(\ell)\}_n$

5 $$\rho = \min_{\ell} \left\{ v_i(k+\ell) - v_i(\ell) \,|\, 1 \le \ell \le n-k \right\}$$

where, in terms of n, k should be a non-decreasing sequence of positive integers satisfying conditions

$$\lim_{n\to\infty} k = \infty$$

$$\lim_{n\to\infty} n^{-1}k = 0$$

6 $$\lim_{n\to\infty} (\log n)^{-1}k = \infty.$$

Note that these conditions embody the usual assumptions made on the properties of the parameter k of the k-nearest neighbor p.d.f. estimator as a function of n (see Appendix A). For example, a possible choice for k is

7 $$k = \text{const.}\sqrt{n}.$$

The value of the p.d.f. estimate at any point within, say, the ℓth bin is proportional to the number of elements from $\{v_i\}$ falling into that bin. The histogram approximation of p.d.f. can be easily inspected for multimodality.

So far we have avoided the problem of determining a suitable coordinate system for faithfully representing the p.d.f. of data by the marginal densities. Unfortunately, such a property of the system of coordinate axes cannot be expressed formally in terms of a criterion function. But we shall use a heuristic argument to define an alternative objective function, optimization of which will hopefully yield a coordinate system satisfying our requirements.

Consider the variance of the ith component v_i of the transformed pattern vector, i.e.

8 $$\mathrm{var}\left\{v_i\right\} = E\left\{(v_i-\nu_i)^2\right\} = E\left\{\left[(\underline{y}-\underline{m})^t\underline{u}_i\right]^2\right\},$$

where ν_i is the projection of the mean vector, $\underline{m}$, onto axis $\underline{u}_i$. It is apparent that axis $\underline{u}_i$ is most likely to satisfy our assumptions if the data clusters projected on the axis be maximally separated, that is when $\mathrm{var}\{v_i\}$ is large. From these observations, it follows that optimal $\underline{u}_i$ should maximize criterion function 8. But, recalling the properties of the Karhunen-Loeve expansion, we know readily the solution for $\underline{u}_i$, namely that $\underline{u}_i$ is the eigenvector of the sample covariance matrix of the mixture population, $\hat{\Sigma} = E\left\{(\underline{y}-\underline{m})(\underline{y}-\underline{m})^t\right\}$, associated with the largest eigenvalue of $\hat{\Sigma}$. Thus as the system of coordinate axes, $U = \left[\underline{u}_1\underline{u}_2,\ldots,\underline{u}_D\right]$, the system of eigenvectors of $\hat{\Sigma}$ should be used.

It should be noted that this coordinate system does not guarantee that clusters projected onto individual axes will not be superimposed. The possibility of clusters overlapping is the main shortcoming of this approach. In particular, unimodal marginal p.d.f.s are insufficient evidence that a data set contains one cluster only (see Figures 11.3 and 11.4). The computational efficiency of the method, however, is a great asset which should be exploited in cluster analysis of any data set. The major consumption of central processor time is due to calculation of covariance matrices to be analyzed and to the eigenvalue analysis.

Once the system of eigenvectors (system of coordinate axes) is determined, data projected onto individual axes are analyzed for multimodality starting with the axes associated with the largest variance (eigenvalue) and working through the others in order of decreasing magnitude of the variances. If a multimodal marginal p.d.f. is found, the data set is partitioned by hyperplanes perpendicular to the appropriate coordinate axis, intersecting the axis at the points of minima between two successive modes. Each resulting subset is considered as a new data set which will then be analyzed for multimodality in a similar manner to that applied to the original data set. This procedure is repeated until the p.d.f. defined on each and every subset is unimodal.

9 The complete mode separation procedure thus can be summarized as follows :

The UNISEP procedure

Step 1: Compute the eigenvector $\underline{u}$ associated with the maximum eigenvalue of the sample covariance matrix and project the data on $\underline{u}$ using Equation 3.

Step 2: Obtain a histogram approximation of the marginal p.d.f., $p(v)$.

Step 3: Determine the points of local minima of $p(v)$ between all successive modes of the p.d.f. and partition the data by

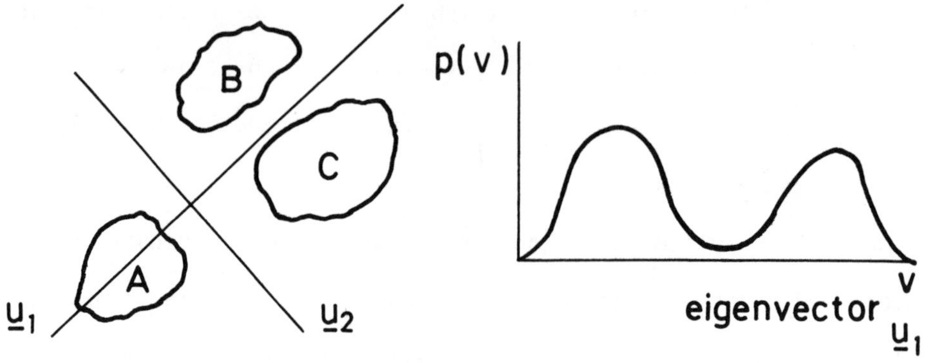

Figure 11.3. The mode separation procedure UNISEP.

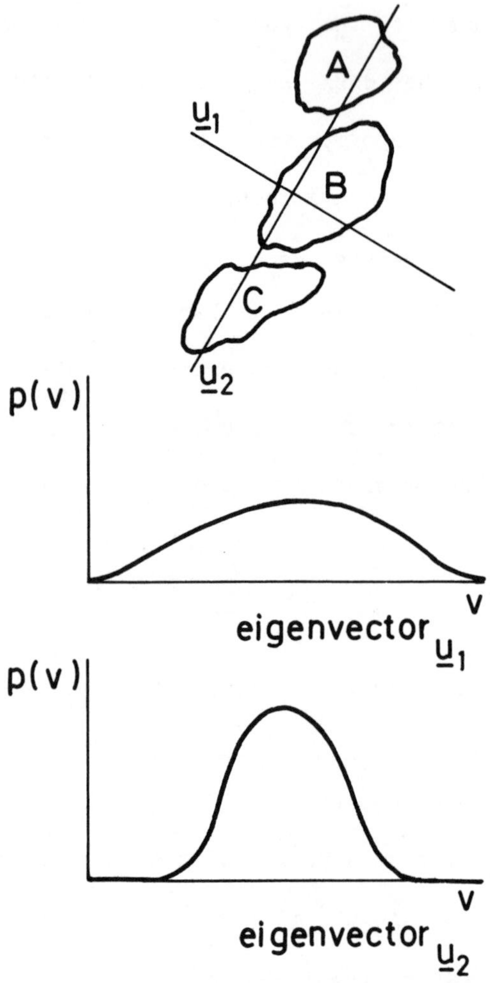

Figure 11.4. Example of a data set for which UNISEP will fail to detect individual modes.

hyperplanes perpendicular to $\underline{u}$ and intersecting the eigenvector at these points.

Step 4: If no such point is determined, repeat the procedure for the next eigenvector.

Step 5: Repeat the procedure for each individual subset that has been obtained by partitioning the complete sample set.

11.2.2. Mode Separation Based on the Properties of Symmetric Sets

Before describing the procedure in detail, we shall examine the concept of symmetric sets.

Denote by $\underline{y}_0$ the mode of the p.d.f., $p(\underline{y})$, i.e.

$$p(\underline{y}_0) = \sup_{\underline{y}\in\Gamma} p(\underline{y})$$

and let $\delta(\underline{\xi},\underline{y})$ represent a metric.

10 DEFINITION: Set Γ is symmetric if, for every two points $\underline{y}_i$, $\underline{y}_j$ in Γ satisfying

$$\delta(\underline{y}_i,\underline{y}_0) \le \delta(\underline{y}_j,\underline{y}_0),$$

the relationship

$$p(\underline{y}_i) \ge p(\underline{y}_j)$$

holds.

It is easy to verify that the p.d.f. over any symmetric set is unimodal. Thus if we partition a given set into symmetric subsets, the original set will automatically be partitioned into unimodal subsets. The symmetry condition is, however, rather restrictive in the sense that it can lead to partitioning of even unimodal sets. In general, therefore, the number of symmetric subsets obtained far exceeds the actual number of modes in the density function. In this situation, we have to determine from among all the symmetric sets those which contain a local maximum of function $p(\underline{y})$; such sets then constitute the nuclei of the modes in the data set. These sets can be recognised quite simply by investigating the neighborhood of the point with a maximum value of the p.d.f., in each symmetric set. If the neighborhood includes the points of the original data set with greater values of $p(\underline{y})$, then the symmetric set cannot contain a local maximum of the density function.

Once the nuclei of the modes are determined, each remaining symmetric set is grouped with an appropriate nucleus. This nucleus is selected by reference to the membership of the points lying in the neighborhood of that point in the symmetric set at which the density function attains a maximum. The essence of the method lies, therefore, in generating symmetric sets which are subsequently grouped to form the minimum number of unimodal subsets of the original data set. The procedure SYMSETGEN which generates symmetric sets is given in the following.

11 The SYMSETGEN procedure

In order to generate symmetric sets Γ_i, it is required to construct an initial sequence S by arranging elements $\underline{y} \in Y$ in descending order of the p.d.f. values, i.e.,

12 $$S = (\underline{y}_1, \underline{y}_2, \ldots, \underline{y}_n \mid p(\underline{y}_k) \geq p(\underline{y}_j), \text{ all } k < j).$$

The symmetric sets, Γ_i, are now acquired with the help of sequences Q_i of ordered candidate points, defined as

13 $$Q_i = \left(\underline{y}_1^i, \underline{y}_2^i, \ldots, \underline{y}_r^i, \ldots \mid \delta\left(\underline{y}_r^i, \underline{y}_1^i\right) \geq \delta\left(\underline{y}_p^i, \underline{y}_1^i\right), \text{ all } p < r\right).$$

Let us now assume, that, by assigning first r elements of sequence S we have generated i sequences Q_ℓ and initiated i sets Γ_ℓ. If $\underline{y}_p^j$ is the current candidate point in Q_j, j=1,...,i, then the point $\underline{y}_{r+1}$ will be assigned according to the following rule:

a. If $\underline{y}_{r+1} \not\equiv \underline{y}_p^j$, j=1,2,...,i, then $\underline{y}_{r+1}$ initiates a new group Γ_{i+1}. The sequence Q_{i+1} is then constructed using 13 from the unassigned points $\underline{y}_s$, s=r+1,...n of sequence S.

b. If $\underline{y}_{r+1} \equiv \underline{y}_p^j$ and $\underline{y}_{r+1} \not\equiv \underline{y}_p^k$, k=1,...,i, k≠j then $\underline{y}_{r+1} \epsilon \Gamma_j$.

c. If the point $\underline{y}_{r+1}$ is equivalent to more than one candidate point $\underline{y}_p^j$, then $\underline{y}_{r+1}$ will be assigned to Γ_j which includes the point $\underline{y}_k$ defined by

14 $$\delta(\underline{y}_{r+1}, \underline{y}_k) = \min \delta(\underline{y}_{r+1}, \underline{y}_\ell) \text{ all } \underline{y}_\ell \epsilon \Gamma_j, \ j \epsilon I.$$

Here I is a set of indices j of the candidate points $\underline{y}_p^j$ which satisfy

15 $$\underline{y}_{r+1} \equiv \underline{y}_p^j$$

and Γ_j is the set of those points $\underline{y}_\ell \epsilon S$, all $\ell<r$, already assigned to Γ_j. After the point $\underline{y}_{r+1}$ has been assigned, it is withdrawn as a candidate point from the sequence Q_j, j=1,...,i.

Once the symmetric sets are generated, we can determine the points of the local maxima of the function $p(\underline{y})$ as those points $\underline{y}_{oi}$ at which the density function attains a maximum value in each Γ_i and which are interior points of Γ_i's. The symmetric sets Γ_i containing the points of the local maxima of $p(\underline{y})$ form the nuclei of the unimodal sets Y_j, j=1,2,...,c in Y. The remaining Γ_i's are added to Y_j according to the rule

16 $$\Gamma_i \rightarrow Y_j$$

if $\underline{y}_k$ satisfying

17 $$\delta(\underline{y}_{0i},\underline{y}_k) = \min \delta(\underline{y}_{0i},\underline{y}_\ell) \qquad \underline{y}_\ell \in \bigcup_j \tilde{Y}_j$$

belongs to Y_j. $\tilde{Y}_j$ is the union of Γ_i already assigned to Y_j by 16.

We can now summarize the procedure for partitioning data into unimodal sets in the following steps :

The SYMSEP procedure

Step 1: Generate the sequence S from $\underline{y} \in Y$.

Step 2: Construct on Y symmetric sets Γ_i according to the procedure SYMSETGEN.

Step 3: Determine among Γ_i's those sets which contain the local maxima of $p(\underline{y})$.

Step 4: Assign the remaining sets $\Gamma_i \subset Y - \bigcup_j \tilde{Y}_j$ to the sets Y_j by applying 16.

11.2.3. Iterative Mode Separation Algorithm

Let set Y be partitioned into c disjoint subsets Γ_i of cardinality n_i, $i=1,2,\ldots,c$. Now let us consider weighted estimates of the conditional probability density functions $f(\underline{y}|\Gamma_i)$, i.e.

18 $$f(\underline{y}|\Gamma_i) = \frac{n_i}{n} p(\underline{y}|\Gamma_i)$$

based on these subsets. For c=2, these functions are illustrated in Figure 11.5. Intuitively, we should like to partition Y so that the pairwise "distance" between $f(\underline{y}|\Gamma_i)$ and $f(\underline{y}|\Gamma_j)$, $\forall i$, $j \neq i$ is maximum. This problem can be formally expressed as one of maximizing a criterion J defined as

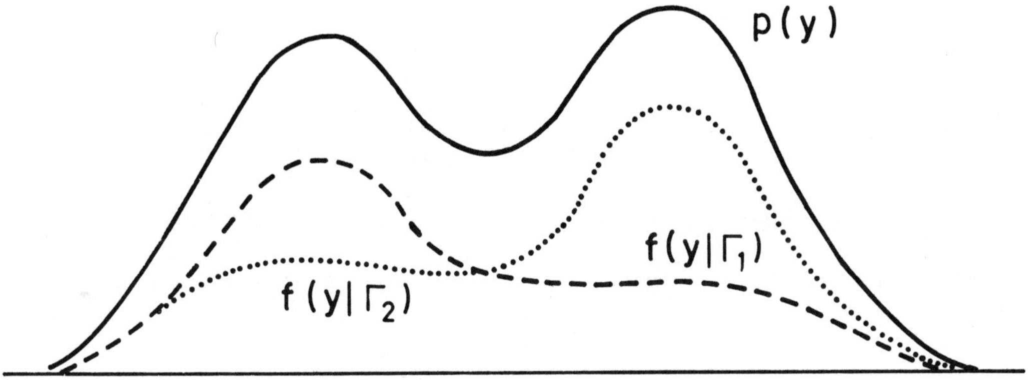

Figure 11.5. Weighted p.d.f.s $f(y|\Gamma_1)$ and $f(y|\Gamma_2)$ of an arbitrarily partitioned data set Γ.

19 $$J = \int \sum_{i=1}^{c} \sum_{j=i}^{c} \left[f(\underline{y}|\Gamma_i) - f(\underline{y}|\Gamma_j) \right]^2 p(\underline{y}) d\underline{y}$$

over all possible partitions of Y.

An algorithm maximizing criterion J can be derived by considering the effect of reassigning a pattern $\underline{y}_k$ from Γ_j to set Γ_i. We assume here that functions $p(\underline{y}|\Gamma_i)$, $\forall i$, in 18 are estimated using the Parzen approach summarized in Appendix A, i.e.,

20 $$p(\underline{y}|\Gamma_i) = \frac{1}{n_i} \sum_{j=1}^{n_i} K(\underline{y}, \underline{y}_j), \qquad \underline{y}_j \in \Gamma_i$$

where $K(\underline{y}, \underline{y}_j)$ is the kernel of the estimator. Then,

21 $$f(\underline{y}|\Gamma_i) = \frac{1}{n} \sum_{j=1}^{n_i} K(\underline{y}, \underline{y}_j) \qquad \underline{y}_j \in \Gamma_i$$

and we note from 21 that the transfer of element $\underline{y}_k$ from set Γ_j to Γ_i, creating new sets $\tilde{\Gamma}_j$ and $\tilde{\Gamma}_i$ respectively will entail

22 $$f(\underline{y}|\tilde{\Gamma}_i) \geq f(\underline{y}|\Gamma_i)$$

and

23 $$f(\underline{y}|\tilde{\Gamma}_j) \leq f(\underline{y}|\Gamma_j).$$

Since the reassignment of $\underline{y}_k$ will not affect other subsets Γ_r, $\forall r \neq i,j$, the resulting change ΔJ in the value of criterion J will be given as

24 $$\Delta J=\int\Big\{\Big[f(\underline{y}|\tilde{\Gamma}_i)-f(\underline{y}|\tilde{\Gamma}_j)\Big]^2-\Big[f(\underline{y}|\Gamma_i)-f(\underline{y}|\Gamma_j)\Big]^2 + \sum_{\substack{k=1\\k\neq i,j}}^{c}\Big\{\Big[f(\underline{y}|\Gamma_k)-f(\underline{y}|\tilde{\Gamma}_j)\Big]^2 - \Big[f(\underline{y}|\Gamma_k)-f(\underline{y}|\Gamma_j)\Big]^2 + \Big[f(\underline{y}|\Gamma_k)-f(\underline{y}|\tilde{\Gamma}_i)\Big]^2-\Big[f(\underline{y}|\Gamma_k)-f(\underline{y}|\Gamma_i)\Big]^2\Big\}\Big\}p(\underline{y})d\underline{y}.$$

Denoting

25 $$f(\underline{y}|\tilde{\Gamma}_i) = f(\underline{y}|\Gamma_i) + \Delta f_i$$

and recalling that

26 $$\Delta f_i = - \Delta f_j = \frac{1}{n} K(\underline{y},\underline{y}_k),$$

we can write

27 $$\Delta J=\int\Big[2c\Delta f_i\Big]^2 p(\underline{y})d\underline{y}+2c\int\Big[f(\underline{y}|\Gamma_i)-f(\underline{y}|\Gamma_j)\Big]\Delta f_i p(\underline{y})d\underline{y}.$$

The first term of 27 will always be positive. The second term, however, could assume any real value. Since for large n, Δf_i will be nonzero only in the vicinity of $\underline{y}_k$, we can assume that this term will be positive and, therefore, result in an increase of J only if

28 $$f(\underline{y}_k|\Gamma_j) \leq f(\underline{y}_k|\Gamma_i).$$

Moreover, note that the greater the difference between $f(\underline{y}_k|\Gamma_i)$ and $f(\underline{y}_k|\Gamma_j)$ the greater the increase of J due to the pattern transfer.

Thus it follows that $\underline{y}_k \in \Gamma_j$ should be assigned to that set Γ_i satisfying

29 $$f(\underline{y}_k|\Gamma_i) = \max_{\ell} f(\underline{y}_k|\Gamma_\ell).$$

The reassignment rule 29 fails only for the point $\underline{y}$ where 29 holds for more than one ℓ so that a unique maximum does not exist. Then for two classes s and t, we have

30 $$f(\underline{y}|Y_s) = f(\underline{y}|Y_t).$$

But 30 indicates that $\underline{y}$ is from the valley of the probability density function $p(\underline{y})$ occurring between the classes ω_s and ω_t. Thus the points occurring along the bottom of the valley can then be assigned arbitrarily to either cluster Y_t or Y_s without incurring a significant error since the p.d.f. at these points is low.

The complete clustering procedure can be stated as follows :

The ITERSEP procedure

Step 1: Choose initial assignment for all points in Y.

Step 2: For each point $\underline{y}_r$, r=1,...n calculate $f(\underline{y}_r|\Gamma_i)$ and assign $\underline{y}_r$ to an appropriate class according to rule 29.

Step 3: If any point is reclassified to a new class, go to Step 2.

11.2.4. Modesp

An alternative approach to determining unimodal subsets Y_i, i=1,2,...,c of Y is based on mapping of data points onto a sequence, S. We shall describe this method with reference to Figure 11.6 illustrating a two modal p.d.f. of a set, Y.

Let us choose any arbitrary point of the data set, say, $\underline{y}_0$, and let

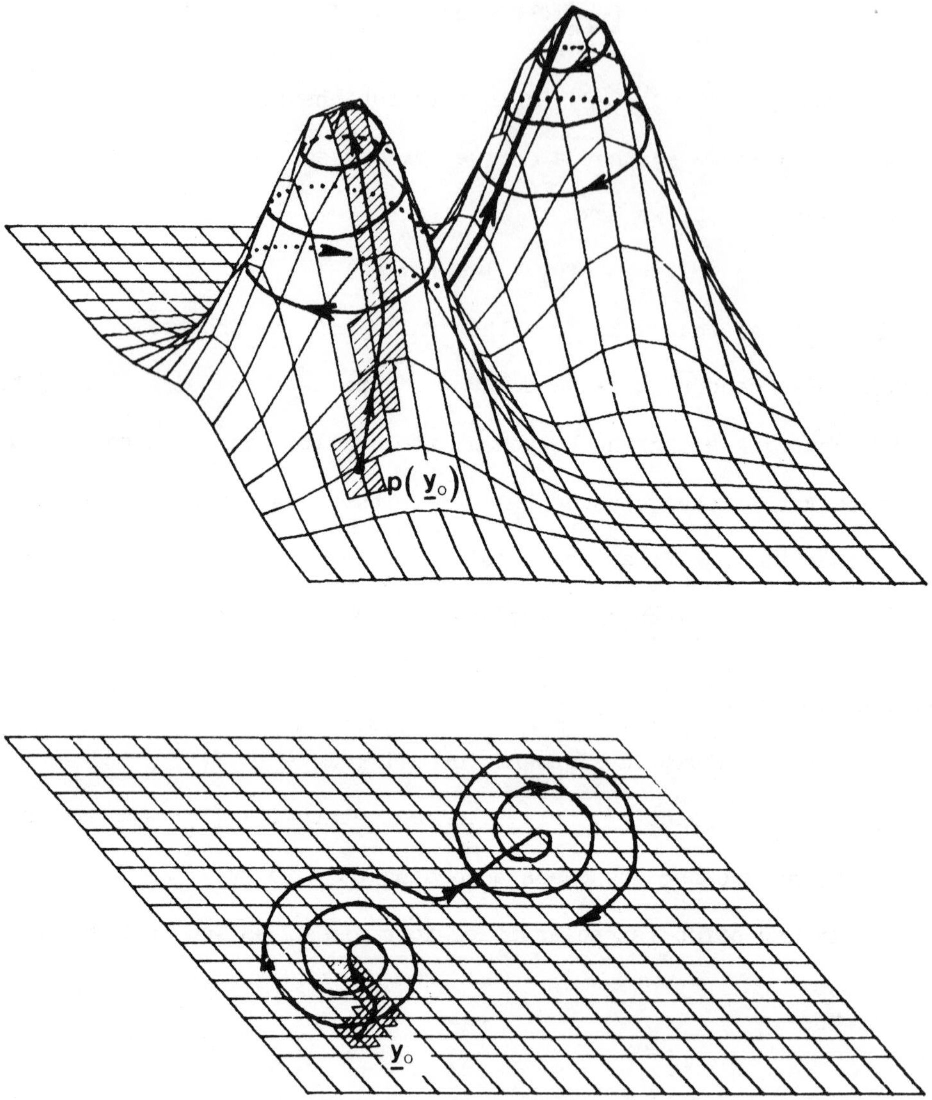

Figure 11.6 The mapping procedure. (From *Pattern Recognition*, Pergamon Press, 1976, Vol. 8, p. 24. Courtesy of Pattern Recognition Society, Washington, D.C.)

this point be the first element of sequence S, i.e. $\tilde{\underline{y}}_1 \equiv \underline{y}_0$. Further, let us construct a hypercube with the centre of gravity at the point $\underline{y}_0$ and the side 2ρ. Suppose that we now select from all the points of Y lying in the hypercubic neighborhood of point $\underline{y}_0$ a point $\underline{y}_k$ which has the highest probability density and denote this point $\tilde{\underline{y}}_2$. By analogy, we can select as the next point of sequence S a point of the data set contained in the union of the hypercubic neighborhoods of points $\tilde{\underline{y}}_1$ and $\tilde{\underline{y}}_2$ with the highest probability density. By repeating this procedure we select points $\tilde{\underline{y}}_4$, $\tilde{\underline{y}}_5$, ... and thus construct a chain of hypercubes in the data set which will eventually reach the local peak of the p.d.f.

Continuing in the same selection procedure after the peak has been reached, we select sequentially points with lower and lower probability density until we reach that point of the valley, $\underline{y}_v$, between the two modes which has the lowest probability density. Since all the points $\underline{y}$ from the first mode with $p(\underline{y})>p(\underline{y}_v)$ have already been selected, the following point, $\underline{y}_r$, with $p(\underline{y}_r)>p(\underline{y}_v)$ will belong, therefore, to the second mode of $p(\underline{y})$. Continuing in this manner, the selected points will subsequently form a chain leading to the peak of the second mode. Further continuation of the selection process will eventually result in selecting all the points of the second mode with probability density $p(\underline{y})>p(\underline{y}_v)$. And once the probability density level $p(\underline{y}_v)$ has been reached, the method will select the remaining points in the data set with $p(\underline{y}) \le p(\underline{y}_v)$, irrespective of the two modes.

Thus at the kth step of the selection process we select, from yet unassigned points of the data set, a point $\underline{y}$ with probability density $p(\underline{y})$ and this will be the kth point of the sequence $S=(\tilde{\underline{y}}_1,\tilde{\underline{y}}_2,\ldots,\tilde{\underline{y}}_k,\ldots)$. We can view this process, therefore, as a mapping of the points from an N-dimensional space onto sequence S.

Suppose now we generate a function, $F(\tilde{\underline{y}}_k)$, on this sequence as follows

31 $$F(\tilde{\underline{y}}_k) = p(\tilde{\underline{y}}_k)$$

and plot $F(\tilde{\underline{y}}_k)$ as a function of k as shown in Figure 11.7. Recalling the mapping process from the beginning we know that $F(\tilde{\underline{y}}_k)$ will first sharply increase until the peak of the first mode is reached. Then the function will slowly decrease while all the points of the first mode are being swept by the selection procedure. Once the valley point $\underline{y}_v$ is reached, the value of $F(\tilde{\underline{y}}_k)$ will rapidly increase, followed by a slow descent corresponding to the selection of the points $\underline{y}$ with $p(\underline{y})>p(\underline{y}_v)$ from the second mode of $p(\underline{y})$. The function $F(\tilde{\underline{y}})$ will continue decreasing even for points $\underline{y}$ with $p(\underline{y})\leq p(\underline{y}_v)$ but these points can now belong to any of the two modes shown in Figure 11.6.

After the mapping of all the points has been completed, a majority of the points from Y will be assigned to one of the two modes. Although the points from the end of sequence S cannot be assigned to any mode, we may use the NN rule to classify these points to their appropriate modes.

Intuitively, it is apparent that, in general, when the p.d.f. is c-modal, all the modes will be detectable from the shape of the function $F(\tilde{\underline{y}})$. In particular, each unimodal interval of $F(\tilde{\underline{y}})$ will

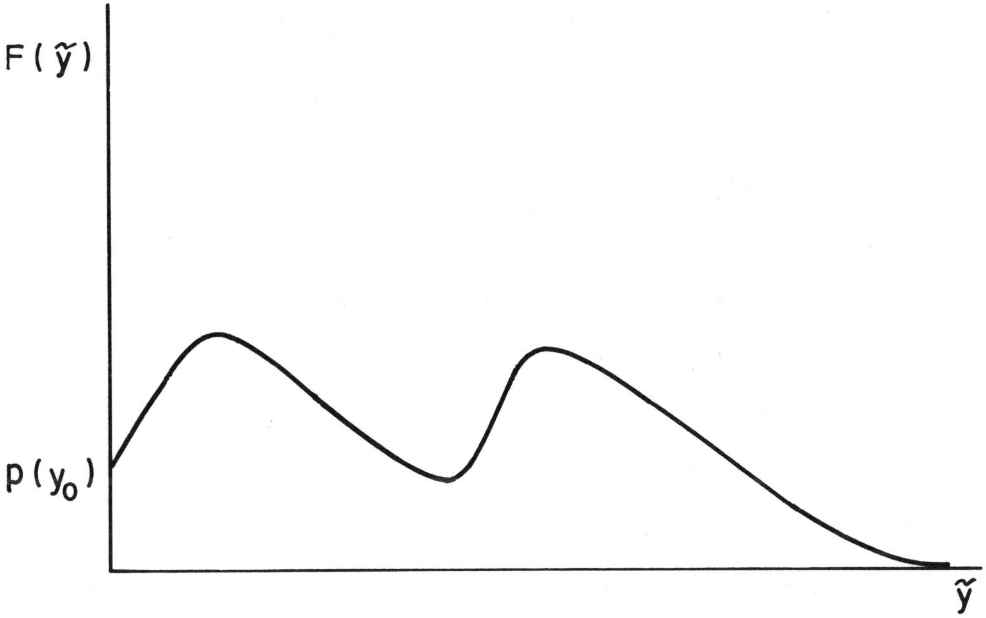

Figure 11.7. Function F ($\tilde{y}_k$) on the sequence S generated by the mapping procedure.

contain a set of points from one of the modes of the function $p(\underline{y})$. This set, which is composed of all those points of the interval having probability density greater than the first point of the interval, can be considered as a nucleus of the mode of the p.d.f., $p(\underline{y})$. Although the membership of the remaining points of the interval is unknown, these points can be assigned later using the nearest neighbor rule.

This process of mapping data points onto a sequence and the subsequent generation of the function $F(\tilde{\underline{y}})$ constitutes a basis of the mode separation procedure Modesp. It can be formalized as follows :

The mapping procedure

a. Choose $\tilde{\underline{y}}_1 \equiv \underline{y}_0 \epsilon Y$.

b. Assume k points have been mapped to form sequence S_k, i.e.,

$S_k=(\underline{\tilde{y}}_1,\ldots,\underline{\tilde{y}}_k)$; then the next point $\underline{\tilde{y}}_{k+1}$ will be an element, $\underline{y}_l$, from set $Y-S_k$ of the remaining points in Y, i.e., $\underline{\tilde{y}}_{k+1}=\underline{y}_l$, such that

32 $$p(\underline{y}_l) = \max p(\underline{y}_j), \quad \forall \underline{y}_j \in (Y-S_k) \subset N_\rho(S_k)$$

where $N_\rho(S_k)$ is the union of the hypercubic neighborhoods, $N_\rho(\underline{\tilde{y}}_r)$, of the points in sequence S_k, defined as

33 $$N_\rho(\underline{\tilde{y}}_r)=\left\{\underline{y}\,\middle|\,\underline{y}\in Y, |\tilde{y}_{ri}-y_i|<\rho,\ i=1,2,\ldots,D\right\}.$$

The parameter ρ which determines the size of the neighborhood must satisfy the unbiasedness and consistency conditions of the Parzen estimator (see Appendix A).

c. Function $F(\underline{\tilde{y}})$ is then defined for all the points of sequence $S=S_n$ as

34 $$F(\underline{\tilde{y}}_j) = p(\underline{\tilde{y}}_j).$$

As mentioned earlier, function $F(\underline{\tilde{y}})$ has important properties for cluster analysis, namely that the number of unimodal intervals of $F(\underline{\tilde{y}})$ determines the number of clusters in the data. Moreover, the majority of the points in each unimodal interval of $F(\underline{\tilde{y}})$ form a nucleus of one of the modes in the probability density function of the data set. More specifically, let $a_1,a_2,\ldots,a_c$ be indices of points $\underline{\tilde{y}}_j$ in sequence S which correspond to the points of minima of function $F(\underline{\tilde{y}})$. These points are, of course, the initial points of the unimodal intervals of $F(\underline{\tilde{y}})$. Then the nucleus of the jth cluster is defined by all those points $\underline{\tilde{y}}_\ell$ in the jth unimodal interval of $F(\underline{\tilde{y}})$ which satisfy

35 $$F(\underline{\tilde{y}}_\ell) > F(\underline{\tilde{y}}_{a_j}).$$

It has been already mentioned that, after the mapping process is completed, the membership of some points in sequence S remains unresolved, that is that of all those points in jth interval with $F(\tilde{\underline{y}})$ satisfying

36 $$F(\tilde{\underline{y}}) < F(\tilde{\underline{y}}_{a_j}).$$

However, using the nuclei of the clusters as reference data, these points can be classified using the nearest neighbor decision rule.

The computation time required by the procedure is considerably dependent upon the structure of the data to be partitioned. In particular, when the modes are disjoint, the procedure is very efficient, since there is a relatively small number of assigned points whose neighborhood must be examined in order to select the next point. This is because all the points of the current mode are exhausted once the procedure terminates.

When the clusters associated with distinct modes of $p(\underline{y})$ are connected, that is the smallest distance between two points of different clusters is less than the mapping parameter ρ, Modesp does not terminate until all the points in Y have been mapped onto sequence S. The computational burden of the method is then substantially increased.

In such cases, it is advantageous to terminate the mapping of the current mode when $F(\tilde{\underline{y}})$ drops below a certain prespecified value. In this way, the speed of the algorithm is made comparable with the disjoint subset case mentioned above. When data set Y is small, the p.d.f. estimate contains a number of small fictitious modes, causing the function $F(\tilde{y})$ to have a noisy appearance. In such situations, we can either specify the permissible deviations from the required monotonicity of $F(\tilde{y})$ on the unimodal intervals by a threshold or discard all those subsets detected by Modesp which contain less than a prespecified number of points.

The choice of the hypercubic kernel with parameter ρ as a basis of procedure Modesp has been based on computational considerations. First of all the absolute value operation is much faster than the calculation required for the evaluation of the Euclidean distance. Second, the presence of pattern vectors in the active neighborhood of the hypercubic kernel can be determined by individually checking the vector components in each axis. Thus a large number of points can be eliminated from further search by a simple test of the first few components of the vector under consideration. From experimental studies, it follows that for small sample sets the spherical neighborhood yields better results. However, the computational time increases substantially. A suitable compromise is to advocate the use of the spherical neighborhood for small sample sets and replace this neighborhood by a more computationally efficient one.

Finally, let us summarize the clustering procedure Modesp :

The MODESP clustering procedure

Step 1: Obtain a Parzen estimate of the p.d.f. based on Y.

Step 2: Generate function $F(\tilde{y})$.

Step 3: Using the nearest neighbor rule classify all those points in S whose membership is unknown.

11.3. INDIRECT METHODS OF MODE SEPARATION

We have formulated the problem of nonsupervised learning pattern classification as one of detecting modes in the mixture p.d.f. and a number of mode separation procedures developed to provide a solution to this problem have been described above. This approach can be viewed as a process of relating respective data points via the values of the density function at these points.

On a number of occasions throughout this text we have resorted to indirect methods of achieving a certain goal and the nonsupervised learning pattern classification problem will be no exception. Here, as an alternative to the direct approach, we shall attempt to partition a given data set into homogeneous subsets (clusters) by considering similarities of data points in each subset and their relationship to the elements of other subsets or by relating data points to the models representing clusters. This approach is referred to in the literature as clustering.

Most of the similarity measures used in practice are based on one of the metrics listed in Section 6.2. The use of these metrics as similarity measures for clustering can be justified by the heuristic argument that points in the same cluster should be close to each other and, at the same time, they should be distant from the elements of other clusters. Note that this particular conceptual basis of data partitioning is not unrelated to the concept associating clusters with modes in the mixture p.d.f., for two points clustered together on the basis of their mutual distance are likely to be associated with the same mode in p($\underline{y}$). After all, an estimate of p($\underline{y}$) itself is defined via intersample distances either directly or indirectly.

There are basically two approaches to data clustering. The first, known as the dynamic clustering method, employs an iterative algorithm to optimize a clustering criterion function. Various criteria of clustering have been suggested in the literature but among these the family of criterion functions quantifying the average affinity of data points to cluster representatives have proved to be most useful.

At each iteration of a dynamic clustering algorithm, data points are assigned to clusters, the number of which must be specified beforehand, on the basis of their similarity with the current cluster representatives. Subsequently, the cluster representatives are updated to reflect any changes in the data point assignments. These new cluster models are then used in the next iteration to reclassify the data and the process is continued until a stable partition is obtained.

The second approach, known as hierarchical clustering, is noniterative. At any stage of a hierarchical clustering algorithm the two of the existing clusters which are most similar are merged to create a new cluster, thus reducing the number of potential clusters by one. After n-1 steps, where n is the cardinality of the set being analyzed, the algorithm terminates. The number of clusters in the data set need not be known *a priori*. Here, natural clusters of points in the data set, for a given measure of similarity, are detected by assessing the relative changes in the values of the measure at various stages of the algorithm.

In the following subsections both of these approaches will be discussed in more detail.

11.3.1. Dynamic Clustering

We shall first consider the problem of partitioning data set $Y=\{\underline{y}_i \mid i=1,2,\ldots n\}$ into c clusters, Γ_k, $k=1,2,\ldots,c$, each represented simply by its mean value $\underline{m}_k$. Let the cardinality of the kth cluster be n_k. Then $\underline{m}_k$ is defined as

37 $$\underline{m}_k = \frac{1}{n_k} \sum_{i=1}^{n_k} \underline{y}_i, \qquad \underline{y}_i \in \Gamma_k.$$

As a measure of similarity between point $\underline{y}$ and a cluster representative, we shall adopt the Euclidean distance given in 6.9. Accordingly, a pattern, $\underline{y}$, in subset Γ_k should satisfy

38 $$\delta_E(\underline{y},\underline{m}_k) < \delta_E(\underline{y},\underline{m}_\ell), \quad \forall \ell \neq k.$$

Among all the possible partitions $\Gamma=\left\{\Gamma_j \mid j=1,\ldots,c,\ \bigcap_{j=1}^{c} \Gamma_j=0,\ \bigcup_{j=1}^{c} \Gamma_j=Y\right\}$ of set Y into c clusters we shall seek the one that minimizes the total square distance of the elements of subsets Γ_j from their representative point $\underline{m}_j$, $j=1,\ldots,c$. Thus, the clustering criterion function $J(\Gamma)$ to be optimized can be expressed as

39 $$J(\Gamma) = \sum_{j=1}^{c} \sum_{i=1}^{n_j} \delta_E^2(\underline{y}_i,\underline{m}_j) = \sum_{j=1}^{c} J_j(\Gamma), \qquad \underline{y}_i \in \Gamma_j,$$

and the optimal solution $\Gamma^{*} = \{Y_j \mid j=1,\ldots,c\}$ will then satisfy

40 $$J(\Gamma^{*}) = \min_{\Gamma} J(\Gamma).$$

To find an algorithm searching for an optimum of $J(\Gamma)$, let us study the effect of transferring a point $\tilde{\underline{y}}$ which is currently in cluster Γ_k into cluster Γ_j. After the reassignment the mean vectors of the resulting clusters $\tilde{Y}_k$ and $\tilde{Y}_j$ will be respectively

41 $$\tilde{\underline{m}}_k = \underline{m}_k + \frac{1}{n_k-1}\left[\underline{m}_k - \tilde{\underline{y}}\right]$$

and

42 $$\tilde{\underline{m}}_j = \underline{m}_j + \frac{1}{n_j+1}\left[\tilde{\underline{y}} - \underline{m}_j\right].$$

Note that, in criterion function 39, only the terms involving mean vectors of the kth and jth clusters will be affected. It is easy to show that the new contributions $\tilde{J}_k(\Gamma)$ and $\tilde{J}_j(\Gamma)$ of these clusters to the value of criterion $J(\Gamma)$ will be given by

43 $$\tilde{J}_k = J_k - \frac{n_k}{n_k-1}\,\delta_E^2(\tilde{\underline{y}},\underline{m}_k)$$

and

44 $$\tilde{J}_j = J_j + \frac{n_j}{n_j+1}\,\delta_E^2(\tilde{\underline{y}},\underline{m}_j).$$

Thus the reassignment of point $\tilde{\underline{y}}$ will result in a decrease of criterion $J(\Gamma)$ only if

45 $$\frac{n_j}{n_j+1}\,\delta_E^2(\tilde{\underline{y}},\underline{m}_j) < \frac{n_k}{n_k-1}\,\delta_E^2(\tilde{\underline{y}},\underline{m}_k).$$

This inequality will be satisfied whenever $\tilde{\underline{y}}$ is located closer to $\underline{m}_j$ than to $\underline{m}_k$.

The algorithm minimizing $J(\Gamma)$ based on the above observations can be stated as follows :

The c-means algorithm

46 Initialization: Choose an arbitrary partition of Y into c clusters Γ_j, j=1,2,...,c and compute mean vectors $\underline{m}_j$, j=1,2,...,c.

Step 1: Select point $\underline{y}$ in Y and assign it to that cluster whose mean is closest to $\underline{y}$, i.e.,

$$\text{assign } \underline{y} \text{ to } \Gamma_j \text{ if } \delta_E(\underline{y},\underline{m}_j)=\min_k \delta_E(\underline{y},\underline{m}_k).$$

Step 2: Update mean vectors $\underline{m}_j$, j=1,2,...,c and go to Step 1.

The algorithm is terminated whenever a complete scan of patterns in Y results in no change of the cluster mean vectors.

47 REMARK: Alternatively, all the points in Y can be reassigned at the same iteration using the current mean vectors. Subsequently, $\underline{m}_j$ are updated taking into account all the changes in pattern allocations. This procedure is repeated until a stable partition is obtained. Algorithm 47 is known as the ISODATA algorithm.

Often the representation of a cluster as provided by the mean vector will be inadequate. However, the above algorithm can readily be generalized to more sophisticated cluster models.

In general, we shall represent a cluster Γ_j by a kernel $K_j=K(\underline{y},V_j)$ with V_j denoting a set of parameters defining K_j. The kernel can be, for instance, a function, a set of points or any other convenient model of the cluster. Further, let $\Delta(\underline{y},K_j)$ designate a measure of similarity between vector $\underline{y}$ and cluster Γ_j represented by kernel K_j. Then, by analogy, the dynamic clustering algorithm that optimizes $J(\Gamma)$,

48 $$J(\Gamma) = \sum_{j=1}^{c} \sum_{i=1}^{n_j} \Delta(\underline{y}_i, K_j),$$

over all possible partitions Γ of Y can be given as follows:

49 The dynamic clustering algorithm

Initialization: Choose an arbitrary partition of Y into c clusters Γ_j, $j=1,2,\ldots,c$ and determine the corresponding kernels K_j

Step 1: Assign each point $\underline{y} \in Y$ to that cluster Γ_j for which

$$\Delta(\underline{y}, K_j) = \min_k \Delta(\underline{y}, K_k)$$

Step 2: Update kernels K_j, $\forall j$; if kernels K_j remain unchanged, terminate the algorithm else go to Step 1.

This algorithm will converge provided the clustering criterion function satisfies the following condition :

50 $$J(\tilde{\Gamma}, \tilde{K}) \le J(\Gamma, \tilde{K}) \text{ if } J(\Gamma, \tilde{K}) \le J(\Gamma, K).$$

where $J(\Gamma, K)$ is the value of criterion function $J(\Gamma)$ in 48 corresponding to the set of kernels, $K=\left\{K_j \mid j=1,\ldots,c\right\}$. In 50 Γ and $\tilde{\Gamma}$ are the partitions obtained by classifying elements of Y using sets of kernels K and $\tilde{K}$ respectively and $\tilde{K}$ is the set of updated kernels, $\tilde{K}=\left\{\tilde{K}_j \mid j=1,\ldots,c\right\}$ corresponding to partition Γ. In other words, convergence condition 50 states that criterion function $J(\Gamma)$ must be such that, assuming the value of the function decreases as a result of updating the kernels representing clusters, a further decrease of $J(\Gamma)$ can be obtained by reclassifying elements of Y using these updated kernels.

For the particular problem of partitioning Y using the mean vector representation of clusters we have

51 $$K = \left\{\underline{m}_j \mid j=1,2,\dots,c\right\}$$

$$\Gamma = \left\{\Gamma_j \mid \forall j\right\} \text{ where } \Gamma_j=\left\{\underline{y} \mid \underline{y}\in Y, \delta_E(\underline{y},\underline{m}_j)=\min_l \delta_E(\underline{y},\underline{m}_l)\right\}$$

$$\tilde{K} = \left\{\tilde{\underline{m}}_j \mid j=1,2,\dots,c,\ \tilde{\underline{m}}_j=\frac{1}{n_j}\sum_{i=1}^{n_j} \underline{y}_i,\ \underline{y}_i\in\Gamma_j\right\}$$

$$\tilde{\Gamma} = \left\{\tilde{\Gamma}_j\right\} \text{ where } \tilde{\Gamma}_j=\left\{\underline{y} \mid \underline{y}\in Y, \delta_E(\underline{y},\tilde{\underline{m}}_j)=\min_l \delta_E(\underline{y},\tilde{\underline{m}}_l)\right\}.$$

It is easy to show that in this particular case criterion 48 satisfies condition 50.

In order to illustrate how the dynamic clustering approach can be used in practice, we shall now give two examples of a possible choice of kernels and of a similarity measure.

52 EXAMPLE 1: One form of kernel K_j which is very important in practical applications is a sample-based estimate of the p.d.f. of a normal distribution. Here the set of parameters, V_j, consists of estimates $\underline{m}_j$ and $\hat{\Sigma}_j$ of the mean vector and the covariance matrix of the distribution respectively. Thus

53 $$K_j(\underline{y},V_j) = \frac{1}{(2\pi)^{D/2}|\hat{\Sigma}_j|^{1/2}} \exp\left\{-\frac{1}{2}(\underline{y}-\underline{m}_j)^t\hat{\Sigma}_j^{-1}(\underline{y}-\underline{m}_j)\right\},$$

where $\underline{m}_j$ is given in 37 and $\hat{\Sigma}_j$ is defined as

54 $$\hat{\Sigma}_j = \frac{1}{n_j}\sum_{i=1}^{n_j}(\underline{y}_i-\underline{m}_j)(\underline{y}_i-\underline{m}_j)^t, \qquad \underline{y}_i\in\Gamma_j.$$

Invoking the Bayes decision rule for normally distributed classes, a suitable measure of similarity can be defined as

55 $$\Delta(\underline{y},K_j) = \frac{1}{2}(\underline{y}-\underline{m}_j)^t\hat{\Sigma}_j^{-1}(\underline{y}-\underline{m}_j) + \frac{1}{2}\log|\hat{\Sigma}_j|.$$

56 REMARK: Note that, using the exponential kernels, it will be possible to recover the components of a mixture of Gaussian distributions. This approach can be considered, therefore, as a parametric equivalent of the iterative mode separation method described in Section 11.2.

57 EXAMPLE 2: In some applications it may be advantageous to represent each cluster by the subspace defined by D_j axes of the Karhunen-Loeve expansion of the cluster centralized patterns, (see Section 9.2). Kernel $K(\underline{y},V_j)$ is then defined as

58 $$K(\underline{y},V_j) = U_j^t\underline{y},$$

where the columns of the $D\times d_j$ parameter matrix are the eigenvectors, $\underline{u}_i$, $i=1,2,\ldots,d_j$ of matrix $\hat{\Sigma}_j$ defined in 54, associated with the d_j largest eigenvalues of $\hat{\Sigma}_j$.

An intuitively obvious measure of similarity between point $\underline{y}$ and cluster Γ_j is the Euclidean distance (or its square) between point $\underline{y}-\underline{m}_j$ and the nearest point to this centralized vector in $K(\underline{y},V_j)$. This point is, of course, defined as $U_jU_j^t(\underline{y}-\underline{m}_j)$. Consequently, there follows :

59 $$\Delta(\underline{y},K_j) = \left[(\underline{y}-\underline{m}_j)-U_jU_j^t(\underline{y}-\underline{m}_j)\right]^t \left[(\underline{y}-\underline{m}_j)-U_jU_j^t(\underline{y}-\underline{m}_j)\right].$$

A geometrical interpretation of this measure is given in Figure 11.8.

Note that updating of kernels K_j in Step 2 of the dynamic clustering algorithm involves computation of each $\underline{m}_j$, $\hat{\Sigma}_j$ and an eigenvalue analysis of $\hat{\Sigma}_j$ to find matrix U_j.

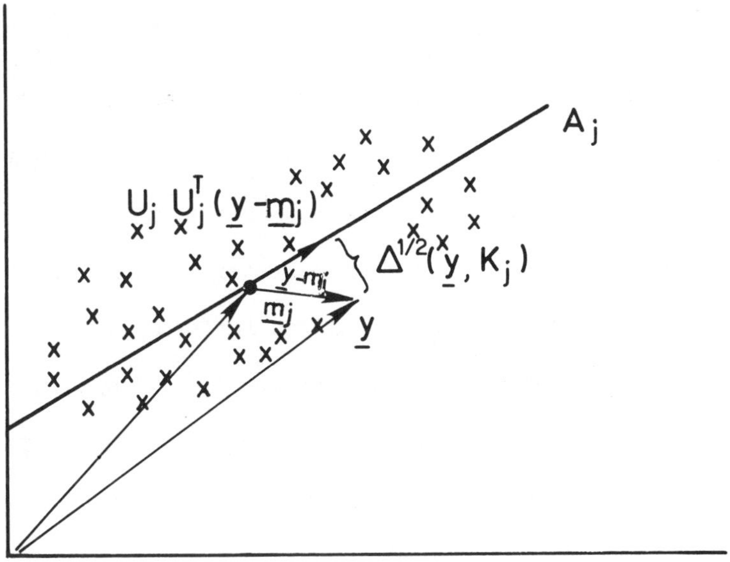

Figure 11.8. Point to cluster similarity measure for Example 2.

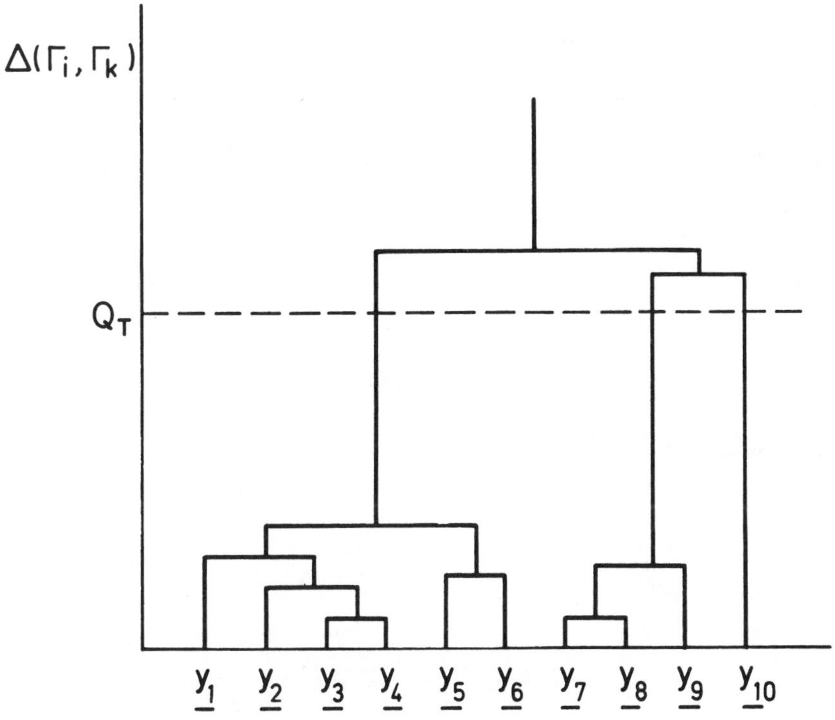

Figure 11.9. Example of the dendrogram for a data set of ten points.

11.3.2. Hierarchical Clustering

It has been already mentioned that the hierarchical approach to clustering involves, at every stage of the clustering process, merging together the two most similar clusters. Initially, every point in the data set is considered as a separate cluster. In the next stage, the two most similar points are combined to form one cluster. This merging process is continued in the consecutive stages of the cluster analysis thus reducing the number of clusters at each stage by one. The clustering procedure is terminated when all the points are assigned to one cluster.

In Subsection 11.3.1 we have introduced similarity measures for relating one data point to a cluster. Here we require a similarity measure, $\Delta(\Gamma_i,\Gamma_j)$, which would enable us to assess the pairwise relationship of clusters. The most widely used measures of similarity for hierarchical clustering listed in the following are defined through inter point distances, i.e.,

<u>NEAREST NEIGHBOR</u>:

60 $$\Delta(\Gamma_i,\Gamma_j) = \min_{\underline{y}\in\Gamma_i,\tilde{\underline{y}}\in\Gamma_j} \delta(\underline{y},\tilde{\underline{y}})$$

<u>FURTHEST NEIGHBOR</u>:

61 $$\Delta(\Gamma_i,\Gamma_j) = \max_{\underline{y}\in\Gamma_i,\tilde{\underline{y}}\in\Gamma_j} \delta(\underline{y},\tilde{\underline{y}})$$

<u>MEAN</u>:

62 $$\Delta(\Gamma_i,\Gamma_j) = \delta(\underline{m}_i,\underline{m}_j)$$

where $\delta(\underline{y},\underline{v})$ can be any metric given in Section 6.2.

The clustering algorithm can now be stated formally as follows :

63 The hierarchical clustering algorithm

Initialization: Set $\Gamma_j = \underline{y}_j$, $\forall j \in I$ where $I = \{j \mid j = 1, 2, \ldots n\}$.

Step 1: Amongst $\left\{\Gamma_j \mid j \in I\right\}$ find the pair of clusters Γ_i, Γ_k satisfying

$$\Delta(\Gamma_i, \Gamma_k) = \min_{\forall j, l \in I} \Delta(\Gamma_j, \Gamma_l).$$

Step 2: Merge Γ_i with Γ_k and delete Γ_i.

Step 3: Remove i from the set of indices, I. If the cardinality of I is two, stop, else go to Step 1.

A graphical representation of the hierarchical structure of clusters yielded by the algorithm is provided by the dendrogram, an example of which is given in Figure 11.9 for a hypothetical clustering problem involving 10 data points. The dendrogram illustrates the cluster merging sequence and the corresponding values of the similarity measure. For any threshold value of the similarity measure, we obtain clusters the subclusters of which have similarity at least equal to the threshold. In Figure 11.9 threshold Q_T splits the data set into three clusters, one point being an outlier. The threshold level should be chosen so that intercluster distances are considerably greater than the intracluster distances.

Note that the use of a particular separability measure will greatly influence the result of clustering. The algorithm employing criterion 60, which is known as the nearest neighbor or minimum spanning tree algorithm, has the disadvantage that it will link together two distinct compact clusters if there exists a path of closely located points connecting the two clusters. The furthest neighbor algorithm based on measure 61 discourages the cluster linking phenomenon but, on the other hand, it suffers from being oversensitive to outliers and from its inability to detect elongated clusters.

11.4. COMMENTS

It cannot be over-emphasized that extreme care must be taken when any of the nonsupervised learning pattern classification methods described earlier are applied to practical problems for the results of the analysis will be affected by many factors such as scaling of the axes, metric used, similarity measure, clustering criterion, number of points in the analyzed set, etc. The result of clustering will, of course, depend also on the particular characteristics of the algorithm used and only very general remarks can be made concerning the various approaches discussed in this chapter.

Broadly speaking, dynamic clustering methods discussed in Section 11.3.1 are usually computationally very efficient and consequently very attractive to the user. The main disadvantage of these methods is, however, that the chosen model rarely reflects the true probabilistic structure of the data. In such situations, the dynamic clustering algorithm can give rise to an unrealistic grouping of data. Although it may be possible to detect inappropriate clustering by further analysis of clusters determined, such an analysis is unlikely to give any indication as to what data representation would be more suitable. Thus we have to analyze data with as many different arbitrarily selected kernels as possible and be content with the most reasonable results obtained.

If we are, however, prepared to trade in computational simplicity for reliability, it is better to use the mode separation methods of Section 11.2 which lay emphasis on local details in the structure of the data as manifested in the probability density function (p.d.f.), $p(\underline{y})$. However, the reliability of these methods is not absolute for they all involve estimation of the p.d.f. This process brings into the analysis an element of subjectivity on two counts which may influence the final decision regarding clustering. First, p.d.f. estimators are functions of parameters whose choice is restricted only by very broad guidelines of p.d.f. estimation theory. It is quite possible that two different sets of parameters, both selected from an admissible range, will result in a p.d.f. with differing number of modes. Secondly, a raw estimate of p.d.f. is usually a noisy function. Consequently it is practically impossible to establish whether some of the peaks in the estimate are genuine, that is whether they correspond to the actual modes in the data.

If the number of points in the data set, n, is very small so that estimation of the p.d.f. becomes meaningless, none of the methods of Section 11.2 should be used for the data analysis. In such situations the hierarchical methods are particularly useful.

To conclude, despite their particular advantages and shortcomings, the methods discussed in these notes should not be considered as being applicable only to problems of a specific type but rather as alternatives voicing an independent opinion about data structure. The only criterion for their inclusion here is the feasibility of their implementation.

11.5. BIBLIOGRAPHICAL COMMENTS

The problem of nonsupervised learning is discussed here in a framework that is consistent with the statistical pattern recognition system model adhered to throughout the book. The emphasis is laid on nonparametric techniques. A detailed treatment of decomposition techniques applicable to mixtures of parametric distributions can be found in Duda and Hart (1973).

The projection method of mode separation is due to Henrichon and Fu (1968). A similar approach was advocated by Eigen, Fromm and Northouse (1972). Gitman and Levine (1970) proposed the mode separation method based on the properties of symmetric sets. The interesting valley seeking algorithm of Koontz and Fukunaga (1972) was probably inspired by the revolutionary ideas of Ruspini (1969). The procedure MODESP was suggested by Kittler (1976).

In the adopted framework, clustering is considered only as an indirect tool of mixture decomposition or mode separation. It is beyond the scope of this book to give an exhaustive account of clustering algorithms whose number probably exceeds the number of typical clustering problems. The interested reader is referred to the texts by Anderberg (1973), Everitt (1974), Hartigan (1975) and the classical work of Sokal and Sneath (1963).

Of particular interest here is the dynamic clustering algorithm of Diday (1974) which is a generalization of the ISODATA algorithm of Hall and Ball (1965), Ball (1965), and the closely related c-means algorithm of MacQueen (1967). The convergence conditions for the dynamic clustering algorithm are given in Diday and Simon (1976).

Supplementary reading on hierarchical clustering, and the original references can be found in Sokal and Sneath (1963), Gower and Ross (1968), and Wishart (1969).

11.6. REFERENCES

Anderberg, M.R., *Cluster Analysis for Applications*, Academic Press, New York, 1973.

Ball, G.B., "Data analysis in the social sciences : What about the details?", *Proc. Fall Joint Comput. Conf.*, pp. 533-559, Spartan Books, Washington D.C., 1965.

Diday, E., "Optimization in non-hierarchical clustering", *Pattern Recognition*, vol. 6, pp. 17-33, 1974.

Diday, E., and Simon, J.C., "Cluster analysis", in *Digital Pattern Recognition*, K.S.Fu, Ed., Springer-Verlag, Berlin, 1976.

Duda, R.O., and Hart, P.E., *Pattern Classification and Scene Analysis*, John Wiley, New York, 1973.

Eigen, D.J., Fromm, F.R., and Northouse, R.A., "Cluster analysis based on dimensional information with application to feature selection and extraction", *IEEE Trans. Systems Man Cybernet.*, vol. 4, pp. 284-294, 1972.

Everitt, B., *Cluster Analysis*, John Wiley, New York, 1974.

Gower, J.C., and Ross, G.J.S., "Minimum spanning tree and single-linkage cluster analysis", *Appl. Statist.*, vol. 18, pp. 54-64, 1968.

Gitman, I., and Levine, M.D., "An algorithm for detecting unimodal fuzzy sets and its application as a clustering technique", *IEEE Trans. Comput.*, vol. 19, pp. 583-593, 1970.

Hall, D.J., and Ball, G.B., "ISODATA : A novel method of data analysis and pattern classification", Technical Rept., Stanford Research Institute, Menlo Park, California, 1965.

Hartigan, J.A., *Clustering Algorithms*, John Wiley, New York, 1975.

Henrichon, E.G., and Fu, K.S., "On mode estimation in pattern recognition", *Proc. 7th Symp. Adaptive Processes*, UCLA, pp. 3-a-1, 1968.

Kittler, J., "A locally sensitive method for cluster analysis", *Pattern Recognition*, vol. 8, pp. 23-33, 1976.

Kittler, J., "A comparative study of five locally sensitive clustering techniques", *Proc. Internat. Comput. Symp.*, North-Holland, Amsterdam, 1975, pp. 1-8.

Koontz, W.L.G., and Fukunaga, K., "Asymptotic analysis of a nonparametric clustering technique", *IEEE Trans. Comput.*, vol. 21, pp. 967-974, 1972.

Koontz, W.L.G., and Fukunaga, K., "A nonparametric valley-seeking technique for cluster analysis", *IEEE Trans. Comput.*, vol. 21, pp. 171-178, 1972.

Koontz, W.L.G., Narendra, P.M., and Fukunaga, K., "A graph theoretic approach to nonparametric cluster analysis", *IEEE Trans. Comput.*, vol. 25, pp. 936-944, 1976.

MacQueen, J., "Some methods for classification and analysis of multivariate observations", *Proc. Fifth Berkeley Symposium on Math. Statist. and Prob.*, Univ. of California Press, Berkeley, 1967, pp. 281-297.

Ruspini, E.H., "A new approach to cluster analysis", *Information and Control*, vol. 15, pp.22-32, 1969.

Sokal, R.R., and Sneath, P.H.A., *Principles of Numerical Taxonomy*, W.H. Freeman, San Fransisco, 1963.

Wishart, D., "Mode analysis : a generalization of nearest neighbor which reduces chaining effects", in *Numerical Taxonomy*, A.J. Cole Ed., Academic Press, New York, 1969, pp. 282-308.

11.7. PROBLEMS

1. Show that the variance of a unidimensional random variable drawn from the mixture of class-conditional distributions is a function of the pairwise distances between the means of these distributions.

2. Consider the magnitude of the variance of a mixture population as a measure of the average intercluster distance. Find the axis in a D-dimensional space which maximizes the intercluster distance of the data projected onto it.

3. Show that the p.d.f. over any symmetric set is unimodal.

4. Show that the number of modes of the function $F(\tilde{\underline{y}}_k)$ defined in

Equation 34 is identical to the number of modes of the mixture p.d.f. $p(\underline{y})$.

5. Show that the condition in Equation 50 holds for the c-means algorithm.

6. Let $\Delta(\underline{y},K_j)=\frac{1}{2}(\underline{y}-\underline{m}_j)^t\Sigma_j^{-1}(\underline{y}-\underline{m}_j)+\frac{1}{2}\log|\Sigma_j|$ be a point-to-cluster similarity measure, where $\underline{m}_j$ and Σ_j are the means and the covariance matrix of the cluster Γ_j. Calculate the change in the value of the criterion $J(\Gamma)$ in Equation 48 resulting from the transfer of a point in Γ_i to the cluster Γ_j.

Appendix A

PROBABILITY DENSITY FUNCTION ESTIMATION

A.1. INTRODUCTION

The application of the majority of the pattern classification and feature evaluation methods discussed in the text presupposes complete knowledge of class conditional probability density functions $p(\underline{x}|\omega_i)$, $i=1,2,\ldots,c$. In practice, the true underlying probability structure of classes as characterized by functions $p(\underline{x}|\omega_i)$ is unknown. The only information assumed available to the designer is a learning set of patterns with known class membership. In this appendix, we shall review various approaches to inferring the unknown probability density functions (p.d.f.s) from the learning data.

A.2. PARAMETRIC DISTRIBUTIONS

Under the assumption that the ith class conditional probability density function is parametric, the problem of estimating $p(\underline{x}|\omega_i)$ reduces to the problem of estimating the parameters of the distribution. The most frequently encountered parametric distribution is the multivariate normal (Gaussian) given e.g. in 7.9, i.e.,

1 $$p(\underline{x}|\omega_i)=\left[(2\pi)^d|\Sigma_i|\right]^{-1/2}\exp\left\{-\frac{1}{2}(\underline{x}-\underline{\mu}_i)^t\Sigma_i^{-1}(\underline{x}-\underline{\mu}_i)\right\}.$$

Given n_i samples $\underline{x}_j$, $j=1,2,\ldots,n_i$, from class ω_i, the mean vector $\underline{\mu}_i$ and the covariance matrix Σ_i of the distribution can be estimated respectively as

2 $$\hat{\underline{m}}_i = \frac{1}{n_i}\sum_{j=1}^{n_i} \underline{x}_j$$

3 $$\hat{\Sigma}_i = \frac{1}{n_i-1}\sum_{j=1}^{n_i} (\underline{x}_j-\hat{\underline{m}}_i)(\underline{x}_j-\hat{\underline{m}}_i)^t.$$

The corresponding p.d.f. estimate, $\hat{p}(\underline{x}|\omega_i)$, of $p(\underline{x}|\omega_i)$ is then given by

4 $$\hat{p}(\underline{x}|\omega_i) = \left[(2\pi)^d|\hat{\Sigma}_i|\right]^{-1/2}\exp\left\{-\frac{1}{2}(\underline{x}-\hat{\underline{m}}_i)^t\hat{\Sigma}_i^{-1}(\underline{x}-\hat{\underline{m}}_i)\right\}.$$

A.3. NONPARAMETRIC DISTRIBUTIONS

When the ith class conditional probability distribution has a general, nonparametric form, the estimation problem is considerably more difficult. In order to appreciate how the information provided by the learning data can be utilized for inference of function $p(\underline{x}|\omega_i)$ let us consider the relationship of the data set and the function $p(\underline{x}|\omega_i)$ in more detail. Note first of all that the elements of the learning set belonging to class ω_i are assumed to be drawn from the same distribution with density $p(\underline{x}|\omega_i)$. The probability that the jth observation $\underline{x}_j \epsilon \omega_i$ will fall into a region, $V(\underline{x})$, of the observation space of volume v is given by

5 $$P\left[\underline{x}_j \epsilon V(\underline{x})\right] = \int_{V(\underline{x})} p(\underline{x}|\omega_i)d\underline{x}.$$

Now suppose that we fix volume v and consider various regions in the observation space. Evidently, in a region where $p(\underline{x}|\omega_i)$ assumes low values, the probability of drawing $\underline{x}_j$ from that region will be small. Vice versa, the probability of observing $\underline{x}_j \epsilon \omega_i$ from a region associated with large values of the density function is high. Accordingly, if we make several observations on random variable $\underline{x}$, the number of these observations falling into a region where $p(\underline{x}|\omega_i)$ is large will be greater than the number of outcomes falling into regions of low p.d.f. values. Conversely it can, of course, be argued that, given a set of observations, the p.d.f. over the densely populated regions is high, whereas the values of $p(\underline{x}|\omega_i)$ over the regions sparsely populated by these observations is low. This intuitive understanding of the relationship between a distribution and a sample set drawn from it is the basis of the p.d.f. estimation methods to be discussed in the following subsections.

A.3.1. Histogram Approach

The conceptually simplest method of estimating a p.d.f. is to construct a histogram. The range of each component x_s of vector $\underline{x}$ is divided into a fixed number, k, of equal intervals. The resulting bins of identical volume v are then inspected and the number of points falling into each bin is counted.

Now suppose that the number of points $\underline{x}_\ell \epsilon \omega_i$ in the jth bin, b_j, be q_j. Then the histogram estimate $\hat{p}(\underline{x}|\omega_i)$, of density function $p(\underline{x}|\omega_i)$ is defined as

6 $$\hat{p}(\underline{x}|\omega_i) = \frac{q_j}{n_i \, v} \qquad \underline{x} \epsilon b_j$$

Note that the value of $\hat{p}(\underline{x}|\omega_i)$ is constant over every bin b_j.

Further, it can easily be verified that estimator 6 is a density function for

7 $$\int \hat{p}(\underline{x}|\omega_i)d\underline{x} = \sum_j \int_{b_j} \frac{q_j}{n_i v} d\underline{x} = \frac{1}{n_i} \sum_{j=1}^{n_i} q_j = 1$$

The histogram p.d.f. estimator is very effective but its usefulness is limited only to low dimensional pattern observation spaces because the number of bins, N_b, grows exponentially with dimensionality d, i.e.

8 $$N_b = k^d.$$

The methods discussed in the sequel are more suited to the high dimensional problems often encountered in practice.

A.3.2. Parzen Estimator

Let us consider the information about $p(\underline{x}|\omega_i)$ conveyed by each individual observation in the learning set. Given $\underline{x}_j \epsilon \omega_i$ we can assert that $p(\underline{x}|\omega_i)$ takes a non-zero value at the point $\underline{x}_j$. Moreover, under the assumption of $p(\underline{x}|\omega_i)$ being continuous, we can infer that $p(\underline{x}|\omega_i)$ will assume non-zero values in the immediate vicinity of point $\underline{x}_j$. But, the further away from observation $\underline{x}_j$ the less can be said about $p(\underline{x}|\omega_i)$ based upon observing $\underline{x}_j$.

Formally, the information about $p(\underline{x}|\omega_i)$ gained by observing $\underline{x}_j \epsilon \omega_i$ can be represented by a function $K(\underline{x},\underline{x}_j)$ centered at $\underline{x}_j$, attaining a maximum at this point and monotonically decreasing as the distance from $\underline{x}_j$ increases. Such a function will be called a kernel. A one dimensional example of it is shown in Figure A.1.

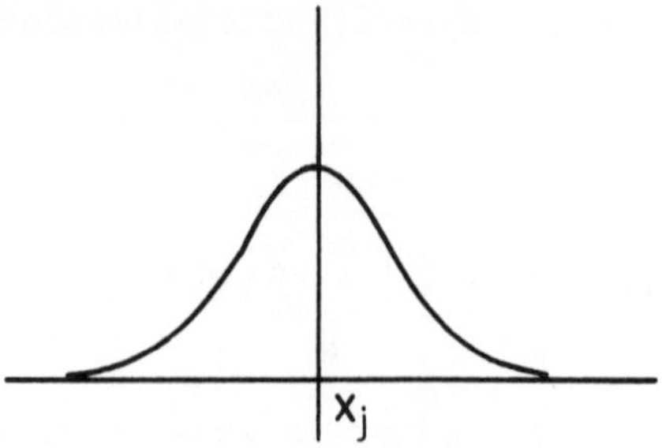

Figure A.1 Example of a kernel.

Obviously, we shall build up our knowledge of $p(\underline{x}|\omega_i)$ not only from observation $\underline{x}_j$ but from all the samples in the learning set from class ω_i. Adding up the contributions of all these points and dividing by their number, we get an estimate of $p(\underline{x}|\omega_i)$ based on the given training set, i.e.,

9 $$\hat{p}(\underline{x}|\omega_i) = \frac{1}{n_i} \sum_{j=1}^{n_i} K(\underline{x},\underline{x}_j).$$

Note that the points close to each other give rise to larger values of $\hat{p}(\underline{x}|\omega_i)$ than points far apart as anticipated (see Figure A.2). Further, the contributions to $\hat{p}(\underline{x}|\omega_i)$ at a given point due to observations $\underline{x}_j$, $j=1,2,\ldots,n_i$ depend on the range of influence of kernel $K(\underline{x},\underline{x}_j)$. If, for instance, the range of influence of $K(\underline{x},\underline{x}_j)$ is very small, the p.d.f. estimate will be a very spiky function, while if the range is large the estimate will fail to detect local variations in $p(\underline{x}|\omega_i)$. Intuitively, when the data paucity is severe, the range of kernel $K(\underline{x},\underline{x}_j)$ should be relatively large to smooth out sampling effects. As the number of samples increases, the range of influence of $K(\underline{x},\underline{x}_j)$ should progressively decrease so as to affect only the immediate neighborhood of $\underline{x}_j$. It can be verified analytically that the kernel function reflecting this intuitive argument should have the form

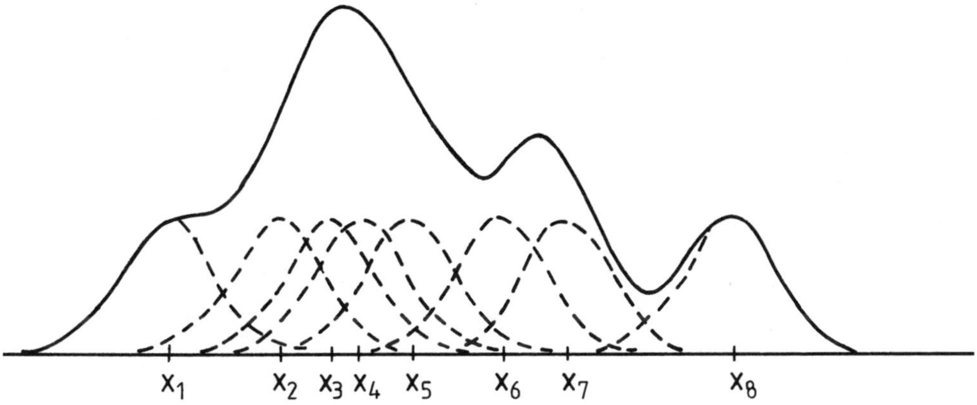

Figure A.2 Summing the contributions of the kernels to obtain a Parzen p.d.f. estimate.

10 $$K(\underline{x},\underline{x}_j) = \rho^{-d} h\left[\delta(\underline{x},\underline{x}_j)/\rho\right],$$

where ρ is a parameter of the estimator satisfying (as a function of sample size)

11 $$\lim_{n_i \to \infty} \rho^d(n_i) = 0,$$

$\delta(\underline{x},\underline{x}_j)$ is a suitable metric (see Chapter 6) and $h[\cdot]$ is a function attaining a maximum at $\delta(\underline{x},\underline{x}_j)=0$ and monotonically decreasing as $\delta(\underline{x},\underline{x}_j)$ increases. If the choice of $h[\cdot]$ is confined to non-negative functions, then the only condition imposed on $h[\cdot]$ is

12 $$\int K(\underline{x},\underline{x}_j)d\underline{x} = 1.$$

Conditions 11 and 12 guarantee that 9 is a density function and that it provides an unbiased and consistent estimate of $p(\underline{x}|\omega_i)$.

The most important kernels are the following :

GAUSSIAN (Figure A.3):

13 $$K(\underline{x},\underline{x}_j) = \left[(\rho^2 2\pi)^d |Q|\right]^{-1/2} \exp\left\{-\frac{1}{2\rho^2}\,\delta_Q(\underline{x},\underline{x}_j)\right\}$$

where $\delta_Q(\underline{x},\underline{x}_j)$ is the quadratic distance defined in 6.11. Theoretically, the scaling matrix, Q, in 13 can be arbitrary. However, when the number of observations n_i in the set is small, a better estimate is obtained if an estimate of the sample covariance matrix, $\hat{\Sigma}_i$, of class ω_i is used as the scaling matrix.

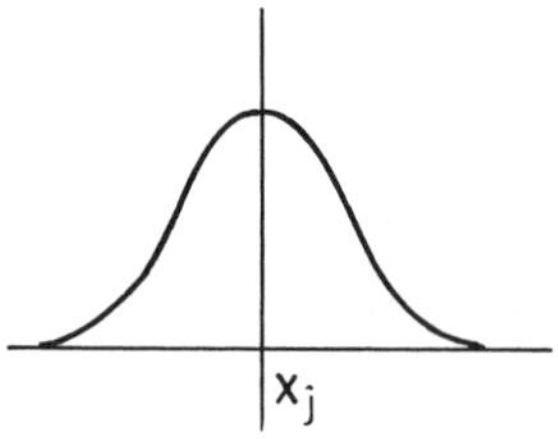

Figure A.3 Gaussian kernel.

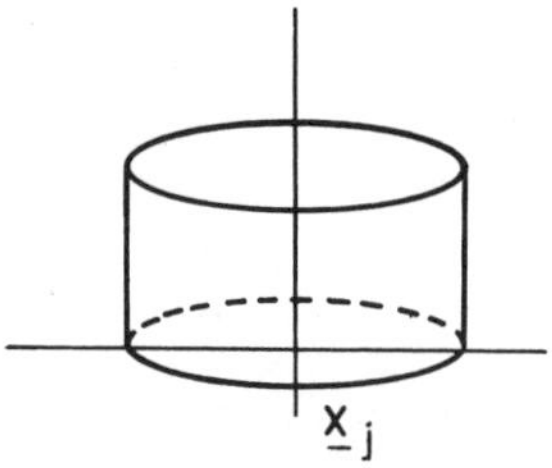

Figure A.4 Hyperspheric kernel.

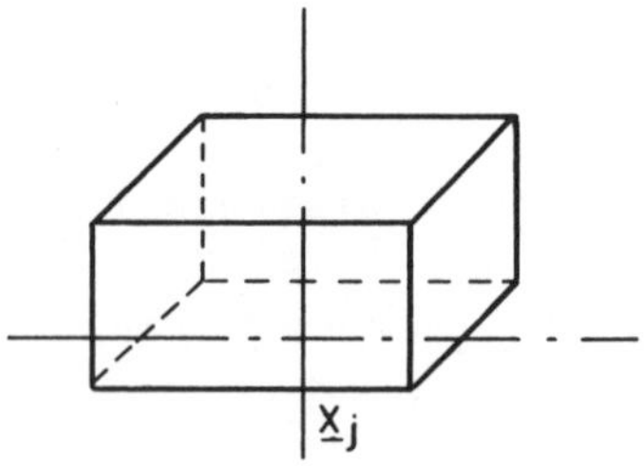

Figure A.5 Hypercubic kernel.

The Parzen estimator employing a gaussian kernel gives a smooth estimate of the probability density function but it is computationally demanding.

HYPERSPHERIC (Figure A.4):

14 $$K(\underline{x},\underline{x}_j) = \begin{cases} v^{-1} & \left\{\underline{x} \mid \delta_E(\underline{x},\underline{x}_j) \le \rho\right\} \\ 0 & \left\{\underline{x} \mid \delta_E(\underline{x},\underline{x}_j) > \rho\right\} \end{cases}$$

where $\delta_E(\underline{x},\underline{x}_j)$ is the Euclidean distance given in 6.9 and v is the volume of a hypersphere of radius ρ.

The hyperspheric kernel gives rise to a piece-wise constant estimate of $p(\underline{x}|\omega_i)$. Also it obviates evaluation of the exponential function in 13 which, from the point of view of the computation requirements, makes the estimator more appealing.

HYPERCUBIC (Figure A.5):

15 $$K(\underline{x},\underline{x}_j) = \begin{cases} (2\rho)^{-d} & \left\{\underline{x} \mid \delta_T(\underline{x},\underline{x}_j) \le \rho\right\} \\ 0 & \left\{\underline{x} \mid \delta_T(\underline{x},\underline{x}_j) > \rho\right\} \end{cases}$$

where $\delta_T(\underline{x},\underline{x}_j)$ is the Chebyshev distance introduced in Equation 6.10. The estimator using 15 is also piece-wise constant and its main attraction is the simplicity and speed of its implementation.

Before proceeding to discuss the k-nearest neighbor p.d.f. estimation approach, the reader should note a few practical points. The first, which applies to Parzen estimators in general, concerns the choice of parameter ρ. As a suitable value for ρ satisfying condition 11 we can take

16 $$\rho(n_i) = n_i^{-\eta/d},$$

where η is from the interval (0,1).

Second, in the case of estimates employing either hyperspheric or hypercubic kernels, contributions to the estimate of $p(\underline{x}|\omega_i)$ at any point $\underline{x}$ are made only by kernels centered at observations in the ρ neighborhood of $\underline{x}$ as defined by the respective metrics $\delta_E(\underline{x},\underline{x}_j)$ and $\delta_T(\underline{x},\underline{x}_j)$. Moreover, the contribution of each of these kernels is identical. To obtain the estimate at $\underline{x}$ it simply suffices to find the number, k, of elements of the learning set from class ω_i lying at distance ρ or less from $\underline{x}$. Thus the estimate is given by

17 $$\hat{p}(\underline{x}|\omega_i) = \frac{k}{n_i} \text{ constant},$$

where the constant depends on the type of neighborhood used. It is particularly easy to determine k when metric $\delta_T(\underline{x},\underline{x}_j)$ is used, for each component of vectors $\underline{x}$ and $\underline{x}_j$ can be considered separately and the search can be terminated whenever the absolute value of the difference between any corresponding pair exceeds ρ.

A.3.3. k-Nearest Neighbor Method

Let us consider a set of samples in a two dimensional space as plotted in Figure A.6. Evidently, the area of the circle which includes a fixed number, say k, of points of the set is much smaller in densely populated regions of the pattern space than in the sparsely populated ones. This behavior, of course, extends to the general multidimensional spaces where the circle becomes a hypersphere. It can be conjectured, therefore, that the volume of the hypersphere occupied by k points is related to the value of the probability density function at the center of the hypersphere, and this can be used with advantage for estimation purposes.

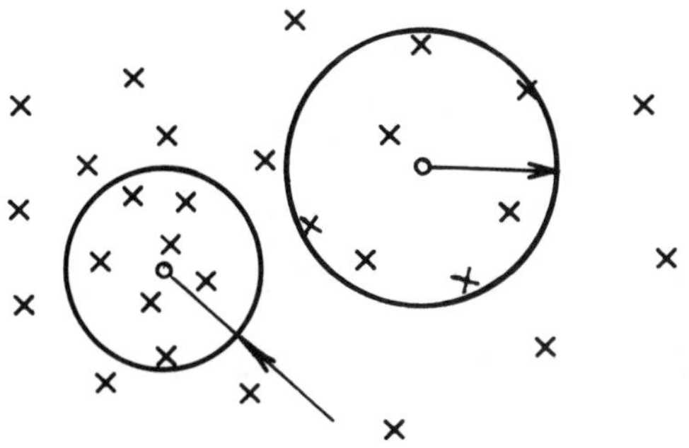

Figure A.6 The volumes occupied by seven nearest neighbors to two different points in the pattern space.

More specifically, let $\underline{x}_j$ be the k-nearest point to $\underline{x}$ from among the elements of the learning set. Then the probability density function at $\underline{x}$ can be estimated as

18 $$\hat{p}(\underline{x}|\omega_i) = \frac{k}{n_i v},$$

where v is the volume of the sphere $V(\underline{x})$ of radius $\delta_E(\underline{x},\underline{x}_j)$ and k/n_i is the proportion of the total number of samples from class ω_i lying in $V(\underline{x})$.

Note that k/n_i plays the role of $Pr\left[\underline{x}_j \epsilon V(\underline{x})\right]$ in 5. Here, however, in contrast to the Parzen method, this probability is fixed and we look for an estimate v of the volume required to ensure that $\underline{x}_j \epsilon V(\underline{x})$ will be observed with this particular probability. The ratio of the probability to the volume then gives a probability density estimate.

It is apparent that the probability level (choice of k) should be fixed in relation to the sample size n_i for, if k is too large, then the local detail will be averaged out over a large region of the observation space. On the other hand, a too small k will result in assigning undue significance to individual observations in the set and, in consequence, the p.d.f. estimate will be spiky. It can be shown analytically that the unbiasedness and consistency of the estimator in 18 will be ensured if the following conditions on k as a function of sample size are satisfied

19 $$\lim_{n_i \to \infty} k(n_i) = \infty$$

20 $$\lim_{n_i \to \infty} k(n_i)/n_i = 0.$$

A suitable choice of $k(n_i)$ meeting these conditions is

21 $$k(n_i) = \text{constant } \sqrt{n_i}.$$

A.4. REFERENCES

Cacoullos, T., "Estimation of a multivariate density", *Ann. Inst. Statist. Math.*, Vol. 18, pp. 179-189,1966.

Fukunaga, K., *Introduction to Statistical Pattern Recognition*, Academic Press, New York, 1972.

Lofstgaarden, D.O., and Quesenberry, C.P., "A nonparametric estimate of a multivariate density function", *Ann. Math. Statist.*, Vol. 36, pp. 1049-1051, 1965.

Parzen, E., "On estimation of a probability density function and mode", *Ann. Math. Statist.*, Vol. 33, pp. 1065-1076,1962.

Rosenblatt, M., "Remarks on some nonparametric estimates of a density function", *Ann. Math. Statist.*, Vol. 27, pp. 832-837, 1956.

Appendix B

DIFFERENTIATION OF SCALAR FUNCTIONS OF MATRIX VARIABLE

B.1. INTRODUCTION

In general, the solving of the linear feature extraction problem involves optimization of a feature extraction criterion function, J(W), with respect to feature extraction matrix W. Recall that any criterion function arising in linear feature extraction applications can be expressed as a function of the trace and of the determinant of matrix functions $F_1,\ldots,F_q$, of the matrix variable W, i.e.

1 $$J(W) = \tilde{J}\Big[\mathrm{tr}F_1(W), \mathrm{tr}F_2(W), \ldots, |F_p(W)|, \ldots, |F_q(W)|\Big].$$

The differentiation of J(W) with respect to W therefore leads to the problem of differentiating the scalar functions of a matrix variable, tr F(W) and |F(W)| respectively.

Let us consider first of all the problem of differentiating matrix function F(W) with respect to W. We shall assume that F(W) under consideration belongs to a class of matrix functions on which the operations of addition, multiplication and inversion (provided the generating matrix is nonsingular) are defined. Further, suppose that F(W) and W are $r\times r$ and $D\times d$ matrices respectively. Then the derivative of F(W) with respect to the (k,ℓ)th component of W is an $r \times r$ matrix, i.e.

2
$$\frac{\partial F(W)}{\partial w_{k\ell}} = \begin{bmatrix} \frac{\partial F_{11}(W)}{\partial w_{k\ell}} & \cdots & \frac{\partial F_{1r}(W)}{\partial w_{k\ell}} \\ \\ \frac{\partial F_{r1}(W)}{\partial w_{k\ell}} & \cdots & \frac{\partial F_{rr}(W)}{\partial w_{k\ell}} \end{bmatrix}$$

Using notation 2, the derivative of any function F(W) can be found by applying the following rules :

<u>$F(W) = G(W) + H(W)$</u>:

3
$$\frac{\partial F(W)}{\partial w_{k\ell}} = \frac{\partial G(W)}{\partial w_{k\ell}} + \frac{\partial H(W)}{\partial w_{k\ell}}$$

<u>$F(W) = G(W) \cdot H(W)$</u>:

4
$$\frac{\partial F(W)}{\partial w_{k\ell}} = \frac{\partial G(W)}{\partial w_{k\ell}} H(W) + G(W) \frac{\partial H(W)}{\partial w_{k\ell}}$$

<u>$F(W) = G^{-1}(W)$</u>:

5
$$\frac{\partial F(W)}{\partial w_{k\ell}} = - G^{-1}(W) \frac{\partial G(W)}{\partial w_{k\ell}} G^{-1}(W)$$

Rules 3 and 4 can easily be verified. The validity of 5 can be demonstrated by considering the identity

6
$$G(W)\, G^{-1}(W) = I.$$

Applying rule 4 to find the derivative of the left hand side of 6, we get

7
$$\frac{\partial G(W)}{\partial w_{k\ell}} G^{-1}(W) + G(W) \frac{\partial G^{-1}(W)}{\partial w_{k\ell}} = 0,$$

since the identity matrix is a constant. Premultiplying both sides of the equation by $G^{-1}(W)$ and rearranging we have

8 $$\frac{\partial G^{-1}(W)}{\partial w_{k\ell}} = \frac{\partial F(W)}{\partial w_{k\ell}} = -\ G^{-1}(W)\ \frac{\partial G(W)}{\partial w_{k\ell}}\ G^{-1}(W).$$

Note that the derivative of matrix W with respect to element $w_{k\ell}$ is an D×d matrix with all the elements zero except the (k,ℓ)th element which takes value one. For brevity we shall denote this matrix $V(k,\ell)$, i.e.

9 $$\frac{\partial W}{\partial w_{k\ell}} = V(k,\ell).$$

EXAMPLE 1: $F(W) = W^tMW$

10 $$\frac{\partial F(W)}{\partial w_{k\ell}} = V^t(k,\ell)\ MW + W^tMV(k,\ell)$$

EXAMPLE 2: $F(W) = \left[W^t\Sigma W\right]^{-1}$

11 $$\frac{\partial F(W)}{\partial w_{k\ell}} = -\left[W^t\Sigma W\right]^{-1}\left[V^t(k,\ell)\Sigma W + W^t\Sigma V(k,\ell)\right]\left[W^t\Sigma W\right]^{-1}$$

We now consider the two scalar functions of matrix F(W) arising in feature extraction, namely the trace and the determinant, and their derivatives with respect to W.

B.2. THE TRACE OPERATION

Inspecting 3 to 5 we find that the derivative of function F(W) is composed of terms each involving the derivative of one of the constituent functions G(W) and H(W). Ultimately, the differentiation of these constituent functions leads to the differentiation of matrix

W with respect to $w_{k\ell}$, thus yielding matrix $V(k,\ell)$. We conclude therefore that each term of the derivative of $F(W)$ has the general form $g_i(W)V(k,\ell)h_i(W)$, that is

12 $$\frac{\partial F(W)}{\partial w_{k\ell}} = \sum_i g_i(W)V(k,\ell)h_i(W),$$

where $g_i(W)$ and $h_i(W)$ are matrix functions and the index i runs over all the terms arising when differentiating $F(W)$. This form is borne out by the examples in 10 and 11.

Now let us consider the derivative of the trace of matrix $F(W)$, i.e.

13 $$J(W) = \text{tr}\, F(W)$$

with respect to $w_{k\ell}$. We have

14 $$\frac{\partial J(W)}{\partial w_{k\ell}} = \text{tr}\left\{\frac{\partial F(W)}{\partial w_{k\ell}}\right\} = \text{tr}\left\{\sum_i g_i(W)V(k,\ell)h_i(W)\right\}$$

and further, as the elements of the matrix product can be shifted around without affecting the value of the trace, i.e. $\text{tr}(gVh)=\text{tr}(hgV)$, we can write

15 $$\frac{\partial J(W)}{\partial w_{k\ell}} = \text{tr}\left\{\sum_i f_i(W)V(k,\ell)\right\}$$

where for brevity matrix $f_i(W)$ denotes

16 $$f_i(W) = h_i(W)g_i(W).$$

It can readily be verified that

17 $$\text{tr}\left\{f_i(W)V(k,\ell)\right\} = \left[f_i(W)\right]_{\ell k},$$

where $\left[f_i(W)\right]_{\ell k}$ is the (ℓ,k)th term of matrix $f_i(W)$. Thus the derivative of $J(W)$ in 17 with respect to the complete matrix W is

18 $$\frac{\partial J}{\partial W} = \left[\sum_i f_i(W)\right]^t.$$

We now illustrate the application of this result on Examples 3 and 4.

EXAMPLE 3: $J(W) = tr(W^t MW)$

Although this example is very simple, we shall find the derivative of $J(W)$ step-by-step to gain some familiarity with the differentiation rules. From 10 we note that the derivative of $W^t MW$ has two terms and that

$$g_1(W) = I$$
$$g_2(W) = W^t M$$
$$h_1(W) = MW$$
$$h_2(W) = I.$$

Thus matrix functions $f_1(W)$ and $f_2(W)$ are given as

$$f_1(W) = MW$$
$$f_2(W) = W^t M.$$

Applying rule 18 and transposing once again the resulting first term we get

$$\frac{\partial J(W)}{\partial W} = [(MW)^t]^t + (W^t M)^t = MW + M^t W.$$

EXAMPLE 4: $J(W) = tr[W^t \Sigma W]^{-1}$

Using rules 5 and 18 we can readily write

$$\frac{\partial J(W)}{\partial W} = \left[\left(\Sigma W[W^t \Sigma W]^{-2}\right)^t\right]^t + \left([W^t \Sigma W]^{-2} W^t \Sigma\right)^t$$
$$= \Sigma W[W^t \Sigma W]^{-2} + \Sigma^t W\left([W^t \Sigma W]^{-2}\right)^t$$

B.3. THE DETERMINANT

We now consider the second important scalar function of a matrix variable, the determinant, i.e.,

19 $$J(W) = |F(W)|.$$

Recall that the determinant can be expressed in terms of the elements of any row or column and the corresponding co-factor. Thus choosing, say, the ith column we have

20 $$J(W) = \sum_{j=1}^{r} F_{ij}(W)F_{ij}^{*}(W),$$

where $F_{ij}(W)$ is the (i,j)th element of matrix $F(W)$ and $F_{ij}^{*}(W)$ is the co-factor of $F_{ij}(W)$. Further, it will be useful to note that the adjoint, $F^{*}(W)$, of matrix $F(W)$ which is defined as

21 $$F^{*}(W) = \begin{bmatrix} F_{11}^{*}(W) & \cdots & F_{r1}^{*}(W) \\ F_{12}^{*}(W) & & \\ \cdot & & \\ \cdot & & \\ F_{1r}^{*}(W) & \cdots & F_{rr}^{*}(W) \end{bmatrix}$$

satisfies

22 $$F^{*}(W) = |F(W)|F^{-1}(W).$$

The derivative of $J(W)$ with respect to element $w_{k\ell}$ of W is given as

23 $$\frac{\partial J(W)}{\partial w_{k\ell}} = \sum_{i=1}^{r} \sum_{j=1}^{r} \frac{\partial J(W)}{\partial F_{ij}(W)} \frac{\partial F_{ij}(W)}{\partial w_{k\ell}}.$$

But from 20 we have

24 $$\frac{\partial J(W)}{\partial F_{ij}(W)} = F_{ij}^{*}.$$

Thus it follows that 23 can be rewritten as

25 $$\frac{\partial J(W)}{\partial w_{k\ell}} = \sum_{i=1}^{r} \sum_{j=1}^{r} F_{ij}^{*} \frac{\partial F_{ij}(W)}{\partial w_{k\ell}}$$

or alternatively, using the trace operation and notation 21, 25 can be expressed as

26 $$\frac{\partial J(W)}{\partial w_{k\ell}} = \operatorname{tr}\left[F^{*}(W) \frac{\partial F(W)}{\partial w_{k\ell}}\right].$$

Finally, from 22 we have

27 $$\frac{\partial J(W)}{\partial w_{k\ell}} = |F(W)| \ \mathrm{tr}\left[F^{-1}(W)\ \frac{\partial F(W)}{\partial w_{k\ell}}\right].$$

Comparing 27 with 14, we conclude that the problem of differentiating the determinant has been transformed into the problem of finding the derivative of the trace of a matrix function.

<u>EXAMPLE 5</u>: $J(W) = |W^t M W|$

$$\frac{\partial J(W)}{\partial W} = |W^t M W| \left\{ MW(W^t MW)^{-1} + M^t W\left[(W^t MW)^{-1}\right]^t \right\}$$

<u>EXAMPLE 6</u>: $J(W) = |[W^t \Sigma W]^{-1}|$

$$\begin{aligned}\frac{\partial J(W)}{\partial W} &= -\ |(W^t \Sigma W)^{-1}|\ \Big\{ \Sigma W(W^t \Sigma W)^{-1} W^t \Sigma W (W^t \Sigma W)^{-1} \\ &\qquad + \left[(W^t \Sigma W)^{-1} W^t \Sigma W (W^t \Sigma W)^{-1} W^t \Sigma\right]^t \Big\} \\ &= -\ |W^t \Sigma W|^{-1} . \left\{ \Sigma W(W^t \Sigma W)^{-1} + \Sigma^t W\left[(W^t \Sigma W)^{-1}\right]^t \right\}\end{aligned}$$

Appendix C

PROPERTIES OF ENTROPY FUNCTIONS

C.1. LIST OF PROPERTIES

Let $\Delta_c = \left\{p_i \mid i=1,2,\ldots,c,\ \sum_{i=1}^{c} p_i=1,\ p_i\geq 0\right\}$, $c=2,3,\ldots$, be the sets of c-ary probability distribution functions. Then for $J_c(p_1,p_2,\ldots,p_c)$, $p_i \in \Delta_c$ to be an entropy function, it must satisfy the following natural and essential properties : the sequence of functions $J_c(p_1,p_2,\ldots,p_c)$ must be

<u>NORMALIZED</u>:

1 $$J_2(0.5,0.5) = 1$$

<u>SYMMETRIC</u>:

2 $$J_c\left(p_1,p_2,\ldots,p_c\right) = J_c\left(p_{k_1},p_{k_2},\ldots,p_{k_c}\right)$$

where k_1, $k_2,\ldots,k_c$ is an arbitrary permutation on $\{1,2,\ldots,c\}$

<u>DECISIVE</u>:

3 $$J_2(1,0) = J_2(0,1) = 0$$

<u>EXPANSIBLE</u>:

$$J_c\left(p_1,\ldots,p_c\right) = J_{c+1}\left(0,p_1,\ldots,p_c\right) = \ldots =$$

4 $$= J_{c+1}\left(p_1,\ldots,p_k,0,p_{k+1},\ldots,p_c\right) = \ldots = J_{c+1}\left(p_1,\ldots,p_c,0\right)$$

CONTINUOUS:

for all c=1,2,... .

and in addition *branching* and *compositive*. These properties can be intuitively justified as follows : Property 1 defines one unit of information as the amount of information we gain by observing the outcome of an experiment with two equally likely alternatives. Symmetry 2 formalizes the requirement that any information must be invariant under a change in the order of events. Decisivity property ensures that the measure yields zero information when there is no uncertainty in an experiment. The fact that additional events with zero probability do not change the uncertainty of the outcome of an experiment is characterized by expansivity. The notion of continuity is self-explanatory. Branching is a generalization of recursivity. Its somewhat simplistic interpretation is that by splitting one event into two, the uncertainty prevailing before an experiment is accomplished will increase. Finally, composivity combines the requirement of weak additivity and quasilinearity.

C.2. REFERENCES

Aczel, J., and Daroczy, Z., *On Measures of Information and Their Characterization*, Academic Press, New York, 1975.

SUBJECT INDEX